SOCIETY
AND DEMOCRACY
IN GERMANY

SOCIETY
AND DEMOCRACY
IN GERMANY

BY RALF DAHRENDORF

W · W · NORTON & COMPANY

New York · London

W. W. Norton & Company, Inc., 500 Fifth Avenue,
New York, N.Y. 10110

Copyright © 1967 by Ralf Dahrendorf. Published simultaneously in Canada by
George J. McLeod Limited, Toronto. Printed in the United States of America.

First published as a Norton paperback 1979 by arrangement with
Doubleday & Co., Inc.

Published in Germany under the title *Gesellschaft und Demokratie in Deutschland* in
1965. Copyright © by R. Piper & Co. Verlag, München 1965.

Library of Congress Cataloging in Publication Data

Dahrendorf, Ralf.
  Society and democracy in Germany.

  Translation of Gesellschaft und Demokratie in Deutschland.
  Bibliography: p.
  Includes index.
  1. Germany—Social conditions. 2. National characteristics, German.
3. Germany—Politics and government—1871—   I. Title.
[HN445.D313 1979b]   309.1'43   79–9553

4 5 6 7 8 9 0

ISBN 0-393-00953-X

For Vera

Preface to the German Edition

Alexis de Tocqueville reported on a distant country, and he was not a sociologist by profession. These facts can hardly be held against him; indeed both tell in his favor. The study of *Democracy in America* would probably not have the same liveliness of observation and ease of style if it had been written by a sociologist. Furthermore, strange lands open their treasures more readily than the familiar world to the eye whose vision is bound by habit, although the latter's treasures may be of no less value. Still it would be a little harsh if one were to conclude from such considerations that the sociologist must not write about his own country.

This is a professional sociologist's study of the country to which he belongs not merely because it is written in his passport. In his *Ortsbestimmung der deutschen Soziologie* [Present Position of German Sociology], Helmut Schelsky noted a few years ago: "In recent German sociological literature no work can be named that attempts to describe the 'whole' of our society" (192, p. 149).* Schelsky calls this deficiency "astonishing," since "this attempt to describe on the basis of investigations undertaken by empirical methods the 'whole' of society would seem to be the conception of 'sociology as an empirical science,' which combines and integrates most appropriately the diverse interdependent modes of experience [discussed by Schelsky before]" (192, p. 83). Outsiders often deplore a characteristic of German sociology appreciated by experts, namely, that the methodological substance of such statements remains in dispute. Apart from that, however, it is my intention with this study to remedy the deficiency stated by Schelsky.

It is a little surprising that Schelsky, otherwise a master of the explanatory aperçu, does not pursue the state of affairs he has named. There are only a few hints here and there, such as his observation: "The Germans have lost nearly all their

* The first figure in parentheses after quotations refers to the number of the source in the Bibliography at the end of this volume.

historical self-confidence, Germany has become an unknown social object" (192, p. 56). There are indeed few modern countries whose citizens are so perplexed by the society to which they belong; there are also few countries in which the prejudices of individuals and groups are so readily taken for information. If it were not for an occasional flare-up of the demand for more exact knowledge, for controllable information, one might be led to believe that the Germans are satisfied with their perplexed state of mind. But this is anticipating questions about which much more will have to be said in this study.

At the present point, two other questions need brief discussion, two conditions of the analysis of total societies (conditions that, where they are missing, explain the lack of such analyses as well). In order to describe the complex reality of a society, and a modern one at that, one needs a guiding thread. This may consist of a map of categories, a catalogue of all the items that make up the society—population, economy, education, etc.—or of a theoretically more ambitious, if methodologically equally irrelevant "system"—"integrative functions," "adaptive functions," etc. In ethnographic reports, such procedures may have a place; but sociological analyses of total societies lose much of their color and interest if one proceeds in either of these ways: they turn into catalogues rather than analyses—that is, their parts may be interchanged and replaced at will.

Good analyses of total societies require, it seems to me, a different guideline. They should start off (like other sociological studies as well, of course) from a problem that removes all statements from the tedious fog of arbitrariness and provides the whole with a beginning and an end. Tocqueville had a problem of this kind: "democracy" in America, to which he related even his literary predictions. This study also has a political thread to guide it; here too, it is the question of "democracy" (although in Germany, of course). By "democracy," however, we mean something different from Tocqueville, to wit, *liberté* rather than *égalité*, a liberal political community rather than an egalitarian society. Or is this shift of emphasis in itself a symptom of social changes that have taken place?

Again we are anticipating arguments that have yet to be developed. I merely wish to emphasize in advance that in my opinion the analysis of total societies requires an attempt to relate the structures of many specific areas of society to an underlying political problem. This attempt should, in turn, provide answers not only to the immediate problem but to the questions asked by the people concerned as well. This is one of the two presuppositions of this study. The other concerns the analyst rather than his subject matter. The advantage of strangeness for the sociologist has already been cited. Whoever attempts a fundamental and comprehensive interpretation of his own society must be capable of some detachment from the world of his daily life. This is rarely the case, for detachment from the familiar and the habitual produces, as well as chances of knowledge, psychological threats to existence. Perhaps the social role of the intellectual must be defined by such detachment. If so, this definition excludes the majority of German intellectuals who, I shall have to show, have always found such detachment peculiarly hard.

How does the individual detach himself from the familiar features of his social environment? By a "series of breaks with primary groups," as the jargon will have it with reference to considerations by Alfred Weber and Karl Mannheim. This means that whoever has been forced by internal or external necessity to abandon what was close and dear to him, whoever has had to break with family and friends, with home and the social world of his parents, cannot help but become an intellectual of sorts. Foreign travel also helps many to experience the world of their daily lives with astonishment, at least occasionally. But, unless the sociology of tourism is mistaken, travel does not modify people's opinions and convictions very significantly; it merely provides them with words to express what otherwise might remain not only unsaid, but also unthought. Travel provides arguments.

Even the most marvelous journey, however, gradually fades into memory. Trips abroad are holidays from one's own society; but as a rule one returns from one's holidays to reality. In order to incorporate the holiday perspective into everyday life, stronger forces are needed than a ticket to Rome. I am fortunate enough to have this holiday perspective in my own home, in the person of my wife, who is not German. Her presence is a permanent reminder of the exciting quality of the familiar. Without this perspective I should probably not have written this book. Detachment from the familiar and habitual, the stranger's view, is not always easy to bear. It is never comfortable, but I have always felt it to be a pure gain. For that reason, above all, I dedicate this book to my wife.

R.D.

Brissago, Spring 1965

Preface to the American Edition

This book was written to stimulate, perhaps to provoke critical thought about Germany's past, present, and future—in Germany. Authors are often mistaken in their mental picture of the audience for which they are writing; but when I finished this book just over a year ago, I felt quite sure that it was addressed to my countrymen, and to the politically alert groups among them. I might have known at the time that German problems are rarely German problems alone, and that even as such they have been a consistent source of concern to the outside world. It was harder to know at the time that the apparent tranquillity of the Federal Republic was to give way to more unstable conditions so soon, and that even in the system of political parties Germany's past was to reappear on the scene. At the time at which this is written, a book on democracy in Germany has acquired a new urgency inside as well as outside the country concerned. Even so, I remain quite unsure whether I have anything of real interest to say to non-Germans.

I might have known also that a sociologist's book, even if it is not presented as a professional piece, would be scrutinized carefully by the profession and its equally professional opponents. Possibly, many an historian will be shocked by the disrespect for chronology implied in the simultaneous treatment of successive events. Political theorists are bound to find the assumed notion of the "constitution of liberty" even more outdated, and certainly cruder, than that of F. A. von Hayek. Sociologists may look aghast at the free and unreserved use of value judgments throughout the book. Need I really state explicitly that this is a book of passion, much as I may have tried to filter emotion by information and reason? The purpose of this book is decidedly not to advance theoretical knowledge in social science; readers of my *Class and Class Conflict* (52) may well suspect the hand of an entirely different author here; that it is still the same person becomes visible only at those points where sociological theories (notably, of conflict) are applied to the German case. For I did want to try to bring the perspective of the social scientist—with its chances and limitations, systematic intentions and practical inconsistencies, advances in precision and deficiencies in detail—to bear on a subject of historical and political interest.

It is gratifying for the author that the book has produced quite outspoken reactions, in terms both of actual political analysis and of its methodological approach. Reviewers have called me an "educator of the people" and a "seducer"; they have praised and condemned the attempted combination of methods. It would be even more gratifying if I could feel that it has rendered a little contribution to making Germans aware of the task of liberty—and non-Germans, of the complexities of the German Question.

I have prepared this English version myself; in other words, I have once again translated a book of mine into a language that is not my mother tongue. Once again, at the end of the work, I am quite sure that I should never have started it; but such insights after the event are rather useless. The translation provided an opportunity for a number of minor changes. Apart from modifications of style and, of course, corrections of mistakes, these changes have been almost exclusively cuts. Where I felt that passages of the original either contained too little information, or provided too little analysis, I have left them out. In this manner, some thirty pages of the German version have been weeded out.

Without the encouragement of a number of institutions and friends, I should probably not have finished the translation. It was begun in New York where the newly founded European Institute of Columbia University, headed by Professor Philip Mosely, provided me with an unusually generous—and profitable—opportunity to consider European problems from an American perspective. The patient encouragement of Anne Freedgood of the publishers, Doubleday & Company, helped me to develop a mixed sense of obligation and worthwhileness that kept me at work. My friend, Professor Fritz Stern of Columbia University, has not only been instrumental in bringing about this translation, but has shaped my thinking about Germany in so many ways that it is almost impossible to tell where his impact on this book begins and ends.

This book is dedicated to my wife. Possibly, all the encouragement I received would not have sufficed to make me finish this English version, had it not been for my wish to present "her" book to my wife in her mother tongue.

R.D.

Constance, November 1966

Contents

THE GERMAN QUESTION

1. THE QUESTION IS POSED

That there is a German Question is a fact familiar to people all over the world. In Germany there are many who think that the only German question to speak of is how the presently "triply divided" country may be united. In this way the German Question turns almost imperceptibly into a question put by the Germans to other people; thus many considerations lapse into possibly welcome oblivion: among them, for example, the fact that there is a question other people put to the Germans, and, above all, that people could do worse than put questions to themselves.

Which, then, are the questions that Germans put to themselves? Here, comparing Germany with other countries yields strange results. In the United States, the domestic debate is dominated today, in the second half of the twentieth century, by problems of civil rights and their implementation. In England, the problems of a society slowly abandoning its own blend of old and new in a painful process with many curious manifestations—the Angry Young Men and the Beatles, scholarship boys and the new working class—absorb the attention of an informed public. Even from the still insufficient reports about the Soviet Union we may infer that problems of internal order, of the relation between consumption and production, or the liberalization of culture, are of primary concern. Nor is this preoccupation with problems of internal social structure confined to big countries; it is hardly less characteristic of Italy and Spain, the Netherlands and Sweden. In Germany, however—more precisely in the western part of Germany—people reserve their political temperament for problems of a different kind: the Oder-Neisse line, the "so-called" German Democratic Republic (DDR), an "abyss of treason," Germany's position in the world. German interest is not devoted to German society and domestic affairs but to the external power structure of world politics and its significance for Germany. German concerns are not social but national.

This preoccupation is by no means a postwar phenomenon,

and it has many ramifications. As it happens, national questions, in contrast to social questions, invariably tend to be
questions posed to others rather than to oneself. Moreover,
while social questions generally call for answers for which
the questioners themselves are responsible, responsibility for
national questions can easily be shirked or rationalized. There
is an even more serious difference. The internal divisions of
a people run very much deeper when they are caused by national questions than they did even at the heyday of the "social question" brought about by industrialization.

Disunity in social matters may be made politically fruitful:
it can lead to conflict and reform and retains a recognizable
significance even as revolution (although, as such, it is bound
to defeat its own ends). By contrast, disunity in national
matters is a struggle of absolute claims. There is no compromise between those who want to recognize the Oder-Neisse
line and those who want to reclaim—at some, or indeed any,
cost—the formerly German territories that are now Polish.
There is no reform into which the hardened controversy about
the attitude of the Federal Republic toward the DDR might
usefully be channeled. Here, every position demands the un-
conditional surrender of the opponent. Thus, differences in
national matters create an all but breathtaking, that is, a
deadly climate of internal politics.

For Germans, their society is an unknown; and this in itself is a version of the German Question: Why do people in
Germany have so little sense of the patterns, hopes, and
frustrations of their social world? Why do they devote so little
energy to controlling their society, which, after all, concerns
the individual much more immediately than the hotly debated
abstractions of "the past," "the future," or "the nation"?
Why does nobody ask the questions whose answers cannot
be delegated to others? While it might be rewarding to try to
answer these questions, it would probably not lead us much
further in our search for the German Question. What, then,
is this German Question?

Here, a reminder seems in place. The German Question
may be unfamiliar to many Germans, but it is neither an invention of others nor their exclusive preoccupation. A hundred years ago, in 1866, Constantin Frantz asserted that, "The
German Question is the most obscure, most involved and
most comprehensive problem in the whole of modern history."
By this statement Frantz certainly meant something quite

different than Wilhelm Röpke did when, in 1945, he used the quotation as a motto for his own essay on the German Question [*Die deutsche Frage* (185)]. And Röpke, a liberal economist, viewed the question in a different light than Gerhard Ritter, an historian of national rather than liberal convictions, who, soon after Röpke, published his study of *Europe and the German Question* (more cautiously entitled in a new edition, *The German Problem* [183]). It would be easy to extend the range of German discussions of the German Question; contributions to it reach far beyond national demands into the swamps of politics, character, and society. But what is the German Question?

There are versions of it that Constantin Frantz was fortunate enough to be spared. How was Auschwitz possible? I do not think that either Hannah Arendt or the Eichmann trial in Jerusalem has succeeded in answering this question; and I am sure that the Auschwitz trials before German and Austrian courts of law have failed even to approach the dimension of the crime committed here, much less to provide an explanation. I am certainly not satisfied with this conclusion; but I cannot derive from it an accusation against either judges or authors. The question is unbearable. At least for the time being it seems to me impossible to answer it without escaping into metaphors—whether those of psychoanalysis or jurisprudence. It is impossible to do justice to the question even by extremes of moral indignation. This is not an argument for eliminating Auschwitz from my study. On the contrary, I shall devote a bitter chapter to some possible explanations. But here, in seeking a precise rendering of the German Question, we must take an easier road if we intend to find answers as well as questions.

There is still the hardly less overwhelming version: How was National Socialism possible? More pointedly perhaps, in an often-heard formulation: How was the victory of National Socialism possible in the country of Kant and Goethe? Without doubt, this is one version of the German Question to which we must address ourselves in this study; but there are too many question marks in it to accept it as *the* Question.

The country of Kant and Goethe has been quoted so often that one cannot repeat this formula without hesitation, if not irony. After the war, the great historian Friedrich Meinecke wanted to cure even the "German catastrophe" by reflection on the "sacred heritage of Goethe's time" (150, p. 21). He recommended the foundation of "Goethe communities" all over the country. In doing so, he contributed to a social structure that accommodated not only the "Rembrandt German" but, eventually, the harmless-looking inhumanity that can be worse than stark brutality. With respect to Kant, one cannot help observing that he did not really survive Hegel in Germany. There were and are many who are less concerned with the departure from self-inflicted infancy than with the vain and dangerous search for the reality of the moral ideal. Such comments do not alter the fact, of course, that Germany is the country of Kant and Goethe among others, but they do cast some doubt on the attempt to formulate the German Question in terms of the contradiction between political failure and cultural fruition.

There is another line of argument that leads to the same conclusion and concerns not cultural fruition, but political failure. What is meant if one asks what were the causes of the Nazi victory? The National Socialist German Workers' Party (NSDAP) was certainly a phenomenon of German politics in the 1920s and 1930s. But much of what it represented was effective in other countries as well. Its anti-parliamentarianism may almost be called a fashion of the late twenties; it had quite a few adherents among English conservatives as well as among Americans of both parties. At least a latent anti-Semitism was widespread in many countries after the First World War, as the sorry history of the so-called *Protocols of the Learned Elders of Zion* before and after the revelation of their forgery by the London *Times* in 1921 testifies. There is many a feature of Italian Fascism, later copied by Spanish Fascism, that found advocates in the Action Française as enthusiastic as those in the NSDAP. It is not easy to find a name for these epochal phenomena. "Fascism" as a concept connected with the corporate-state notions of the Italian Fascists, seems almost too precise for the mixture of ideas that dominated the "innovators" of the twenties. Even so, one must concede to Ernst Nolte that we are indeed facing an epoch here.

All this must emphatically not be misconstrued as an apology for National Socialism; the apparently quantitative difference between nearly and wholly successful anti-parliamentary movements has made world history in too unforgettable a way to think of such an apology. The attempt to formulate the German Question as one of National Socialism does, however, seem unsatisfactory. We will have to look rather for a formulation that, without casting the events of 1933 into a milder light or even obscuring them, sets the Nazi rise to power in the wider context of modern German history and society.

Among the many versions of the German Question suggested by Röpke, there is one that seems to satisfy this demand. At one point, Röpke speaks of the necessity "to protect Europe against Germany as Germany against herself" (185, p. 15). In the same year in which this was written, A. J. P. Taylor, in his essay on *The Course of German History*, which, more than anything else, earned him the reputation of Germanophobe, put his case in very similar terms: "The 'German problem' has two distinct sides. How can the peoples of Europe be secured against repeated bouts of German aggression? And how can the German people discover a settled, peaceful form of political existence" (214, pp. 8 f.). Like their author, these questions are less Germanophobe than Machiavellian, as the following sentences make quite clear: "The first problem is capable of easy solution and has often been solved. It was solved by Richelieu and by Metternich. . . . [The solution] is, in general terms: unity of Germany's neighbours, disunity among Germans" (214, p. 9). For Taylor, the German Question is essentially a practical one: How can we protect ourselves from the wolves? We can kill them, but that would be cruel. We therefore have the choice of domesticating them, driving them away, or caging them and letting them tear each other apart. Machiavellianism is inevitably unhistorical, so the historian Taylor formulates his theses unhistorically.

But, it might be argued, is not Taylor right, at least in so far as there is today, after the Second World War, no longer really a German Question? Taylor's own satisfaction with the outcome of the war was short-lived; he has begun again to warn of the new, old "German danger." But is this realistic? Must we not conclude that Taylor's wishes have in fact come true? Has Germany not become a small country, or, to be more precise, two small countries, neither of which would be capable of upsetting the balance of world politics? And is not—to push the cynicism of these questions to the extreme—the internal order of both Germanies comparatively "quiet" and "peaceful"?

At this point it is necessary to remember that although

Germany is no longer a big power, she continues to be one of the great sources of unrest in world politics. Germany belongs to the relatively small group of countries in which all the leading groups question the territorial status quo. For that reason, if for no other, she is still feared in many other nations, including the Soviet Union. In addition, people in many countries have an almost mystical belief in Germany's capacity to accomplish a spectacular return to power. Moreover, the apparent stability of the political regimes of East and West Germany may well be deceptive. Even its friends admit that the balance of power in the DDR is highly precarious; but the Federal Republic, too, has a wider range of potential directions of political development than the current positions of its parties would make one believe. I am not asking at this point whether such facts are desirable or not. What they show, apart from their evaluation, is that there is still a point in seeking the German Question and its answers. But what *is* the German Question?

One version, which has gained wide currency since the Second World War, may, if we examine it more closely, help us in our search. This is the statement of a contrast between Germany and "the West," and its implications. There are many observations to support the statement. As early as 1935 Helmuth Plessner, for example, argued in his study of German intellectual history (republished after the war under the title of *Die verspätete Nation* [The Belated Nation]) that Germany tried to compensate for her inferiority in the First World War by dissociating herself from the value system of the victors. Thus she achieved in her own, characteristically spiritual way what she could not achieve by political or military means. "She thus adheres to her line of struggle against the political humanism of the Western world, whose development and national consolidation occurred in the seventeenth century, that is, at the time of the decay of the old German Empire" (172, p. 32).

This is a subtle and indeed somewhat involved explanation of a German attitude that is both older than 1918 and more concrete than any "struggle against humanism." Like a shadow, a mood of cultural pessimism accompanied industrialization in Germany. The spokesmen of this mood were widely read authors of the fin de siècle. Their search for a truly German character went hand in hand with resentment of everything Western, as Fritz Stern has shown in his study,

The Politics of Cultural Despair (210). In the minds of ordinary people this detachment from the West assumed simpler, more direct forms. Karl Buchheim recognizes this when he refers to the widespread "notion that the mind of the German people and the character of German culture are of a kind different from the mind of the West European countries, so that for the sake of his soul the German has to beware of fashioning the political patterns of his country on those of the West" (35, p. 5). Buchheim adds to this point a telling and insightful remark: "In this respect, the ideology of many Germans showed traits related to the ideology of the Russians."

Germany as a mediator between East and West was and, I would venture, is one of the most widely entertained self-images of German politics, to which nearly all its great protagonists and theoreticians bear witness. While this notion was temporarily silenced by anti-Communist enthusiasm and Adenauer's policies after the war, and therefore seems buried today, it is probably still as alive as ever under the cover of the Western alliance—and, for that matter, under the cover of the Eastern ties of the DDR as well. This is even more true culturally than politically, on the popular level. Unlikely as it may seem, even former prisoners of war tend to blend with their accounts of suffering and terror a trace of the "Russian experience" that has joined the traditional "Italian experience" of artists long before Rilke and Barlach. Germany not only differs from the West, she wants to be different. This is an observation that may well serve as a point of departure for reflecting on the German Question.

The first step of this reflection, however, is one of critical self-evaluation. The "alienation between German and Western thought" to which Hans Kohn refers (117, p. 23) is certainly a version of the German Question. Gerhard Ritter chooses this version when he emphasizes the question of "how it happened that a strongly felt contrast of political thinking and political patterns of life emerged between Western Europe and us in modern times" (183, p. 11). A score of others might also be cited on this particular version. Their number unfortunately adds little to the precision of the question.

Possibly, "the West" is an historical reality. There may be certain features shared by Breslau and Seattle, Aberdeen and Palermo, Helsinki and San Diego, Dublin, Cherbourg, and Prague, which at the same time distinguish the people of these cities from those in Murmansk and Tiflis, Rangoon and Bangkok, Peking and Tokyo, Addis Ababa and Lagos. Actually, it is not easy to name very many common distinguishing features of this sort. Even Christianity can be described as a Western force only historically; its ambitions and contemporary realities are more complex. The "respect for life," which Albert Schweitzer never tired of demanding, may evoke a more immediate response in Western European and North American culture, which is oriented to the protection of human life; but it is by no means a "Western" prerogative. In any case, one hardly dares refer to the application of this principle in Germany. Moreover, the Western advantage (quite uneven in any case) is diminishing rapidly with respect to the accomplishments of modern civilization, such as medicine, technical development, educational opportunity, the system of law. In the end, all that seems to remain as its real possession is capitalism, the Communist image of the West, and the impression that, however we may choose to define "the West," Germany has deviated from it in the last decades and is thus only precariously part of it.

But we cannot stop here. It is clear now that "the West" is in many ways less than an historical reality. When Ritter refers to "Western Europe," he hides the incompatible behind the appealing façade of a single concept: the Cartesian rationality of French Enlightenment and the economic rationality of British political theory. Or is Ritter also using the notion of "the West" as a somewhat embarrassed circumscription of what Charles de Gaulle calls "the Anglo-Saxon character"? For here, and perhaps here only, there are indeed identifiable common patterns that can be used as a standard to measure developments elsewhere. If this is done, Germany will not always stand as alone as most discussions of the German Question would suggest. For de Gaulle's reasoning was less absurd than his conclusions when he contrasted the "Continent," that is, France and Germany, with "Anglo-Saxon traditions" in order to block Britain's entry into the Common Market. Do we have to conclude, then, that the German Question is in fact a "continental European," or indeed a "Franco-German" one?

We do not; yet this brings us close to the conclusion of this involved discussion of an involved problem. There is a German Question. But summary terms such as "Western Europe" or "the West" do not lend themselves to a very precise formulation of it. Why are Germany and the West compared in the first place? What is the point of such comparisons, considering that most Germans in the past and many even today are quite unconcerned about belonging to the West? The questions are evidently rhetorical. While "the West" may appear to be an historical or geographical notion, it is, in fact, intended to suggest a set of values. Germany's alienation from the West is an alienation from certain valued attitudes and patterns of social life. To note the contrast between Germany and Western Europe is to apply a moral standard to German history. Underlying such analyses is the desire to lead Germany back to the path of virtue from which she strayed at some point—with Luther, with Frederick William I of Prussia, with Hegel, with Bismarck, with William II, whatever the author's idiosyncratic thesis may be.

These are laudable intentions. There is nothing fundamentally wrong with this approach even as a method of analysis. Indeed, it proves the important truism that any analysis that fails to bring value judgments to bear on its subject is bound to remain barren. But it is preferable to formulate such value judgments explicitly rather than to disguise them under complex historical concepts. Such explicitness leads incidentally to a more cautious evaluation of Luther and Frederick William I, Hegel and Bismarck, because they are no longer needed as precursors ex post facto. And the explicit formulation of values provides, also incidentally, a standard by which other countries, too, may be measured and found lacking. Our main intention at present, however, is to find a precise way of posing the problem, and it is here that a statement of values has its greatest use. What then, finally, is the German Question?

There is a basic political attitude of which much more will be said in this study. Briefly, it may be characterized by three premises: (1) All men are imperfect in the sense that no one can know for certain what is good for himself and everyone else. The substance of justice is uncertain. There are, to be sure, firm convictions, and it is evidently possible to convince others, either by argument or by demagoguery; but nobody can establish the binding validity of his convictions except by force. (2) There is thus always a plurality of proposals for short-term and, especially, long-term solutions of social and political problems. Without forcible suppression, all proposals are competitive. (3) It is possible that any design of a socio-political nature has a propensity to absoluteness.

If this is so, we can follow Theodor Eschenburg in expecting institutions to protect us from the badness of men. In any case, political institutions exist to make sure that no single design, no single idea of justice will prevail at the expense of all others. Political institutions serve to canalize and thereby maintain the competition of designs. This involves, among other things, the effective control of those who themselves control the means of force.

Such a brief summation of so important a matter is bound to be misleading. Since, however, I intend to elaborate on these suggestions later, the inevitable first impression of superficiality may be corrected. After all, one of the minor themes of this study is the chances the constitution of liberty has in the modern world. There are three labels—terms may be a more attractive word—I shall use throughout to describe the attitude just outlined. The first statement made to characterize it is of an anthropological, or perhaps an epistemological kind. It concerns one assumption of the experimental or *empirical* approach, which declares that all knowledge is potentially false. The second statement relates to social facts. It describes social conditions as intrinsically *pluralistic*. Here I am very hesitant in respect to the choice of the word, for in contemporary public debate pluralism has all but lost any definite meaning. But it is the third statement about which I feel most strongly. It concerns political theory and formulates as a general principle a position that in the history of theory has been called *liberal*. The value attitude underlying this study then is one of liberalism.

The concept of liberalism has had both a social and a national history; the same holds for democracy, which, in order to complete the temporary confusion, I now want to connect with it. Neither concept can be used today entirely without irony. So far as their German pathology is concerned, this may be illustrated by a single sentence of Gerhard Ritter's: "Democracy in its original, strict sense not yet softened by liberal admixtures is not the safeguarding of personal liberty against arbitrary rule and relentless force, but the immediate rule of the people" (183, p. 45). That this sentence with its remarkable mixture of naïveté of theoretical substance and maliciousness of political effect could have been written by an important historian, leads us directly back to the German Question.

Democracy means many things to many men. There is an

egalitarian version as Tocqueville understood it; there is a totalitarian version, which J. L. Talmon has shown originated from precisely that democracy in its "original, strict sense" praised by Ritter; there is a liberal version. In this study the term democracy will be used with discretion, but always in the sense of "softened by liberal admixtures." There is no shortage of discussions about the aroma of these admixtures either. There are classical liberals and neo-liberals, national liberals and social liberals; one is almost inclined to compliment Ritter for not regarding the word as an epitheton ornans. Since I am going to use the word "liberal" frequently in this study, it seems useful to emphasize in advance that I understand this epitheton ornans in a classical rather than a neo-liberal, and certainly in a social rather than a national sense.

But we have played with concepts long enough. There is a basic attitude, political in intention and effect, that is characterized by the search for institutional means to control the powerful in order to keep the political system open for ever new solutions. Underlying this attitude are an empirical theory of knowledge and the sociological insight into the pluralist character of social reality. One may describe the institutions built on these assumptions as those of a liberal democracy. What the constitution of liberal democracy looks like and has to look like in detail cannot be determined, either for all countries or for all times; the same principle permits of many different historical forms. But the principle remains the institutional safeguarding of liberty by effective protection from the dogmatic establishment of one-sided positions.

This is doubtless a partisan principle; but it is not partisan in terms of political parties. Its goal is certainly not everybody's goal, but it is the realistic goal of any policy of liberty: the greatest happiness of the greatest number. True, it is almost as difficult to measure the happiness of men as it is to create it. But perhaps these are difficulties of rather less consequence than the ones facing those for whom the relative best does not suffice because they are plagued by a propensity for absolutes. To oppose them, the liberal attitude takes a partisan stand as the party of relative but real liberty against its absolute but abstract version. When I use the word "liberal" in this study I am not referring to the rather unfortunate history and present state of German liberalism, but to what F. A. von Hayek has called the *Constitution of Liberty* and what has been wished for so long and so vainly by "the demo-crats not established by party membership" in Germany (to use Carl Amery's phrase).

Thus we are at last able to formulate the German Question and launch our investigation: Why is it that so few in Germany embraced the principle of liberal democracy? There were enemies of liberalism everywhere, and there still are to-day. There may even be or have been other countries in which liberal democracy has found as little recognition as it did in Germany. Since we are looking for a general standard that will permit us to establish the liberal potential of any country, no initial deprecation of Germany is implied by our question. But in this study we want to find out what it is in German society that may account for Germany's persistent failure to give a home to democracy in its liberal sense. This is not, of course, a new idea. It probably does not differ sub-stantially from that of many authors who contrast Germany and the West. Therefore, the skeptical question remains whether we are not ourselves guilty of dogmatizing a one-sided value attitude if we take this course. Does not the pro-cedure we recommend contradict its own moral principle? There is no question that I should be glad if, by this study, I were to succeed in converting some to a more liberal approach to politics. After what has been said it will not come as a surprise if I assert that I regard the principle of liberal democracy as the only safe basis of any constitution of lib-erty. In addition, it seems to me that social, economic, and political history in the last two centuries or so all tell in favor of the liberal principle. Thus this study is, among other things, a plea for the principle of liberal democracy. But I hope that it is not a naïve plea. One need not accept the value attitude for which I am pleading; one can keep the household of one's political ideas free of all liberal admixtures. Moreover, if one does so—and this, above all, is important in the pres-ent context—this will not affect at all the way in which this study is arranged, or its questions and answers. Quite apart from its substantive value, the principle of liberal democ-racy proves a master key to the light as well as the dark cor-ners of the unknown society, and as such I intend to use it here.

Tocqueville described the United States as a country in which, surprisingly, (egalitarian) democracy existed. In this study, we are concerned with Germany as a country in which, surprisingly, (liberal) democracy did not exist. Tocqueville wanted to explain what it was in American society that produced and supported the democratic order. I want to explain what it was in German society that continued to prevent the establishment of a democratic order. The comparison, however, is a lame one. By his description of America, Tocqueville wanted to contribute to the discussion of the "French question" of his time. My own concern is to apply an instrument of knowledge to the analysis of German society that may also promote its change: What has to happen to make liberal democracy possible in Germany? This, too, is a version of the German Question.

Two ambiguous points in this version of the German Question must be clarified before we embark on our analysis. Asking for the causes of the National Socialist victory in Germany means raising a question that is both definite and concrete. We shall certainly not evade this question—indeed we could not do so—since the events of 1933 are the most striking single symptom of the malaise of the liberal principle in Germany. But by phrasing the German Question more generally, we have admittedly, and somewhat annoyingly, made it much less definite. Are we trying to determine why liberal democracy *was* or *is* lacking in Germany? Are we concerned with the conditions under which the Federal Republic of Germany or the German Democratic Republic may become a country of liberal democracy? Or are we concerned with the conditions under which Imperial Germany might have been more liberal? In short: When is Germany? And where is Germany?

Since there are no correct answers to these questions, we need considered decisions rather than long discussions. The sociologist is not always on the best of terms with the historian or the geographer; his colleagues in these neighboring disciplines tend to blame him for the generosity of his intercourse with time and space. Yet the sociologist would abandon his freedom of analysis, were he to renounce this generosity entirely. German society probably has more continuity in the dimensions of time and space than the breaks of historical events and territorial changes would lead one to suspect. The German Question is posed in this study for Imperial Germany and for the Weimar Republic, for the Third Reich and for Germany after the Second World War, for the German Democratic Republic and for the Federal Republic.

Naturally some explanations are specific, others describe a common substratum of all parts and periods of German society in the last century or so. That there have been changes in this period is, of course, one of the themes of this study. That the structures of German society were not, and are not, as uniform as the singular "society" promises, will perhaps not always be as evident as the historian might wish. Mentioning this here may to some extent excuse the deficiency. But the fact that it would also be possible to write books about democracy in the Hanseatic towns or in Prussia, in the Weimar Republic or in the DDR, can not invalidate the attempt to deal with democracy in Germany. When is Germany? Roughly speaking, in the last hundred years. Where is Germany? In all territories that belonged to Germany during this span of time.

Questions are like revolutions. Once one gets started, it is hard to find an end; both seem to breed incessantly. Thus there is something arbitrary in putting an end to them. In this chapter, many questions have been raised in order to pose one. John Locke was no German; neither was Adam Smith nor John Stuart Mill. *The Federalist Papers* were not written in Germany, and pragmatism was not invented there. Immanuel Kant unfortunately stopped short of the crossroads that would have forced him to consider the political consequences of his theoretical philosophy more radically than was possible in occasional essays. What happened at writing desks was symptomatic of other, more important things that happened in cabinet chambers and parliaments, in election campaigns and political demonstrations. There is an experimental attitude that allows anybody to propose new solutions, but rejects any dogmatic claim to truth. There is a liberal doubt that seeks to build fences around those in power, rather than bridges for them. There is a competitive spirit that can lead to progress only when there is a struggle for predominance in every field. There is a conception of liberty that holds that man can be free only where an experimental attitude to knowledge, the competition of social forces, and liberal political institutions are combined. This conception has never really gained a hold in Germany. Why not? This is the German Question.

2. POLITICS, CHARACTER,
AND SOCIETY

The impatient reader who is in a hurry to find out the answer
to the German Question may as well skip this chapter. Here I
want to devote some reflections to matters of methodology,
that is, to examining the way in which we may be able to
answer our question and, above all, the various ways in which
a satisfactory answer is at least improbable. In the literature,
there are many memorable attempts to master the German
Question; but quite often these carry as little conviction as the
political attempts to master the question practically. This assertion has to be proved. And, a few remarks may be in order
about the precise meaning of our promise to provide a
sociological analysis of German society with a political
perspective.

In keeping with the experimental approach, let us begin
with the refutations. Most of the many attempts to answer the
German Question may be localized somewhere on a scale that
ranges from Hitler to Tacitus. Strictly speaking, the combination of names is unfair; it is obviously largely symbolic. There
are explanations in terms of short-range historical developments, even individual events or men on the one hand ("Versailles," "the Depression," "Hitler the seducer"), and in terms
of historical universals, archetypical phenomena removed
from change altogether on the other ("even the ancient Germans as Tacitus described them . . ."). It may be worth looking at a few points on this scale a little more closely.

Since the Second World War, a conception of Germany's
recent history has become established in the Federal Republic,
in which professional historians largely agree with the authors
of school textbooks and which for that reason, if for no other,
is gaining an ever firmer hold on the public. The point of
departure for this conception is the thesis that all the countries involved more or less "slithered" into the First World
War. Nobody is really responsible for the outbreak of war in
1914, or else responsibility is equally divided between all.
Germany lost the First World War; she had to accept a harsh

peace treaty. However—so the story continues—the Treaty of Versailles, which ascribed responsibility for the war to Germany and imposed severe territorial, military, and economic measures, did not correspond to the common responsibility of victors and vanquished. It was an overreaction from which all other overreactions had of necessity to follow. The severity of the Versailles treaty was bound to give rise to a national countermovement, which took the form of National Socialism. A number of additional problems, largely of an economic nature, such as the inflation of 1922 and the depression of 1929, helped National Socialism to its victory. Then a terrible aberration of German history began, unpardonable in its dimensions, yet understandable in its origins. The worst of these aberrations, however, do not implicate the German people, but are entirely the work of its seducers. The Second World War, then, was largely Hitler's doing, although even here responsibility is not distributed as one-sidedly as many want it . . .

This is rather a tranquilizing instrument of self-interpretation, in so far as German history permits of tranquillity at all. Is it also a legitimate instrument? Indeed, is it an answer to the German Question?

So far as the legitimacy of the alleged sequence of responsibility and innocence is concerned, Fritz Fischer's book, *Griff nach der Weltmacht* [The Grasp for World Power], has convinced us that it is at the very least precarious. The case is of considerable interest; Fischer has published documents proving far-reaching imperialist designs on the part of leading German politicians before the First World War and has drawn from them the conclusion that Germany was, in fact, largely responsible for the outbreak of the war. The reaction of the historical profession to this book by one of its members was and is astonishing. Its bitterness and intensity are understandable only if we remember that Fischer has pulled the center piece out of the whole, useful conception of history the profession has built up.

If the First World War did not come about by accident or (which is in effect the same) by some superior inevitability, or even the common responsibility of all, then the Treaty of Versailles appears in a different light and with it the emergence and victory of the National Socialist movement . . . But is a scholar trespassing if he questions an ideology of justification? Is it not one of his tasks to do so whenever he can?

It would be of little help here to meddle in this professional conflict. For us, it is the range of the explanations offered that is of primary interest. For even apart from the highly dubious assumption that National Socialism was an inevitable reaction to the Treaty of Versailles, it can be demonstrated that the range of this explanation is short and that, in this as in other respects, Fischer has touched a sore as well as a crucial point. The ultimate basis of the accepted historical explanation of Germany's recent history is an accident, or at least an event removed from any definite responsibility of concrete persons—the parthenogenesis of the First World War. What appears here is Mephisto's hand in history, a beginning preceded by nothing, nothing in any case that would have a decisive bearing on the consequences. One does not, to be sure, have to go on asking questions in order to go on living. But to suggest an explanation of this kind is taking an easy way out of a very hard problem.

When Fischer's book was discussed at the Berlin meetings of the German Historical Association in 1964, the American historian Fritz Stern rightly pointed out that it is a grotesque misunderstanding of the problem to substitute a discussion of the genuineness and weight of documents for a serious explanation of historical events. He also raised another question. By comparing the catastrophic turns of recent German history with a series of work accidents in industry, he asked whether such a series could happen anywhere without somebody suspecting that something must be wrong somewhere in the enterprise (cf. 211). The question, rhetorical though it obviously was, embarrassed German historians, because it touched on the foundations of prevailing historical explanations.

Not all historians have allowed their vision to be narrowed by the somewhat pathetic and remarkably ideological textbook perspective. Increasingly, great historiography has turned to looking for continuities in German history. Stern's own contribution, his study of the political potential of German cultural pessimism, has been mentioned before (cf. 210). Other historians around Hajo Holborn—and including himself —have followed a similar line of historical analysis. Leonard Krieger's study, *The German Idea of Freedom* (119), which explores the connection between small-state notions of sovereignty and the German misconception of liberalism, may serve as an example. A. J. P. Taylor is also exploring continuities, if with different intentions. Even Gerhard Ritter has made many contributions to this undertaking, including the derivation of the German catastrophe from the "one-sidedly authoritarian tradition of the military-bureaucratic authoritarian state" of Prussia (183, p. 40), and from Lutheranism as that version of the Reformation which became established not against, but by the princes. This search for continuities and derivations has found entry into more comprehensive historical writings by Golo Mann, Paul Sethe, and others (although less into those by members of the German historical establishment).

There can be no doubt about the significance of such middle-range historical research. But if we are looking for explanation, it shares the limitations of all historiography. One can learn from history, but one cannot apply the lessons. Both the greatness and the limitation of historical presentations accrue perhaps from the force of uniqueness; they can try to revive the color and richness of events, but the process by which they do so is one of reproductive understanding and of artful presentation of secondhand experience. The most that an historical presentation of the antecedents of 1914, 1933, 1940 can hope to achieve is the affirmative nod of the reader: Yes, now I know how it came about. This nod need not be forgotten. Knowledge by understanding certainly forms a good part of any man's mental habitus; it changes us, as all education changes us. Yet understanding remains inconsequential in a decisive sense: it does not tell us what we have to do to prevent the return of the false and to help achieve the advent of the right.

There is yet another objection, which applies to even the most grandiose historical explanation. The nod of understanding documents a feeling of evidence; however, a friend, a neighbor, and above all an enemy, a stranger may not share this feeling. It is always possible to say: No, this is seen quite wrongly. What is worse, there is no agency and no method capable of deciding who is right, friend or foe, neighbor or stranger, Fischer or Zechlin. There is an element of arbitrariness in even the most penetrating historical analysis. And this arbitrariness cannot be removed by further research, for it comes not from any lack of evidence but from the logical status of interpretive statements in an epistemology aimed explicitly at evident insights rather than testable theories.

All this holds a fortiori, especially in its critical undertones,

for the type of historical analysis that since Dilthey and Meinecke has been favored in Germany: the study of intellectual
history as a clue to social and political events. It may not be a
very serious objection to this type of analysis to say that it is
particularly liable to dilettantism. But it does make one wonder that so many believe that *Der deutsche Geist von Luther
bis Nietzsche* [The German Mind from Luther to Nietzsche
(203)]—as a book by the Frenchman Jean-Edouard Spenlé is
called—has revealed itself to them and solved the German
Question for them. Friedrich Meinecke is clearly no dilettant,
nor would it be fair to judge him on the basis of his "reflections and memories" about *The German Catastrophe* (150)
alone. But are the following sentences really merely the fool-
ishness of old age and not of method?

> From decade to decade this stronger tie to reality proceeds,
> and the need recedes to live in a superreal, higher and eter-
> nal [realm]. Today, Goethe once observed to Zeller, all that
> people want is wealth and speed. The new magic arts of the
> steam engine and the railway create the new cult of coal and
> iron. The new realism takes a hold of intellectual life too,
> sets an end to a form of life oriented purely to the improve-
> ment and spiritualization of one's own individuality and di-
> rects the mind more to people's common life in masses, to the
> social entity and the nation as a whole. In addition [there are]
> the well-known motive forces of domestic policy, the revolt
> against the police state, the demand for constitutions in order
> to help the middle class to power. Thus the way is prepared
> for the revolution of 1848 which was not merely a cry for
> greater liberty, but, as Dahlmann once said, in its greater part
> the cry of the nation for power.
>
> But the modern man of power in Germany, as we have
> finally experienced him among ourselves to our horror, was
> not yet completed by any means. There were many intermedi-
> ate stages left in German humanity from the time of Goethe
> to the time of Bismarck, and from the time of Bismarck to the
> time of Hitler. . . . (159, pp. 30 f.)

This, too, is a contribution to the German Question.
Whether it is also a contribution to its explanation would
seem rather doubtful. Doubts are raised, in the first place, by
the syntactic meaninglessness of the sentences and the vagueness of the concepts (two sins, incidentally, that are not in-
frequent in the writing of intellectual history). A glance at
the grammatical subjects of the statements tells a story of its
own: "[the] tie to reality," "the need . . . ," "the new magic

arts," "the new realism," "the well-known motive forces," "the revolution," "the modern man of power," etc., There are many references to reality, but hardly anything that is said is real in any definite sense. In fact, the style could be described as a technique to accomplish the evaporation of all reality into metaphor. What makes such statements dubious is not that they are not true, but that they cannot be false. There are times when intellectual history appears as the catch-as-catch-can of historical scholarship, where anything goes because everything is arbitrary in any case.

Explanations that do not explain, statements that do not state anything—these are two weaknesses of many analyses of the German Question. We must now add a third: a deficient sense of history, a failure to understand that change is probably the only persistent quality of the social works of man. Not surprisingly, this third deficiency is rarer among historians than it is among philosophers and sociologists. Yet even historians occasionally fall victim to it. If, for example, Gerhard Ritter asks for "the meaning of German history," even the quotation marks (found in the original) cannot mitigate the impression that here an historian is engaging in history-less metaphysics. Hegel, of course, also thought that his sequence of the four world empires (with the "Germanic Empire" at the point of culmination) was an expression of the law of all history. But what kind of history is it that adumbrates territorial boundaries, about whose accidental nature and variability the historian himself has many a story to tell, with an almost religious sanctity?

It is an ancient and indispensable philosophical problem to ask the meaning of history. But why should "German history" have a peculiar meaning, different from that of French, English, American history? And why after all "German," and not "Prussian" or "Bavarian" history? The invocation of a "meaning of German history" is not designed for such questions. It contains an element of that historical metaphysics whose decisive weakness is not that it is metaphysics, but that it is not history. It is only a step from some imaginary "meaning of German history" to the "eternal nature of German man."

While it is easy to pour irony on such approaches, we must not overlook the fact that probably no explanation of the German Question is more widespread than that which invokes the "German character."

Over and beyond all changes and shifts of historical situations, the following basic properties of the nature of Germans have proved to be particularly unchangeable, unassailable, or (when they were temporarily modified or obscured) to be always returning:

1. the urge to work,
2. thoroughness,
3. love of orderliness,
4. aversion to formalism,
5. self-willedness,
6. romanticism. (96, p. 171.)

This, too, was written by an aging, but important man—Willy Hellpach, long-time professor of psychology in Heidelberg who, as candidate for Reich President in 1925, managed to gather no less than a million and a half votes on the first ballot. Wilhelm Röpke's feelings for his former compatriots are not quite as friendly. He is looking for a "constant means of proof accessible to scientific analysis" by having recourse to the "spirit of German language," but his conclusions differ little from those of Hellpach:

The German language mirrors the unbound, anarchical, soft, indefinite, romantic-unclassical, sentimental, brooding and vague which has been peculiar to the German as long as his language. It confirms the trait of involution, of the Gothic and the Baroque which has struck every acute observer of the German and which the German has to admit to himself. It is at the same time the dreaming and brooding quality, introspective and staring into the unexplorable, which makes Dürer's "Melancholy" one of the most German of all works of art. It is the irrational which, as we shall see a little later, time and again breaks through in the history of the German soul and contrasts so strongly with the Latin rigidity of form and clarity. . . . (185, pp. 140 f.)

It is difficult to avoid satire in the face of such formulations; the superlative of "German" is no less tempting here than the "history of the German soul." But once again we have to remember that this was not written by a youthful court reporter or a first-term student of German literature, but by one of the most highly regarded contemporary social scientists. The problem is therefore rather more serious than satire would have it; and we shall have to explain why, in this study, we are not going to adduce an eternal, substantively defined "German character" in order to answer the German Question.

Helmuth Plessner advances one significant argument against the concept of national character in his study of the German Question, namely, that this kind of approach tends to be tautological. Often, what has happened in national history is simply imputed to national character. "National character, regarded as a quasi-prehistorical system of dispositions, thus contains nothing but what has been recognized and retained as essential for the formation of national peculiarities from the history of a nation: the Varus battle, the Reformation, the impetuosity of Storm and Stress." Plessner rightly adds: "But to hold such immutable character traits responsible for the actions and sufferings of a nation—by way of apology or accusation, as required—means to turn upside down the history in which and by which they have been formed" (172, p. 22). Prehistoric national characters have a status somewhat similar to that of instinct theories: they repeat an observed state of affairs in terms that are removed from the control of intersubjective experience, and thus manage to add nothing to the original observations except a mystical air of obscurity.

There is another point also. The crude notion of national character we have discussed so far is not merely tautological, it is also remarkably defeatist. Even Taylor, who is otherwise careful to avoid the unreflected mythology of a German character, is not very encouraging when he says: "It has taken about four hundred years to build the Germans into their present frame of mind; and there is no knowing how long it will need to take the frame down again" (214, p. 9). Taylor's "German frame of mind," however, has at least come about gradually and is therefore historical. The real problem begins with those "basic properties" that have survived "all changes and shifts of historical situations." Who could so much as think of changing them? On the other hand, if there are such solid properties, why is there something like education at all— or history for that matter? Its defeatism may not be a very strong argument against the notion of national character; but its obvious lack of an historical quality leads us to the decisive objection against this approach.

There is a sophisticated notion of national character, which has emerged from modern sociology and social psychology but which cannot be dismissed as simply. Here, national character appears as one of many social roles, a complex of expectations by which any incumbent of the relevant position is

surrounded at a given time. We will have occasion later to
explore the substance of this role in detail and even to take
up ironically the title of Hellpach's book (cf. 96), *The German Character*. But we can anticipate the methodical principle of this treatment here. "The German" is expected to
behave in a certain manner, much as "the man," "the
secondary-school teacher," "the fellow clubman" is. One can
learn this role; one can also deviate from the demands attached to it. Moreover, the expectations hold here and now;
they are strictly historical. Barely a decade and a half after
the beginning of Germany's "economic miracle" (for which
Röpke incidentally laid much of the theoretical groundwork),
Röpke's character mask of the German has turned into an
historical reminiscence. Even if one does not regard today's
young Germans as a "skeptical generation," one searches in
vain among them, apart from all "romanticism," for traces of
"thoroughness" and "love of orderliness." Of course, Röpke's
comparative use of the adjective "German" might prompt the
objection that the Germans of today are simply less German
than their forefathers; but such rescue attempts of lost theories refute these more thoroughly than any direct test or argument could do.

We have passed along the scale of errors in the treatment
of the German Question—a little quickly perhaps, but in proportion to the importance of the errors. The scale ranges, as
I have said, from Hitler to Tacitus. At one of its end points
there is the attempt to hold a single man or event responsible
for all that happened; at the other extreme are authors who
have recourse to the most distant causes removed from all
historical change: "Everything is Hitler's fault"; "The Germans have always run true to the type described by Tacitus."
Methodologically, the error of specificity is no better than
that of generality; neither of them helps us to a satisfactory
understanding of the German Question.

It is an open question, of course, whether an approach informed by sociology can avoid both fallacies, as well as the
numerous minor weaknesses of all approaches between the
extremes. The fact that the sociologist tends both to reorgan-
ize history as the textbook authors present it and to disor-
ganize the myth cultivated by the apologists for national character describes merely the destructive part of his work.
Fortunately there is a constructive part as well, a way of deal-

ing with the German Question without falling into the traps
of misplaced specificity or generality.

The case is simple, and familiar to any student of society.
We have defined the German Question as a question of the
obstacles to liberal democracy in Germany. Liberal democracy is a political principle. But historical political structures
are not suspended in mid-air, as anybody knows who has ever
said or thought: It is obvious that democracy in the Western
sense cannot work in the Congo. Why should this be "obvious"? The reasons given—lack of preparation for independence on the part of the Belgian colonial masters, the low
educational standard of the people, economic difficulties, the
absence of an indigenous elite—are not always very convincing, but they show that at least with respect to the new nations
people are aware of the fact that constitutions require an infrastructure in order to gain a hold. Political constitutions
need certain social structures in the sense that they cannot
become effective unless the society for which they are designed is organized in certain ways. Here as elsewhere there
is no simple one-way determination; given social structures
do not "create" their own constitutions (a most imprecise
metaphor in any case), but social structures do set fairly narrow boundaries to the effectiveness of political institutions.
One can give South Vietnam the constitution of the Federal
Republic of Germany, but one cannot make it work the same
way, or indeed bring it to life at all, without fundamentally
changing Vietnamese society.

There is no reason to assume that what holds for new nations is any less true in the older ones. In other words, we are
now no longer concerned with spatial or temporal peculiarities, but with the possibility of a general theory. Under which
social conditions will the liberal principle become established
in a country? This is the question the sociological theory of
democracy must answer.

This theory is as old as the notion of the constitution of
liberty itself. Indeed, a notable feature of the history of political theory is that analysis of the social conditions underlying political constitutions is most frequently associated with
the theory of democracy; the sociological theory of tyranny
is by comparison a recent invention. One may, of course,
doubt whether Aristotle really had a liberal society in mind
when he designed his mixed constitution based on a strong
middle class, but the figure of thought is there—as it is in the

works of Montesquieu and again of Tocqueville, to mention but three great political theorists of liberty with a sociological bent.

In recent years, the sociological theory of democracy has made great strides, and the present study is implicitly a contribution to the debate about this theory. Theoretical development has profited greatly from the fact that authors reared in diverse disciplines have added to it: economists from Joseph Schumpeter to Kenneth Arrow and Milton Friedman, political scientists from Harold Laski to David Truman and Robert Dahl, sociologists from Karl Mannheim to Raymond Aron and Seymour Martin Lipset. In looking at this list of names —which is unquestionably idiosyncratic, and yet not arbitrary —one is struck by the fact that the older authors in it (Schumpeter, Laski, Mannheim) all had, at some stage or continuously, socialist leanings; they were therefore liable to emphasize the egalitarian preconditions of what they called democracy and to propose activist, practical theories of politics. The younger authors on the other hand incline more to a liberal conception of democracy; as a consequence, their theories have become more subtle and complex, with equality figuring as but one of many elements in them. I need not add at this point that I share without reservation the inclinations of these "younger" authors.

It is a debatable point exactly how profitable a general theory of democracy is likely to be. If we look at the literature, political and sociological thought seems most advanced where it concentrates on specific relations: the connection between industrialization and liberal institutions, or international relations and democracy, or the process of maximizing political support under marketlike conditions. To the extent that such specificity may be called advanced, the present study is backward; here I shall confine myself to a general and thus almost by necessity rudimentary approach to the sociological theory of democracy (and, moreover, leave out entirely the important current problem of the relation between internal liberal structures and the system of international relations). As a result, I will employ what can barely be called a theory, but is, rather, a pre-theoretical orientation informed by the discussion of the subject in politics, economics, and sociology and designed to guide us to areas of social structure relevant to the anchoring of the constitution of liberty. It seems to me that four such areas are of central importance, and their analysis may provide a starting point for the formulation of more specific and methodologically satisfactory theories:

1. First of all, the relation between political constitution and social structure is determined by the ways in which individuals participate in the life of their society. These are crystallized in the generalized membership role. In more political terms, this means that the extent to which the social role of the citizen is realized provides us with a first index for the chances of political democracy in a given country. If one wants to describe this basis of the system of social differentiation traditionally, the notion of *equality* of opportunities of participation occurs—actually a misleading concept, which, as we shall see, is in contrast to infancy rather than to inequality.

2. Equality of citizenship rights is a necessary, but not a sufficient, condition for establishing the constitution of liberty socially. It is on the foundation of certain equalities associated with the status of citizenship that the institutions within which citizens act are built. These, however, are characterized by one feature highly relevant for the realization of the liberal principle of democracy, that is, internal tensions and antagonisms. Societies differ markedly in the ways in which they deal with their *conflicts,* and these differences are possibly a main cause, in any case a symptom, of variations in political structure. The extent to which conflict is regulated rationally is probably the most significant dimension of variability in this context.

3. Metaphors are a slippery ground for argument; but having said this I suggest we turn our view from the foundation of equality and the structure of conflict to the rooftop of elites. These, too, assume a great variety of characters in different societies. Of the many ways of classifying them, the most relevant for the theory of democracy is in terms of their uniformity or *diversity* in relation to the social interests and groupings reflected by them. This is still a simplified and preliminary discussion, but there is—or so we assert in this approach—a positive correlation between diversity of elites and working democratic institutions.

4. After foundation, structure, and roof there remains the seemingly even more vague "atmosphere," which pervades the building. This consists, of course, of values—valid or ruling, established by consensus or enforced by authority—the favorite topic of modern sociology. There is no dearth of

classifications of values; but the public-private dichotomy, which I want to take up in this study, is relatively unburdened by theoretical claims. The constitution of liberty works, then, to the extent to which a society is dominated by *public virtues*.

This statement of the theoretical perspective employed in this study is as general as it is superficial. It refers in principle to the social limitations imposed on any political constitution, and it tells us little more than how we can hope to find points of orientation for an analysis of the social structure of politics in the ocean of social reality. If we try to be a little more precise and relate the perspective to the constitution of liberty, a sequence of four statements emerges, which the sympathetic reader may regard as the beginning of a sociological theory of democracy: liberal democracy can become effective only in a society in which, (1) equal citizenship rights have been generalized; (2) conflicts are recognized and regulated rationally in all institutional orders; (3) elites reflect the color and diversity of social interests; and (4) public virtues are the predominant value orientation of the people. If this is rather less than a theory, it still provides a workable perspective and guideline for our study.

The relative modesty of this claim is not a mere captatio benevolentiae. I realize fully that if I judge the theoretical perspective offered here with the same ruthlessness as I have the attempts of others, the balance is only very slightly in favor of this approach. A series of four statements is considerably less than a theory. Nothing has been said about the relative weight of the problem areas, and little about their precise features or even the ways in which an intersubjectively binding ("operational") identification of "equality," "rational conflict regulation," "diversity," and "public virtues" becomes possible. It is easy to see in advance that a "theory" of this kind will frequently force us to make statements that cannot satisfy the rigorous demands of empirical science. Indeed, there will be many points at which theses developed here will closely resemble the vagueness of intellectual history and employ methods of *Verstehen* rather than of theory and test. Perhaps the demand for a rigorous sociological theory of democracy transcends the possibilities of social science at the moment. Perhaps it simply transcends my own abilities. In any case I will not be able to satisfy the demand.

This leaves us with a very modest conclusion to the methodological argument. Reducing the German Question to specific events or individuals as causes or culprits yields little in terms of general knowledge. But middle-range historical derivations also leave much to be desired; they describe what happened in terms that defy the test of controllable experience. This holds a fortiori for the derivations of intellectual history, which are arbitrary almost by definition. But the other extreme, the grasp for superhistorical constants of national character is no less unsatisfactory, since its tautological statements ignore the fundamental and pervasive historicity of all things social. Strictly speaking, we need a theory, or several theories, of the relation between democracy and social structure. Until we have these, an orientation, a theoretical perspective, which may help us avoid some of the cruder fallacies of other approaches as well as organize and relate the endless descriptive material about a given society, has to do.

3. IMPERIAL GERMANY AND THE INDUSTRIAL REVOLUTION

Liberal democracy is not as old as its sympathetic historians would have it. If we look at the reality of its institutions rather than at the theory of its principles, it is a very recent discovery indeed, which barely takes us back to the Jacksonian revolution in the United States, much less to the French Revolution, and certainly not to the English revolutions of the seventeenth century. In fact, if this were not too confusing a thing to say, one might well assert that up to the present day liberal democracy did not and could not become real anywhere. The reality of the liberal principle presupposes the completion of those two revolutions that Marx combined in a brilliant turn of thought—although only in our century did they in fact occur together in some places—that is, the French and the Industrial revolutions, the principle of equal citizenship rights and the dissolution of the rigid orders of traditional dependence. Formally, liberal democracy must remain a model en miniature without these revolutions, a test game in the inherited sand pit in which—as in the Greek cities or in modern England—only a minority may participate. Substantively, these revolutions set in motion the interplay first of an old and a new, later of two new classes, which filled the political system of the institutionalized alternative with life (a conflict that, incidentally, in a rather discouraging loop, has brought with its fulfillment the slackening of its own dynamics, so that today, once again, one feels the need to "get the world moving"). If this is correct, it follows that the question of the relationship between liberal democracy and certain social structures could not emerge before the nineteenth century, and that the German Question has its definite origin in the decades determined by the political activity of Bismarck.

To be sure, the beginnings of the realization of the liberal principle have their historical antecedents. That the conditions for realizing this principle were and are different in different countries is indeed our subject here. If we therefore fix a terminus a quo for our investigation, this is not meant to im-

ply that everything that happened before did not matter for
what followed. The crossroads of decision for the development of liberalism may, however, be found in the age of industrialization. It is only at this point that a society decides
which political path it is going to take; a nation, which social
path it will follow. At the very least, industrialization is the
great filter through which the history of a society has to pass
before it faces the modern problem of liberalism. We therefore begin with the assumption that the formation of German
society was determined first of all by what happened, and did
not happen, at the time of industrialization. What, then, did
happen at that time?

In 1915, at least three of the "heroes" of sociology published remarkable works about Germany: Max Weber, his
essays on Bismarck's *Foreign Policy and the Present;* Emile
Durkheim, his book *L'Allemagne au-dessus de tout* [Germany
above All]; and Thorstein Veblen, his study on *Imperial
Germany and the Industrial Revolution.* The German problem
is, in other words, a traditional preoccupation of sociologists.
Of the three mentioned, Veblen's study is most relevant in
our context. It is a curious piece of work, characterized
equally by acuteness and ignorance, insight and naïveté. The
imaginative sociologist manages to construct a neolithic national character of the "Baltic peoples"; he then proceeds to
employ a somewhat abridged cultural history of the Germans
to bridge the gap between prehistory and the present, and to
depict the present with numerous marvelously wild generalities. But underneath this cloak of abstruseness there is a
kernel of acute analysis. Veblen compares the social preconditions and consequences of German and English industrialization. His conclusions may not seem very original today; but
it is to Veblen's credit that he formulated them at an early
date:

> Germany carried over from a recent and retarded past a State,
> of the dynastic order, with a scheme of detail institutions
> and a popular habit of mind suitable to a coercive, centralized,
> and irresponsible control and to the pursuit of dynastic
> dominion. Quite unavoidably, the united Fatherland came
> under the hegemony of the most aggressive and most irrespon-
> sible—substantially the most archaic—of the several states that
> coalesced in its formation; and quite as a matter of course the
> dynastic spirit of the Prussian State has permeated the rest of
> the federated people, until the whole is now very appreciably

nearer the spiritual bent of the militant Prussian State of a hundred years ago than it has been at any time since the movement for German union began in the nineteenth century.

This united German community, at the same time, took over from their (industrially) more advanced neighbors the latest and highly efficient state of the industrial arts—wholly out of consonance with their institutional scheme, but highly productive, and so affording a large margin disposable for the uses of the dynastic State. Being taken over ready-made and in the shortest practicable time, this new technology brought with it virtually none of its inherent drawbacks, in the way of conventional waste, obsolescent usage and equipment, or class animosities; and as it has been brought into full bearing within an unexampled short time, none of these drawbacks or handicaps have yet had time to grow to formidable dimensions.

Owing in part to the same unprecedentedly short period of its acquirement and installation, and in part to the nearly unbroken mediaevalism of the institutional scheme into which the new technology has been intruded, it has hitherto had but a slight effect in the way of inducing new habits of thought on institutional matters among the German population, such as have formed the institutional counterpart of its gradual development among the English-speaking peoples.

Nevertheless, Veblen remains a moderate optimist in this respect. He continues, almost apologetically: "Such institutional consequences of a workday habituation to any given state of the industrial arts will necessarily come on by slow degrees and be worked out only in the course of generations" (220, pp. 249 f.).

We shall have to see as we go on whether Veblen is right here; at present, Veblen's other suggestion is more relevant—that in Germany industrialization has formed a fruitful misalliance (if the expression is permitted) with the "dynastic state" and has therefore taken a course entirely different from that of England. In dealing with the problem this raises, we may also be able to correct, or render more precise, many of the remarks Veblen throws off rather easily.

Compared with its historical precursors in England and France, industrialization in Germany occurred late, quickly, and thoroughly. Even if one chooses to follow Hans Mottek and fix as dates of the German industrial revolution the decades from 1834 to 1873, this is a late start compared to England and France. In 1840, the production of pig iron amounted to 1.5 million tons in England, 0.4 million tons in

France, and 0.2 million tons in Germany. But the most concentrated process of industrial expansion, the industrial revolution proper, occurred in Germany only after a few decades of "quiet self-collection, idyllic tranquillity" (to quote Sombart's in itself somewhat idyllic statement) in the seventies and nineties of the nineteenth century. If we once again take the index of pig-iron production in the years from 1870 to 1910, this nearly doubled in England, trebled in France, and increased tenfold in Germany. These figures give an indication of a second characteristic of industrialization in Germany: its speed. While industrial expansion proceeded gradually in England, the process was compressed in Germany into a comparatively short span of time. In England, the index of total industrial production rose (1913 = 100) from 34 in 1860 in fairly even rates to 53 in 1880 and 79 in 1900. The corresponding figures for Germany are 14 in 1860, 25 in 1880, and 65 in 1900 (cf. 228).

That German industrialization was not only late and rapid, but also thorough may be demonstrated most easily by a comparison with France, where, after an early start, the process lay nearly dormant for a century. A look at the occupational distribution of populations illustrates the point. In the beginning of the nineteenth century the proportion of the total population in non-agricultural occupations was probably around 30 per cent in France, and around 20 per cent in Germany. A century later, this proportion amounted to little more than 50 per cent in France, but 65 per cent in Germany. Germany's late industrialization advanced quickly in one single comprehensive process, which ramified into all areas of society.

These are familiar and important facts. Many statements about the economic potential and social structure of the countries concerned may be derived from them. If one thinks, as many authors do, that in the case of German industrialization "late, quick, and thorough" means "too late, too quick, and too thorough," these statements provide a lever for a critical analysis of German social history. But I do not think that these are the facts that would enable us to describe the peculiar, if not unique, patterns of industrialization in Germany and their social and political consequences. In order to do this, we must reach beyond the external features and even the rhythm of the process of industrialization to a set of factors that may be documented in terms of five phenomena.

The first is the order of magnitude of the economic units that emerged in the course of industrialization. If we compare statistics of joint-stock and limited-liability companies in 1910, we find that in Germany there were about 5000 such companies with a capital of approximately 16 billion marks; in Great Britain, on the other hand, there were about 50,000 such companies with a total capital of 44 billion marks. In other words, while the average company capital amounted to less than 1 million marks in England, it was more than 3 million marks in Germany (cf. 207). This observation does not stand alone. One of the decisive differences between industrialization in Germany and in the Anglo-Saxon countries lies in the role of banks, which themselves combined into mammoth financial empires at an early stage, carried by their credits and investments a considerable part of the weight of German industrialization and at the same time facilitated the rapid growth of large industrial units. Apart from giant banks and near-monopolies in production, we soon find powerful economic combinations in the form of syndicates, trusts, cartels, all of which were not only tolerated, but in fact furthered by the state in Germany. A contemporary English historian found these words to describe the consequences of such developments:

> It is a striking fact that a large part of the natural resources, industry, and wealth production of that unresting workshop of Germany is under the control of a dozen men of commanding business genius—men of strong and masterful character, born rulers of the sternest mould, without sentiment, not insusceptible to justice yet never going beyond it, inflexible in decision, of inexhaustible will-power, and impervious to all modern notions of political liberalism. (55, p. 122.)

Perhaps the twelve men were not quite so Teutonic as Dawson would have them. But the fact remains that large economic units and a powerful but small group of industrial leaders emerged so early in German industrialization as to leave no place for the traditional liberal infrastructure of medium-sized enterprises and bourgeois entrepreneurs. It has already been mentioned that government agencies favored large economic units. In other respects, too, industrialization in Germany—and this is the second important phenomenon— met from the beginning with the benevolence of the state. Sombart certainly has a case when he transfers Hardenberg's

dictum about Russian administration by comparison to that
of France to German industrialization by comparison to that
of England: "We have to do from above, Your Majesty,
what the French have done from below!" The benevolence
of the state found many expressions, ranging from the granting of loans without interest for the erection of enterprises
through benevolent laissez faire to the protectionist policy
that replaced the brief bloom of free trade at the end of the
1870s. We have to remember here, of course, that the state
concerned is not that of Joseph Chamberlain or of Glad-
stone, but one of leadership groups whose origin was as pre-
industrial as their social and political outlook. Thus, despite
his use of the polemical imprecision of Marxist terminology,
Mottek has a point when he says:

> The common business deals between Prussian state and bour-
> geoisie as well as more directly between *Junker* and bourgeoi-
> sie are one cause for the betrayal of the bourgeois democratic
> revolution of 1848 on the part of the bourgeoisie, just as later
> its profitable collaboration with Imperial Germany contributed
> to the rapid decay of the original liberalism of the bourgeoisie.
> (158, pp. 35 f.)

One way in which the state took a definite part in the process of industrialization in Germany—and this is the third phenomenon of great social and political consequence—is state
property. Since the country was for a long time divided into
numerous principalities, whose lords often engaged in economic affairs, state property played a relatively large part in
Germany at an early date. Soon traditional state property was
supplemented by new and more powerful forms. The Reichstag debate about the nationalization of the railroads might
be taken as a turning point here; its immediate consequence
was the resignation of the liberal minister of trade, Delbrück.
But state property was not confined to railroads and canals.
In 1913, Prussia owned no less than forty coal mines and
twelve blast furnaces. Local communities frequently took the
supply of gas, electricity, and water as well as transportation
into their hands.

In addition, there was a large number of mixed public and
private enterprises in which local communities and the central government had their share, to say nothing of the influential state banks and the public domain in agriculture and
forestry. At what should, in terms of the English model, have

been the heyday of private enterprise and liberal social and political patterns, the state was, in Germany, the largest single entrepreneur. The administration of economic enterprises was frequently in the hands of civil servants or other men dependent on government agencies, who were therefore supposed to act in terms of a problematic public interest rather than economic profit. Gustav Stolper's bitterness may be exaggerated but is by no means implausible in his observation that "Imperial Germany . . . had gradually created for itself an economic order of mixed private and public property. . . . This historical epoch laid the foundations upon which the war economy, the experiments of the [Weimar] Republic, and in the end the National Socialist system could later be built" (212, p. 50).

A fourth phenomenon, and one that at first sight seems to stand in a paradoxical relation to those discussed so far, leads us even more deeply into the peculiarities of German industrialization. From almost the earliest beginnings of industrialization a kind of state socialism corresponded to the prevailing system of state capitalism. In contrast to the applied Social Darwinism of publicly tolerated misery of industrial workers, their wives and children in England, which Marx took as the emotional point of departure in his demand for state action, public agencies in Germany consistently felt responsible for the welfare of workers. There was poverty, illness, and misery in industrializing Germany as elsewhere; but the official attitude to the social question strikingly documents the preindustrial combination of a severe and benevolent paternal authority.

The three great institutions of sickness, accident, and old age and invalid insurance are as much a part of the Bismarck era as the great foreign-policy decisions about war and peace. Moreover, these measures of social policy, in contrast to those of foreign policy, outlasted Bismarck's resignation; they were completed by the legal limitation of working time, the protective laws for women's and children's work, and other state interventions in favor of the weak. Here, too, government interfered with economic process. Entrepreneurs certainly recognized, and resented, this fact; but it is part of the tendency that they did not determine either public opinion or government decisions. An organization like the Association for Social Policy (*Verein für Sozialpolitik*), founded in 1872, was much closer to both; and it was at least symptomatic that

the founding charter of the Association included the demand
for "the well-considered intervention of the state in order to
protect the legitimate interests of all participants" in the
economy.

The Association for Social Policy did not demand this without specifying its reasons. It was concerned with fulfilling
"the highest tasks of our time and our nation." And here we
encounter the fifth, and possibly the most significant, peculiarity of industrialization in Germany. Many of the characteristics of German social history described here seem perfectly
reasonable, at least at first sight. Are not large economic units
much more efficient under modern technical conditions than
small and medium-sized ones? Is not the benevolence of the
state a necessary condition of industrialization in any case? Is
it not plausible to withdraw from the interests of private owners certain economic enterprises supplying basic services to
the people? Is not Bismarck's social legislation one of the
glories of modern German history?

While these questions have been phrased in a suggestive
manner, affirmative answers are by no means inevitable. But
whatever one may conclude about the phenomena discussed
so far individually, their social and political significance ac-
crues from the fact that they stand in a context. As a first
illustration of this context, let us take two well-known examples. The first concerns Bismarck and the nationalization of
the Prussian railroads. In 1876, in a letter to the Prussian
minister of trade, Achenbach, Bismarck expressed his urgent
wish "that the Royal Prussian government should immediately
[conduct] the further extension and consolidation of its state
railway system" and added:

> It is precisely the energetic endeavor of Prussia to secure for
> itself a dominant railway power and to pull the reins of state
> control tightly, that will guarantee the most advantageous
> solution for the national tasks of the *Reich* in the field of
> railways, and the most beneficial execution of the latest law
> promulgated by Prussia but standing on the national ground.
> (187, p. 334.)

The second example concerns Max Weber and the economic and social policy of the state. One must certainly not
judge Weber on the basis of his justly infamous Freiburg inaugural lecture, yet its very effect makes it impossible to ignore. "Not peace and human happiness we have to pass on

to our descendants, but the maintenance and upbreeding of our national kind" (225, p. 14). After National Socialism such statements sound even more macabre than they were at the time, but it is hard to deny their symptomatic significance. "It is not the purpose of our work in social policy to make the world happy, but to unite socially a nation split apart by modern economic development, for the hard struggles of the future" (225, p. 23). It may well be that the authors of public social policy in Imperial Germany were as little motivated by humanitarian intentions as the author of this statement. Germany embarked on the road to social reform, "not by self-help, but by the state and for the sake of the state," as Rothfels expresses it (187, p. xlv). Or, to quote yet another sympathetic witness, Carl Jantke: "What Bismarck meant was thus not a federalist economic and social order independent of the idea of the state, but a movement toward a corporate representation of interests which, despite a high degree of differentiation of occupations, groups, and strata in the modern economy, would be able to bring about public co-responsibility, national-state feelings, and adaptation and subordination to the interests of the whole as represented by the state" (106, pp. 272 f.).

There are certain words that come up time and again in connection with economic and social policy in Imperial Germany; and whoever cares about the greatest happiness of the greatest number, freedom of the individual and his rights, autonomy of social groups, liberalism, and competition, must note them with surprise: nation, state, tight control, the interest of the whole, adaptation, and subordination. Not even industrialization managed, in Germany, to upset a traditional outlook in which the whole is placed above its parts, the state above the citizen, or a rigidly controlled order above the lively diversity of the market, the state above society. Wherever one would hope for the word "rational," the other one, "national," appears instead as an argument for policy decisions. Instead of developing it, industrialization in Germany swallowed the liberal principle.

Here, however, we have to pause for a moment. The reality of Imperial Germany was clearly not so simple as such formulae make it appear. Bismarck may be cited as a witness for many cases; among them, even that of liberalism, which he defended more than once, and not only in his free-trade period. For Max Weber, the Freiburg inaugural is to some extent a youthful aberration rather than an article of faith. Furthermore, Imperial Germany was by no means only the country of Bismarck and Max Weber, or even of leaders of economic combines and socialists of the lecture hall. There was a strong tendency toward liberalism at work in it; there were more than just beginnings of the formation of a politically conscious bourgeoisie; there was the conflict between a late feudal tradition and capitalist ambition. Possibly, this conflict even provided the overriding source of tension and change in Imperial Germany. The strong colors in which I have painted the propensity of German industrialization toward the gigantic, toward state intervention and national interpretation, have to be understood as an attempt to balance another—at least as misleadingly one-sided—picture, of which more will be said presently. It is the mixture of feudal and national elements with features familiar from the English experience that makes for the peculiar and consequential pattern of industrialization in Germany.

The most striking characteristic of this pattern is in fact a surprising deficiency: in the full sense of the term, it is not capitalist. There are many concepts of capitalism, and it would take little effort to find one that covers the German example too. But we need think only of the disappointed Marxist illusion with respect to the German revolution to see how little there is to be gained by such an extension of terms. If we follow a more realistic man, Raymond Aron (10, p. 80), a "capitalist system" requires, first, that the means of production are "the object of individual appropriation." Germany had a large and growing sector of state property throughout industrialization. For that reason also, Aron's second requisite, that "the steering of the economy . . . is decentralized" and occurs on the market, holds for Imperial Germany only within surprisingly narrow limits. It might be stretching a point somewhat to say that the phenomenon of "wage labor"— Aron's third characteristic of capitalism—was also perverted in Germany by the survival of traditional ties, and therefore not fully present. "The predominant motive" of the capitalist system is, for Aron, "the profit motive"; Bismarck frequently denounced this motive, as in the railway debates in the Prussian diet, and he found much applause from the benches as well as from a wider public. Thus, Germany never displayed "that which is polemically called capitalist anarchy"; indeed, it remained the permanent goal of those running the state to uphold a more rigid notion of order, by force if need be, against the "threats" of capitalist anarchy. To be sure, "there is no capitalist economy which would be capitalist in an absolute or ideal sense" (10, p. 80). Moreover, the capitalist traits of the German economy before 1944 are unmistakable, if compared, say, with the Soviet economic system. But one may well doubt whether these traits were not only present, but dominant. To that extent it remains true that Imperial Germany developed into an industrial, but not into a capitalist society.

How was this possible? Veblen had a scurrilous theory to explain it, which is too amusing to be suppressed here. Even in the Stone and Bronze ages—so Veblen argues—one of the notable characteristics of the "Baltic peoples" was a propensity for "borrowing," that is, for taking over the achievements of others for their own purposes. "These peoples borrowed permanently and with great ease" (220, p. 19). The bad habit persisted throughout the cultural history of the Germans, and is the dominant feature of German industrialization: Germany borrowed the achievements of her Western neighbors without these fitting into her own social and cultural context. At the same time she knew how to exploit what was taken over for her own purposes, that is, for the purposes of her inherited institutions.

There is a more serious side to Veblen's theory, which is otherwise as naïve in terms of cultural history as in those of sociology. The motif of "belatedness" plays a part in many interpretations of modern Germany. Usually, this refers to the formation of Germany as a unified nation. Germany is, in Plessner's formula, a "belated nation," and many of the peculiarities of German politics, society, and culture are, so to speak, the outcome of social-psychological complexes caused by national retardation. Others use the notion of Germany's belatedness to explain economic development. Here, being late has certain advantages (as Veblen saw). Whoever follows can avoid the mistakes of those who preceded him; whoever industrializes late may begin at a stage of technical development and organization that countries industrializing earlier had to spend much time and effort to develop. Because of the catastrophic destruction caused by the Second World War, Germany experienced this particular advantage a second time; it is thus one of the causes of two German economic miracles. But the technical and economic advantages are more than balanced by the disadvantages accruing from the fact that economic development is merely stuck onto an existing social structure so that, while the economic superstructure (as one might say in an ironic reversal of Marx's terms) is assimilated, the social and cultural context remains unchanged.

Even so, all theories of German belatedness retain an element of the naïveté of the mechanical. Can it really happen that an industrial economy remains entirely without social context? We may get further with respect to such questions if we try a somewhat different approach. Lipset has claimed that there is a sense in which the United States may be called the "first new nation," the first developing country of history. It is indeed the first modern nation that has freed itself from colonial tutelage. Lipset shows that many features of contemporary American society may be understood as those of a developing country. If one is less optimistic with respect to the future of the developing nations, however, one might suspect that Germany rather than the United States was the first new nation, at least so far as the contrast of economic development and internal modernization is concerned. Because Germany was a latecomer on the stage of the industrial nations of Europe—or so one might argue—she could not afford the luxury of a gradual capitalist development. Because she industrialized late, she had to industrialize quickly and thoroughly. This could be accomplished only if the state took a strong hand in the process, that is, by tighter organization and control than the capitalist principle would permit. Thus came about a combination of modern economic patterns and an authoritarian political order.

I am not sure precisely how far an explanation of this kind will carry. In any case, the real lesson of the German example is of a different order. In sociological lectures about modern society all over the world, students are told today that there is such a thing as an "industrial society," a basic social structure of the modern world, which is determined by the patterns of an industrial economy. This conception presupposes that industrialization is a great leveler, which evens out all, or most, traditional social differences within as well as between countries.

One may trace this notion back to Max Weber whose concept of capitalism with its preconditions in economic attitudes and consequences in bureaucratic organization displays traces of an historical necessity à la Hegel. Beyond Weber, the concept of uniform social structures in the modern world derives from Karl Marx who, while he could know only English capitalism in full bloom, generalized and dogmatized this historical experience into a necessary law of development. In doing so, Marx was not particularly radical; he expressed what many felt and said at the time, and all feel and say today. The assertion of the convergence of all societies that have undergone the economic process of industrialization today unites scholars in East and West, indeed Eastern Marxists and revisionists, Western liberals and socialists. The concept of the irresistible steamroller of industrialization is a basic dogma of the social self-interpretation of our time. However, is this notion right?

The consequences of the dogma are as numerous in scholarship as in politics. For example, interpretations of the conflict between Communist and capitalist countries display a curiously divergent convergence of thought: If the West relies on the inevitability of an internal liberalization of Communist countries with growing prosperity, this presupposes the same "historical necessity" of social change on the basis of economic developments that lies at the basis of Communist confidence in the internal breakdown of the capitalist system; and the same holds for the common assumption, however different in substance, that the new nations are bound to develop into one or the other supposedly prescribed directions.

Such hopes and explanations are still current, much as confirmed evidence contradicts them. But fortunately we do not need debatable contemporary experiences in order to demonstrate that the dogma of irresistibility as well as the image of a uniform and leveling process of industrialization behind it is false: it is sufficient to think of the example of the industrial revolution in Imperial Germany. Germany turned into an industrial country without thereby becoming any more similar to England than she was before. Industrialization has not led to rendering German and French, French and American, American and Japanese society more alike, unless one sees, with the superficial perception of the cultural pessimist, likeness and leveling in the simple fact that there are, in all these countries, foundries, cities, tractors, and cans. Contrary to the beliefs of many, the industrial revolution is not the prime mover of the modern world at all.

Once again, this is too general and extreme a statement to be upheld without qualification. Let us remember therefore

that we are here concerned with the peculiar patterns of industrialization and its consequences in Germany. There are
clearly corollaries of industrialization observable in all modern
societies (although even here many versions are possible).
But the theory that such social structures and cultural attitudes
are invariably drawn into a given context, rather than the
notion of an "industrial society," seems plausible in view of
the German case.

Every country absorbs industrialization into its own tradition; every country assimilates the process in a manner
peculiar to it alone; in every country there emerges an amalgamation of cultural traditions and ramifications of industrialization characteristic of it alone. There are as many modes of
industrialization as there are industrializing countries, and
every one of them needs to be understood in its own terms.
Comparing Germany to England can therefore be meaningful
only in order to expose differences by confrontation, not in
order to apply an assumed standard case to others. And analysis of the German case with the instrument of Marx's laws of
development of capitalist society, like analysis in terms of a
general notion of industrial society, must lead the analyzer
astray. In any sense, the astonishment over the fact that Germany was an industrial society but went her own way politically, merely refutes its own assumption. Imperial Germany
simply brought the specifically German amalgamation of inherited social structures and correlates of industrialization.

This argument is not directed against the possibility of establishing social laws; it is directed against false social laws,
and the assertion of the leveling force of industrial development and its necessary consequences is false. Ironically, this
conclusion leads us back to Veblen in one important respect.
Imperial Germany absorbed industrialization quickly and
thoroughly. But she assimilated this process to the social and
political structures by which she was traditionally determined.
There was no place in these structures for a sizable, politically
self-confident bourgeoisie; for that reason large economic
units played an important part from the outset. The state held
a prominent place in the traditional structures; for that reason
it took part, as promoter and owner, in the process of economic development. The state (accepting its German personification for the moment), which thus managed to use the new
power of industry to strengthen the old power of tradition,
was itself characterized by an authoritarian blend of severity

and benevolence; for that reason, welfare measures of social policy accompanied industrialization. In Germany, not even industrialization has led to the autonomy of civil society vis-à-vis the state; as a motive force of social change the idea of national power remained effective among politicians, their ideologists, and their public.

All this resulted in a perplexing and contradictory mixture. Perhaps the amalgamations of new economic patterns and inherited social structures were and are no less contradictory in some other countries. Our argument suggests that Germany is not unique in her development. But to explain the German Question it is not the fact of uniqueness or of internal contradictions that matters, but their kind. We can discover, in the industrial society of Imperial Germany, the explosive potential of recent German social development and its political consequences. It is neither the speed and lateness of industrialization as such, nor the inherited structures of the "dynastic state"—of Prussia, of a long and painful process of national unification, of Lutheranism and the craving for authority, of Junkerdom and militarism—but the encounter and combination of these two strains of development in Imperial Germany that form the explosive core of a society in which the liberal principle could settle only haltingly and occasionally. Here therefore we find the point of departure for a sociological analysis of modern Germany.

4. THE FAULTED NATION

One of the consequences of the peculiarly German blend of social tradition and modern industrialism is that many of the correlates of industrialization, so often assumed to be inevitable, appeared in Germany only partially or in strange deflections. Without much exaggeration, the history of industrialization in Germany could be written as a history of non-industrialization. Throughout, the industrial revolution carried within it a counterrevolution—and strangely, the counterrevolution did not arrest the progress of the revolution or prevent active resistance against it. Here again we are led to conclude that allegedly incompatible forces, such as feudalism and industrialism, may in actuality combine into new, if perhaps not very encouraging, historical compounds. This conclusion deserves to be illustrated by a few examples.

It is generally believed that industrialization means the mobilization of people. Factory production demands that people be freed of some of their inherited social positions, so that "contract" may take the place of "status"; at the same time industrialization, by its changing fortunes, promotes such mobilization, especially under conditions of free enterprise. In Germany, the process of industrialization was accompanied by large-scale migration, as a rule from East to West, from country to town, but this is only part of the story. "It is regrettable," said Kirdorf, the uncrowned king of the coal and steel syndicates, at the Mannheim meetings of the Association for Social Policy in 1905, "that our workers are in a position to change their places at any time. An enterprise can thrive only if it has a stationary labor force. I do not demand that legislation come to our assistance, but we must reserve the right to take measures in order to stop this frequent change of employment" (cf. 55).

Kirdorf's demand is astonishing in several respects. Capitalist industry needs a mobile labor force; and once again it appears that German industry was more nationalist than capitalist, even where it was privately owned. Furthermore, the legislation invoked by Kirdorf did in fact exist, and, characteristically, was never opposed very fiercely by German entrepreneurs; I mean, of course, social legislation. It is the rationale of all state-inaugurated social policy of the European type to immobilize people by providing for them, at the place at which they happen to be, until their dying day and thus make it unnecessary for them to act rationally, that is, to explore the market of life chances themselves. Moreover, the mobility of German workers was very restricted. There were—and still are today—characteristically immobile groups, like the "worker-peasants" of the Saarland and the "side-job peasants" of Württemberg to mention only two examples.

In this manner one has to add a "Yes, but . . ." to nearly every allegedly general consequence of industrialization if one wants to describe Germany; here, these consequences, if they were present at all, had notable modifications and limitations. Urbanization is another corollary of industrialization. Between 1871 and 1939 the proportions of the population living in rural communities (with less than two thousand inhabitants) and in larger communities (with more than two thousand inhabitants) were reversed in Germany: in 1871 two thirds of the population lived in rural communities; in 1939 the same proportion lived in larger communities. Yet the town, in particular the large city, has never really been accepted in Germany as an environment worth living in. Where writers dealt favorably with city life, their works were soon denounced as "asphalt literature." The simultaneous glorification of the country as the home of everything healthy and denigration of the city as the root of all evil is a solid stereotype of a cultural pessimism that appears in the elementary-school primer as well as in the parting speech of the principal on graduation, and indeed in declarations of government policy; and it is a symptom of a lack of urbanity.

Industrialization involves profound changes in occupational structure, especially, of course, a shift from agricultural to manufacturing occupations. In 1871, nearly half the population of the German Empire was employed in agriculture; at the beginning of the First World War, the proportion had shrunk to one third; and today employment in the primary sector amounts to little more than 10 per cent. Yet Stolper's observation that Germany "in contrast to the approach of England . . . by no means [sacrificed] its agriculture to the extension of industry" (212, p. 25) is still correct. It is not exactly popular to refer to this "sacrifice" in England; more-

over, the German experience is paralleled in many ways by
that of France and the United States. But so far as the consequences of industrialization are concerned, and even by
comparison with countries of similar occupational structures,
there is another "Yes, but . . ." in the facts that, simultaneously with industrialization, agriculture experienced an economic upswing in Germany, and that its political representatives continued to set the tone throughout this period.

Industrialization destroys the family. Among its consequences are the breaking up of traditional family ties, the
separation of home and place of work, the entrance of women
and children in the work force and the perversion of traditional patterns this produces, and the final obsolescence of
the idyllic country family. Again a "but" has to be added for
Germany, in this case a familiar one, since indigenous and
foreign images of the German family are agreed in their emphasis on the patriarchal home of the Wilhelminian era, in
which the mother is restricted to *Kinder, Küche, Kirche* and
the children are held on tight reins. This is, to be sure, the
image, or indeed the caricature, of a bourgeois family; with
workers things probably looked different even at that time.
But there are dominant values and patterns in any society,
and in industrializing Germany these laid great stress on the
"intact" community of the family as the "germinal cell of
the nation." Nothing demonstrates the effectiveness of such
ideologies more clearly than the fact that, even after the Second World War, a German sociologist, Helmut Schelsky, asserted the integrity and stability of the family in Germany as
against most other industrial countries.

Marx saw the revolutionary aspect of capitalism in the fact
that the free labor contract presupposes the formal equality
of the partners. Ever since wage labor has existed, this has
held true for Germany as it has for England. But we shall see
as we go on how little this formal equality means, not only in
view of the persistence of social relations of super- and subordination, but especially because of the extent to which traditional ties and expectations can render it ineffective. If, for
example, a change of residence transcends the social horizon
of a worker, his formal equality means little for his work in
the coal mine of his home town; he has no choice in either
an objective or a subjective sense.

Many other illustrations could be given of how allegedly
general correlates of industrialization combined in Germany

with specific traditions into new patterns of social structure. Among these there is one that merits particular emphasis, because it is of more general relevance. Just as the economy of Imperial Germany became industrial, but not capitalist the German society of the time did not become bourgeois, but remained quasi-feudal. Industrialization in Germany failed to produce a self-confident bourgeoisie with its own political aspirations. In so far as a bourgeoisie emerged at all, it remained relatively small and, what is more, unsure of itself and dependent in its social and political standards. As a result, German society lacked the stratum that in England and America, and to a lesser extent even in France, had been the moving force of a development in the direction of greater modernity and liberalism.

Possibly the history of the independent middle class advancing to an upper-class position is brief everywhere. It contradicts more than our sense of linguistic consistency to have a middle class become an upper class. Possibly the struggles of the independent middle class with the late feudal lords of the preindustrial world, the time, in other words, at which the bourgeoisie merely claimed power and represented demands and aspirations rather than achievements, were historically more effective than the eventual success of these claims. But in Imperial Germany the middle class was not only not successful; even its aspirations were individual desires for recognition rather than solidary demands of a new political class. As the power of the state increased through the industrial economy, the traditional leading stratum managed to turn the rise of the entrepreneurial middle class to its own uses and thus rob it of the revolutionary potential of its social position and mentality. At this point, the social and political significance of the peculiarities of German industrialization become fully apparent—the part played by the private and public masters of large economic units, the persistent social and economic weight of agriculture, the continued preference for things national rather than things rational, the insistence on an allegedly non-partisan common good as superior to all partisan interests.

As a result, there emerged a bourgeoisie that was not really a bourgeoisie, which rightly became the laughingstock of cartoonists and novelists. Max Weber who was, at least on the brighter side of his political existence, one of the most eloquent representatives of the bourgeoisie in Imperial Germany, pilloried the failure of this bourgeoisie time and again as emphatically as unsuccessfully: "With us, the broad strata of the bourgeoisie are still excluded from power by that feudalism which rules ministers and factory owners and makes them accept aristocratic titles" (225, p. 109). Germany's would-be bourgeoisie was not encouraged by such criticism. It continued to seek "that feudal prestige . . . which with us [is symbolized] by the capacity to give satisfaction in duels and become a reserve officer, which in turn is acquired by wearing student colors, a face disfigured by fencing, and in general leading the traditional student life distracting from intensive work" (225, p. 107).

In the end, resorting to sarcasm was all that even a man like Max Weber could do: "However, it is in keeping with the wisdom of the state ruling in Prussia today, to reconcile the bourgeois purse with the minimal political influence of the bourgeoisie by granting a kind of 'second-class right of admission at court,' and in the interested circles nothing would be more unpopular than if difficulties were created for the 'nobilitation' of capital acquired in commerce, in industry, in the stock exchange by their metamorphosis into the form of the landed estate" (225, p. 40).

Such "nobilitation" of capital also existed in other nations, including the mother country of industrialization, England; here, too, members of the bourgeoisie strove for landed property, whether with or without aristocratic title, once they had acquired wealth. But while in England the traditional nobility was fundamentally changed by this bourgeois invasion and a middle-class-become-upper-class emerged, the entry of some middle-class elements had little or no impact on the mentality of Germany's upper class. Ernest K. Bramsted has described the difference between the apparently similar developments:

> In England the aristocracy maintained an organic contact with the other strata of the nation by sending its younger sons into the business world, and also by the bestowal of knighthoods or peerages on successful middle-class business magnates. In Germany, however, the process was one-sided, for although a number of wealthy industrialists, bankers and leading civil servants ascended into the feudal stratum, the aristocracy, for its part, adjusted itself only slightly to the new economic structure and often disdained to engage in middle-class occupations. (33, p. 229.)

Thus the German elite confidently maintained its values and demanded complete submission from its new members. And the number of these new members remained small in important places; of 600 corps fellows of the Bonn student corporation Borussia between 1840 and 1904, only 20 came from middle-class families; of 435 members of Göttingen's Saxonia between 1854 and 1904, there were 35; and among 740 of Heidelberg's Saxo-Borussia between 1853 and 1904, 177 (cf. 178). But the success of the nobility and failure of the middle class is not a question of numbers. Contrary to that of England, the German bourgeoisie never formed into a class. It remained a set of aspiring individuals in the class-destroying situation of competition for status. Such competition does not create anything new; it is the movement of the parts that confirms the pattern of the whole; what is changed by it is never the map of society, but merely the individual's place of residence on it. This need not be a bad thing; it may also be a sign of the stability, and to some extent even of the flexibility, of a social constitution. But in the German case substitution of numerous titled nouveaux riches for the bourgeois revolution meant the persistence of relations of authority that stood in an explosive relation to the rapidly changing economic conditions. There is no doubt that the result became effective in subsequent history, but there will be few who describe these effects as desirable.

Every society has its own faults of new and old, economy and society. Social units are too much alive to permit the geological symmetry of a simple stratification, a smooth relation of basis and superstructure, pluperfect and perfect. Certainly these strata of social reality are present. Difficult as it may be at times, it is even possible to identify them. But strata of historical evolution and elements of social structure are exposed to such strong percussions at any time that we encounter them only in scurrilous faults in which the new appears as old and the old as new, and base and superstructure begin to look alike to the point of interchangeability. In this sense, any society is a faulted society.

For German society, however, this holds true in a special sense, and by this I do not mean only the metaphysical ambiguity of faultiness. The society of Imperial Germany was consistently determined by faults to such an extent that it must be described as volcanic. The English notion of an establishment that holds all reins of political decision in its hands, or the British monarchy define faults of historical strata that can be localized, are thus accessible to observation and control, and may even be abolished by political decisions. That there are few who want to abolish them and that even the Labour Party cherishes a secret love for the Public Schools merely proves how unvolcanic these faults are.

A somewhat more explosive compound can be found in France with her paradox of administrative centralism and emotional regionalism. The "mayors," being the traditional representatives of regional political empires, can, and do at times, turn French politics upside down. They are—in the language of the *18th Brumaire of Louis Bonaparte*—the political "small-lot peasants" of French history. In the United States, such volcanic faults are especially characteristic of the Deep South. Their eruptions require the concentration of all the forces of the nation, but they are localized and may, therefore, be controlled. In Germany, however, there is hardly a phenomenon that does not display the faultings of old and new, of social traditions and economic requirements, of centralism and regionalism, of nationalism and rationalism. What is merely present in other societies is dominant in Germany, as can be demonstrated by many examples.

As Thorstein Veblen did during the First, Talcott Parsons wrote about Germany during the Second World War. His essay on "Democracy and Social Structure in Pre-Nazi Germany," while clearly very different from *Imperial Germany and the Industrial Revolution,* shares with Veblen's book an alert dilettantism, which skillfully combines definite observations with indefinite generalizations. The observations at least are of interest, if only because they are those of the visitor who is surprised where the native no longer raises an eyelid.

In every country there is one rank order that provides the standard for its prestige hierarchy. In Germany—so Parsons observes—this is, or rather was, the rank order of the military, and he adds not without understandable surprise: "The status of the officer was one of maximal social prestige, although not particularly impressive in normal times in terms of wealth or political influence" (166, p. 106).

As we know, the rank orders of prestige, wealth, and power do not have to coincide; but the surprising fact remains that under modern economic and social conditions the standard of rank is provided by a status that is determined neither economically nor politically. There was little change in this re-

spect when the state employee (*Beamte*) replaced the officer
as the model of social status, as Parsons notes (not entirely
consistently perhaps) when he states: "Generally speaking,
the civil service represented the highest prestige element of
the bourgeoisie especially in Prussia" (166, p. 108). Officers
and civil servants or, more generally, the military and the
bureaucracy, have one important feature in common, which
has struck Parsons as well as other foreign observers in Germany to the present day, that is, a high degree of formalization of status. There is an extensive system of titles, so that
"the number of people who are mainly Mr. Brown or Mr.
Smith is relatively small" (166, p. 111). Titles are, moreover,
used all the time, in letters, in address, on the name plate
outside one's front door, and in private conversation.

The separation of the occupational from a strictly private
realm implied by this extensive use of titles is one of the pre-
requisites for the strangely exclusive and romantic German
notion of "friendship," which begins with the familiar form
of address, the ceremonious *Du* of what is characteristically
called "brotherhood." The fact that formal titles are transferred to wives documents the particular, that is, lesser rank
of the German housewife. Parsons elaborates a syndrome of
faults—as we can say now—in German society before 1933
and, more particularly perhaps, before 1918, which to him
are causally relevant for the success of National Socialism.

Herbert Spencer's distinction between "industrial" and
"military societies" provided self-interpretations of the fin de
siècle with a welcome alternative. Imperial Germany was no
exception here; a lively discussion was carried on about industrialism versus feudalism. But this abstract alternative did
not correspond to reality at all, for in fact German society
was both industrial and military, industrial and feudal. The
much-cited "matter-of-the-house approach" of the captains
of industry, represented in an extreme but not unique fashion
by the Saar entrepreneur von Stumm-Halberg, bore witness
to the translation of feudal notions of dependence into the
contractual sphere of modern industry. It is even more telling
to look at the peculiar combination of military and industrial
virtues in Germany. W. H. Dawson, the English historian of
the time, was probably right in suspecting: "If a German
manufacturer in close touch with his men—or, better still, the
practical manager of his works—be interrogated on the point,
he will invariably answer in words like these: 'Military service

makes men of the recruits, and they come back to us far more efficient as workers than when they left. For they learn obedience, discipline, regular habits; they are more alert, quicker to understand, smarter in every way' " (55, p. 151).

These are indeed phrases often heard in Germany. But they have a deeper significance, which is rarely emphasized in the literature. When Max Weber studied the relations between a Protestant ethic and the spirit of capitalism, he was thinking above all of entrepreneurial success, the origin of the profit motive and the motive force of a steady growth of needs. But an industrial economy does not consist of entrepreneurs alone. Among its conditions, the preparedness of workers for the discipline of labor is at least as important as the initiative of capitalists. Today, the difficulties of industrializing the new nations of Africa or South America remind us of the extent to which people have to accept the habit of discipline, if not domestication, in a modern economy.

What is it that brings about this discipline? It may be "rational" in the sense that without complying with its demands a person cannot get very far in a modern society. But industrial discipline more strongly implies another kind of rationality. It is no accident that some of the first factories, even in England, emerged from orphanages and prisons. The discipline of rigid organization, the habit of subordination and obedience, as it is bred not only in orphanages and in prisons but even more in large armies, is a very favorable condition of industrial discipline. While it is not very likely to teach people how to think and act by themselves—by starting up an economic enterprise, for example—military discipline is all the more suited for fitting workers into large industrial enterprises, which in any case relieve the individual of the burden of independent decisions. We are beginning to see what kind of society results from such conditioning, but in preparing for industrialism, military training of the Prussian pattern is clearly at least as useful as Calvinist articles of faith.

The two conditions of industrialism are incompatible in more than the obvious ways, for they point to an ambiguity in the notion of rationality that even Max Weber, the great sociologist of rationality, failed to see clearly, which describes another characteristic and unfortunate fault in him and, through him, in his society. The market is rational in that it brings about an optimal result by the competition of the interests of all involved; but the plan is rational, too, in that available knowledge is used to determine in advance who has to do what and when. Market rationality involves rules of the game and referees; plan rationality involves a bureaucracy to design lines of action and control their execution.

In terms of market rationality, plan rationality is not rational; all plans may err, and reliance on them therefore means a gigantic chance of error. In terms of plan rationality, market rationality is not rational; competition means a considerable waste of resources. Smith's theory of political economy is market rational; but List's theory of national economy is plan rational. The political theory and practice of liberalism imply an attitude of market rationality; the authoritarian and, more recently, the totalitarian state are based on an attitude of plan rationality. Thus Weber may well be right in speaking of the pervasive rationalization of modern society; but the statement carries little weight so long as the ambiguity of the terms is not cleared up. German society, in any case, was not characterized simply by rationality, but by the institutionalized ambiguity of the two forms of rationality, the mixture of free trade and state bureaucracy, private economy and interventionism, bourgeois and military order.

"After Bismarck," J. P. Mayer asserts, "no other German reflects the political life of his country more fully than Weber" (148, p. 13). This is a bold assertion, but it certainly holds for our context that Bismarck and Max Weber, half a century apart, carry in their dynamic personalities those faults of German history that lie at the basis of the German Question. They are different and yet similar, both of them on the borderline between theory and practice, but guided into opposing directions by talent and early inclination. We are not here concerned with their biographies, but there are significant features of German society and its political structures that become visible through the lives of these men. Their environment tells in them—and both might have been liberals in an environment different from theirs.

On January 29, 1886, Bismarck fired off, in the Prussian diet, at the Center and Progressive parties some of those phrases that made him well hated among liberals (including Max Weber):

In England, the weapon against an opposition of this kind is very easily given; one says to the leaders of the opposition involved: All right, I resign; you be so good as to take over the ministry. In England it is regarded as unpatriotic, indeed I can say as indecent, to make opposition if one is not prepared to take the government out of the hands of those whom one opposes and into one's own in order to do better. I, however, now find myself faced for nearly a quarter of a century exclusively with a fruitless, negative criticism, and never yet have I been in the position to summon my opponents with any hope of success: All right, you try it; let me sit down for once on the benches of the opposition, and while you go on acting the play on the stage, I am going into the stalls and watch and applaud or boo. (187, p. 285.)

The cynicism of this remark (in which contemporaries may recognize a recent successor of the Iron Chancellor) is hard to surpass, but cynicism is not its only characteristic. Bismarck often emphasized the liberal principle of control of power. He was far too fond of fighting to be fundamentally hostile to the idea of an opposition. But he increasingly found himself in the awkward position of having not only to make government decisions, but to create the resistance against these decisions as well. He was acting before a background of subservience and illiberalism. Thus he could afford to insult a parliament with the statements quoted without its rising against him to a man; probably the gentlemen thought Bismarck's comparisons funny. Can one blame those in power for their subjects' failing to offer them any resistance?

Bismarck may not be exactly an authoritarian malgré lui, although certainly the social and political environment in which he acted aggravated his inclinations. But there is another side of his political personality, which Bismarck himself would have described as the "primacy of foreign policy," and which appeared to many others as a hollow nationalism. "Let us first create a solid structure, secure to the outside, firmly built inside and joined together by the national tie, and then you ask me for my opinion about how the house should be furnished with more or less liberal constitutional institutions, and you may find that I answer: Well, I have no preconceived opinion on this; you make your suggestions to me and if the sovereign whom I serve agrees you will not find any fundamental difficulties with me" (187, p. 70).

With respect to how people should live, the Chancellor, otherwise no Hamlet, has "no preconceived opinion." After all, it does not matter so much what the house looks like inside. What really matters is the firmness of its external as well as internal construction. Here the other symptomatic figure, Max Weber, comes to mind. He was a sociologist, but his Freiburg inaugural address of 1894 seems to take off exactly where Bismarck stopped. As Wolfgang Mommsen has conclusively shown (cf. 153), Weber, often cited as a crown witness of German liberalism, built his political convictions on the foundation of the primacy of the national and the national-political. Mommsen's central thesis has met with opposition, but nobody has as yet been able to refute it: national state power was always the last, if not the only, point of reference of Weber's political thinking. Indeed, Weber was, if anything, more "nationalistic" than Bismarck.

To be sure, one has said little about so dynamic and broad a man by calling him a nationalist; and with him, too, we have to consider the context in which he wrote. Even to say that he was an adherent of power politics does not tell us very much, but concerns merely one facet of the man. So one has "to derive the extreme tendency to think in terms of power on the part of Max Weber from the general intellectual situation of German liberalism, which had run aground in 1848 with its great and ideal goals for lack of physical political power and then had to watch Bismarck accomplishing with the power of the Prussian military state and without shunning civil war with Austria the great goal of the liberal movement, the German national state" (153, pp. 46 f.). It is then that we see that, in the context of German politics, Max Weber was indeed a liberal. It was a strange liberalism, to be sure, which desired above all the German national state—but then this is precisely the context with which we are here concerned. There were in Imperial Germany national-nationals like Treitschke, national-socials like Schmoller, national-liberals like Weber, and many versions and shadings of these positions— but all groups stood under the spell of the primacy of the national, which in August 1914 caught up with even German Social Democracy.

Bismarck and Weber are for us merely illustrations of the assertion that the political fronts of Imperial Germany followed lines no less peculiar than those of the social structures and economic patterns of the time. Here the ideas borrowed from elsewhere acquired a different meaning, as did the names by which they were called—and yet they were not disfigured or misused, but merely fell into a different social context, which assimilated them in peculiar ways.

If one wants to give the social structure of Imperial Germany a name, it would be the paradoxical one of an industrial feudal society. This is no more than a name, of course; that is, it gives an indication, not a description, of substance. Speaking of feudal conditions in nineteenth-century Central Europe always involves an escape into metaphor. The traditional patterns of dependence that formed an explosive compound with the industrial form of the economy can be traced back only partly to more strictly feudal relations.

On the other hand, describing features of one's own society as "feudal" was quite common in Imperial Germany. The industrial feudal society penetrated social relations everywhere. It described the formalized status hierarchy of a system of social stratification modeled on military or bureaucratic orders of rank. It was reflected in the patriarchal family with the woman in a servile role. The specific traits of the German Gymnasium of Wilhelminian times found their literary expression in Heinrich Mann's *Blue Angel* and many other novels. The church, especially the quasi-established Lutheran church of Prussia, was only too ready to adumbrate the industrial feudal society with a transcendental ideology. In discussions of military questions, including the "fleet question," the dilemma of the two concepts of rationality may be discerned. The economy itself betrayed the faults of feudalism and industrialism in its basic patterns as well as in individual enterprises.

There remains the realm of politics. Corresponding to the industrial feudal society we find, or found in Imperial Germany, a peculiar constitution of politics, which we have so far but hinted at, although its effect reaches all the way to the present. We may describe it by another apparently paradoxical name as the authoritarian welfare state. Is not the welfare state a specifically modern, and authoritarianism a specifically traditional phenomenon? There may be a basic error in this question. Sometimes it would seem that the champions of the welfare state—the Social Democratic parties particularly of Sweden, England, and Germany—have borrowed more than policies of national insurance from Bismarck's Germany and indeed have their origin in this period. And from here it is only a step to the suspicion that, along with the welfare state, they might revive its authoritarian political context. But however that may be, Imperial Germany managed to combine the two.

Imperial Germany was politically authoritarian. "Authoritarian" means something entirely different from "totalitarian." The authoritarian state rests on the undisputed claim to leadership of a stratum generally legitimated by tradition. Those in power are not exposed to any decisive control by representative institutions, but instead prevent the many from political participation. At the same time, the authoritarian regime is not one of arbitrary power. Its leaders do not rule by terror, but by that mixture of severity and benevolence that characterizes the patriarchal family. William I expressed this blend with almost endearing naïveté in his message to the Reichstag of November 17, 1881: "Even in February of this year We have had Our conviction expressed that the healing of the social damages cannot be sought exclusively by way of the repression of Social Democratic riots, but will have to be sought equally in the positive promotion of the welfare of the workers" (178, p. 360).

A policy may then be called authoritarian if it does not use "repression" alone but is at the same time concerned about the welfare of the subjects. The combination of the (Anti-) Socialist Law and social legislation to which William I referred here is an impressive illustration of the pattern. But at all times the benevolence of the state and its born lords was authoritative. The state did not need the participation of those concerned in its decisions. The Imperial Reichstag with its mixture of rights (in matters of the budget) and impotence (in matters of the composition of the ministry) already marked an extreme point of compromise beyond which authoritarian power would run the risk of jeopardizing its basis. The many might, within certain limits, talk; they might even express wishes; but action remained the prerogative of the few who were called upon to take it.

Authoritarian government is hardly a modern political form. In many ways this is its strength. Authoritarianism is, and certainly was in Imperial Germany, comparatively enlightened. It is neither tyranny nor despotism, and does not grant absolute power. There is, in the authoritarian welfare state, a serious concern about the welfare of its subjects. Possibly, or even probably, social legislation also serves to strengthen the authority of the state; but acts of social policy or humanity are not invalidated by their latent consequences. Imperial Germany made life very difficult for many an inhabitant of the country; but by and large it was possible to live in it with some degree of liberty.

There is one thing the authoritarian welfare state does not and cannot permit: the development of the subject into the citizen with all the rights of this social character. Its basis is the minority of those who live in it, who are treated like children of the patriarchal family. This is not a condition of liberalism. In terms of political theory the faults of the society of Imperial Germany are as many compromises and grudging concessions; and it cannot be denied that even the greatest representatives of the time accepted these compromises of their environment without protest, if they did not applaud them or even contribute to bringing them about. One may hold in their favor that they could not recognize at the time the volcanic nature of the faulted society.

Such conclusions strike the theme that pervades the painful history of Germany in the last century, which thus reveals more continuity than is often seen in it: the departure of the German from his self-inflicted infancy—as one might call it, not without bitterness, in modification of Kant's famous definition of enlightenment. What is remarkable about Imperial Germany is that throughout the industrial revolution it managed to miss the road to modernity and instead consolidated itself as an industrial feudal society with an authoritarian welfare state. Even in the Weimar Republic, Germany did not embark on this road; the revolution to start the journey had not occurred. In its place, the earthquake of National Socialism was to push German society to the point of its social development that made modernity and liberalism a real possibility. But before we pick up the thread of history again at this point, we have to turn to the central and sociological parts of our study.

EQUALITY *OR*

THE LONG ROAD TO MODERNITY

5. THE CITIZEN AND THE CLASSES

In its social aspect, the revolution of modernity may be summarized in a single word: "citizen." The formation and spread
of the character mask of the citizen marks an historical
change whose like would be hard to find. Revolutionary upheavals were not the only way in which this change came
about; indeed possibly those societies are happiest in which
the replacement of the subject by the citizen proceeded in
almost unnoticeably gradual steps. Moreover, the citizen's
role is by no means a specifically modern one in every respect.
Its prehistory extends beyond Christian theory to the Stoa,
for whose numerous immigrant Greeks universal equality was
more than a philosophical problem. But it is only in the
eighteenth century that the citizen, as a real figure of history,
slowly enters the scene here and there; and even today there
is many a stage without him. We would not be concerned with this role here if it were not for its unfortunate
absence, or to stretch the metaphor somewhat, for its most
incomplete presence in German society.

The character mask of the citizen is its bearer's title to participation. Citizenship rights are so many chances of participation. This is not to be misunderstood. Today, we know that
the maximum of, say, political activity on the part of every
citizen is by no means the optimum; it is a signal of crisis
rather than an index of stable democratic conditions. By participation I obviously do not mean the enforced organization
of every individual for the purposes of the total state, either.
This is why it might be clearer to speak of chances of participation rather than the act of taking part. What makes
citizenship effective is the possibility it offers the individual to
take part in the political as in the more inclusive social process, that is, to carry his interests to the market of politics as
he does his goods to the market of the economy, and his
idiosyncrasies to the market of society. In this sense, the role
of citizen is an element of liberty; the citizen is able, through

a world of choices, to develop his personality in a way and to a degree that the majority of men could not do throughout history.

The revolutionary aspect of the citizen's role is that by its very essence it cannot be exclusive. In principle citizenship means citizenship for all. It means "that no man shall be so placed in society that he can overreach his neighbour to the extent which constitutes a denial of the latter's citizenship" (H. Laski: 125, p. 153). As it is, the large number of men stand in the shadow of history; and so far as the collective memory of peoples is concerned, they may well do so forever. But in all past centuries the many also stood in the shadow of events themselves; they were denied not only the chance of political participation but their share in the rewards and facilities of life as well. It would be unfair to hold Aristotle responsible for this state of affairs, on the grounds that he prescribed to some a practical life of toil in order to enable others to enjoy the theoretical life of leisure; but until the revolution of citizenship there were in all history unsurpassable boundaries and barriers between men: God made them high and lowly and ordered their estate. The citizen has liberated the many from the prison of closed opportunities, and thus marks the turning point of the road from inherited position to autonomous decision, from status to contract.

The role of citizen involves rights of equality; and here a clarification is necessary. There is an important difference between equal citizenship rights on the one hand, and equality of social status or even of social character on the other. Citizenship rights provide chances of participation without determining the outcome of such participation. Thus, equal opportunities in the selection of higher education are a requirement of citizenship; equal school degrees for all, however, have nothing to do with this right. Equal rights to a minimum income, which secures the social subsistence level, are a citizenship right; but equal incomes are explicitly not. Indeed, the significance of citizenship is that it makes inequality possible in so far as this does not affect people's basis of life. Equal citizenship rights replace inherited privilege by inequalities of acquired rank. Equality, therefore, belongs to the character mask of the citizen only in so far as it must be regarded as a condition of full participation in the social and political process.

This has to be emphasized and stands in deliberate contrast

to those—and, especially in Germany, there are many of them —who prematurely denounce the civil society of citizens as a mass society. The "tyranny of the majority," less in its Platonic than in the rather more cautious version of John Stuart Mill, that is, the society of the nouveaux riches of citizenship rights, certainly poses many a difficult social and political problem. But with all its problems, it is a necessary condition for the unfolding of the principle of a liberal democracy, which promises to all, and not merely the chosen few, a lively competition of political interests and effective control of power.

If this political form should prove unrealistic under conditions of general citizenship rights, its theory would be refuted and liberalism finally revealed as an ideology of semimodernity. This is why I should like to stress once more that I am not advocating a utopia or a fiction. I am not concerned with an electoral participation of 99.9 per cent, or with people who spend their entire leisure time reading newspapers and carrying on political debates. Apart from the borderline situations of massive protest, politics will always remain a domain of active minorities. But I am concerned with the fact that in a liberal democracy as it is here understood, everybody counts, everybody can participate and has the right to secure the range of his existence against the claims of others, whether people or institutions, including the state.

There are many who object to defining the citizen role in terms of the rights it confers. What about the obligations and duties of the citizen? In part, the objection is justified. Equal rights are only one side of the medal of citizenship, and, what is more, they are—as we shall soon see—the less problematical one. It is much more difficult to bring about a state in which people in fact participate in the political process as citizens, and as citizens only. If the citizen role may be described as epitomizing the principle of modernity, this is not because of the rights in its theory, but because of the facts in its reality; for apart from the privileges in which social ranks have become crystallized, citizenship excludes those traditional ties that condemn men who were born for freedom into a structure of bondage. If German society failed to advance on the road to modernity, it was these ties of tradition as much as, if not more than, the absence of rights that account for it.

But this is anticipating. Let us return to citizenship rights themselves and to their reality in Germany. In doing so, I should like to follow T. H. Marshall's discussion of the development of citizenship in England, at least part of the way:

> I shall be running true to type as a sociologist if I begin by saying that I propose to divide citizenship into three parts. But the analysis is, in this case, dictated by history even more clearly than by logic. I shall call these three parts, or elements, *civil, political* and *social.* The civil element is composed of the rights necessary for individual freedom—*liberty of the person, freedom of speech, thought and faith, the right to own property* and *to conclude valid contracts,* and *the right to justice.* The last is of a different order from the others, because it is the right to defend and assert all one's right on terms of equality with others and by *due process of law.* This shows us that the institutions most directly associated with civil rights are the courts of justice. By the political element I mean the right to participate in the exercise of political power, as a member of a body invested with political authority or as an elector of the members of such a body. The corresponding institutions are parliament and councils of local government. By the social element I mean the whole range from the right to a modicum of economic welfare and security to the right to share to the full in the social heritage and to live the life of a civilised being according to the standards prevailing in the society. The institutions most closely connected with it are the educational system and the social services. (142, pp. 10 f.)

England makes it easy for the historian of the citizen role. Without forcing interpretation unduly, T. H. Marshall can ascribe the development of each of the three elements of citizenship to one century, "civil rights to the eighteenth, political to the nineteenth, and social to the twentieth" (142, p. 14). Characteristically, this would at best describe the evolution of the theory of civil rights in Germany; and even then, Hegel's "supersession" of civil society by the state would blur the picture. The process of implementive citizenship rights began late in Germany; and its early difficulties, more than its incompleteness today, distinguish German society from other countries.

Considering the long history of the idea of the "rule of law" (*Rechtsstaat*) in Germany, one might think that at least the legal elements of the citizen role are firmly established. However, the assumption implies a consequential error. The rule of law is not the same as democratic institutions, and insistence on it is as such no testimony to the basic attitude of modern liberalism. That everything, including the actions of those in power, should be done in accordance with codified rules, or at least be limited by these, is certainly an important condition of an acceptable political order; but it leaves the substance of the rules quite open. Thus the belief that the establishment of the rule of law must bring about democracy more or less automatically is in itself a German misunderstanding. This conclusion leaves out of consideration the fact that the rule of law as a condition of equal rights for all remained incomplete for a long time. Civil equality was not realized to any notable extent before the Weimar Republic, and again in the Federal Republic.

In part, the deficiencies of equality before the law were of a technical nature. Even at the time of Bismarck's social legislation, parliamentary and legal debate focused on the somewhat academic point of whether such enactments would not create indefensible special rights for certain groups. This debate gained in intensity, and in substance, after the establishment of labor courts in the Weimar Republic. Since then, the old institution of disciplinary courts for state employees giving them a special—if probably especially difficult—position before the law, has raised new problems. It certainly casts doubt on the reality of equality before the law if there are several—in Germany seven—branches of law courts, some of which are exclusively geared to certain social groups.

But these are subtle and on the whole probably harmless restrictions of equal citizenship rights in German society in comparison to, say, the explicit statutory discrimination against certain groups. Although the "problem of nationalities" was one of the persistent themes of public debate in Imperial Germany, in whose parliament there were, even during the First World War, eighteen "Poles," nine "Danes," and one "Alsace-Lorrainer," it took a long time before this debate resulted in equal legal rights for minorities. At least at the time of the "culture struggle" one cannot really speak of full citizenship rights for Catholic priests, and indeed for a large part of the Catholic population. In 1917, Walther Rathenau wrote, with good reason, to Mrs. von Hindenburg: "Although myself and my ancestors have served our country as best we could, I am, as you would presumably know, as a Jew a second-class citizen" (178, p. 259). Equal rights for women were granted by constitution and law only after the Second World War. And these are examples illustrating legal—as against even more pervasive social—privileges and disadvantages.

The picture of Imperial Germany—to say nothing of that of Nazi Germany—looks even darker with respect to the civil liberties of speech, thought, and faith. There was censorship; there were court rulings against the practice of even the liberties guaranteed by the constitution; there were manifold discriminations for reasons of conviction or of membership in certain groups. In terms of the Federal Republic it is easy to conclude that Germany has no civil-rights problem that reaches the dimension of the color problem in the United States. But this perspective is clearly very distorted. It excludes no less than fifty-nine of the seventy-four years from 1871 to 1945, and in the years since the Second World War it excludes one half of the country.

An analogous case can be made so far as the development of the political rights of citizenship is concerned. Article 20 of the Constitution of the German Empire of 1871 promised: "Parliament is constituted by general and direct elections in secret ballot." In this, the national parliament differed laudably from that of Prussia, where up to the First World War a three-class franchise remained in force, which subdivided the people according to the oldest criterion of stratification into tax classes and meant that one third of all members were elected by 3 per cent of the electorate, a further third by 12 per cent, and the remaining third by 85 per cent.

But equal suffrage on the national level needs to be taken with a considerable lump of salt; while it may have been equal for some, it was certainly not universal. Approximately 10 per cent of the total population actually took part in the first election for which the law of 1871 held; about 20 per cent had the right to vote: men who had completed their twenty-fifth year and satisfied certain residential qualifications. Actual participation is no less telling in this period than the right to vote, since there were numerous obstacles preventing the realization of rights that were granted in theory. Participation rose to about 15 per cent of the population in 1907, and 19 per cent in 1912. Incidentally (and as a demonstration of the limits of this statistical analysis), in terms of political participation Germany led nearly all other countries in the world before the First World War, when only in Australia and New Zealand, where women already had suffrage, more than 20 per cent of all people participated in elections. In Great Britain, the proportion of the population going to the polls amounted to about 12 per cent at this time, in the United States, as in Germany, to about 19 per cent.

There were other restrictions of equal suffrage, some of which remain in effect to the present day. Among these is, above all, the ancient problem of electoral districting. Although there were in Imperial Germany, in contrast to England, no university constituencies (which would probably, if unjustly, have seemed suspect to the conservatives), there were rotten boroughs, depopulated constituencies, which for that very reason had become safe seats for the conservatives. The size of constituencies in late Imperial Germany varied between 9500 (Schaumburg-Lippe) and 247,500 (Teltow) voters; in 1902, 18,000 votes were needed for every seat of the German Conservatives, 21,000 votes for every seat of the Center Party, and 76,000 votes for every seat of the Social Democrats.

In the Weimar Republic, most restrictions on political equality were abolished. The proportion of the population that went to the polls rose in Germany (as in most other countries) to between 50 and 60 per cent, a rate that may be called normal in view of the demographic structure of European societies. Both the introduction of woman suffrage and the lowering of the voting age contributed greatly to this change. Thus the realization of the political rights of citizenship would seem a problem of the past in Germany; they were missing for too long and at too many points. Where they were granted by law and constitution, there was not, after 1918, a Mississippi, not even in the easternmost provinces of the Empire.

But this tranquilizing picture soon gives way to one of dramatic colors if we take the step from the legal and political to the social rights of citizenship. T. H. Marshall is surely right in his claim that the status of citizenship is fully achieved only when certain social rights are granted. Equality before the law is an empty promise for those who cannot find or pay for legal counsel; equal suffrage remains fictitious for people who cannot read and write. Nor are inaccessibility of legal counsel and illiteracy the only problems. How the social rights of citizenship were held back, or distorted, becomes fully apparent if we consider the two examples Marshall suggests as decisive: social policy and education. In doing so, we will also encounter one of the keys to the persistent structures of German society.

Not surprisingly, English liberals of the nineteenth century were rather less than fond of the full status of citizenship and, above all, of its social ingredients. T. H. Marshall has demonstrated this in a lecture devoted to his great namesake, the English economist Alfred Marshall. Alfred Marshall, otherwise an emphatic opponent of state intervention, including state social policy, nevertheless permitted one exception, education. For him, education was, even if it involved compulsory schooling enforced by the state, "bound to compel [the working classes] and to help them to take the first step upwards" toward a society in which everybody is, "by occupation at least, a gentleman," a civilized being (142, pp. 6 f.). Both the dislike of social policy and the demand for education here serve the same liberal ideal of autonomy. In Germany, social policy was less unpopular. Its rationale was, however, not the establishment of citizenship rights, but the maintenance of human minority. It sufficed, therefore, for the national ideal to create a system of general primary and vocational schools, which opened the path to the institutions of higher learning only to the chosen few. The rhetoric of equal educational opportunity was, and still is, missing in German politics of all parties, because none of these has ever emphatically espoused the liberal ideal of autonomy for all.

With respect to social policy, this conclusion has its paradoxical side. In Germany, those minimum guarantees of status that form the social side of the citizen role were provided earlier than anywhere else, while at the same time the role of the citizen advanced rather more slowly than in many other countries. Upon closer inspection, however, the paradox can be dissolved. In order to contribute to the establishment of civil rights, state social policy must be informed by liberal principles; but in Germany its principles were those of the welfare state, of "state socialism." Social policy need not immobilize subjects; it may strengthen the sense of responsibility in citizens too. Here, social policy in Germany always went too far in holding citizens in tutelage. On the other hand, it never went far enough in terms of respect for a civilized human existence. Its guiding ideas had little to do with the image of the gentleman, into which every man wants to develop. To the present day, social insurance agencies have put considerable difficulties in the way of modern medical treatment; in many luxurious-looking new hospital buildings the dying are still pushed into lavatory rooms; work accidents are regarded by many as an inescapable fate; invalids and old-age pensioners can hardly be said to live a civilized life in the throes of state social policy. Thus the conclusion has to be upheld in substance: apparent civil rights, although old, have not become effective as such; an early social policy serves to prevent rather than to promote the reality of the citizen role.

Essentially the same holds for the German educational system. It offers little to all, and everything to a few. If one works on the assumption that education is not only a fundamental civil right by itself (a notion written into the constitutions of most German states), but also a necessary condition for the effective exercise of nearly all other civil rights, including equality before the law and equal suffrage, then the obstinate survival of extraordinary inequalities of educational opportunity constitutes a fundamental deficiency in the establishment of equal civil rights in Germany. Here, moreover, we are no longer concerned with deficiencies remedied after 1918, or even 1945; at least in Western Germany, inequalities of educational opportunity are still a striking and shocking fact.

General education in Germany is old. This is a merit, but no advantage. Once one leaves the cities, one rarely finds, especially in the South German states, fully developed primary schools. In terms of numbers, schools in small places with but one or two classes dominate; in such schools, children may learn certain elementary skills, but can hardly hope to be educated according to their abilities, or indeed to be guided onto the road to higher education. In the Federal Republic, this is still true for every seventh child (1964: 13.2 per cent) and almost every other school (45.5 per cent).

These schools are often the pride of villages, but their equipment and teaching are a shame to a civilized country. It is not known how many children leave these schools as quasi illiterates. Unfortunately, it is also not generally known —and cannot be derived from official statistical sources—how large the proportion of real illiterates is in Germany. All we know is that there are exceptions to compulsory schooling that permit, especially in the country, subnormal and handicapped children to live a life in the twilight without ever having attended a school, to say nothing of having received the chance to be educated for the crafts and skills that they would have been able to learn. These are German problems of civil rights that do not yield much to those of Mississippi or Notting Hill in significance or in shamefulness.

Inequalities of educational opportunity become starkly evident in institutions of higher education. Here we encounter three great categories of German society in ever diminishing proportions: children from the country, children from working-class families, and girls. A fourth group, Roman Catholics, must be added to these under certain conditions, although here recent changes are most marked. Two thirds of all German children have parents either in agricultural or in working-class occupations; but barely 10 per cent of all university students are recruited from these groups. Even at the point of transition to secondary schools at the age of ten plus, these groups are markedly underrepresented, as against the overrepresentation of children of professional people, state employees, and clerical workers. In the course of secondary school itself their proportional number is almost systematically reduced further. Only one out of three children of workers and peasants who enter secondary school complete the degree taken at its end. Contrasted with the relative size of these groups in German society and also in terms of international comparisons, the number of students from these groups is so strikingly small that the favorite German explanation of educational inequality—differentials of ability—is evidently inadequate.

A similar argument can be advanced with respect to educational opportunities for girls. Germany is one of the few countries in which it has been regarded as necessary to include women's claim to equal rights explicitly in the constitution; but, in fact, a role image of the woman, which grants women at best derived civil rights, has survived all changes of the last decades. For girls, an intermediate-school final degree is considered sufficient; women should get married and have children; women do not need an occupation—familiar notions such as these are still widespread. The reality of this role image is not only unjust, but also painful.

This is what girls who dropped out of universities before completing their degree had to say: "If my husband were a professional man or had at least finished secondary school, I would certainly have taken my degree. But he only went to primary school. If I had taken the degree, the educational difference would have become even greater. . . . My husband was also very much in favor of breaking off. He never made it a condition really, he never said, 'You stop now.' But I noticed that he would not have liked to be married to an economics graduate." In marriage too, the educational differential serves to demonstrate the traditional rank order of men and women: "He always said, I should not allow myself to be pushed out. He did not want to pull me down. But finally I simply could not have a higher social standing than my husband. After that, continuing my studies had become entirely pointless" (82, pp. 48 f.). These quotations from interviews provide a first indication of the complexity of the causes of the phenomenon in question. But we are not concerned with causes yet, nor with the search for culprits, but simply with documenting inequalities of educational opportunity in Germany.

Where there are deprived groups, there are usually also privileged ones. It is not very surprising, of course, that the children of professional people are among those apparently preferred in the institutions of higher education. But, more significantly in terms of our analysis, we here encounter again the group we have already mentioned as forming the unhappily solid backbone of the German system of social stratification: state employees (*Beamte*). More than one third of all German university students are (in 1962/3) the children of state employees, an occupational group that comprises approximately 6 per cent of the population. Moreover, a number of these children (20.8 per cent) come from the families of lower-echelon state employees. Their fathers are not university-trained, and many of them are bound to find it as difficult as workers to finance the education of their children. At this point the study of educational opportunity confirms the historical suspicion that the bureaucracy of the state assumes a peculiarly prominent position in German society.

Even in view of these facts, speaking of unequal educational opportunity is by no means a matter of course. Do not all children in Germany have formally the same chances of access to higher education? We are indeed not concerned here with formal privilege by a planned policy of selection or even by law. Such statutory distinctions may indeed be more widespread in countries where actual privilege is at the same time much less pronounced. In the German case, we are concerned rather with those inequalities that undercut and undermine legal equality of opportunity. It need hardly be emphasized that such flagrant differences in the educational standard and

educational opportunities of social groups are incompatible
with the principle of equal citizenship rights.

But this does not imply that equal opportunities of education must under all circumstances and by themselves lead to
political liberalization. In the German Democratic Republic,
inequalities of opportunity have been abolished in so far as
they have not, after a quasi-revolutionary initial stage, already
been replaced by new kinds of privilege, but the detailed
planning and control of education by a dogmatically partisan
government serves thoroughly illiberal purposes. This is an
observation of consequence, for here we see for the first
time that the principle of citizenship is politically ambiguous;
it serves as a basis for liberal democracy only in conjunction
with other social conditions. Otherwise, and more simply put,
the generalization of citizenship is a necessary, but not a sufficient condition of liberal democracy.

For a long time, there have been "second-class citizens" in
Germany. This phrase of Rathenau's is evidently a contra-
dictio in adiecto; the notion of citizenship excludes all class
structures based on formal privilege. But there were, in fact,
people of several classes in Germany, and at least in terms of
educational opportunity, if not also in those of hospital treatment and treatment in a court of law, there still are. Worse
than that, there were inequalities between men in Germany
for which even this is too idyllic a description. Men of different classes do not cease to be men, human beings. But
German society has, at times at least, gone beyond such human differentiations and denied certain people who should
have been its members not only their civil, but also their human rights. The German language has permitted not only the
"superman," but also the "subman," *Untermensch*, who no
longer counts as human, and may therefore be disregarded,
trampled on, expelled from home and hearth, put out to
pasture, and if need be even killed. This is a bitter subject to
which we shall have to return time and again, and it concerns
not only the Jews.

There is no country in which 100 per cent of the inhabitants enjoy full citizenship rights. Certain groups remain outside the rights of this status under all conditions: children and
juveniles; immigrants who have, as we say, not yet acquired
citizenship; foreign citizens resident in the country; the mentally ill as well as certain persons, often delinquents, who have
lost their citizenship rights either temporarily or permanently.

All these exceptions add up to a sizable proportion of the people, which in most societies is probably somewhere between one third and one half. Now it may well be that the reality of the rights of citizenship in a country is proved most clearly by its negation, so that the ways in which those who are not full citizens are treated would enable one to tell how the liberal principle of basic equality fares. If this assumption is correct, the balance that results in Germany offers a pitiful picture.

Any analysis of German society might well include a chapter on the social role of the child. It is unlikely, however, that this chapter would lead to the conclusion that in Germany children are taken seriously as future citizens and treated as such. Instead, the child's role of minor in the family epitomizes the position that is by implication imputed at least to women as well in the society, and that the majority of men have had—and not merely in Imperial Germany. There is a hypocritical praise for such infancy, too; "childish" children are better than "precocious" ones who try to do as the grown-ups do. While elsewhere many assumptions of the citizen role are extended to children at least by analogy, the reverse tendency may be observed in Germany: adults are treated as children.

The condition of other groups with restricted rights does not testify to any greater sense of civic equality. There are the foreigners living in the country. As "nationalities" they have existed as long as there has been a German Empire, although its presumably definitive destruction by National Socialist initiative has reversed the situation so that today there are German minorities in all the countries bordering on Germany. But the demands of German minorities abroad have often stood in grotesque contrast to the treatment of foreign minorities in Germany.

Workers from abroad are also a familiar feature of German society. Their countries of origin have changed since 1880; after Poles, and later Poles and Russians as well as Hungarians and Rumanians, there are today Turks, Greeks, Italians, and Spaniards. What has not changed is their number of nearly one million (whose manpower was only temporarily replaced by that of the German expellees from the East) and, more significantly, their treatment in the country that, while it calls them "guests," only tolerates them from six o'clock in the morning to four in the afternoon, that is, as long as they work. Other countries may not do much better in this respect; but this is no excuse for the nearly complete disregard of this large, external, yet internal proletariat.

Then there are the more extreme examples: delinquents, inmates of prisons and mental hospitals, gypsies, Jews—all those toward whom far too many Germans regard everything, including murder (for which there are so many euphemisms) as justified. The disproportion between the visible and the invisible part of the German legal system, that is, between courts of law and prisons, could hardly be greater. While judges still express their hope that the accused will be improved by imprisonment, a penal system is already waiting that excludes improvement from the outset by treating its victims not as failing citizens, but as semihumans. And afterward, the civil service society reacts accordingly. The mentally ill count for even less. Even nurses, to say nothing of doctors, whose calling is the loving care of patients, killed, in Nazi Germany, hundreds of the mentally ill: euthanasia, murder out of care, horrible perfection of the welfare state for minors. It is easy to get into the snake pit in Germany, but difficult to get out, and there are few who dare discuss either problem in public.

Anti-Semitism has many layers. It is present in nearly every country in which Jews are living, and it has a long history. But it is a far cry from the religious antagonisms between Christians and Jews to the gas chambers of Auschwitz. The social figures along the road between these points are many. Among them is the stranger, who by his marginality confirms the central position of the others. Then there is the conspirator, who provides a transparently simplistic explanation of the unexplainable. There is the enemy, who is responsible for all the evils of the times. These are figures that Jews have had to assume with Englishmen and Americans, Frenchmen and Italians as well, although in general not by way of official government policy. But the figure of the Jew as a creature devoid of human rights, as no longer human, is a German invention. And it is this notion that provided a motive and a horrible excuse for those many thousands of Germans who directly or indirectly took part in the great mass murder after 1940. "Thou shalt not kill"—of course—but the commandment means men and not vermin, which must be exterminated. After the war, some of the murderers awoke to a more humane perspective and thereby documented the full horror of an official policy defining some men as not human.

We will not be able to explain the ghastly consequences of this distinction between men and "submen." But recalling it to consciousness is inevitable in a discussion of the pathology of civic equality in Germany. Germany has no problem today as strikingly apparent as that of Commonwealth immigration to Britain or of Negroes in the American South. This is just as well—not for Germany, for such problems serve to keep alive an awareness of the incompleteness of citizenship rights—but for those who are spared the fate of being rightless minorities in Germany. For citizenship rights are by no means general in German society even today. There still are second- and third-class citizens who are lacking many requisites of civilized life and chances of full development. Furthermore, it is hard to dispute the suspicion that the ability to distinguish not only between men of different classes but also between men and "submen" is still slumbering in many Germans.

In such deadly distinctions a familiar motive recurs. It cannot be the intention of our analysis to accuse; but occasionally strong colors have to be applied to the picture of German society. This is especially so if we enter areas that are left blank by political as well as scholarly discussion. Underlying the class distinctions cited here, we encounter once again the "primacy of foreign policy," the predominance of the national, the house whose furnishing is a matter of no consequence to its architects: the German question of reunification seems more important than the German question of educational opportunity, or of the treatment of the mentally ill or gypsies. Considering that questions must not only be raised but should also be answered, might it not be that the two German questions, one clamored about so noisily, the other repressed so effectively, are more closely connected than many believe—and too closely for it to be possible to settle them with national recipes?

6. SOCIAL STRATIFICATION OF THE GERMAN PEOPLE

The citizen is the enemy of classes, since he does not tolerate second-class men beside him. A possible definition of class is "a hierarchy of status, [in which] the difference between one class and another is expressed in terms of legal rights and established customs which have the essential binding character of law." In a class structure of this kind, T. H. Marshall's assertion is plausible: "The impact of citizenship on such a system was bound to be profoundly disturbing, and even destructive. The rights with which the general status of citizenship was invested were extracted from the hierarchical status system of social class, robbing it of its essential substance" (142, p. 30).

In the terminology of sociology (which cannot altogether please the historian), the "classes" destroyed here would have to be called estates, that is, status groups protected by privilege. An estate society cannot survive the onslaught of citizenship; the invention of the role of citizen was historically and continues to be today the epitome of protest against an estate order. But the abolition of such privileges does not mean the disappearance of all inequalities. Distinctions of classes and strata remain, and the part they play in the day-to-day lives of people is hardly less prominent than that of the older ranks.

At least in Germany, this needs to be emphasized. The community of the whole people has for some time been one of the preferred German ideologies; and those who claimed that they no longer recognized any parties or that there were no classes left any more could hope to be popular. We will have a closer look at this German ideology a little later; for the moment, our concern is with reality. All known societies display at least rudiments, and often elaborate structures, of two types of inequality. One of these, the productive one, is the seed of social conflicts and thus of change; not the least of its many effects is to produce the other inequality. Productive inequality is inequality of power, which gives rise to the formation of classes and to their struggles. The other inequality is distributive; it concerns the unequal distribution of social rewards, such as income, prestige, and, under certain circumstances, education and power too, although the latter straddle the border between productive and distributive inequality. The social system of distributive inequality we call social stratification.

But is not social stratification an outdated notion in the affluent society of today? And how can the persistence of social stratification, if it is a fact, be reconciled with the equal status of citizenship? The first question is a very German one, the answer to which is obvious. There are people who have sleepless nights trying to devise ways of receiving parcels from mail-order houses without their neighbors' noticing these symbols of inferior status; there are (as we have seen) girls who abandon their careers as students because they "simply cannot stand higher socially" than their husbands; there are people who can tour the Caribbean in a private yacht, and others who have yet to go on their first holiday trip; there are hungry nights for the sake of acquiring status symbols, stomach ulcers from status anxiety, and suicides because of a "failure," which can be called such only if the dichotomy of Above and Below continues to be a hard fact of social life. In short, there is social stratification in modern as in any other society.

The other question is not quite so easy to answer. There are indeed two points at which contradictions between citizenship rights and social stratification are likely to exist. One of these has to do with the top positions of social status. There are conceivably, and actually, positions that stand out so far from the general range of status that their paraphernalia enable their incumbents to dispute the citizenship of others. This holds for wealth as it does for respect where and when these are so concentrated that they can be translated into social power, that is, for monopolistic property and for charisma. The other point at which civil rights and status differences may become incompatible lies at the foot of the pyramid of stratification. There is a degree of status deprivation, that is, of poverty and of social contempt, that makes full participation as a citizen impossible. This is why the implementation of citizenship rights demands a certain amount of what is often called leveling, that is, a reliable floor and a protective ceiling for the building of social stratification. A policy designed for this end may well be conceived as a liberal social policy. It would remain a liberal policy, for its proper goal would be to keep the space between ceiling and floor as wide as possible, so that the multiplicity of human talents and achievements could be expressed in the language of distributive inequality. But whether policy or, on the contrary, institution is selected for abolition, a system of social stratification has emerged everywhere.

Our question is then: What does this system look like in German society? As a basis of information, the distribution of people according to various criteria of status is of interest. There is, to begin with, income. In 1963, the main earners in German households were distributed over various income groups in the following way: less than 250 DM (a month), 5 per cent; 250–399 DM, 12 per cent; 400–599 DM, 34 per cent; 600–799 DM, 27 per cent; 800–999 DM, 12 per cent; 1000 DM and more, 10 per cent (104, p. 4). All these figures, but especially the last, would require a much more differentiated analysis in other contexts. Thus the 10 per cent with monthly incomes of 1000 DM and more include the many with incomes of little more than 1000 DM, that is, annual incomes of 12,000 to 15,000 DM, as well as those 12,000 men who, in the same year, had a taxable income of more than 1 million marks. Why we nevertheless confine ourselves here to crude general figures will soon become evident.

The income structure confirms a general observation that K. M. Bolte has put into the graphical terms of an onion-shaped system of stratification, which has succeeded the traditional pyramid of status (24, pp. 248 ff.). While in the past the largest number of people were probably situated near the foot of the scale of social stratification, the greatest concentration today is found in the middle. While this may hold for income, however, it is not characteristic of the distribution of power, nor is it true in terms of educational achievement. In 1962, 82 per cent of all Germans had received only primary-school education, 13 per cent had finished an intermediate-type school, and 5 per cent had acquired university entrance qualifications (104, p. 4). Probably rather less than one half of all secondary-school graduates have also got a university degree.

A quantitative distribution of social prestige is much harder to assess, although it would be of considerable interest to know more about this seemingly imponderable and yet crucial element of social stratification. In 1951, that is, before the onset of affluence (and in an untypical part of the country), Bolte conducted a survey about the relative prestige of thirty-eight possibly symptomatic occupations. The result is charged with all the problems of this kind of study; its information value is therefore strictly limited:

1. University professor
2. Physician
3. Factory manager (e.g., foundry manager)
4. Higher civil servant (*Regierungsrat*)
5. Secondary-school teacher
6. Electrical engineer
7. Landed proprietor
8. Priest
9. Primary-school teacher
10. Technical designer
11. Army major (active service)
12. Car mechanic (own shop, two assistants)
13. Opera singer
14. Bank employee (accountant)
15. Textile businessman (owner of shop, one salesman)
16. Skilled industrial worker (e.g., fitter, turner, etc.)
17. Tailor (own business, no assistants)
18. Peasant (medium-sized farm)
19. Carpenter (employed in furniture factory)
20. Hairdresser (own business, one assistant)
21. Grocery shop owner (own business, two salesmen)
22. Butcher (employed in sausage factory)
23. Postal clerk
24. Machine tool fitter (journeyman)
25. Sergeant (active service)
26. Insurance agent (representative)
27. Mason (journeyman)
28. Musician (in a dance band)
29. Writer (author of cheap novelettes)
30. Male nurse
31. Sailor
32. Waiter
33. Salesman (in a food shop)
34. Conductor (tram, bus)
35. Tradesman
36. Agricultural laborer
37. Messenger (office messenger)
38. Unskilled laborer   (23, p. 42.)

Attractive as it might be to reflect upon the considerations that went into this scale, or to find out the probable rank of one's own occupation (which, for the professor, is as simple as it is gratifying), such endeavors would not really help us gain a reliable picture of social stratification in Germany. All they would prove would be an obvious and familiar fact: the various scales of social stratification do not coincide. Many people in modern society have discrepant statuses. The professor does not earn more than the physician and certainly not more than the factory manager. The average educational level of factory directors is lower than that of secondary- and primary-school teachers. It is thus difficult to present a unidimensional picture of social stratification, or to identify social strata as such, as desirable as both these efforts might appear.

There have, in fact, been a number of attempts to construct unidimensional models of stratification for Germany after the Second World War (cf. p. 83 below). These proceed in different ways. The American sociologist Morris Janowitz has subdivided positions into four strata in terms of a combination of various criteria of stratification. His upper middle class includes the professions, leading white-collar workers, higher civil servants, wealthy businessmen; in the lower middle class we find clerical workers and state employees of the middle and lower echelons, independent small businessmen and craftsmen as well as peasants; the upper lower class is composed of skilled workers and craftsmen in dependent positions; the lower lower class consists of semiskilled and unskilled workers as well as agricultural laborers. Janowitz also interviewed a representative sample of Germans about their self-evaluation in terms of a given set of strata; here he found a pronounced polarization into two strata, middle class and working class, in which more than 90 per cent of those interviewed placed themselves. The result, and its problems, remind one of R. Centers' study of *The Psychology of Social Classes* in the United States.

Another, rather more differentiated model has been developed by H. Moore and G. Kleining in terms of the social self-estimation (SSE) of the population. It is based on numerous surveys among varying samples, on the basis of which Moore and Kleining were able to construct a self-image as well as an image of social strata; their model has been applied most frequently in market research. In the context of German stratification research, the model developed by E. K. Scheuch according to American precedents is without doubt the most refined. Scheuch has used data from a representative sample

Model of Social Stratification of German Society after 1945
(All figures are percentages)

Janowitz (105)	Self-ranking (according to Janowitz)	Moore/Kleining ("SSE," 155)	Scheuch ("Cologne Index," 195)
UM 4.6	U 1.9	U 1	U 2.6
LM 38.6	M 43.2	UM 5	UM 9.9
		MM 15	MM 18.9
		LM 30 — industrial 13 / non-industrial 17	LM 23.3
UL 13.3	W 48.5	UL 28 — industrial 18 / non-industrial 10	UL 33.6
LL 38.6		LL 17	ML 10.2
	U 5.3	SD 4	LL 0.6
ND 4.9	ND 1.1		ND 0.9

U = Upper class; UM = Upper middle class; M = Middle class; MM = Middle middle class; LM = Lower middle class; W = Working class; UL = Upper lower class; ML = Middle lower class; LL = Lower lower class; L = Lower class; SD = Socially despised; ND = No data.

(For explanation, see text.)

about their occupational groups (one aspect), their economic
position (four aspects) and their cultural level (four aspects), and has then applied a complex index based on a
point system of evaluation of the nine aspects to assign individuals to one of seven strata.

There are other, on the whole less important, models of
social stratification in Germany; but presenting them would
serve only to aggravate the impression of willful diversity
which, more than anything else, confuses the intelligent layman. And unless he has an infinitely benevolent attitude toward sociology, he may suspect that this diversity is simply
another example of academic quarrelsomeness. The layman is
right and wrong at the same time. The differences between
stratification models are an involuntary demonstration of the
fact that, in contemporary German society, there are no social strata whose boundaries are so clearly defined that any
observer can identify them. But this is the only good reason
for divergences between the models; in all other respects they
are a sign of weakness. Stratification models such as those
discussed here are in fact only moderately fruitful analytically.

It is often said that the number of social strata distinguished
depends on the purpose of the investigation. But which purpose justifies which distinction? None of the various models
of stratification is really any better—more correct, more useful—than another; they are all equally construed. And this
provides the reason for a second objection. Because the models
are construed, and thus do not even aim at marking real
boundaries, they are arbitrary even for descriptive purposes.
Put less academically: they do not describe contemporary
German society at all. In order to get such a description, we
have to follow an altogether different path.

K. M. Bolte thought he could overcome the dilemma of
the methodological limits of available sociological tools on
the one hand and the intention to describe real inequalities
on the other only by renouncing entirely the attempt to develop one stratification model for the whole of society. He
therefore sketched four distinct "stratification types" for
purely rural, rural-urban, small-town, and large-town areas
(cf. 24). But here legitimate doubt in a method seems exaggerated into defeatism. In any case, there is in the history
of German sociology a model for the analysis of social
stratification that satisfies our demands, the more so since it is
also tied into a total analysis of German society with a political

intention: Theodor Geiger's 1932 study, *Die soziale Schichtung des deutschen Volkes* [Social Stratification of the German People], which he himself described as a "sociographic
attempt on a statistical basis." Taking up Geiger's study
provides our analysis with some historical depth as well as
offering a methodological precedent worth emulating.

Geiger's material is the occupational census of 1925. In
an analysis as extensive as it is subtle he opens up this material for sociological understanding. The analysis proceeds in
three steps. The first step involves the articulation of occupations by economic position into three categories (further differentiated in an "articulation in depth") of "capitalist,"
"intermediate," and "proletarian" positions. The second step
leads from the economic to the social sphere, to social strata
such as the "middle class" or the "proletariat." But it is the
third step that really distinguishes Geiger's approach and
continues to be useful. In addition to determinants of position,
he introduces a social-psychological category, "mentality."
"Mentality . . . is mental-psychical disposition, it is immediate formation of man by his social environment and by the
experiences of life emanating from it and made in it" (79, p.
77). Geiger's concept of stratification is characterized by the
idea that social strata are groups with a common social mentality, from which we may therefore expect specific patterns
of economic and political behavior. In this sense, strata are
real groupings, if complex ones, which are differentiated
within themselves and merge at their borders with neighboring strata. The model of social stratification that results from
this approach is clearly construed also; it is the work of a
scholar. Here construction aims at the description of identifiable modes of group behavior and at the same time serves
to explain such modes of behavior in terms of common
socio-economic position. In the final analysis, Geiger distinguished five main strata for German society at the time of
the Weimar Republic:

Capitalists	0.92%	
Old middle class	17.77%	
New middle class	17.95%	
Proletaroids	12.65%	
Proletariat	50.71%	(79, p. 73.)

Geiger's categories betray—as does his substantive discussion of them—a heavy emphasis on economic aspects of posi-

tion and behavior and a Marxian accent characteristic both
of Geiger's sociological habitus at that time and of the time
itself. In the present study the attempt to develop a mentality
model of social stratification for contemporary German society will have to follow different paths. But before we begin,
Geiger's strata are worth closer inspection.

The highest stratum in Geiger's model includes large-scale
entrepreneurs, landed proprietors, and wealthy capitalists;
their mentality is characterized by the "crisis of capitalist
thinking." "The crisis of late capitalism has shaken status-
confidence to such an extent that the core of the stratum has
shrunk considerably" (79, p. 84). This, however, is even more
markedly true of the old middle class. Despite all differences
between the small self-employed in commerce, manufacture,
and agriculture, "the three main elements of the old middle
class have . . . in common that they are at present in a state
of defense," in which Geiger believes that the defense of
"social prestige" is at least as important for the old middle
class as defense against "economic pressure" (79, p. 87).
In other ways, this is equally true for the new middle class,
to which Geiger devotes his special attention because in this
rapidly growing group of white-collar employees, he sees
(in 1932!) the social soil on which National Socialism thrives.
"The typical character trait of the stratum would then be:
the ideological uncertainty of the settler on new social land;
still unsure and uneven with respect to the mentality typical
of its place, the 'new middle class' is the natural field of attraction for 'false ideologies' " (79, p. 105). The proletaroids
are "downward-mobile old middle class," self-employed without independence, "day laborers for their own account." In
their mentality they are very uneven. "In the terms of party
politics one might say: National Socialists, *Stahlhelm,* Center
Party, and Communists share this mass, and recently National
Socialism seems to have gained considerable advantages here"
(79, p. 90). There remains the mass of workers in industry
and agriculture to whom Geiger ascribes a Marxist ideology,
not without indicating different potentials of behavior as they
may be sensed among "young workers" (79, p. 97).

Clearly this picture of stratification is much more alive
than the constructions of contemporary sociology, and it
achieves vitality without any loss of exactness. Not the least
advantage of his approach is that Geiger was able to use it in
an explanation of the progress of the Nazi Party in the late

years of the Weimar Republic. The notion of stratum or class mentality is plausible too: there are certain economic, political, and social attitudes that adhere to social positions just as role expectations do. Whoever becomes an entrepreneur is faced with these attitudes as a demand on him, and so is the clerical worker, the industrial worker, the peasant. Class mentalities are never completely uniform. And not every member of a stratum displays the expected mentality at any given time; here, as with other role expectations, there are deviants, outsiders, marginal figures, and strangers. Thus, while the approach is sound, it is highly questionable whether the actual strata distinguished by Geiger still describe the contemporary scene. Along with the capitalist, there emerged captains of industry without capital, managers, and experts. The new middle class has proved too heteromorphous after all to be described as a single mentality stratum. Even the working class—which today can hardly be called a "proletariat" any more—requires further differentiation. In describing the contemporary mentalities of social strata, it might be useful to replace Geiger's socio-economic and marginally socio-political emphasis by a pronounced socio-political emphasis with socio-cultural overtones.

The picture of German social stratification that I would suggest in the light of such considerations is not backed up by statistical analysis. In so far as quantitative statements are made, they are based on informed discretion, that is, reasoned estimate—a procedure that, in view of the fleeting boundaries between the strata, may be appropriate even in principle. So far as the description of mentalities is concerned, it is subject to Geiger's own reservation that it does not yield "any final results": "For an exact investigation of mentalities would require empirical material in great quantities" (79, p. 80). Since in social research such data have today become available at least in greater quantities than in 1932, it may be somewhat excusable if, contrary to Geiger, we venture "too far into the realm of interpretive construction." Which, then, are the strata and stratum mentalities of contemporary German society?

The top of society consists of the elites. These—almost literally—upper ten thousand need not be, and probably never are, the select in the sense of the best; the term "elite" simply describes the leaders of the various institutional orders of society. We will devote several chapters of this study to this highly significant group, so at this point a few remarks may suffice.

In Germany in particular, it is necessary to refer to elites in the plural, for there is little coherence, little objective and subjective solidarity among the leading groups. There is no consciousness of belonging to an upper stratum, much less an elite, among those who are nevertheless by their positions a part of it. This may well be the reason for the otherwise surprising fact that its elites determine contemporary German

Social Stratification of the German People
(All figures are percentages)

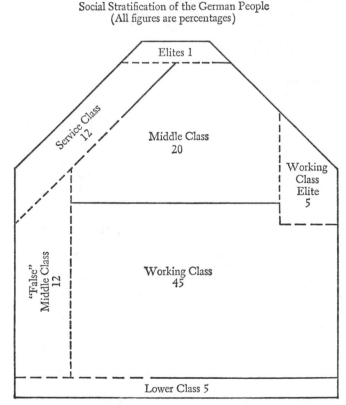

Elites 1

Service Class 12

Middle Class 20

Working Class Elite 5

"False" Middle Class 12

Working Class 45

Lower Class 5

(For explanation, see text.)

society only in a formal sense, by institutional mandate so to speak; substantively they take over the behavior, the social and political orientations of another stratum whose traditionally crucial position in German society has if anything gained significance through modern economic and occupational developments, that is, the service class. This class above all, therefore, requires our attention if we want to describe the social stratification of the German people.

The service class is not very large. One of its primary components is that part of the new middle class that is engaged, by occupational position, in bureaucratic activities proper, that is, non-technical clerical workers and state employees of all ranks. These ranks are numerous. It is a long journey from the administrative assistant to the undersecretary of state, and from the clerk to the vice president of a large company. But it is a journey on the same road, even if this road is barricaded at several points by nearly unsurmountable barriers, such as, in Germany, the required laissez-passers of degrees from intermediate schools, secondary schools, and universities. All the way, the road leads in one direction—service to those in power. The concept of service class (terminologically inexact, if one distinguishes strictly between classes and strata, which is, however, rather cumbersome in this case) has been stated by Karl Renner:

> In addition to all the changes discussed so far, there is another of no less consequence: the capitalist uses paid helpers who gradually replace him in his function as capitalist. The civil service has served as a model of this development for capital. According to this model, the functioning capitalist pays his helpers and, in so far as he leaves his function, his substitutes as well as the helpers' helpers, the executive organs, which he rightly does not describe as workers, but as employees, as officials or servants. Besides the working class (in the strictly technical sense) there has emerged the service class. (181, pp. 211 f.)

The origin of the service class can thus be found in that process of the division of the labor of power that, following the laws of the increasing social obligations of state and economy—and those of Parkinson—has caught hold of not only public administration, but other institutions as well. As a result, every member of the service class has a share in the exercise of power; a fact of which he is well and confidently aware, however imperceptibly small it may be. There is a colorful characterization of this mentality in Geiger's study with respect to civil servants:

> They are not a class, hardly an estate, but—especially in our bureaucratically overburdened German world—almost a caste. What weighs most heavily from a sociological perspective is that even for the official who is subordinate in the last position, the unbuttered bread acquired by a starvation salary is spiced tastily: by that minimal share which he has in the omnipotence of the state represented by him as well. It is so easy to explain psychologically that this tiny share of power means the more and is demonstrated the more studiously as prestige, guarded and defended the more jealously, the more oppressed the position of the individual official is in terms of level of remuneration and internal function. The less a person is capable of asserting his position and developing his personality in the occupational sphere of activity, the more he is hampered in his initiative by strict subordination and the more he is subject to the commands of those above him, the more unapproachably does he protect the counterdistance toward a public which has to be "dispatched," the more he is delighted by shoulder-pieces, swords, and other insignia of an official-impersonal aloofness; the more he is also hurt by the deprivation of these symbols of social recognition. (79, p. 98.)

This is a caricature, to be sure, but one in whose distorted picture the intended reality becomes recognizable. Since the 1920s, such civil-service ideologies of status have rapidly spread from the world of work to the whole of society. Interwoven throughout with the silk threads of status symbols, modern society provides the service class with many an occasion for displaying its social mentality: makes of cars and places of vacation, choir stools in the living room, and seven dwarfs in the front garden, the wife's coat and the children's toys. Members of the service class are the original status seekers; from them the infectious habit has spread to nearly all other social strata.

In political terms, one consequence of the mentality of the service class is particularly significant. There is a civil-service association, and there are white-collar workers organized in trade unions; but for both these groups collective action is atypical, and strikes are unlikely. If state officials or white-collar workers want to get ahead, they try as a rule to do so individually and by their own efforts. Bureaucratic social contexts are invariably hierarchical and pyramidal; not all those who start at the bottom can reach the top, but all roles are defined in relation to it. This is the structural condition for a competition between individuals that constitutes one of the main sources of organizational discipline in bureaucracies and at the same time makes life full of frustrations for those involved, especially if they are not successful.

Because individual competition takes the place of collective solidarities in the lives of members of the service class, they do not constitute a class in the strict sense: class actions on their part are improbable. Moreover, because individual competition is carried on in a context of dependence, so that the service class as a whole is ultimately dependent on leaders who are not part of it, it cannot even represent itself politically. It must be represented; and this is a condition amounting to an invitation to the usurper who borrows its name and thus helps its members to extend the basis of their dubious legitimacy.

Such assertions would be exaggerated in their harshness were it not for the fact that the service class has so evidently managed to spread its mentality to all other strata in modern and a fortiori in modern German society. By now, this diffusion of a bureaucratic mentality has reached even the old middle class of those who are working in their own enterprises. This old middle class stands out in contemporary societies as Marx's error turned into structure, for Marx prophesied its early end between the grindstones of capital and labor. England is the only country in which the self-employed have been reduced to almost insignificant proportions, except for their role as a charming and cherished ornament of the past in a totally industrialized society. In France, the small self-employed continue to be a political force, which nobody underestimates with impunity; their condition is still the dream of many industrial workers who frequently rationalize their positions of dependence as a mere step on the way to independence. Germany occupies an intermediate position in this respect.

In no country, however, does the middle class of the self-employed have much in common with its legendary historical predecessor, the bourgeoisie of early capitalism. In Germany, as we have seen, there has never been a dynamic bourgeoisie of this kind. Thus the self-employed middle class is not a seat of liberal convictions but, on the contrary, one of the main claimants for the protective hand of the state. As a group, it is not adventurous but anxious, not expansive but defensive, not liberal but protectionist, not an element of progress but a retarding force. It is no accident that the arguments of peasants demanding subsidies are political rather than economic, national rather than rational. A propensity for estatelike closure, coupled with a temerity, if not resignation, from which only the demand for state protection occasionally awakens it, characterizes Germany's old middle class from the professions right down to small peasants and shopkeepers.

The old middle class includes the independent entrepreneurs of industry. Not all of them have become large entrepreneurs or dependent managers; there is still a considerable number of medium-scale entrepreneurs in Germany. But their attitude, too, is predominantly defensive. Although they clamor less often and certainly less noisily for state protection than peasants, craftsmen, and shopkeepers, it would be an exaggeration to characterize them by initiative and daring. Even in their relations to organized labor the attitude of German entrepreneurs is often one of insecurity based on the underestimation of their own position. This is even more strikingly true if we leave the narrowly economic realm beyond which entrepreneurs hardly dare say a word. In any case, most independent entrepreneurs present anything but the vulgar-Marxist caricature of the unscrupulous individual who supplements his economic power by the political power he has bought. If the self-employed middle class fails to shape German society according to its image, the defensiveness of entrepreneurs is not the least reason for this failure.

One can obviously not describe the working-class elite as shaping the whole of society either. But it does determine, today as in the past, the social character of that subculture from which it stands out, that is, those who are situated "below" in society. For a long time, the working-class elite provided the most important reservoir of labor leaders. This group of dependent craftsmen and skilled workers has, however, a paradoxical mentality; it did produce the exponents of political radicalism, but its members were also capable, once they had acquired office and status, of adapting quickly to their new roles. Today, the working-class elite—master miners and foremen, printers and fitters—once again gives directions to the rest of the working class, but these directions are no longer contradictory. Instead of leading to political radicalism, they lead today to the individual search for happiness which, as embourgeoisement, is as intensely scorned by some as it is conspicuously praised by others. We do not know very much about the mentality of the German working-class elite today; but many an observation supports the impression that it is above all the skilled men, those who "have an occupation," who regard themselves as belonging to the middle class and assume a middle-class style of life.

There is one group in our model of stratification whose very name contains an element of criticism: the "false middle class." It includes those nominal white-collar workers whose peculiar position and mentality is responsible for the fact that the term "new middle class" has lost nearly all meaning. Basically, the false middle class consists of the workers of the tertiary industries, that is, those who occupy subordinate positions in the ever growing service industries: the waiter and the salesgirl, the conductor and the postman, the chauffeur and the gas station attendant. Here, a wide and new range of occupations is emerging. Its incumbents are distinguished from all others, inter alia, by the fact that their work forces them to maintain contact much of the time with other people of diverse social circles; superficially, there may well be less social distance between the false middle class and other social strata than there is between any two other strata. But describing this group as "middle class" is justifiable in one respect only, namely, its consciousness of self.

Members of the false middle class are not self-employed; this distinguishes them from the middle class proper. But they do not contribute to the subdivided process of authority either; this is how they differ from the new middle class of clerical workers and officials. If on the other hand one looks for signs that distinguish this stratum from the working class, that is, if one asks what the difference between the positions of salesgirl and seamstress, waiter and bricklayer is, the only sign to be found is that of social self-evaluation. The sociologist has learned to take such seemingly subjective realities seriously, even if they have little basis in the positions of people and are "false" in this sense. Nobody defends middle-class rights and interests more noisily than the problematic members of this stratum, the workers of the tertiary industries. Moreover, the contradiction between social position and social consciousness makes this stratum a particularly unreliable category in political terms; no party that has won the support of this group can be very confident of its strength. It is no accident—and it has consequences for the mental make-up of professionals of these trades—that conversations at the hairdresser's, or across the counter, at gas stations and in restaurants, are stereotyped as few other social situations are. Workers of the tertiary industries help to create the conditions of a civilized existence in the modern world; but they can hardly be envied their social roles.

In Germany, those who are not part of it themselves like to doubt the fact that there is any working class left. "The boundaries between blue and white collar have become hazy today." "Most workers earn more nowadays than the average salaried employee." "There are really no workers in the proper sense left." Thus the largest stratum of society evaporates to pleasing nothingness, for the professional man "knows how difficult it is in a particular case to describe those belonging to given occupations with such general terms as 'worker' in an appropriate way" (215, p. 42).

Many facts and arguments might be held against such partly misleading, and partly false, stereotypes. "Who in your opinion is more highly regarded in the population in general: a clerical employee earning 450 marks a month, or a foundry worker who takes home 600 marks a month?" an opinion research institute tried to find out. Some 26 per cent were "undecided," 23 per cent pleaded for the foundry worker, but 51 per cent for the clerical employee (104, p. 367). It is not, however, only facts like these that count. The disappearance of the working class from the social image of the others also testifies to the prevalence of that German ideology of social harmony that makes it possible to ridicule those concerned with the social position of workers as hopelessly antiquated, if not to calumniate them as being infected by communism.

It is, of course, true that in Germany as elsewhere the working class is not a homogeneous social stratum. The old distinctions between the skilled, the semiskilled, and the unskilled, or craftsmen, specialists, and laborers, form but one, and possibly no longer the most important, principle of differentiation. The working class is divided into workers in large and in small enterprises, miners and automobile workers, pieceworkers and timeworkers, old and young workers, industrial and agricultural workers. However, although the working class turns out to be, upon closer inspection, a stratum of considerable internal differentiation, it is still a stratum with its own culture and mentality.

German official statistics make it difficult to prove this point by their aversion to subdividing the population by social strata and by correlating social status with other data. Otherwise, the demographic peculiarities of the working class would stand out even more clearly: earlier marriage age, a higher average number of children, greater infant mortality, lower life expectancy by comparison to other strata. Survey statistics can supplement such findings. Workers do not travel abroad as often, they have fewer holidays anyway; they spend a greater proportion of their incomes on food, and differ in their habits of consumption as in their patterns of opinion from other strata. Inequalities of educational opportunity with respect to workers' families have already been mentioned; the question of how equal their treatment is before courts of law, or in hospitals, touches upon a German taboo. There are deeper social-psychological differences of mentality, too. Workers have a different sense of time. They lack the middle-class pattern of deferred gratification, the ability to forego immediate minor pleasures in favor of greater but distant gratifications. Workers have other attitudes toward child rearing, another relation to the experience of security, a greater distance from the ruling social values than middle-class people.

Until recently at least, workers also had a peculiar image of society, which Heinrich Popitz has described on the basis of an interview study among German steelworkers. Workers experience society as "dichotomous," that is, divided into an Above and a Below, and in this they differ characteristically from white-collar people. "All workers with whom we have spoken and who develop any image at all of society in the sense defined by us, see society as a dichotomy, unchangeable or changeable, unbridgeable or capable of mediation by 'partnership.' . . . Clerical employees on the other hand recognize an Above which is higher, and a Below which is lower than their own position. They see themselves in the middle and develop a remarkably acute sense of distinction for new graduations. One can assume therefore that they do not see society dichotomously like industrial workers, but hierarchically" (177, pp. 237 and 242).

A dichotomous image of society is the subjective counterpart to a structurally similar position of a large group of peo-

ple; for this reason, it constitutes a condition of solidary social and political action. But even in the working class solidarity is no longer as pronounced as it was in the 1920s; indeed
it is questionable whether one can still apply the strict term
of "class" to workers. What, then, is the future of labor going
to be? Will there be (to use an English expression) a "new
working class" in Germany too? Or is the working class going
to be caught by the mentality of status-seeking and individual competition that is characteristic of the service class?
It has been claimed that a "new type," particularly among
young workers, is emerging. K. Bednarik and H. Kluth have
ascribed to young workers a propensity for middle-class
behavior, as exemplified by the same aversion to collective
action, the same lack of a pronounced consciousness of class.
But the studies quoted were all conducted in the early 1950s.
It appears that the working class is no longer an exciting object of sociological research in the Federal Republic, as it has
apparently lost its attractiveness for political parties. The result
is that we know very little about this large and significant social group.

This, however, is even more clearly true for the seventh
stratum of our model, the lower class. It consists of those who
are sometimes described as the "dregs" of society, the un-
employables, unsteady types, notorious delinquents, semiliter-
ates, and others who appear in the model of H. Moore and
G. Kleining as the "socially despised." I have already referred
to the implications of such notions in terms of equal citizenship rights. A common mentality cannot be discerned in this
stratum. Characteristically, it is individual rather than structural patterns that bring about its existence; that is to say, it
emerges not from the impact of identifiable social mechanisms
on a group with a common position, but from a multitude
of individual (if in each case obviously socially mediated)
fates. This *Lumpenproletariat* has no formative potential or
force either socially or politically.

The edifice of social stratification has more than the seven
rooms described here. And every one of these rooms has corners and niches that might well be called rooms themselves;
every stratum has subgroups with their own mentality traits:
the state officials in the service class, the peasants in the middle class, etc. Moreover, the walls between the rooms can not
only be shifted, they are penetrable too; there are groups with

a common mentality in some respects who, by position, are distributed over various strata: professional people may be found in the elites, the service class, and the middle class; craftsmen in the middle class and the working-class elite. Finally, there are some groups we have not mentioned at all, such as the intellectuals, who are hard to accommodate in the house of social stratification in any case. But then, a description of this kind could not possibly claim to be comprehensive or final.

Among many open questions, one at least cannot be adjourned: Is the picture sketched in this chapter in any sense peculiar to German society? In other words, what does it contribute to our study? The contribution is clearly modest. On the one hand, the picture does not describe even the whole of German society. By that I mean not only regional differences or stages of historical development, but, above all, East German society, which would certainly have to be described in very different terms. Although here, too, the ascendancy of a service class may be observed, the mentality of a service class of party functionaries is bound to differ significantly from that of state employees. The self-employed middle class —as if to demonstrate that false theories can be proven only by force—has been destroyed almost entirely in the DDR. The mentalities of all other strata are clearly formed by the ruling values of the political system in ways rather different from those of the more liberal environment of West German society.

On the other hand, our picture certainly does not describe West German society alone. In essential features it may well resemble that of social stratification in other Western societies. Even the paradoxical trend toward a domination of the subordinates, the formation of the whole structure of stratification by the mentality of the service class, is not a German prerogative. But it may be suspected that in view of the formative force of bureaucratic social structures in German society, the service-class mentality finds easy and thorough access to all other social strata here. In addition, there are many details by which stratum mentalities betray the nationality of the people, such as the snobbery of professional people and the nationalism of peasants, the anti-industrial ideology of craftsmen and the shoulder-pieces of status. But in important respects the picture remains admittedly unspecific. In order to return to our central problem, we have to advance to the questions that follow from this picture of German social stratification: How securely do people stand in their strata? How easy or difficult is it for them to leave their rooms in the edifice of social inequality?

7. UNMODERN MEN IN A
MODERN WORLD

The social role of the citizen has two dimensions, and these are not necessarily linked. Both may be described as chances. The first is the set of objective chances that may be offered by granting rights: Every man has the same right to vote as every other one. But this is only one side of citizenship. Objective chances need to be supplemented by a set of subjective chances that provide the realistic possibility of making use of one's rights and that cannot be given by granting rights alone. If the landlord advises his laborers not to go to the polls; if the sanctioning force of the husband follows the wife to the solitude of the polling booth; if the dogmatic association "A good Catholic has to vote for the Center Party" keeps believers under its spell—then the objective chance is nullified by the absence of its subjective interior. This is what I meant before by asserting that if the social role of the citizen has become real, people participate in the social and political process as citizens and only as such.

A sociological category may help to clarify what is meant here. Among the many positions each of us occupies in society are some that we have acquired for ourselves (achievable positions) and others that have come upon us without our doing anything about it (ascribed positions). Memberships in clubs and associations are usually achievable, but those in sex or age groups are invariably ascribed. Between the extremes there is an important range of social positions that may be more or less achievable or ascribed depending upon the social-historical context. Among these we can count occupation, which has increasingly become, in the course of modern economic development, an achievable position rather than an unquestioned family heritage. We may include here religious affiliations, the abandonment of which offered difficulties of a very different order in medieval than in modern times and which still has a different meaning in Germany than, say, in Spain. Class position also belongs in this intermediate category; in a caste society it is almost completely ascribed, whereas in the ideal-typical open class society it is almost completely achievable. Using these notions we can say that the reality of civic equality in a society is threatened to the extent to which the social personality of people is determined by ascribed positions and their behavior is restricted by that inescapable horizon of experience that ascribed positions provide. The citizen needs the open society.

Reality, however, is not that consistent. The distinction between formal and substantive citizenship suggests a strange possibility of social structure. There may be societies that are formally developed in the sense that they promise equal rights to their citizens, but that remain substantively traditional because the citizens, chained to ascribed social positions, are unable to exercise their rights. The social universe is modern, but its inhabitants have remained unmodern, and the road to liberalism remains barred. These are extreme and obviously abstract statements; yet they describe a noteworthy feature of German society, which documents once again those explosive faults left behind by Imperial Germany and the industrial revolution.

As we try to support this assertion we may, to begin with, return to our model of the social stratification of the German people (cf. p. 88 above). We have yet to explain why the lines between strata, the walls between the rooms of the house of class, are partly continuous, partly broken or even dotted. The graphic device indicates degrees of openness of strata for entry and exit, thus gradations of the achievability or ascription of class positions. By the same token, chances and avenues of (vertical) social mobility as well as barriers on the ways up and down the status scale become evident. Despite a certain crudeness of presentation, both mobility within generations, that is, the social biography of the individual, and between generations, that is, the status path of children in relation to their parents, have been taken into account.

First, some general observations are indicated. Between elites and service class there is frequent exchange both within and between generations; employees in public and private bureaucracies are one main reservoir of leadership groups. The false middle class is open in all directions; it is a dispersing stratum. It is easy for the girl working in a factory to become a salesgirl, and vice versa; the gas station attendant can switch to repair work and, more rarely, vice versa. By contrast, the self-employed middle class is fairly closed; a notable exchange occurs only across the border to the working-class elite, that is, by craftsmen shifting from self-employed to dependent occupations, and vice versa. The ordinary working man dreaming of independence for himself or for his child is generally detoured by way of the false middle class or the working-class elite.

To render such indications reasonably definite and reliable, we would need studies that in fact we do not have. The only empirical support of our model that can be found at present consists in its application to data about the recruitment of German university students (1959/60). In this manner, we get a clearer view of barriers to social mobility. Even here, translation of the statistics of fathers' occupations into our categories of stratification forces us to resort to estimates at some points. These have been kept deliberately conservative, especially in so far as recruitment from the upper strata, and more particularly from the elites, is concerned. Even so an impressive picture of the mountain landscape of upward and downward social mobility in Germany remains (see table below).

As in all countries, social self-recruitment is most pronounced at the peak of the status pyramid. Nobody likes his children to be downwardly mobile; whoever has got to the top usually finds ways and means to preserve this status for his family. The service class and, to a much lesser extent, the

Recruitment of German Students by Social Stratum (cf. 110)

Social Stratum	Size of Stratum	Students by Origin	Index of Representation
Elites	less than 1%	5%	50
Service class	12	53	} ca. 1–5
Middle class	20	32	
Working class elite	5	2	} ca. 0.1–0.5
False middle class	12	5	
Working class	45	3	
Lower class	5%	0%	0

middle class still provide an important reservoir of future professional people; in terms of formal statistical measures, they are considerably overrepresented among the recruitment groups of students, too. All other groups, however, are strongly underrepresented in this respect. So far as the working class is concerned, the degree of this underrepresentation is even more striking than is generally known, if we except the working-class elite. Nearly one half of all workers' children in German universities are the children of craftsmen. The lower class can be ruled out entirely as a recruiting ground of academic leadership groups in Germany.

I have used the image of a mountain landscape. Let us imagine then the system of social stratification as the hiking route of a man who starts at the very bottom, in that stratum from which almost no one ever reaches a university, and aims at the very top—not a normal case, to be sure, and perhaps not even a model one, but an instructive example nevertheless. As he sets off, our hiker has in front of him a slope of medium altitude which leads him from the lowlands of social contempt to the plateau of belonging, of social participation. Once he has reached this plateau, however, there rises in the distance before him a forbidding rock face, which he has to scale, a mountain wall after two thirds of the way, which can be mastered only with extreme effort, great skill, and a good portion of luck. Even then, our hiker has not reached the peak, but a high plain below it, so that another, final effort is required before he has reached the top.

Let me emphasize once again that nobody has to undertake this difficult expedition except by the motive force of his own ambition: one can stay at home; but beyond that, there are many walks along the way that, while they do not lead from the very bottom to the very top, are hardly less rewarding. On the wide plateau of the working class, its elite, and the false middle class, there are many easy slopes permitting gradual rise on the scales of income and prestige, in terms of education and influence, in the personal range of liberty and happiness. The same is true within the service class and the self-employed middle class. There are other, typical routes of ascent that are mastered in two generations, such as the road from the workers' family to a civil service position in the first, and from the civil servant's family to university and a profession in the second generation. There are rewarding detours and scenic walks, which may even make descent bearable. Thus the picture of social mobility is much more complicated than the hike from the marshes to Mount Everest makes it appear. Nevertheless, the long hike is worth our special attention.

The mountain hike is in fact but a comparatively harmless metaphor for what is really a very serious matter. German society is stratified in such a way as to create three barriers. Two of these are medium-sized and may, therefore, be overcome with some effort by those who reach them; similar barriers may be found in any modern society. In the German case, these are, first, the borderline between the elites and the adjoining reaches of service class and middle class; and, second, the boundary between the lower class and the adjoining lower ranks of the working class and the false middle class.

But there is a third barrier, and this is very much harder to overcome. It divides an Above from a Below—namely, approximately the upper third of the edifice of stratification from the lower two thirds—and it runs (to remain within the spatial metaphor) from the lower end of the service class along the line between the working class and the middle class. On either side of this line, social mobility is not uncommon. But so far as movement across the border, and therefore belonging to one of the two sides is concerned, we have to conclude that class positions are still largely ascribed in German society.

Whether an individual stands on one side of the barrier or the other, is a position falling to him without his doing, and one he can escape only in the exceptional case. In this sense, German society continues to be a divided society: divided into an Above that knows little of the Below, and a Below that knows equally little of the Above. Only psychoanalytic theories could explain why a society split in this fashion systematically compensates for its internal divisions by ideologies of the community of the German people and of national unity.

These are far-reaching assertions, in which an aftertaste of the *Threepenny Opera* may be sensed:

> For the ones are in the darkness
> and the others in the light,
> one can see those in the light,
> those in darkness no one sees.

The aftertaste also makes one suspicious. Is not this the history of a time gone by? It is not; but on the other hand history is not as simple as Brecht could afford to make it. In presenting it we cannot dispense with paradoxical formulations altogether, much as we may dislike attractive imprecisions.

In a sense, every society is a divided society. Participation in the exercise of power or exclusion from it divides the great classes whose dynamics create the direction and rhythm of social development. There is also, in every society, a distance of information and of affection between social groups, which grows with the distance of groups from one another in the mountain landscape of stratification. One might even concede to the ideologists of community that this division must appear less pressing in Germany than in many other societies. The formative force of state officials, strengthened today by a much broader service class, has for a long time impeded the establishment of group solidarities and thus promoted that competition between individuals that represses awareness of social divisions. But it is precisely this lacking awareness of social inequality that illustrates the peculiarity of the divided society in Germany. The question of how the other half lives is rarely raised in Germany. Existing conditions are accepted without protest; they are as they are, and nobody can do much about them. It is part of the order of the world, and no reason for doubt, that there is a borderline between Above and Below.

This is the point at which our suspended explanation of the flagrant inequalities of educational opportunity in Germany becomes possible. We have seen that certain groups—workers' children, children from the country, girls—are heavily underrepresented in German secondary schools and universities. We have moreover seen that they are not formally underprivileged, so that their condition must have reasons other than legal. These form a complex pattern. They range from the financial preconditions of education to the availability of schools, from the mentalities of social strata that are hostile to education—such as the absence of a sense of deferred gratification—to aspects of school and university life that discriminate against certain groups. But there is much to be said for seeking one of the main causes of the inequalities of educational opportunity in Germany in the minds of those hit hardest by them, that is, with workers and peasants and with parents of girls, as well as with their children. Among all these people, an attitude of traditionalism prevails that prevents them from perceiving the chance to shorten and simplify the mountain hike to the peaks of stratification by using the funicular of educational institutions. Part of the same attitude is the failure to recognize any necessity to move more than a few steps from one's place in society. This is a social, not an individual attitude, of course; we are not trying to charge workers with willful neglect of their opportunities, but are merely looking at their motives as an expression of social patterns.

In detail, these motives are complex and involved. So far as workers are concerned, their social consciousness is dominated by a sense of dichotomy and of the distance associated with it: "The people with money, well, they send their children, never mind if they are dim or not. And they get through, too. And not only in school; where good apprenticeships are concerned too. Among the poor there are sure to be good people left, but they do not get through. We have seen that ourselves in my firm. There were sons of rich people too, who got in all right, but they were certainly not as good as others, who had no money. That is why they did not get in. This is how it is in secondary schools too. Just go and look how many children of rich people there are!" (53, p. 21). This from a forty-three-year-old smith and father of several children of school age, resigned rather than aggressive in his mood.

There is more in such remarks than the mere distinction between poor and rich. The rich and "their" secondary school present themselves as distant and strange. "Strange, threatening, unpleasant, rigid, demanding"—this according to a survey conducted by J. Hitpass, is how the secondary school appears to German workers; and the university seems to them "situated in space, sinister, incomprehensible like Picasso" (cf. 97). There is a familiar and there is an alien world. They are separated by an enormous social distance, which means that one has little real knowledge of the alien world and therefore gets along with simple stereotypes, whose objective falsehood does not impair their subjective effectiveness. The distance and the substitution of stereotypes for information holds the other way too, of course. While the geography of societies permits that distance from Below to Above is greater than that from Above to Below, it is questionable whether this is the case in Germany. But on either side of the fence, lack of information and strangeness is easily translated into a feeling of threat. The conclusion drawn from this product of strangeness and anxiety is the conclusion of traditionalism:

people refuse to be drawn into the venture of the road to the unknown.

The case of country children and girls resembles that of working-class children in many respects, except that in the former case parents can more easily be held personally responsible for the persistence of traditional ties. If peasants want to keep the one-class school in their village at the risk of blocking the road to the top for their children, they do so also because they fear that the traditional patterns of village life might be endangered if their children received a higher education in distant places. (This is not so different from the concerns of Catholic priests who, worried about the secularization of the faithful, confined their educational zeal to those who promised to become priests themselves.) Parents who remove their talented daughter from school before she takes her degree because they want her to help at home deliberately perpetuate the traditional role of the woman, which is defined by the absence of independence, motivation, and initiative. In all these half-conscious restrictions a traditionalism becomes evident that prefers the conservation of the heritage to the rise into the unknown heights of modernity.

In the long run, traditionalism needs homogeneous social structures in order to thrive. A mentality that rejects novelty and initiative is most easily upheld in groups that are uniform in their ethnic origin and religious affiliation, their regional and occupational attachment, their dialect and their collective memory. H. Peisert has been able to show that motivation for higher education decreases as the social contexts in which people live become more homogeneous, regardless of the basis of such homogeneity: homogeneously Protestant regions are as traditionalist as homogeneously Catholic ones; in all cases, inherited likeness in kind is an obstacle to development (cf. 169). This may be demonstrated e contrario as well: among refugees who have all been torn out of their inherited social contexts, the proportion of children attending secondary schools is higher than among families born in the Federal Republic, although the former's economic position is on the average somewhat lower (cf. 208).

The mention of refugees also gives rise to a puzzling question: Are there, after the Second World War, any homogeneous social contexts left in German society? Did not the immigration of millions of people and the internal migration of further millions whirl society around and destroy all traditional homogeneity? One quarter of all West Germans are immigrants, that is, refugees from the formerly German regions in the East or migrants from the DDR. Every year, about 6 per cent of the population of the Federal Republic change their place of residence, among them 2 per cent change their state of residence too. Purely by statistical extrapolation one would have to conclude that under such conditions there can be almost nobody left who, twenty years after the Second World War, is still living in the place where he grew up. It is all the more surprising, therefore, to learn from a representative sample survey among adult Germans that 55 per cent grew up in the place where they are living today (57 per cent of the men and 54 per cent of the women in the still "patrilocal" society!), so that only 45 per cent have moved. Indeed, in the case of 32 per cent, that is, one third of the population, both parents were born in the place where their children are living today; and for a further 16 per cent this holds for at least one parent (104, p. 5). This documents an astonishing immobility in restless times and under conditions of an industrial economy, and it can give some plausibility to the seemingly anachronistic notion of homogeneous social conditions.

Such figures and analyses must nevertheless not be overstated. It would be perfectly plausible to interpret them quite differently and point out that there is considerable vertical mobility in Germany, and that in certain groups, such as state officials, a motivation for upward mobility is systematically inbred. The fact that almost one half of all people did not grow up in the place where they are living today may be taken, by comparison to strictly traditional conditions, as a sign of remarkable mobility. In other words, the persistence of a basic attitude of traditionalism is not the whole truth of contemporary German society.

This can be put in more dynamic terms. The mixture of modernity and unmodernity, rationality and traditionalism, in the mentality of large social groups once again displays the faults that Imperial Germany and the industrial revolution have bequeathed to German society. Alongside a nearly immobile peasant estate there is alleged modernity in the form of the civil service; next to mobile metropolitan Berliners there are firmly rooted small townspeople unprepared to move at any price. Admittedly, this is one of the respects in which the volcanic surface of German society has been shaking for some time. While state social policy is still trying to chain people to their social places, the dynamics of economic development, the brutal struggle of National Socialism against tradition, as well as more sensitive and courageous measures by farsighted reformers in churches, other institutions, and the state have lowered many of the barriers of traditionalism in Germany. The threshold holding back the assault of modern rationality is therefore no longer very high today. There are examples in the field of educational policy that show how little may suffice to make people who never even considered a higher education for their children change their motives. The traditional attachments of the Germans' social psychology are probably on the whole relics of a passing epoch, striking as their vitality may still appear at some points.

This reminder adds a reservation to our thesis, but does not invalidate it. Nor is the advent of modernity in Germany to be secured solely by the dissolution of traditional motivations with respect to education. Groups that are at a factual disadvantage in the exercise of citizenship rights merely document extreme cases of a far more general pattern. When David Riesman distinguished between three social characters —inner-directed, other-directed, and tradition-directed—he, like others who used similar distinctions, left the notion of "tradition" residual without paying much attention to it. Yet it is far more descriptive of some apparently modern societies, including Germany, than Riesman and others seem to think. The core of traditionalism (and in this it differs from all modern mentalities) is the notion that we cannot do much about things because they have always been as they are. There is a defeatism about traditional attitudes, which can hardly encourage the spread of citizenship, or indeed of civilization. Where people might feel motivated to act and change unsatisfactory conditions, one hears instead in Germany the resigned comment that they are "fate" (*Schicksal*), accompanied by a helpless shrug of the shoulders. It is in contrast to this defeatism that the notion of modernity (which we are using rather freely and perhaps seemingly indefinitely here) has to be understood.

How about the implication that modernity makes men happier than tradition possibly could? What reason is there to believe that a more modern, active mentality is preferable to a traditional one? The question is remarkably patronizing in the first place: Who can presume the right to decide for others what is good for them and what not? But apart from this matter of taste, the fact remains that modernity is a liberation of men from unquestioned ties, and therefore opens up new avenues of self-expression for people. Such optimism, it is true, creates its own frustrations, whether they result from problems of discrepant status, of rapid mobility, or from other sources. But by making all problems, including these, appear manageable, modernity transcends the subtly paralyzing hopelessness of tradition.

Such hopes are, however, promise rather than analysis. In our context, another version of the question of the price of modernity is more relevant, and may also help us give some sociological substance to the praise of modernity: What are the political consequences of a society that shuns the road to modernity? What were, and are, these consequences in German society, past and present? We are still concerned with restrictions of citizenship by social roles that accompany ascribed social positions. What happens then if people make their political decisions not on the basis of their interests and a rational calculation of the gains and losses involved in various political lines, but allow themselves to be guided by expectations in which they have become entangled without being able to free themselves by their own efforts? Class position is not the only possible form of politically relevant ascription, of course; there are other positions that might acquire such relevance. What follows for a political system, if these positions determine the form of political participation?

The answer may be clothed in an example. It is a familiar fact that the political preferences of men and women differ. There were 161 women to every 100 male voters of the Catholic Center Party in the German parliamentary elections of 1924. At that time, nationalist parties had not as yet found much favor with female voters; but in 1932 and 1933 the proportion of women among the supporters of the Nazi Party was higher than that of men. In the Federal Republic, women are inclined to prefer the Christian Democratic Union (CDU). Sex is without doubt an ascribed position. Let us assume for purposes of argument that its influence on voting was not—as it is in fact—limited, but determined it totally, so that all men would vote for party M and all women for party W. In this case the political process of parliamentary democracy would obviously have lost its meaning. One would need neither election campaigns nor elections; the possibility of an alternative government would turn into a problem of demography, that is, of the quantitative relation of men and women in a society.

It is tempting to spin out the example and consider the possibilities of a great coalition, or the use of wars for the W party, and the like. But the example is not meant facetiously. It illustrates an extreme case of what Dutch sociologists call *verzuiling,* pillarization. The immovable pillars on which Dutch politics rests are those of the denominations, that is, Calvinists, Catholics, and "humanists"; and since denominational memberships are at least tendentially also ascribed positions, it is no accident that demographic arguments ("The Catholics have too many children . . .") play at least an undercover part in Dutch election campaigns. There are other forms of pillarization, such as on the basis of regional divisions, or of entrenched political groupings. And there are countries in which the tendency toward such pillarization is particularly weak, because in them ascribed positions lost their relevance for individual decisions at an early date; this is true for England as well as for large parts of American society. What are the pillars on which German society rests?

European societies like to compete in their claims for internal diversity introduced by regional traditions; thus it is only with a grain of salt that the assertion may be offered that regional differences and persistent political attitudes based on them play a larger part in Germany than elsewhere. Nevertheless, it is worthy of note that in the Reichstag elections of November 6, 1932, 31.3 per cent of the electorate in Berlin, 37.2 per cent in the area of what is now the Federal Republic, 45.1 per cent in what is now the DDR, and 51.6 per cent in the eastern territories that are now Polish and Russian gave their vote to parties of the extreme right. These boundaries are, of course, artificial, as are those of all the states (*Länder*) that make up the Federal Republic. Even here, however, regional differences continue to play a significant part in politics; Bavaria provides an extreme, but by no means the only, illustration of this fact.

More than region, religion continues to determine the people's political habitus. The principle of the Augsburg Peace of 1555, *cui regio eius religio,* epitomizes what we mean by pillarization; it was designed to render religious struggles superfluous by establishing the existing distribution regionally. Such regional homogeneity of religious denomination has since been largely destroyed; but within villages as well as cities religion still divides people culturally and politically. One of the historical reasons for this fact was that Catholicism had a minority position in the German Empire, despite the fact that nearly one third of the population was Catholic. As a result, Roman Catholics closed their ranks; the Catholic Center Party was the most stable political party right up to 1933. In the Federal Republic (and, if with converse effects, in the DDR), the proportion of Catholics has changed greatly; they are no longer a minority in West Germany, which is almost equally divided between the two great denominations. At the same time, this division has increased rather than decreased the dangers of pillarization.

The question of whether or not this process has in fact taken place in the Federal Republic is in dispute. At first sight, the very creation of the Christian Democratic Union (CDU) and its success tell against the thesis, since the party was conceived as a union between Protestants and Catholics. On the other hand, it may be pointed out that within this party, as in the allocation of positions elsewhere, proportionality of denominations is often the guiding principle: where there are two positions, both denominations have to be represented; if there is but one chairman, the vice chairman has to belong to the other denomination. Then again, it may be pointed out that party politics at least are free of pillarizing effects, quite apart from the fact that in an increasingly secularized society religious denomination steadily loses significance as a criterion of distinction. In this manner, argument may be added to counterargument. If there is any result to the debate, it is that while there may be tendencies of pillarization, these are probably less pronounced in the Federal Republic than in many other countries of the contemporary world.

We are moving here on the narrow line between stability and stagnation of political structures; and the question of how strong the forces of tradition are in German society has its meaning in relation to this issue. Stability is a fine thing to have; but if it degenerates into stagnation, as it would if ascribed positions and traditional mentalities determined the ways in which people participate, it would soon produce so much resistance that revolutionary upheavals would be imminent. The liberal dream of a society whose members make their political decisions rationally has a sociological reason too. If unmodern men would merely make unmodern politics, and if traditional structures would merely preserve traditions, one might argue for or against them, according to taste and temperament. But part of politics in terms of ascribed social positions and unquestioned dependencies is the erratic rhythm of change, which characterizes a large part of all previous history, but which seems characteristic of German history even at a time when it is no longer necessary. German society is certainly no longer unreservedly traditional; it is still threatened by pillarization, but there are worse examples in the modern world; still the journey to modernity is made impossible if there are too many unmodern men. In Germany, it is still necessary to remind people that the road to modernity may be hard and painful for many, and in many respects; it means a departure from many an old love. But it also means a departure from those experiences of the "good old times" that the glorifying memory forgets, even though they were uppermost in the consciousness of those who lived during them.

Both aspects of the chances of liberty intended by modern citizenship rights, the external and the internal, are under-developed in German society. But here the fact that there is a system of social stratification is not the most relevant; every society has one, and even the liberal dream cannot and need not abolish it. Men are different in kind, and a society trying to force all their differences into the strait jacket of equal position would not be worth living in. But men are not different in rank; and equality is therefore a condition of liberty at those points at which inequalities of social position may be turned into inequalities of power, so that some are prevented from participating fully in the social and political process while others are capable of denying the citizenship of their neighbors.

There are such inequalities of opportunity in German society; there are people of several classes in this sense, and there were people who did not even count as human. Germany still is a society divided by a gulf of social distance, which prevents the parts from realizing their civil rights together. This is what we called the external side of civic equality in Germany.

The internal side remains in the shadow; if one lights it up, it reveals even starker colors. What distinguishes German society from others is less the objective inequality of opportunity, which in varying degrees may be found in every country, but its subjective counterpart, the persistence of traditional ties in determining people's behavior. Many people have equal formal rights but are chained to ascribed social positions to an extent that makes it impossible for them to realize their chances. This is why it is misleading to speak of the survival of social privilege in Germany. Unless one wants to describe the modern mentality itself as a privilege in the faulted society, one is faced with the paradox of a modern country populated by people whose simple-minded motives are closer to the spinning wheel than to the spinning jenny, much less to the automatic spinning machines of our time.

The connotations are familiar but, as we have seen, misleading. Technical development is not the cause of human attitudes; each of its stages may be reconciled with far more diverse patterns of behavior than traditional social science would have it. The inherited inequalities of industrial Germany reveal one of the explosive faults that determine its structure throughout; if they have to some extent been removed from attention, this was because, unlikely as it might appear, they have proved perfectly feasible.

Perhaps this feasibility and the habits of thought resulting from it are some of the reasons one does not hear very much about the problems of this part of our study in present-day German sociology. Indeed, if these problems are discussed at all, it is usually in order to prove that they do not exist. In this respect, German sociology faithfully reflects the visible and audible parts of public consciousness. This may not be the whole of public consciousness, nor need it be right consciousness. The "postideological age" has so far not prevented social groups and strata, and dominant groups and strata in particular, from finding ways and means to foster and adumbrate their position by useful arguments. One may call these ideologies or not; the usefulness of a general disinterest in problems of the internal order for certain social groups is almost calculable. It seems worth having a somewhat closer look therefore at the ingredients of the striking German aversion to recognizing existing inequalities.

There are many witnesses of the German ideology whom it is easy to attack. But at least one important sociologist has, in a number of essays since 1953, defended a position that resembles the German ideology in many respects—Helmut Schelsky. His theory of the "classlessness" of German society (as he himself called it, not without self-irony, in 1961) has found a broad, if varying echo, which ranges from enthusiastic agreement (particularly in Germany) to astonished headshakes (particularly outside Germany) and intense criticism. Its reception alone would warrant its discussion.

Schelsky starts off with an unspecific image of the past as a class society in more or less the Marxian sense. "Thus, class theory was a legitimate social-science interpretation of social reality" (194, p. 338). But it no longer is such today. This is because of, above all, "comprehensive and structurally pervasive processes of upward and downward mobility" (194,

p. 339), among which Schelsky lists the "collective rise of industrial labor," the "rise of the white-collar worker in technical and administrative positions," and the "broad processes of downward mobility and déclassement" that "have struck the strata of the former bourgeoisie by property and education" (194, p. 332). The result is the much-cited "leveled-in middle-class society" (194, pp. 332 and 340), the "social leveling into a relatively uniform social stratum, which is neither proletarian nor bourgeois, that is, which is characterized by the disappearance of class tension and social hierarchy."

The resulting style of life is uniform and "certainly no longer determined by the substance of a constitution of society articulated or stratified hierarchically in any sense" (194, p. 332). The "relative equalization of economic positions and the far-reaching equality of political status is followed by an equalization of social and cultural patterns of behavior and desires of existence in a design of life that, in terms of the old rungs of stratification, must be localized somewhere in the 'lower middle' " (194, p. 340). Old class distinctions survive only in ideologies, and in a "ceremonialized" version. The new society has its own tensions; it is by no means a utopia of social harmony become real; but these tensions run along different lines and they, therefore, demand different concepts of analysis:

As in the middle of the last century the concept of "class" moved to the center of the debate in politics, philosophy, and social science, so social science in the highly industrialized countries today seems to place the structures of consumption and leisure-time behavior in the center of the interpretation of contemporary society. It appears that instead of class status, consumer position becomes the central determinant of all patterns of behavior, in child rearing, in politics, or in the cultural realm, so that the negative process of the leveling of class society would have to be defined positively as the formation of the highly industrialized leisure and consumption society. (194, p. 341.)

Do we have to take it then that our analysis was fundamentally mistaken? Has the divided society long been joined, and have all inequalities of opportunity and of class mentality thus been leveled in? Does our presentation merely testify to one of those "ideological restorations" to which, according to Schelsky, the "leveled-in middle-class society . . . is inclined"? Or is Schelsky wrong? Speaking of a "relative equalization of economic position" is not altogether unambiguous (who sets the standard?), but it is certainly daring in view of the 12,000 millionaires and the 90 per cent with an annual income of less than 12,000 marks in the Federal Republic in 1960.

The "far-reaching equality of political status" is, as we have seen, at best an equality of objective chances. The "equalization of social and cultural patterns of behavior and desires of existence" seems suspiciously like an optical illusion to which those whose vision is so blurred by past patterns of social differentiation that they do not perceive the emergence of new ones fall victim. This is how the mistaken belief can come about that any car is like any other, a place of vacation simply a place of vacation, and that interest in a higher standard of living means the same for the ball roller, the postal clerk, the department head, and the university professor. But the basic phenomenon to which Schelsky refers time and again documents an almost incredible error of information for a sociologist. We have seen that the "social leveling in a very broad, comparatively uniform social stratum" is, for Schelsky, the result of an "extraordinary increase in social mobility" (194, pp. 339 and 332).

Can anyone seriously maintain this assertion in a society in which only one out of every ten children from working-class families has the chance of moving upward, and conversely, at the most one out of every ten children of professional people has to step down a few rungs on the ladder of status? Speaking of an "increase" in mobility is relative again; but reality is distorted to a grotesque extent if at one point Schelsky even refers to an "excess of upward and downward social mobility" in contemporary German society (194, p. 345). The distortion at the same time betrays its author.

Schelsky's thesis documents a baffling and yet symptomatic reduction of perspective. It implies, quite without reflection, the whole range of social distance of which we have spoken and amounts to nothing less than the image of society characteristic of the service class. Realities disturbing this harmless image are simply not perceived as such, but fittingly suppressed or silently adapted. Can one be surprised that this civil-service image of society was accepted by those who could use it to support their own somewhat shaky position? One is reminded of Theodor Geiger's characterization of the new middle class: "A class denies with indignation being a class and leads a bitter class struggle against the idea and reality of the class struggle" (80, p. 168). There are social groups that abhor not merely the productive tensions of classes but also the distributive differences of strata.

It is not true, of course, that an uneven ground like that of stratification has to be volcanic; rather, it becomes a threat only by the denial of its unevenness, so that the German ideology to which Schelsky has added a new version is not in any sense a very rational tool. The theory of the classless present provides the slightly frightened service class with a soft pillow; and behind the screen of this ideology the elites can conduct their business undisturbed by awkward questions and worries—a business that may often be harmless enough, but always also serves the preservation of their own power position and thereby the cementing of the status quo.

Helmut Schelsky is not that easily dismissed, however. He is well aware of most objections to his theses, and he has therefore made them immune to all criticism in a counter-critique a procedure that, while it does not raise the quality of the theory, tells greatly in favor of the brilliance of its author. Schelsky concedes that his thesis is "purely negative as a structural statement" (194, p. 355), "a preliminary antithesis . . . which in the long run proves too crude and summary for an intensive analysis of contemporary social structure" (194, p. 356). He also admits that his thesis may be useful ideologically to the strata he prefers. Then, in a characteristic figure of thought, he makes this very usefulness the principle of his further considerations. According to Schelsky, the fact that his theory may be exploited ideologically merely proves a phenomenon general in the "scientificated world," that is, that sociological analyses are "subject to sinking down into immediate social consciousness and thus into ideology" (194, p. 370). Schelsky then describes West German society as one in which—in the language of our own analysis—collective solidarities are increasingly replaced by individual competition, and remarks disarmingly: "The ideology of classlessness is the general social background ideology that supports this differentiation, individualization, and privatization

of social positions of interest and the social mentalities associated with them" (194, p. 375).

This means nothing else but that Schelsky has relativized
his own former theory into a social ideology and detached
himself from it by demanding, with his characteristic irony,
"a social consciousness that is ambivalent in principle with
respect to the substance of all its ideas": "A social consciousness of this kind would be 'scientific' to a higher degree than
previous ideologies in that it would have to emulate by its
ambivalence the fundamental openness or unfinishedness of
modern scientific thought, although in the process of this the
accustomed forms of social and political action would also
have to be questioned" (194, p. 381). Here, the critic has lost
his last point of attack by the evaporation of all statements
into a dialectic for which everything may be right—unless he
wants to turn to methodology or ignore Schelsky's ironical
self-detachment. It will be profitable for our own argument if
we do both.

The methodical question is: Which society is Schelsky
talking about? As he likes to confront a past, which the historian seeks in vain, with a present, which appears strangely
alien to the contemporary, and to derive a brilliant sociological aperçu from the confrontation of two unrealities, Schelsky
prefers to leave his readers guessing as to the particular society with which he is concerned. He leaves little doubt,
however, that when he talks of the classless society he means
that of Germany above all: "Independent of the radical
breaks of political systems, there have thus been constants in
the changes of social structure of our German society from
the twenties to the present, which have led to rendering class
theory no longer applicable" (194, p. 354).

There have indeed been such constants in Germany; but
these do not concern consistent changes so much as a lasting
aversion to the notion of social inequality, which ranges from
William I's "harmony of classes" (appropriately invoked in
the preamble to the "Socialists' Law") to Hitler's "people's
community" in which the "workers of the mind" combine
with the "workers of the fist" in a fundamental equality that
means turning large groups out of the country, locking them
up in concentration camps, or even killing them. Schelsky
does not think very highly of the ideology of the "people's
community" either; his self-commentary is all the more sur-

prising: "We seem to be led to these insights primarily by an analysis of contemporary German society in which, due to the radicality of social and political events, the supersession of the former class structure of bourgeois society has perhaps progressed furthest, and which may therefore be a model of the current general laws of change of European industrial civilization, even if it remains specifically German in many essential traits" (194, p. 331).

There is indeed something specifically German about this astonishing avant-gardism. The assertion that the realization of the rights of citizenship and the reduction of class distances is more advanced in Germany than elsewhere stands in such evident contrast to all observations that it is probably ineffective even as a tranquilizing ideology. That Schelsky nevertheless advances it seriously merely shows that sociologists are not immune to the German ideology that holds that classes are dead and Germany is the best of all possible worlds in any case.

The classless society provides the ideology to cover the outside of the lack of equality of opportunity in Germany. But here, too, there is an inside, an ideology of unmodernity that belongs to the ideology of classlessness, which supplements the image of an illiberal reality by an illiberal consciousness of self. There is yet another point at which Schelsky lets down his defenses: "Despite all successes of advancement, despite all provisions of security, the individual can no longer develop within him a sense of social order and of the placing of his person. From this hopelessness of their basic motives there results not only the permanent unrest and insecurity, but above all the steadily growing dissatisfaction of men in our society. Ultimately, only a system of social status and a membership in social groups stable through generations in a society that embodies within it a socially transcendent set of values is probably able to spread persistent and well-founded feelings of social security" (194, p. 346).

The question of exactly how happy modernity makes people is perfectly legitimate; we have discussed it ourselves. But the way Schelsky puts the question, it bears suspicious resemblance to cultural pessimism in the name of a romanticized past that never was. Since in Schelsky's own work concern about the lost security of social place is combined with the image of a classless present, its author cannot be charged with stereotyped anti-modern cultural criticism. But one cannot spare him the charge that two of the main ingredients of the ideology that we have here described as the German ideology appear in his works: the classlessness of his own society, which is thereby distinguished from others, and a melancholy nostalgia for security, which denies the modern world the ability to make people happy.

However, for this other, deeper, and worse side of the German ideology, Schelsky is certainly not the appropriate crown witness. Here another sin of German sociology comes to mind, one of those unfortunate dichotomies in which German thought is rich, and of which the contrast between a higher literary "culture" and a lowly technical "civilization" is but one example—dichotomies that are virulent because in their terrible simplicity they are eminently suited for "sinking down into immediate social consciousness and ideology." I mean, of course, the untranslatable dichotomy of *Gemeinschaft* and *Gesellschaft,* which was invented by a man who also liked to confront good and evil in the form of culture and civilization and was one of the most effective cultural pessimists in German sociology, Ferdinand Tönnies.

Tönnies had no shortage of negative attributes when, in 1887, he described the state of *Gesellschaft,* society, in which men are either hostile to each other or bound by mere contract in a state of civilization. He did not even spare us the pun by which the *liberum arbitrium* of men may be called arbitrary: society is a mere arbitrary relation of men. By contrast, *Gemeinschaft,* community, is founded on an essential sympathy and provides a "natural" union of men in which force and civilization are equally absent. Tönnies claims originality for his perfidious dichotomy (217, p. xxix), but many ancestors and contemporaries represented rudiments and variations of it. The idea that an original human *Gemeinschaft* is threatened by an artificial *Gesellschaft* is part of the folklore of German self-consciousness; that this development is unfortunate and should be arrested, if not prevented, adds an element of political zeal to the philosophical interpretation of the world.

The world called *Gesellschaft* by Tönnies resembles more than superficially our concept of modernity (and, of course, Hegel's "civil society," which in any case anticipates Tönnies' notion in a much more differentiated fashion). Here, the relations between men rest on willfulness. The word, like many another, was probably not chosen without evaluative undertones; instead of willfulness, one might speak of free agreement, rational choice, autonomy. The institution characteristic of society is the contract. Society has internal tensions and clashes, but also institutions within which these are conducted. It is civilized. But despite society's connection with technical progress and modern science, Tönnies clearly prefers the older form of *Gemeinschaft*. Its cohesion is not willful but grown, so that it rests on an organic co-operation of parts (which Durkheim, a more rational sociologist, would have called "mechanic"). It is a world of human nest warmth, held together by "harmony," "custom," and "religion," thus not merely external and rational, but founded on the "will of nature." Our intention here is neither the intellectual history of German irrationalism nor the critique of cultural pessimism. We are still concerned with the German ideology as a barrier on the road to modernity. But it is part of this concern to show that Tönnies' dichotomy is historically misleading, sociologically uninformed, and politically illiberal.

The confrontation of a sweet community of minds in the past with the heartless contractual society of the present is historically misleading in at least two respects. It is unlikely that a community of this kind has ever existed; and it is certain that the reality that is idealized as communal was, in fact, much less agreeable than its glorification suggests. All human societies have social structures of deliberate agreement, whether these come about in village or kraal, with ancient Germans or Tikopians. There are always and everywhere those who are able to lay down the law and those others who are bound to obey. Possibly for this reason, there are always conflicts. But if the notion of community refers to the traditional world of a more or less distant past, it should be stressed that the image of the village idyll is quite incomplete without mentioning sickness and early death, starvation and war, dependence and humiliation, and those many other results of man's "will of nature" that to those involved were probably very much more relevant than pleasure in the natural and the familiar.

Sociologically speaking, the contrast of a harmonious "community" with the struggles of "society" is convincing only in so far as community is indeed an unsociety, that is, a social form unable to survive. For with contract and inequality, with the state and with conflict, history, too, has been suspended in the world of *Gemeinschaft*. But history is not legislated away with impunity. He who tries to stop social change will soon be overwhelmed by it. We have seen earlier that an authoritarian political order is neither rational nor efficient; by denying it, one removes change from human control. It is understandable perhaps that under these conditions change appears to people not as an instrument of controlled progress, but as an inescapable destiny by which they abide with their heads bent in useless humility.

The aurea aetas of peace and harmony that the community ideologies of cultural pessimism prefer to the bellum omnium contra omnes in order to depreciate contract and conflicts, law and human autonomy, betrays the basic illiberalism of this ideology. The consistent liberal starts off with the badness, or at least the incompatible self-interests, of men, which make it necessary to invent institutions capable of making these divergent interests fruitful for all. To the liberal therefore, the golden age of the past is no less suspect than the utopia of a classless present or future. He gets impatient with the illusion of a community that robs the individual of his opportunities for decision and reduces him from a free person to a bee tied to the hive. In terms of liberal theory, the contractual basis of all society provides the starting point and hope of developments toward a greater happiness of a greater number.

This leads us back to the German ideology and its uses in a society that embarks on the road to modernity with great hesitation. Widespread preference for the word *Gemeinschaft,* including the undertones of meaning given to it by Tönnies, reflects the lasting effect of traditional social ties. The evaluative rank order of community and society is the ideological counterpart of the missing option for modernity. But all this describes the impersonal side of the German ideology. In fact, its uses are far more concrete than the depiction of a faulty reality. There were and are social groups hoping to profit from this ideology, and actually doing so. By promoting an ideology of *Gemeinschaft,* these groups have contributed to hindering the advent of modernity in Germany.

If one recognizes that every society including one's own generates within it inequalities and tensions, one accepts by the same token the probability of change into an uncertain, open, in any case different future. Calling social inequalities and traditional ties by their names means questioning their legitimacy and making a beginning for their transformation. But the leadership groups of German society could have little interest in this, because any change was bound to threaten the basis of their position (even though these leadership groups were not by any means the most conservative stratum in Germany). Moreover, a service class of plan-rational character and a bureaucracy of Prussian virtue and discipline also had to suspect a threat to their power in the destruction of tradition. They found possibly unexpected support in that middle class of unhappily self-employed who saw their only chance of survival in the maintenance of the economic, social, and political status quo. Thus there emerged a coalition of the antiquated and the illiberal against modernity and liberalism, and the German ideology of inner harmony as a fact or a point of direction served as a convenient program of defense.

This may explain the production and supply of the German ideology on the market of social self-interpretation. But how can we understand the demand and sale of this unpromising commodity? Why was the German ideology of social harmony so successful? Why was there no resistance to it? In fact, there was such resistance. Among German sociologists of the 1920s, for example, it would be hard to name one representative of this harmonizing doctrine. Tönnies was still alive, of course, and he temporarily found, in the shadow of the National Socialist movement, a co-fighter in Sombart; but from Max Weber and Robert Michels to Karl Mannheim and Theodor Geiger critical analyses of modern class structure and its ideologies dominated the scene. At that time, alas, sociologists evidently were not yet typical representatives of their society, for the demand for *Gemeinschaft* remained large, and the scale of this artful product grew with the improbability of its utility. Here we are once again on the trail of a strange feature of German social development, if one that is by now familiar.

In political debate, the ideology of an inner unity of society generally appeared encased in the other ideology of a state of national emergency. Because the nation is surrounded by enemies, it must close its ranks inside and form a "forsworn community." Thus the social psychological law according to which pressure from without produces solidarity within was abused for the creation of an unreal world: self-made, frequently only asserted pressure served to distract from the internal disorders of society. Possibly the success of the German ideology of social classlessness and national community consisted less in the power of conviction it carried than in its advocates' ability to distract people's interest from the immediate, real, and acutely threatening and turn it to the more distant and obscure. Thus society and its classes disappeared behind the nation and the fictitious community of its people.

Germany's road to modernity was long for many reasons. The faults of industrial, economic, and traditional social structures proved vital and surprisingly resistant. A persistent traditionalism of thought weakened the effects of formal rights of equality, which were gradually granted in law, politics, and society; chances objectively given were not realized subjectively. There were strata who were tied by interest to the state of semimodernity. They were helped in their struggle against modernity by a German ideology of the classless community, which was as useful for them as it was symptomatic of 'the society as a whole. As a consequence, equal citizenship rights remained incomplete for a long time, and chances of participation have continued to be, to the present day, more unequally distributed than the status of citizenship would permit. In this way, German society has made it difficult for liberals to make their conception of rational politics the dominant principle.

If there is any consolation in this picture, it is that Germany's road to modernity may after all be described in categories of movement. German society has advanced some way on this road, and the signs are favorable for further progress. That, in the eastern part of Germany, this has to be paid for once again by the freedom of people, may reflect, apart from external influence, the weakness of resistance against a minority in a society still dominated by traditional and authoritarian patterns. That West Germany will succeed in following the road in freedom, one can so far hope. Among the four elements of the social structure of democracy that we have taken as our guideline in this study, equality of citizenship is no longer the most relevant. But its analysis has led us to the border of a second sphere in which the aversion to tension and the false love for community assume even more consequential forms, and where we encounter a nearly unmoved constant of German social structure: that is, the sphere of conflict.

CONFLICT *OR*

THE NOSTALGIA FOR SYNTHESIS

9. CONFLICT AND LIBERTY

One of the great dramas of human life in society may be found in the courtroom where the man who has failed to observe the ruling norms is faced with his trial. Such failures betray the pleasing reliability of the structure of social roles; their punishment is therefore celebrated in a ritual role play, which lends the general drama traits that are both peculiar to and symptomatic of the society. If, for example, anyone trained in the English tradition of legal thought followed the preparation and conduct of a German criminal case, he would notice a number of telling differences. In fact, each of the three principal characters involved in the trial—judge, counsel for the defense, and counsel for the prosecution—differs in important details, in both the theory and practice of criminal law, from its English counterpart. It will prove rewarding to look for the principle behind these differences.

To begin with, the judge, far from being the referee in a contest of parties or, in Erving Goffman's delightful description of this role, a chairman who, as "go-between," provides his audience (in this case, the jury) with cues as to their appropriate reactions to the evidence and arguments presented, is more like an "actor-manager"—and one who is, of course, always on the winning side. A German judge not only guards the rules of the game, he takes an active hand in the examination of witnesses. No critical undertone is intended if a professor of law reports that the judge is "required to determine the facts and elicit the production of evidence for all facts that in his opinion are essential for judgment. He thus combines the offices of investigator and judge" (15, p. 52). Once the trial comes to a close, the investigator withdraws with the jurors so that he can continue to direct the proceedings and not relinquish to others his position as "master of the trial" at any time.

The judge is a civil servant; so is counsel for the prosecution, but counsel for the defense is usually a private citizen. In both the general social and the specific legal context this status tends to become a disadvantage, which is aggravated by the fact that often counsel for the defense does not have access to all the evidence before the trial. To make matters worse, the decision as to which part of the evidence may be made available to counsel for the defense without "endangering the purpose of the investigation" is, according to the German law of criminal procedure, up to his later opponent, the state attorney. They are thus hardly equal opponents; rather, counsel for the defense becomes a beggar for clemency (and indeed the most frequent plea of the defense is that of extenuating circumstances).

It is symptomatic that until quite recently, counsel for the defense was physically placed, in many German courtrooms, somewhat below counsel for the prosecution, whose very title of state attorney (*Staatsanwalt*) connotes an air of authority. The state attorney's is clearly the crucial role in a German criminal case; it is indeed two roles, which may be regarded as barely compatible. Before the trial opens, the state attorney represents what a widely used legal commentary describes, without irony and indeed with some justification, as "the most objective authority in the world." The office of state attorney is an institution whose like we will encounter often in this part of our study. According to criminal-law procedure, it has the contradictory but telling task "to investigate not merely the circumstances incriminating, but also those exonerating the accused." The state attorney has every conceivable means —files and witnesses, laboratory tests and police information, etc.—at his disposal to determine "the truth"; for nothing less than this ambitious intention stands behind his office. Evidently, this usually takes a long time—which is one of the reasons why many months, and sometimes years, elapse between the original arrest and the opening of the trial in Germany. Evidently, too, the trial itself loses in importance since "the truth" has been worked out beforehand—which explains in part why critics of German criminal-law procedure so often feel that the accused is assumed guilty once the case has been brought to trial. Most important of all, the state attorney undergoes a curious change of character when, on the day the trial opens, he slips from the role of an impartial "objective" investigator of "the truth" into that of a naturally partisan counsel for the prosecution.

Even from this brief description of its characters the course of the drama may almost be guessed. But this is not my intention here. Much less do I want to praise or condemn any system of legal rules and modes of procedure. Such easy value judgments can hardly do justice to complex traditions; they ignore, moreover, the actual similarities of seemingly widely divergent institutions. A clever defense counsel may transform a German criminal trial into a contest of the English type, just as a clever English judge may influence the course of the trial far beyond his role as referee. Rather than being a starting point for an analysis of legal systems as such, this brief sketch of criminal-law procedure serves as a useful metaphor for a feature of German social structure we want to explore in this part of our study: Wherever opposing interests meet in German society, there is a tendency to seek authoritative and substantive rather than tentative and formal solutions. Many institutions of German society have been and are still set up in such a way as to imply that somebody or some group of people is "the most objective authority in the world," and is therefore capable of finding ultimate solutions for all issues and conflicts. In this manner, conflict is not regulated, but "solved"; and in the following remarks and chapters I want to examine the social patterns, political implications, historical causes, and philosophical bases of this procedure in Germany.

Let us return for a moment to the example of criminal-law procedure. A criminal case, and in particular the drama of the trial, may be thought of in terms of a conflict of interests. In its crudest interpretation, it involves a clash between the interest of the prosecution to prove and that of the defense to disprove the guilt of the accused. In German criminal law, however, the task of finding out who was guilty is accomplished before the trial, by setting up an elaborate machinery of research and investigation—the position and office of the state attorney. In this manner, what might be regarded as a situation of conflict is in fact conceived as one of a concerted search for truth. As a consequence, the function of the trial is less that of a contest for the judgment of common sense as embodied in the jury than one of making "the truth" public, considering extenuating circumstances, and drawing the conclusions stipulated by the legal code. In place of debate and argument, an agency is set up to find the ultimate solution. The procedure is guided not by the "principle of party presentation" (which in Germany is confined to civil proceedings), but by the "principle of investigation"; it is thus not a

competition between equals, but the search for an authoritative solution.

But we risk being misleading if we do not stop our interpretation here. In an important sense, the example of criminal law can be no more than a metaphor for social modes of
dealing with conflicts. There is a fundamental difference between the clash of interests in a criminal case—this would
not be equally true for civil lawsuits—and, say, the clash of
interests in a wage dispute or an election campaign. In the
legal situation, there is no fundamental uncertainty, at least
in respect to one of the issues at hand—the question of fact:
"the truth" is in principle available in the sense that the crime
has been committed, and that somebody has committed it.
A long history of judicial mistakes, few well known and many
unknown, demonstrates with oppressive pregnancy how difficult it is, in fact, to discover even this "truth"; there is thus
much to be said for implanting the metaphor of uncertainty
into all institutions, that is, to borrow, along with the criminal-
law procedure characteristic of common law, the ethics of
uncertainty from those other areas in which it is more evidently appropriate. But this would not alter the fact that, in
comparison to the subject of investigation in a criminal case,
"the truth" is fundamentally uncertain in industrial or political conflicts (as, of course, it is in respect to questions of
right in law as well). There is no authority capable of rec-
ommending a universally valid solution of a wage dispute
or a clash between political parties that is realistic as well as
morally just.

In addition to its authoritarian procedures, the German
legal system illustrates the resistance to the assumption of
uncertainty by its tendency (founded in the tradition of Roman law) to remove all quaestiones juris from dispute by
complete reliance on a given code of answers. But a peculiar
attitude toward conflict in the institutions of German society
is not confined to the legal system, as will soon become evident if we turn now to the other great institutional orders.

Conflict begins at home. The family, like any other institution, may be regarded as a system of conflict regulation. And
indeed the authoritarian character of the German family has
become a favorite stereotype of all political and literary critics
of German society from Heinrich Mann and Curt Goetz to
Max Horkheimer and Theodor W. Adorno. Occasionally, one
encounters the notion that the German father is, or at least

used to be, a combination of judge and state attorney: presiding over his family, relentlessly prosecuting every sign of deviance, and settling all disputes by his supreme authority. There is an element of caricature in many descriptions of the German father. In so far as it is descriptive of reality at all, the reality concerned is that of Wilhelminian times rather than contemporary Germany; and the Wilhelminian father had probably more in common with his Victorian counterpart and the father of other societies of the fin de siècle than with his compatriot half a century later, the German father of 1960. This is not to deny that the caricature does strike peculiarly German conditions in some respects, as in the notion, long embodied in the structure of the family, that the others, the children, the wife, are minors in every respect. It is no accident that Tönnies, like Hegel before him and the vulgarized sociology of the Nazis after him, took the family to be the purest form of *Gemeinschaft*. It is ruled (at least in the world of ideologies) by love, not justice; biological ties, not social agreement. Since conflicts happen nevertheless, in the family as in any social institution, the applications of such theories are no less authoritarian than the political reality of the German ideology of community. Treitschke has stated this clearly and without a spark of irony: "Even in the family we find the state's principle of subordination. The father is the sovereign, he executes the law" (219, p. 26).

Nevertheless, the internal structure of the German family is not the most striking illustration of the perverted attitude to social conflict that permeates German society and prevents the spread of the democratic principle in it. The consequences of this attitude stand out rather more clearly, for example, in the organization and methods of education. When Max Weber advanced his thesis of the desirability of a value-free approach to social science, and in particular his demand for a complete abstention from value judgments in academic teaching, one of his main points was the slightly ironic, yet not seriously questioned reference to the "discussionless tranquillity, carefully protected from all contradiction, of the lecture room privileged by the state" (224, p. 478), in which the listeners do not have a fair chance to defend themselves against the lecturer. But may it not be that the educational situation described by Weber is as dated (and placed) as, say, Freud's notion of the superego as the internalized father? Is it not conceivable that academic teaching is now conducted in such a way that the students do not "have to be silent" (as Weber says elsewhere) and that the lecturer is exposed to questions, objections, debate, and discussion?

We will presently examine more thoroughly the institutions of science in terms of uncertainty, conflict, and German misconceptions of these. But the fallacies that will have to be explored then, and that are recognizable in Weber's implications, determine education in German schools, too. It is clearly possible to exaggerate the significance of discussion in education; although the dubious occasion of the first Russian sputnik intensified the process, enthusiasm for the author of *Democracy and Education* has been on the wane in the United States for years, and for good reason. But one error does not justify the other. The traditional picture of the German Gymnasium as a prison, which children enter with a sense of oppression and leave with a sigh of relief, is probably not worth much more than the stereotype of the Wilhelminian father. But the very principle of the school as a place of disciplined learning involves a rigid separation of roles between those who are capable of teaching and those who have to be taught. We can but note in passing here that a rather mechanical notion of the "material" that is being taught is part of this educational principle: the material, originally in the possession of the teachers, is dished out to the pupils like a school meal in well-measured rations, until all have their part (and those who brought along some from home, correspondingly more). It is evident that this kind of rigid separation of roles excludes conflicts, which assume an approximately equal rank among the groups involved; the teacher's monopoly of possession and distribution provides him with an overpowering authority whose counterpart is the subservience of those in need of teaching. In a school of this kind there may be room for modest questions, but not for objections or indeed permanent discussion.

It is almost too obvious to need emphasis that this is not the whole reality of the school, nor perhaps its characteristic contemporary style. At a later point, we will examine school and family as the mediators of ruling values in Germany in greater detail (cf. Chapter 20). Modes of conflict regulation do not provide the key to the whole reality of a third great institution, the military, either. Indeed, one may well ask whether the military does not have to be, by its construction and purpose, a place of discipline rather than discussion.

However, the greater the force is that holds together a social organization and the more the obedience that is demanded, the more the latent conflict produced by force gathers in intensity and momentum. This has been a problem of military institutions at all times. So far as professional soldiers are concerned, the permanent state of discipline may have no other safety valve than the old triad of wine, women, and song. In modern armies, however, the role of soldier is a temporary one for most. The "total institution," as Goffman calls it, which devours the individual, becomes bearable by the calculable chance of leaving it. But total institutions remain symptoms, because they can vary considerably in their structures. For that reason, it makes a difference for those involved, as well as for the surrounding society, whether, in the military, conflicts are canalized, or whether blind obedience is demanded and enforced. For Germany, the citizen in uniform is still a new social figure; the parliamentary ombudsman for the military, a new approach to the rational regulation of conflict in an exceptional social condition; and it is questionable whether these deviations from Prussian military tradition have really gained a hold.

If I may be permitted to add a last to this rag bag of examples before we begin to explore their common features, we might think of church organization. It is a striking fact that, in the past, liberal democracy seems to have flourished in countries in which there was also a fairly widespread interest in so-called non-conformist churches and sects. It is more than daring to offer generalizations about the large number of such religious groups that exist in the present world. With this warning, however, it may be argued that while some non-conformist groups are more dogmatic in their theology, many of them tend to be more democratic in their organization than established churches. By "democratic" in this rather loose sense I mean the influence of the lay element in church affairs, the ways in which dignitaries are elected and controlled, the amount of discussion permitted, widespread lay participation on the basis of what may be described as church citizenship, and the like. Before this background it may therefore be relevant to remark that German Protestantism has always, especially in the eastern provinces, tended toward the established type. Where this was not the case, as in Württemberg, where sectarian formations played a large part, the liberal principle gained a deeper hold on the population. On the whole, however, non-conformist groups have never played a significant part in Germany. Even today—at a time, that is, when they are under no public pressure and when interest in them is growing—only about 3 per cent of the population of Western Germany are not members of the two great churches, Lutheran and Roman Catholic, and many of this minority do not belong to any church at all.

In political debate, if not in political theory, the claim that political democracy presupposes the "total democratization of society" is often heard today. The word offends the ear; more than that, it involves a very imprecise notion of both democracy and society. Schumpeter was not a liberal, but we do not deviate from our own understanding of the concepts if we follow him and understand by parliamentary democracy "that institutional arrangement for arriving at political decisions in which individuals acquire the power to decide by means of a competitive struggle for the people's vote" (197, p. 265). It can be shown, I think, that this distinctive arrangement is strictly appropriate only to the political community. All other institutions have features of social structure that either exclude the democratic procedure from the outset or reduce it to a metaphor and thereby transform its effects more or less radically.

It is hard to see how an army could serve its purpose if its officers had to campaign regularly for office among their soldiers. While a strict council system of army organization is eminently suitable as an instrument for the total exchange of leaders in a revolutionary upheaval, it is no accident that it disappeared like a ghost after 1917 and 1918. However liberal a school system may be, the election of teachers and professors by pupils and students would hardly enhance the quality of teaching. The separation of roles, which is so exaggerated in German schools, is based on a drop of authority inherent in the educational situation in which the ones know by virtue of their acquired office what the others cannot know yet by virtue of their ascribed age position. Even in the most democratic church, the transcendent substance of faith requires, at least temporarily, such as during services, a similar drop, which ascribes to some the chance to communicate or interpret a divine truth, which the others feel bound to accept. While some children may dream of electing their parents, the resulting family system would presumably be a novelty for even the most widely traveled anthropologist.

The claim that a similar basic drop characterizes economic enterprises, too, is more controversial; we will discuss it more thoroughly a little later. It will emerge, then, that the requirement of continuity, and even more the unavoidable fact of property (which may be private or public, called capitalist or socialist, but which always gives some a fundamental advantage over others) stabilizes a structure of authority in the economy that cannot be abolished as such by democratic procedures. The common feature of all non-political institutions is that a basic authority drop is built into their structures, which cannot be overcome by periodic elections, party struggles, and parliamentary control. It is not surprising, therefore, that the many attempts to democratize these institutions that have been made in our experimentative century have all failed to achieve their utopian ends and returned nolens volens to older forms.

This is the negative presupposition of any program of the "total democratization of society," but not the last word on the subject. Positively speaking, there is one possibility of change, that is, a structural variability of the non-political institutions, which we have already discussed at some length: the replacement of the subject by the citizen. Although it may seem indicated, and certainly was the rule in history, to translate the basic drop of authority in family and school, church, military, and industry into a drop of rights of participation, this is neither necessary nor adequate for a society in which the liberal principle is supposed to blossom. Germany's road to modernity has been long not only because the transformation of political subjects into citizens turned out to be very difficult, but also because the attempt to realize independent and equal participation in the other institutional orders met with a great deal of resistance. To use current slogans and catchwords: the citizen in uniform, the adult church, the child taken seriously, the democratic school, and industrial and economic citizenship were all long in coming.

There is yet another realistic possibility of "democratizing" institutions with a prescribed authority structure, and it is this that we are concerned with in the present part of our study. Equality of citizenship rights creates the potential of a democratic constitution; but its actuality depends on other patterns. Implicit in the institutions of parliamentary democracy is an attitude to socially structured conflicts of interest, which may be transferred to non-political institutions. If one reduces this attitude to its abstract core, it involves (1) recognition of divergences of opinion and interest as inevitable; (2) a consequent concentration of action on the forms rather than the causes of conflict; (3) the creation of institutions that offer conflicting groups binding forms of expression; and (4) the development of rules of the game acceptable to both conflicting parties in that they do not put either of them at an advantage or disadvantage.

As we turn to specific institutions, we encounter a variety of patterns satisfying these principles. Thus, systems of conciliation and arbitration in work disputes, teaching procedures based on dialogue and discussion in schools and universities, a machinery of complaint and legal hearing in the army, and many other ways of canalizing differences of interest may be full equivalents of parliamentary government in the political field. But while there is a great variety of institutional arrangements of conflict regulation, it is our contention that liberal democracy can work only in the context of a society whose institutions are characterized throughout by the recognition and rational canalization of conflicts.

Wherever there is human life in society, there is conflict. Societies do not differ in that some have conflicts and others not; societies and social units within them differ in the violence and intensity of conflicts. But while this sociological law —if it is such—would lead one to conclude that the indicated liberal attitude to conflict is the only realistic, and perhaps even "scientific" one, the history of mankind has seen this law violated far more often than recognized. Techniques designed to suppress conflict are much older than the word "totalitarian" with which we describe them today; and at least by appearance these techniques are also much more successful than our law would permit.

In theory there are at least two other, in our terms nonrational attitudes to conflict. One is the cynical approach, which is unconcerned about the inevitability or avoidability of conflicts but wants them suppressed as an awkward obstacle to the (arbitrary) exercise of power wherever they occur. The other, and rather more sophisticated attitude is characterized by the search for solutions to conflicts. By this I do not mean the perfectly rational solution that may be found for an individual case of conflict, a specific wage dispute, for example, by skillful conciliation or arbitration, but solutions in a more ultimate sense, affecting the roots of conflict.

One of the basic assumptions of all utopian constructions is that conditions may be created under which conflicts become superfluous. Indeed, the resulting state of harmony is the theoretical basis of the persistence of the social structure of utopia. But in reality these conditions do not exist. In fact, with the terrible dialectics of the non-rational, it happens that utopia first requires and then glorifies suppression. For if in a supposedly realized utopia—the people's community, the classless society—that which is forbidden nevertheless occurs, if, for example, resistance against power does not disappear, saving utopian theory requires the practice of terror in order to suppress what cannot be talked away, as a relic of a superseded past, or as an attempt to subversion by alien powers. Soon the beautiful but false theory turns into a Sunday dress of arbitrary rule.

The suppression of conflict has seen many forms in history, none of which was as pure as its concept. In Imperial Germany, for example, suppression was mixed with benevolence and a modicum of rationality, which denied existing conflicts only their impact, not their expression. Imperial Germany remained authoritarian where the Nazi Germany of the Third Reich and the Communist Germany of the DDR chose totalitarian forms. But even totalitarian rule leaves some room for conflict. The state party also acts as a gigantic institute of opinion research; there are ritualized forms of complaint and criticism, there is passive resistance, which effectively blocks the realization of arbitrary measures. Such unwanted intrusions of reality and rationality demonstrate even more convincingly than the properties of liberal constitutions (whose reality is no freer of alien admixtures than that of authoritarian or totalitarian forms) the inevitability of conflicts and the desirability of their rational regulation, so our presupposition may indeed be called a sociological law.

Such remarks must not be misunderstood. Despite all impurities of real constitutions, differences between them remain great, and they are expressed in different rhythms of national histories. The rationality of the liberal attitude to conflict comes ultimately from the fact that it alone does justice to the creativity of social antagonisms as motive forces of change. Conflicts determine the speed, depth, and direction of change. Whoever domesticates conflict by recognizing and regulating it may thus hope to control the rhythm of history. Whoever scorns such domestication has this rhythm as his enemy. Wherever conflicts are suppressed as awkward obstacles to arbitrary rule, or declared abolished once and for all, these fallacies produce unexpected and uncontrollable responses of the suppressed forces.

Bismarck's disappointment that the Socialists' Law did not diminish but multiplied the number of adherents of German Social Democracy, shows up a rare blind spot of naïveté in the great man. Suppressed conflicts not only become virulent unexpectedly, they also take the reins of change from those in power. Change then assumes unforeseen radical forms, which moreover tend to reproduce themselves in a vicious circle. The erratic changes of political systems in German history of the last hundred years may be described as a consequence of a fallacious attitude toward conflict in politics, as in the other institutional orders of society.

This is one—the sociological—side of our argument. The political-theory side or, more simply, the evaluative critique of German society, corresponds to it, here as elsewhere. Different attitudes toward conflict have ramifications for views and policies of liberty. In so far as a rational approach to the regulation of conflicts is a pragmatic implication of parliamentary government, it is also a condition of the development of the individual that the constitution of liberty promises. But this is only part of what I mean here. Different attitudes to conflict imply different interpretations of the human condition. If one is prepared to recognize the permanent reality of contrasting opinions and regard conflict as a moving force of social development, this implies the conviction that man is living in a world of inherent uncertainty. In the terms of the economist, we are always, and not accidentally, lacking some of the information that would be necessary to decide ultimately what is true and what is good. Since no man knows all the answers, it is all-important to avoid the dictatorship of false answers. The best way to accomplish this is to see to it that at all times and everywhere more than one answer may be given. Conflict is liberty, because by conflict alone the multitude and incompatibility of human interests and desires find adequate expression in a world of notorious uncertainty.

This was not, however, at least in the past (to quote the title of Leonard Krieger's important study), the German idea of freedom. The suspicious liaisons of freedom and necessity, or freedom and authority, in German political philosophy have often been remarked upon; Krieger adds to them the historical liaison between the notions of freedom and the idea of the sovereignty of the numerous provinces and principalities before the creation of the Empire. We will try to trace the consequences of such unfortunate marriages primarily in three areas of German social structure: science, the economy, and politics. In all of them we will find the same nostalgia for a world whose uncomfortable conflicts have been replaced by ultimate solutions. If there are antinomies, a synthesis must be found; if Kant had to be, a Hegel has come to "supersede" him. We will encounter many versions of the Baconian view of man on which such convictions are based; but first of all we will look at institutions.

Liberal democracy is government by conflict. As such it cannot be suspended in the thin air of constitutional theory. Even if all other institutions have predetermined structural limits that rule out the principle of government by conflict for them, they must meet conflicts, which are as inevitable in them as in politics, with the same rationality as political institutions in order to provide a basis for the constitution of liberty. It is, however, hard to find more than traces of this in German history up to the present day; and in view of the slowness of their development the traces can scarcely be called beginnings. "Man wants concord," says Kant, and he is certainly right about the wishes of German man. "But nature knows better what is good for his kind; it wants discord" (109, p. 32). The question why nature, with which Germans otherwise boast of being on such good terms, failed to impart its better knowledge to them will accompany us throughout the following chapters.

10. THE GERMAN IDEA OF TRUTH

When Wilhelm von Humboldt presented his *Proposal for the Internal and External Organization of the Institutions of Higher Learning in Berlin* in 1870, he met the wishes of Fichte, Friedrich August Wolf, and the Royal Prussian Chief of Cabinet Beyme to the extent of distinguishing between two tasks of the "institutions of higher learning" and ascribing them to two separate institutions: the "university" and the "academy." Humboldt may well have realized that this distinction has social and political grounds apart from those of theory:

> The university always stands in a closer relation to practical life and the needs of the state since it always undertakes practical jobs for it in directing the youth; the academy, however, is concerned purely with scholarship in itself. The teachers of the university stand in a merely general relation to each other about matters of the external and internal order of the discipline; of their own concerns they inform each other only in so far as their inclination leads them to do so. The academy is, by contrast, an association truly designed to submit the work of each to the judgment of all.
>
> In this manner, the academy has to be maintained as the highest and last refuge of scholarship and the corporation most independent of the state, and for once one has to run the risk that a corporation of this kind will prove, by too little or too one-sided activity, that what is right will not always come about most easily under the most favorable external circumstances. . . .
>
> There thus arises between university and academy a competition and an antagonism and such a mutual effect that, whenever one has to be concerned about an excess or a lack of activity in them, they will restore equilibrium to each other by themselves. (103, p. 307.)

This is the liberal conclusion of an intelligent argument, which contains more than it reveals at first sight. In the introduction to this part of our study, I have claimed that politics is the only institutional field in which the social conditions that demand the rules of parliamentary democracy without metaphor are present. There is one respect, however, in which this analysis was incomplete. A dividing line of functions and patterns runs straight through the traditional university, making it one of the most formative institutions of history. On the one hand, universities perform part of the task of socializing individuals with which educational institutions (among others) are entrusted. In universities, the skills for certain specialized professions, and sometimes the general qualifications for leadership as well, are imparted. In tasks of this kind, the university is, like the school, tied to and bound by the values and ruling powers of the time, that is, it is close to the "needs of the state." From this perspective the social structure of the university has, in principle, the same drop of authority that characterizes schools and armies, churches and business enterprises; in this side of their activity, universities are essentially conservative institutions. This is not to say that the German lecture course, whose audience is forced to remain respectfully passive, and other characteristically authoritarian patterns are, after all, legitimate; but the lecture course, too, has its origin in the conservative, that is, the training aspect of academic society.

There is, however, another side to universities—scientific research. In contrast to teaching, research can, in principle, not be fettered by predetermined validities, whether these are social values, existing distributions of power, or even historical "authorities" in the world of scholarship. It requires openness and freedom, which can be provided only in "the corporation most independent of the state." In so far as scientific research always seeks new horizons of knowledge, it is oriented to the future and in principle progressive; in this aspect of their social structure universities invariably become uncomfortable rather than useful to those in power. Most significantly in our present context, the organization of research provides no justification for a drop of authority; here indeed rules of the game are possible (if not necessary) that correspond exactly and fully to those of political democracy. Science and politics—truth and justice—are the two realms in which the constitutional uncertainty of human existence becomes manifest, and in whose organizational forms its liberal mastery is therefore possible.

Possibility is not reality; this triviality has to be emphasized quite often where German history is concerned. Fichte did not get his way. No "superuniversity" of research grew out of the traditional university; university and academy remained united, and the threat of the academy was domesticated by the reliability of the university. Humboldt was enough of a politician to leave this development open when he invoked the "blessing of German universities" in almost the same breath as the need for a refuge of research: "If one wants to confine the university to teaching and the spreading of knowledge alone, and the academy to the extension of knowledge, one obviously does an injustice to the former" (103, p. 305). Humboldt spoke in favor of a close connection between university and academy based on mutual inspiration, and the result was the University of Berlin, whose founding idea of the "unity of teaching and research" spread to all other German universities and beyond. This is the unity of the incompatible, of conservative stateliness and progressive liberalism; as such it might be fruitful. Why this has not always been its effect is a question that may advance our argument.

There were many reasons why the German university was badly in need of reform in the beginning of the nineteenth century; the "university frozen in corporate ties" fulfilled hardly one of its tasks adequately. Among its many problems, however, was the fact that the unity of research and teaching had broken up: universities had become largely teaching institutions. One hundred and fifty years later a similar picture presents itself. The mutually inspiring competition of "university" and "academy," which Humboldt had hoped for, has very nearly driven one of the competitors from the market. Once again teaching has proved the stronger of the two pillars on which the university is built. Do we have to assume from this the superiority of the conservative, of the forces of persistence? Is there in the long run a kind of gravitation away from research and toward teaching? Or is the reason much more simply the presence of students, which makes teaching hard to avoid whereas one can always stop doing research?

There may be yet another reason why German universities were threatened time and again with being reduced to elevated schools. This concerns the substance of scholarship and research in German universities rather than its relation to teaching. The German idea of science (*Wissenschaft*), more precisely the concept of science that has dominated German universities since the foundation of the University of Berlin, offers little resistance to the temptations of the forces that be. The refuge of the "academy" has to be filled with the life of science to become effective; but not just any science will accomplish this, and the kind of science Humboldt had in mind could not do so. These are far-reaching assertions that we can make good here only in a rather daring tour de force of argument. The assertion and its foundation are, however, equally indispensable for the progress of our considerations.

Humboldt rightly adds to his presentation of the "spirit of genuine science" that his understanding of this spirit is controversial. What he regards as science some call meaningless speculation. Thus he can say as early as 1814 that "this is the cause for the never fully conciliated quarrel between the Germans and the foreign world." Fortunately he adds, "But it has become a source of dissent among ourselves" (103, p. 315). The German who speaks of *Wissenschaft* usually means something quite different from the Englishman or American speaking of science. For the latter, a notion of "empirical science" is characteristic; actually, Humboldt was still using the term in this sense. However, after Dilthey's dictum, "all science is empirical science" (60, p. vii), this specification has become insufficient too; let us proceed, therefore, from names to things.

There is a conception of the goals and methods of science according to which science is concerned with explaining observable phenomena by general statements whose correctness or falsehood may be tested by new observations. Science aims at theory, although its starting point is the description of facts and its most time-consuming activity is the experimental test of the consequences of theories. This concept of scientific method excludes statements that cannot be refuted by controllable experiences as unscientific. Sensual experience, extended and refined by the developed techniques of scientific perception, provides the intersubjective agency of decision about theories; but the path of science itself leads to the general, to constructive statements that have binding consequences for observable reality.

The concept of empirical science is familiar, much as any statement of its precise meaning may provoke controversy. We can ignore this, however, since our intention here is not epistemology but sociology. Our concern is not with the logic of scientific inquiry as such, but with an analysis of the social attitudes and institutions associated with different concepts of science. The concept of empirical science carries with it an experimental attitude of doubt and a rejection of all authorities, as well as institutions of debate and mutual criticism. We can use a familiar metaphor to illustrate this.

If a criminal trial is conducted on the principle of party presentation, its procedure follows almost exactly the rules of empirical science. This is especially the case when the evidence is circumstantial. A crime has been committed; from diverse observations the prosecution develops a theory from which it follows conclusively that the accused has committed it; the defense seeks to refute the theory by looking for observations that contradict it. In this manner, the criminal trial becomes a metaphor for the road to truth as well as for that to justice, and this means, for scientific method as well as for the regulation of social conflicts. The principle on which it is based is not to hold anything to be finally true and to regard even confirmed theories as but temporarily correct.

The institutions of science demonstrate that this concept has always found more critics than friends in Germany. It would be tempting to quote Hegel here, but we can equally effectively stay with two authors already familiar in this context, Humboldt and Dilthey. Their works are a century apart, but either of them documents in its own way the German idea of truth. Moreover, they can stand for many others who start out with a superior notion of the intrinsic insufficiencies of empirical science. Even Humboldt cannot conceal a patronizing superiority when he says: "We do not want to censure the effort to clarify and extend experience within its own sphere by any means. All empirical sciences, history, and the knowledge of nature, may proceed undisturbed in this way, and although in this form they do not constitute true science, they may yet contribute infinitely to its construction" (103, p. 313).

Humboldt stood at the beginning of the century often called, in retrospect, the century of natural science, although in Germany at least it is very questionable whether the label describes the facts. For Dilthey, a century later, the scorned notion of science was already identical with that of natural science. This narrow concept enabled Dilthey to spread the myth, for all disciplines that, without being natural sciences, follow similar methodological principles, of a "transfer of natural-science principles and methods" (60, p. xvi). In this way he added his own to the numerous bothersome dichotomies of German intellectual history: the "difference between our relation to society and to nature." "The facts of society are understandable to us from inside. . . . Nature is mute to us. . . . Nature is alien to us. For it is only an outside to us, no inside. Society is our world. We experience the play of interdependence in it with all the strength of our whole nature, since we perceive in ourselves from inside, in the most lively movement, the states and forces that make up its system" (60, p. 37).

And the "simpler peoples" whom German anthropology likes to describe as "natural"? And the biochemistry of human metabolism? And scientific neurology? That there are value judgments involved here, so that "external" means, if not evil, then at least "bad," and "internal," "good," is evident, and would hardly be denied by an author who revives the cave metaphor by describing "our image of nature" as a "mere shadow cast by a reality concealed to us" and confronts it with "reality as it is" which we have "merely in the facts of consciousness given in inner experience" (60, p. xviii).

Humboldt and Dilthey are clearly right in pointing out that experimental science does not provide the only access to truth (and that positivism, thus narrowly and dogmatically understood, is a particularly unimaginative fallacy). There are other ways of acquiring knowledge, among them divine revelation and artistic beauty as well as modes of thought one may call scientific. But the rejection of dogmatized empiricism can neither justify the rejection of all empiricism nor the construction—characteristic of both Humboldt and Dilthey— of a rank order of value of modes of knowledge in which the non-empirical favorites of the architects come out first.

Substantively, Humboldt and Dilthey recommend two very different remedies for the experimental approach, and if one wanted to do them justice as philosophers one would have to distinguish them carefully and analyze them extensively. But in their institutional and political consequences these recipes have much in common. "Genuine science must be pervaded and vitalized by the sense of a basic force, whose essence presents itself, as in a mirror, in an original idea, and it must attach to it the totality of phenomena. The path to this depth, the swing to this height, need not always be ventured, the circle not always be completed; but the avenues must remain open, the will to proceed on them must be present, and false pride in a worthless property must give way to the modest search for the genuine" (103, p. 313). Humboldt wants speculation, as he calls it himself, that is, classical metaphysics. For him, Kant is already superseded and metaphysics has been moved to its old, or possibly almost to its new Hegelian position.

For Dilthey, too, Kant is but a pathetic rationalist. "In the veins of the subject seeking knowledge as constructed by Locke, Hume, and Kant, there runs no real blood but the diluted juice of reason as a mere activity of the mind" (60, p. xviii). Dilthey, too, prefers a less rational epistemology; but his medicine is, rather than speculation, understanding, historical interpretation—*Verstehen*—or the triad of "facts, theorems, and value judgments and rules," that is, description, explanation, and judgment, connected by empathy. "Only if the theory of sentence, statement, and judgment, is informed by this insight, does an epistemological basis emerge that, instead of compressing the subject matter of the humanities into the narrow search for uniformities by analogy to natural science and thus mutilating it, understands and grounds it as it has grown" (60, p. 27).

Speculation and understanding, apart from being answers to the same alleged malady of science, have this in common: their results, the propositions emerging from them, cannot be refuted by intersubjective experience. From speculative or interpretive statements nothing follows for the real world in which we are living. They may be true, but they remain arbitrary; for they do not appeal to our reason or experience, thus not to the rational side of our existence, but to our sense of evidence or our benevolence. The "sciences" that emerge from such methodological preferences may be poetic and pleasing, profound and thought-provoking, but they are lacking in definiteness and in reality, that is, they are lacking in necessity.

This is, once again, not to deny the legitimacy of non-experimental modes of knowledge. These (like all others) are a subject of critical attack in our context only when they are dogmatized; for it is then that their institutional implications have detrimental political consequences. This was the case with the non-experimental concept of science in German universities throughout the nineteenth century. The philosophical faculty, in which speculation and understanding had their home, occupied the center of the academic corporation. The natural sciences, equally misunderstood in their methods by positivists and by humanists, gradually grew out of the philosophical faculties after 1863, without ever acquiring a more than marginal position in German universities. Characteristically, the technical disciplines were, in Humboldt's conception, defined out of the universities into special technical academies; a growing part of basic research followed after the foundation of the Kaiser Wilhelm Society in 1911. The social sciences, claimed by the humanities and thereby hampered in their chances of experimental development, fared even worse; they had to subsist at the margin of all other faculties, unless they betrayed their own potential. Such institutional developments may well be a contributing cause of the rather backward state of social psychology and economics, anthropology and sociology, social statistics and political theory, criminology and medicine in Germany.

But there are other institutional consequences of the dominance of an anti-experimental conception of science in Germany, which lead us even closer to the thread of our argument. All science needs liberty; but the combination of solitude and liberty demanded by Humboldt is certainly more useful for speculation and historical understanding than for experiment and empirical research. Indeed, it is difficult to dismiss the suspicion that for the humanities an "inner freedom" that allows the scholar to work in peace is sufficient, whereas the experimental sciences necessarily require the political freedom that permits publicity and exchange.

Under conditions of freedom thus understood, even the problem of scientific objectivity, which has vexed humanistic scholars in Germany for so long, would lose its urgency. If one wants to be free in solitude, one must, of course, try to produce within oneself a sterile equilibrium of objectivity, that *Ding an sich* of the psychology of science; by contrast, a social structure that might be described as one of dispute and liberty produces what objectivity it is possible to reach almost by itself, as the fallible but open result of mutual criticism. Solitude and liberty is a principle that allows the individual scholar to fence himself in and thus further the subdivision of the world into innumerable little front gardens, one of which is allotted to each scholar with his Ph.D. subject to put up his garden dwarfs in, after he has made sure in the property register of the history of science that nobody else could possibly advance a claim for his particular lot. Experimental science does not permit such fencing-in; it demands, on the contrary, that one tackle subjects of research on which others have worked before, so that accepted theories may, if possible, be refuted. In this sense, experimental science may appear a rather destructive business; its greatest triumphs lie in the defeat of seemingly proved laws. Correspondingly, speculation and understanding have, for more naïve minds, a tranquilizing flavor of the constructive; their insights are never made at the expense of others.

It is no accident that this appearance reminds one of ideologies of political conflict. The two notions of science we have contrasted here, the experimental and the German, have political consequences as well as political implications. One of them has already been mentioned. Research in the humanities may be conducted in the quiet chamber, thus under authoritarian and even totalitarian political conditions; empirical sciences can thrive only in a liberal political context, unless they violate their own rules of the game. But the contrast has a more subtle implication, which we have intimated in our polemics against Humboldt's "liberty and helpful solitude." The method of empirical science is strictly analogous to that of the political constitution of liberty. Knowledge by conflict corresponds to government by conflict. More precisely, knowledge in the empirical sciences is possible only through the concert of the many: interrelations between scholars, which assume manifold forms from co-operation through competition to conflict. Of these forms, the principle of conflict, that is, the refutation of theories held to be confirmed, is the most important for the progress of knowledge. Cumulation of knowledge comes about from the supersession of old theories by new and generally better ones. At any given time, a lively conflict of minds provides the market of science with the best possible result of knowledge.

The forms of organization suggested by the self-appointed "real" sciences are very different in kind. If everybody cultivates his own little garden, there will be some who manage to do this better than others ("good" and "bad" being debatable matters of taste, of course). Others imitate them in other places. In this manner, "schools" emerge, which derive from individual "teachers" as "authorities." Knowledge in the sense of both speculation and understanding does not require debate. If such nevertheless takes place, it inevitably assumes the form of personally injurious scholarly polemics. Essentially, however, knowledge is a matter for the individual and his concentration on his problem. It requires those virtues

for which older German scholarship was rightly praised—
profoundness of thought and thoroughness of work. Experimental imagination and theoretical brilliance, on the other
hand, are praised rather more rarely in German science.
Knowledge in the sense of the speculative or historical humanities is thus by its very social structure not far removed
from the structures of teaching. It, too, involves a drop of
authority, or suggests it at least; it also lacks the lively dynamics of knowledge in the experimental natural and social
sciences. This may well be the missing reason for the persistent inclination of German universities to their own conservative side, as well as for the contribution of German
scholarship to that nostalgia for synthesis that makes it hard
for liberal political institutions to gain a hold.

If we permit ourselves—for experimental reasons, of course
—a moment of speculation, we may surmise that, underlying
the different traditions of science and their organizational
and theoretical consequences, are different ideas of truth.
"The whole is the untrue," Theodor W. Adorno says in a
sentence that, quoting himself, he uses as the motto of his
Aspekte der Hegelschen Philosophie [Aspects of Hegelian
Philosophy]. Neither Hegel nor Adorno have let this consideration prevent them from consistently reaching for the imaginary whole, versions of which constitute the goals of speculation and understanding as well. James B. Conant has a
point when he remarks that in Germany people refer "with
enthusiasm to the 'total image,' the 'great order,' the 'great
overview,' to what is 'universally valid,' and they feel a certain
disquiet about the confusing and somewhat disorderly diversity and ambiguity of things and events" (40, p. 8).

We have spoken of the fundamental uncertainty of human
existence with respect to justice and truth. This assumption
not only provides a basis for the theory of government by
conflict, the meaning of the experimental approach in science
may also be derived from it. If truth cannot be known, or if
at least we cannot know whether what we know is true, then
we have to find ways and means to avoid dogmatizing the
false. One may call this attitude critical, if the concept is used
in the sense of Kant and Karl Popper, rather than in that of
Bruno Bauer and Adorno.

The counterconcept is not easily formulated. What Popper
calls the "theory of manifest truth" (cf. 176), the conviction
that reason and senses put us in the position to acquire true

knowledge and only a "conspiracy" of internal and external circumstances can prevent truth from becoming manifest, concerns a part of German science, above all classical empiricism. But while by some strange inconsistencies classical empiricism could have those enlightened and liberal consequences that Popper concedes to the Cartesian errors, speculation as well as empathetic understanding in the German sense are characterized by a variant of the theory, which might be called the elite theory of manifest truth. There may be certainty; but there cannot be certainty for all. In historical fact at least some are called upon to discover and communicate such certainty; thus some acquire an especially intimate relation to truth.

Speaking of "acquiring" this relation is sociologically imprecise, of course. Like "charismatic leader," "genius" is presumably an ascribed social position, and it is this quality, rather than intellectual craftsmanship, that opens the gates to the sanctums of knowledge. The Calvinism of this notion goes further: one cannot be sure whether one has genius; not everybody who seeks truth, finds it; success alone reveals the chosen few; meanwhile the many have to console themselves with an ideology of the "search for truth":

> Whoever searches tirelessly,
> to him salvation comes.

Speaking of genius has gone out of fashion nowadays, but the theory according to which truth becomes manifest to the chosen few, continues to flavor many works of the non-experimental sciences.

The term "elite" as such implies neither praise nor condemnation. In so far as speaking of an elite theory of manifest truth is meant critically, it is not the elite, but the privilege of certainty that prompts our doubts. But the elite theory of manifest truth has an immediate relevance for the ways in which political decisions are made in Germany, that is, for leadership. The political application of this theory documents and at the same time explains a notorious German misunderstanding of the relation between theory and practice. Schelsky has characterized contemporary society as a "scientificated world," in which even the primary experience of men is preformed by categories of science, and science and reality merge in the self-awareness of people, as knowledge and decision do in the political order of society (cf. 192 and 194).

Might it not be that here again Schelsky describes less a general feature of the times than a trauma of German reality, which is made to appear legitimate by its generalization?

The distinction between the expert and the actor is simple; the rational relation between the two, obvious. The knowledge the expert can impart enters into the conditions surrounding the actor's decisions. Sensible decisions require careful information about possible consequences. But information and decision cannot replace each other. The substitution of decision for information has at least an intellectual history in Germany, as Christian von Krockow has shown in his analysis of the "decisionists" Ernst Jünger and Carl Schmitt. But here we are concerned with the other, structurally more interesting fallacy, the apparent replacement of decision by information, that is, the search for the expert in decision-making.

This search has two very different sides, although a common error connects them. If we say that somebody knows something well, this may refer to a definite area of knowledge, such as economic theory or machine-tool construction or perhaps strategy. It would cause surprise and raise objections in Germany if the minister of justice were an economist, the minister of economic affairs a classical philologist, and the minister of science a peasant, or if the trained economist became the technical executive, and the trained engineer the business executive of an enterprise. Objections would be unjustified; the dilettant may prove an excellent actor, the more so if his department is far removed from what he has learned. It is rather small-minded to mistrust men as soon as they leave the narrow field they may well have studied for more or less accidental reasons. On the other hand, expertise need not disqualify for decision, of course, and it is at least understandable in view of the complexities of leadership in the modern world that there is a search for the expert.

But the principle becomes suspicious if the things people know well include the great uncertainties of our existence, that is, if the search is extended to those who are experts in truth, in justice, perhaps in decision. Yet this inclination, too, is characteristic of German society. Political discussion is dominated by the search for the specialist of the general, for those who are specially qualified for the necessarily diffuse tasks of leadership; and the same error occurs in non-political institutions as well. While most of us may remain in a world of uncertainty—so one could formulate the rationale of this attitude—some have certainty. Thus, rather than pursuing abstract goals, such as establishing the freedom of accepted conflict, political institutions ought rather to help in the search for the "right people," that is, the experts of certainty. Authority belongs to them, for they are made for its possession.

In terms of such misunderstanding of expertise, even the more specific expert begins to look suspect: the scientist whose opinion determines the outcome of the trial, the industrial-sociologist-become-executive on the dubious basis of his diagnosis of, say, the causes of labor turnover, the economist as minister of economic affairs, and the general as minister of defense. Whoever prefers experts in all positions, removes decisions from general control and takes a big step toward the formation of an authoritarian oligarchy. The expert as actor must make decisions that can in no way be derived from his specialist knowledge; yet his specialist knowledge constitutes a possibly welcome veil, which removes these decisions from the public eye. Even in the most favorable case the society run by experts is not a world of technical necessities praised by the technocrats of the scientificated world, but an authoritarian order, which gives the few their rights at the expense of the many.

In its political version the elite theory of manifest truth means, above all, the distrust of common sense. This distrust is one of the widespread German ideologies, and it assumes ever new forms and versions. Every man has an ability to make decisions, to distinguish right and wrong, to carry his judgment to the market of political conflict. It does not invalidate this judgment that it is mixed with self-interest, prejudice, and many other so-called "subjective" motives; plain subjectivity is preferable by far to its camouflaged version decorated by refined ideologies. Thus common sense is not in itself a source of truth or of certainty. It means little more than the ability to represent a self-interest, enlightened by recognition of useful rules of the game. In Germany, not only is it frequently doubted that every man has an ability of this kind, but a political system that is supposed to work by the market competition of such crude talents is ridiculed. This is understandable. Corresponding to the applied elite theory of manifest truth is the belief in the continued minority of those who live far away from all certainty; this useful ideology is threatened by common sense as well as by equality of opportunity.

But we are here concerned primarily with the German idea of truth as a way of dealing with social conflict. Science may be understood as the transposition of the rules of the game of liberal democracy to the realm of knowledge; in both areas, the principle holds that human existence is constitutionally uncertain. Since we cannot have truth we need the institutions of conflict that prevent the dogmatization of error. The German idea of truth is, however, not precluded from all. For the speculative mind and the empathetic understanding there is a way to certain knowledge, at least for the chosen few. Since in the history of modern German universities this concept of science has outdone the other, more experimental one, we cannot be surprised that the institutions of critical empiricism never gained a hold either. In Germany's institutions of higher learning the forms that demand or at least permit a drop of authority between teachers and student have had the greatest chances of survival. These include academic teaching and those types of science that promote the formation of schools. The authority drop reflects the assumed hierarchy of access to truth, so that the lack of an experimental attitude and the distrust of common sense may be called causes of the hierarchical stagnation of the German university. But the effects of such deficiencies go further. The absence of institutionalized liberal procedures in the academic sphere is one of the structural obstacles to liberal democracy in Germany.

It would be vain to expect much understanding for the statement that family and school, church and university, are institutions in which conflicts have to be regulated and whose structure may therefore reflect the constitution of political democracy. Such lack of understanding is not strictly a German problem either—even in the perspective of this study there are some problems that are not German—but one of everyday language. Whoever hears the word "conflict" is led to think of violence, bloodshed or at least strife, threats and ultimatums, demonstrations and riots. Yet there are reasons why we are using the term here in a wider sense. Negotiation, discussion, dispute, threat of violence, demonstration, and armed clash as well as many other phenomena of social discord may all fruitfully be understood as manifestations of the same social force we call conflict, and they constitute only a limited catalogue of its direct expressions. A single theory may therefore include their causes as well as the chances of their regulation, and thus at least by implication the significance of conflict in non-political institutions for the social foundation of liberal democracy.

With respect to industry, however, it might appear superfluous to emphasize this wide concept of conflict. Even those who otherwise prefer to interpret the world in terms of harmony and order cannot deny the existence of conflict in industrial enterprises. Here we find violence too, political general strikes that paralyze the life of a nation, lockouts on the part of employers, which may be enforced by an armed works-police force. We shall see as we go on that in industry, too, there are many more quiet, almost inaudible and yet effective manifestations of conflict. However, the cruder manners of industrial relations are no doubt the reason why the translation of political concepts to the field of industry is almost as old as industry itself.

Among these concepts there is, above all, that of "industrial democracy" (frequently reinterpreted in Germany as either "works' democracy" or "economic democracy")—a notion that since it was launched in the great work of Sidney and Beatrice Webb, has assumed almost as many nuances of meaning as the idea of "political democracy." Is there at least one of these nuances that has proved useful? Is there one that may guide us both in arranging industrial relations rationally and in constructing them in such a way that they support the institutions of political democracy? And is this rational version of industrial democracy its German version too?

If the purpose of industrial democracy is to prevent industrial civil war, that is, strikes and lockouts, the Federal Republic of Germany need not fear comparison with other countries. Since the Second World War, the number of strikes and lockouts, the number of those involved in them, and the number of workdays lost by such strife were all lower in Germany than in comparable countries. Comparing the Federal Republic with some countries of approximately equal size in the years from 1955 to 1961 may give an indication of this fact (cf. 208):

Country	Employees involved (annual average)	Workdays lost (annual average)	Empl. involv. workdays lost
Germany	137,000	637,000	4.7
France	1,523,000	2,196,000	1.5
Great Britain	762,000	4,154,000	5.4
Italy	1,761,000	6,202,000	3.5
Japan	1,255,000	5,102,000	4.1

This table tells more than one story. The relation between employees involved and workdays lost, for example, betrays the comparatively great significance of short-term political strikes in France and Italy as against more long-term work disputes in Great Britain and the Federal Republic. If one were to add figures for the United States, Canada, and Australia, one might even be tempted to work out an average strike frequency characteristic of functioning liberal democracies. But here we are concerned with the more specific conditions of Western Germany. How peaceful conditions are in West German industry remains conspicuous by comparison not merely to other countries, but to the German past as well. In the years from 1920 to 1924, for example, the annual average of strikers amounted to nearly 13 million, the number of workdays lost to nearly 20 million (which means

a quotient of 1.5—as in France after the Second World War!).
By contrast to their fellows in the Weimar Republic, as well
as in most other industrial countries of the present, the majority of German workers today have never experienced a strike
or a lockout.

Are these facts the result of a working system of industrial
democracy in Germany? Here, the comparisons raise some
doubts and suggest that other factors must be at work as well;
but let us follow our thread until it tears by itself. Otto Neuloh
uses an illustrative metaphor to describe the history of industrial relations in Germany in what he himself calls "a
greatly simplified sketch," which "cannot correspond to the
highly differentiated reality of the process," but which nevertheless provides a useful point of departure:

> The play begins with a long monologue by the entrepreneur
> whose commands are executed by mute creatures. Then the
> state enters the scene. Its occasional dialogue with the entre-
> preneur is accompanied by the slowly forming social move-
> ment, as by the approach of a thunderstorm. In the third act,
> the conversation between entrepreneur and state is frequently
> interrupted by disturbances and interventions of a third
> partner of social and political activity, the parties and the
> trade unions. The scenery changes, in that the weight of con-
> flict is shifted, with the state taking more or less of a hand
> in it, to the relation between employer and worker, until the
> state itself negotiates with the employers' opponents, first in a
> very conciliatory, later in a hostile mood. In the third phase,
> one finally sees them all sitting at one table under the threat
> of a danger threatening them all, war. The worker, represented
> by his union, gradually acquires equal rights and an immedi-
> ate representative in the enterprise, the works councilor. New
> percussions of a political and social nature finish the talk at
> the round table. Disobedience by workers is answered by the
> closing-down of the factory by the employer. The act ends in
> an economic catastrophe, from which a new power over-
> shadowing all others draws the advantage of complete domin-
> ion of economic and social life. The employer is reinstituted
> in his old rights, but subjected to permanent control in their
> execution.
> The last act begins with a monologue of the trade union,
> now under the control of a foreign overlord, until the em-
> ployer, supported by the order of the gradually restrengthened
> state, returns as a negotiating partner of the unions in a re-
> verse relation of recognition from before. Clashes about the
> distribution and relative weight of the mutual roles are often

influenced by the state as the referee of the power struggle, but they remain undecided. In the minor parts of this clash the churches, the parties, science, research, and the public appear. (161, pp. 11 f.)

This dramatic metaphor has its greatest interest for us between the lines. For example, the importance of the national motive as an overpowering impersonal destiny, which breaks through at several points, is familiar to us from other contexts and will occupy us again. Here I want to use Neuloh's presentation to make points not intended by its author that nevertheless describe industrial relations in Germany in terms of their mastery of social conflict.

One of the characteristic features of the entire history of industrial relations in Germany is that it may be described as a series of surgical operations on the structure of industrial enterprises. While Neuloh refers to the round table at which all concerned are sitting, and to negotiating partners, the frequent mention of the state leaves no doubt that we are facing massive government interference all the way. The subject of attack of such interference provides the central theme of Neuloh's own research: the "constitution of the enterprise" (*Betriebsverfassung*), which he has supplemented recently by the "style of the enterprise," which includes its legal basis as well as its social reality. Instead of industrial relations, the main issue in all clashes between employers and workers in Germany was and is the constitution of industrial enterprise.

One has to realize its alternatives in order to recognize the peculiarity of this approach. Industrial relations mean that, while all parties accept existing property relations and the legal as well as social structures of enterprises as they are, the conflicts of interests continually arising from them are regulated in institutions of negotiation, conciliation, and (voluntary) arbitration. The approach of those involved in German industry is characteristically different. Here, the search for ways and means to change the internal structure of economic enterprises dominates, since all participants expect such changes to mitigate, if not abolish altogether all work disputes.

In Neuloh's presentation, the different stages of the constitutional history of German industry are invariably recognizable by the appearance of "the state" on the scene. Even in Imperial Germany, legislation restricted entrepreneurial

rights. More far-reaching interventions occurred in the unstable years after the First World War; the council ("Soviet")
idea had the strongest effects here. One lasting heritage of
the German council movement is the institution of works
councils (*Betriebsrat*) which were originally set up in all
enterprises with twenty, and today with five employees.

First stipulated in 1920 and enriched with new substance
after the Second World War, the works council is by law given
the double task of defending the interests of employees vis-à-
vis the employers on the one hand, and of supporting the
employer in realizing the purposes of the enterprise on the
other. The latter aspect of the explosive role of works councilors elected by the employees involves specific tasks, particularly in the sensitive area of hiring and firing. The
National Socialist regime replaced such representative side-
hierarchies by other, more partisan and authoritative ones.
But after the Second World War they re-emerged and were
indeed supplemented by the last great act of government
interference in the constitution of enterprises, the right of
co-determination in heavy industry. Since 1951 the boards of
coal mining and steel firms have been composed of equal
numbers of representatives of the shareholders and the employees (plus a supposedly neutral "thirteenth man" as chairman); furthermore, one of the executives, invested with the
full rights of this position, has to be a labor manager (*Arbeits-
direktor*) who may not be appointed against the votes of
the labor representatives on the board. Initiatives on the part
of individual entrepreneurs, also directed to changes in the
constitution of enterprises, might be added to this list of
government initiatives, for the various experiments of co-
ownership and shared administration of enterprises, often
described by the notion of "partnership," also transcend the
proper sphere of industrial relations.

Between the lines of Neuloh's parable appears a second
peculiar feature of the history of industrial relations in Germany: industrial relations are largely settled on two levels,
that of the state on the one hand, and that of the individual
enterprise on the other. At first sight the two appear to be
incompatible; but the fact that preference for regulations on
the level of the individual enterprise is often, as in the case of
co-determination, the result of government initiatives proves
how easily this division of labor works in its co-operative
aspect as well.

We have seen earlier that the economy of Imperial Germany had, from the beginning, certain state socialist traits. With the single (if for that very reason remarkable) exception of the Federal Republic after 1949, these elements of state socialism have grown in strength throughout the century. They include compulsory arbitration by government agencies, in the Weimar Republic as well as the German Labor Front under National Socialism, and the conversion of nearly all firms into the so-called People's Own Enterprises in the DDR. However, so long as this state socialism did not turn totalitarian, it was coupled with another tendency, which may almost be called syndicalist, and which gave the individual enterprise considerable scope in settling problems of industrial relations within its own boundaries.

Once again, the peculiarities of German methods stand out most clearly if we contrast them with alternative possibilities. The point about the subdivision of attention between the state and the enterprise is that, in this way, the whole area between the two—that of industrial relations in the strict sense—is bound to remain underdeveloped. This is the level on which workers organized in trade unions meet with entrepreneurs organized in employers' associations, the level of conflicts involving whole branches of industry, or regions, or occupational groups. Here as elsewhere reality is, of course, not as extreme as such simplifications may make it appear. Many wage disputes in Germany are, in fact, settled on the level of industrial relations; in the Federal Republic, there is a clear tendency to expand this intermediate area. But the assertion is still valid that, in the history of German industry, all participants—workers organized in unions, employers organized in associations, and the state—have avoided as best they could the level of autonomous industrial relations and preferred other ways of dealing with conflict.

The result of such preferences is regrettable. It has led, in the first place, to the absence of a developed rational system of industrial relations in which it is possible to canalize and thereby control conflicts. Instead, we find more and more indistinct and costly structures of industrial organization, which do not serve anybody concerned. There are traces everywhere of the deep aversion of all participants in industry to conflict, and the untiring search for ultimate solutions. Industrial democracy in Germany has always been the search for an industrial utopia. Changes were motivated by the reach for solutions that might be once and for all, that is, the same search for certainty and the same fear of the contradictory diversity of reality that, in another dress, determines German science. Here, as there, this does not provide a condition for the establishment of the principle of liberal democracy in the political community.

These are far-reaching statements, which may well appear unwarranted in view of the comparative strike statistics of the postwar era. To support them we need more evidence as well as a theoretical presupposition that, while it is not undisputed, especially in German sociology, is nevertheless unrefuted and has considerable explanatory power.

Why are conflicts between employers and workers a persistent reality of the industrial world? One can no longer assume today that the answer may be found in the social condition of the working class. Work disputes have ceased to be motivated by claims for the physical subsistence minimum of the workers; instead, they are about the maintenance and improvement of the standard of living, indeed about a share in the profits of the firms. This has led industrial sociologists to suspect that in many disputes wages have an indirect and symbolic rather than an immediate function. Money is the lingua franca of the economy; in it one expresses less what one wants than that one wants something; thus workers translate all their wishes and complaints into the vernacular of financial demands.

Property relations as such do not explain industrial conflicts either. Strikes may, of course, be outlawed; but even in Communist countries we know that workers advance demands in many concealed and in as many ritualized open forms. The riots of June 1953 have shown that in the DDR the People's Own Enterprises are no solution to industrial conflicts. The many variations of private, mixed, and public property in economic enterprises in the modern world have not abolished the clashes between those who stand above and those who are below. And the same is true of the constitution of the enterprise and trade cycles, systems of industrial relations and changes in the technical basis of production: not one of these factors decides the presence or absence of industrial conflict.

It seems likely, therefore, that industrial conflict is built into the structure of enterprises; and the relevant feature of this structure would seem to be power and its distribution.

There are industrial conflicts because enterprises are held together by power; there will be industrial conflicts so long as
no other way of co-ordinating them is invented. Neither
conflict nor power mean the same under all conditions; there
are numerous and, as we can see now, mutually dependent
manifestations of both. In his *Work and Authority in Industry,*
Reinhard Bendix has distinguished four ideal types of the
structure of power, which he exemplifies by industrial organization in England and Russia in the nineteenth century,
and in the United States and the DDR today. But Bendix
also assumes that "wherever enterprises are set up, a few com-
mand and many obey" (17, p. 1). The dividing line between
rulers and ruled at the same time marks the front of industrial
conflict, with the service class of white-collar workers who
have an often minimal share in the exercise of authority blur-
ring the picture somewhat.

Power also provides the most general issue of industrial
conflict; ultimately, it is always the distribution of power and
its legitimacy that are at stake. In contrast to those of politics,
however, an element of incurable hopelessness is built into
industrial conflicts. Possibly the management of economic
enterprises is more clearly dependent on continuity and competence—as distinct from common sense—than that of the
political community. But above all there is the right of control
conferred by property, whether public or private, decentralized or monopolistic; and this gives economic enterprises
something of the character of colonial territories: their leaders have to look not only to those they lead, but also to the
proprietors. For this reason industrial firms do not permit a
clash of parties based on the possibility that government and
opposition change places every now and again. In industry,
both government and opposition are permanent. I suspect
that this structurally predetermined drop of authority is the
reason why even the most rational system of industrial relations cannot hope to prevent violent conflict—strike and lockout—in industry altogether.

German industry, however, has a long way to go before it
reaches this most rational system. A second look at some of
the characteristic methods of industrial democracy in Germany will soon prove this point. The works council is, as
Friedrich Fürstenberg has plausibly put it, a "border institution" in the triangle of management, labor, and trade unions.
On the explosive borderline between management and labor

it has taken over from the foreman his most unrewarding tasks and itself moved into the "cyclist's position" of the man in the middle: bending its back to the handlebars above, but treading on the pedals below. Works councilors may, of course, behave otherwise, and they frequently do, but as long as it remains possible for each side to ascribe the council to the other as a kind of double scapegoat, they can contribute little to the canalization and regulation of conflicts.

In addition, they lean heavily on a third side, which also leans on them—the unions. The law does not stipulate anything about the union membership of works councilors; while many, especially in large enterprises, are union members, there is also the official union representative in the enterprise. Thus representation is sufficiently confused to make the response of a steelworker who was interviewed about the tasks of the works council symptomatic, if not typical: "They are supposed to represent and realize our demands before the powers that be, or at least make it clear to them who is in the wrong. But everything passes without a song. They get wonderful posts and do not want to commit themselves 100 per cent. This is what I condemn about the German trade union" (177, p. 210). And from here it is only a step to bitter resignation: "Once they have feathered their nests, you know how it is. If they have their contract [!] in their pocket, that is all they care about for them for the time being; they hardly bother about the worker. . . . The works councilors get their 500 to 600 marks a month and stick to their place, of course, like stockfish" (177, p. 203).

Undeniably the works council has found its place in the constitutional reality of German enterprises. Possibly it is more efficient in some respects than the traditional foreman as he exists elsewhere. This might hold with respect to passing on information, not merely from the top to the bottom but even more from the bottom up, and also in regard to mediation in personal quarrels, and possibly even in the way in which hiring and firing is handled. But all these laudable effects of the border institution leave the other, more important task of industrial relations unsolved.

In a short-term sense, the works council is possibly more useful for management than the shop stewards and stewards in England and the United States or the *comités d'entreprise* in France, because it is more easily manipulated; for the effective control of industrial conflicts, however, and thus in the long run for all concerned, the unambiguous roles of stewards as representatives of the workers' interests and little else, are certainly preferable to the ambiguities in the works councilor's role.

Essentially the same is true of the institutions of co-determination in the German coal and steel industry. In so far as the new institutions have proved useful, this was generally unintentional; in respect to the intentions behind them, they have done more harm than good. Thus, it is argued in favor of a board of directors composed of equal numbers of workers' and shareholders' representatives that most of these boards did not experience a single contested vote in ten years' practice. But can anybody be satisfied if a union leader consents today to the annual balance of a firm, including the dividend, in order to attack tomorrow before his members the profits of entrepreneurs and their unfair distribution?

It is sometimes entered on the credit side of co-determination that the boards have proved a useful forum for discussions of all controversial issues between management and labor. This may well be the case; it presumably enables boards of directors to act as a mediating institution in industrial conflict. But who then carries out the proper tasks of the board, which have, after all, not been invented at random? Possibly, a growing proportion of labor representatives on the boards of coal and steel firms will in due course be qualified for these tasks too. In 1956, very nearly one third (31.5 per cent) of the 574 directors of this group were skilled workers or mining foremen; even at that time these were balanced by numerous union employees (22 per cent) and other white-collar workers (14 per cent); and again almost one third of all employees' representatives on boards of directors consisted of top-level administrators, executives, higher civil servants, ministers, or academic experts (31.9 per cent). Representation certainly does not mean statistical representativeness; and it is hard to avoid the suspicion that the less the directors represent specific group interests, the better they do their jobs, and vice versa. But who, then, represents the vital interests of employees without the admixture of responsibility for the management of the enterprise, and where and how?

The labor manager is hardly in a position to do so. On the contrary, it is equally true of him that the less he plays his role as representative of the interests of labor, the better he administers his office. It is a hopeful sign therefore in terms of the office that even in 1956 almost one half of the ninety-six labor managers were recruited from the higher civil service, top-level white-collar occupations, the professions, and academic and technical positions.

Theo Pirker has pointed out that the labor manager has filled a gap in the role system of the German enterprise by assuming the function of the personnel manager, well known in other countries for some time (cf. 170). This is, of course, a perfectly normal executive position. Possibly labor managers can fill it particularly well because of the way the position is guaranteed by the law and the method of their appointment. But these unintended useful consequences of reform have little to do with the idea of co-determination; indeed, since all these unintended successes must by the same token disappoint the expectations of legislators, lobbies, and the workers themselves, they serve to worsen instead of improve a condition that is unsatisfactory in any case. In the place of rational regulation and open conflict we find confused fronts and attitudes of insecurity and resentment.

Quotations are no proof; but this is the mood of one out of every four of the six hundred steelworkers interviewed by Popitz about co-determination:

> The employees are supposed to co-determine with capital. They are supposed to control the initiatives of capital. But that we shall never get, for money rules the world. . . . Whatever has happened so far, has been done by capital. In reality they say: "We decide and nobody else." That would be even nicer than nice.

> The workers' representatives may be bribed. Where there is money, there is power. And if the workers' representatives have really pushed through a decision, one can rig the working-out of it in such a way that nothing comes of it.

> All that is merely talk. We have nothing to co-determine. This has been managed by the unions, and if anybody co-determines, it is at best the union functionaries and bosses. . . . Those up there do not care anyway.

> One only wants to pacify the workers. They are to think that now they are well off. But in reality they are only tolerated up there. . . . The works council has its people sitting on the board. But how are they supposed to open their mouths there? . . . In reality it is only capital that governs. Labor cannot compete. (177, pp. 202 f.)

These quotations are not taken from the most radical quarter in terms of Popitz's typology. They show that the unintended uses of co-determination are more than balanced by the (equally unintended) harm done in the very area for which they were intended. Much the same is true for other efforts in the same direction, such as union programs to put property in workers' hands, or experiments of individual entrepreneurs in shared ownership and partnership administration. They all may produce good effects in unexpected quarters; but in respect to the order of industrial relations they do little but harm.

Under these conditions—or, rather, if this analysis is correct—we must wonder why this search for the Holy Grail continues to find so many supporters in German industry. Employers may view the extension of co-determination critically today, but in 1951 they accepted without protest the law jointly passed by the Christian Democratic Union (CDU) and the Social Democratic Party (SPD). The unions still regard changes of the constitution of the enterprise as a core of their program. And even those concerned, the workers, have preserved, underneath all disappointment, a desire for an arrangement of industrial things that overcomes the dichotomy of Above and Below. If there is any conclusion to be drawn from empirical studies of co-determination in Germany, it is that while the workers are generally dissatisfied with the practice of co-determination (about whose details they know very little) they still approve of this principle. Where does this love of utopia stem from?

It is certainly insufficient to quote Kant here once again: "Man wants concord. . . ." But the quotation has its justice, for it explains why the constitutional history of German industry is of great interest all over the world. However, apart from the general, there is the specific side: German man wants concord above all. This is a very crude generalization, which obviously applies neither to all nor to everything. Opinion surveys have shown, for example, that the majority (57 per cent) does not regard a strike to achieve the forty-hour week as justified, but a similar majority (52 per cent) would support a strike to prevent nuclear armament of the German army. This is an interesting finding. One of its interpretations would be that the normal application of this industrial weapon to industrial problems is widely disapproved. During the prolonged wage dispute in the metal industry of

Baden-Württemberg in 1963, 39 per cent of a representative sample interviewed spoke out against the strike; 35 per cent were for it; 18 per cent remained undecided; and 8 per cent had never heard of it. Not surprisingly there were great differences in this respect between the adherents of different parties (*pro: contra,* CDU 23:46, SPD 59:28, FDP [Free Democratic Party] 11:72) and between various occupational groups (workers 52:32, white collar 34:41, self-employed 20:60).

In our context the answer to a long-term question is even more significant. People were asked whether they thought it likely that there would still be strikes in twenty, thirty years' time. Almost equal parts of the population answered in the affirmative, in the negative, or remained undecided (cf. 104, pp. 374 ff.). This is one of those findings that may be interpreted in several, and even contradictory ways; but there clearly are many who support the inherent tendency of industrial relations in Germany to try to solve conflicts once and for all. As a result, existing divisions are not regulated rationally, but repressed and redirected.

Much as the analysis of industrial relations in Germany may suggest this conclusion, it is clearly contradicted by the facts from which we set off. Comparative statistics of industrial disputes show a remarkably favorable picture for the Federal Republic. One might go further and argue with Neuloh that, until 1960, there was in German heavy industry "not a single strike since the introduction of co-determination, with the exception of a one-day stoppage of work to defend co-determination" (161, p. 55). How can these facts be reconciled with our analysis?

First of all, we have to explain the incidence of industrial disputes. Why, in the German Federal Republic, is the number of disputes decided by strike or lockout so low by comparison to other countries and also to the Weimar Republic? Five observations seem relevant for an explanation:

(1) West German economic development has experienced, since 1948, an unheard-of upswing from an extraordinarily low starting point; this also holds for private consumption. Even without growing incomes most people improved their standard of living consistently and noticeably after the currency reform, so that the sting was taken out of what dissatisfactions there were.

(2) But most incomes did not remain fixed by any means.

Since 1948, two thirds or more of all blue- and white-collar workers have received wage or salary increases each year. This testifies to an unusual readiness of the employers to accept, if not to anticipate, the demands of employees. There are other illustrations of this attitude. In the years of the Weimar Republic about 30 per cent of all strikes ended with the complete defeat of the employees, whereas in the Federal Republic (apart from the one great exception of the metal workers' strike in Schleswig-Holstein) this is true for only 5 per cent (208, p. 336).

(3) Increasing prosperity in a service-class society does not increase the sense of solidarity. Since prosperity is spread more evenly in Germany than in the comparable countries of Great Britain, France, Italy, and Japan, or than it was in the Weimar Republic, this is part of the explanation of industrial peace in Germany.

(4) Prosperity and the German version of industrial democracy both lead to the redirection of industrial conflicts, such as the translation of a collective situation into a mass of individual reactions. Thus we find instead of work disputes, individual actions whose connection with social conflicts is barely recognizable at first sight. Sinking work morale, growing fluctuation, indeed even sickness and accident rates may be indicators of such redirections of industrial conflict.

(5) In these manifestations, the redirection of conflicts (which has, after all, the effect of a safety valve) approaches repression of its energies. Some of the workers quoted before display an attitude of almost hopeless resentment; this may become manifest unannounced and in ways removed from all chance of control, such as wildcat strikes, or the election of declared Communists to works councils, and also political activity directed against the system as such.

All this means that the dislike of industrial disputes in Germany is no cause for satisfaction. It is a symptom of an unfortunately rigid and unimaginative attitude toward the adversities of industrial life that is often coupled with utopian hopes, and is for that very reason unprepared for real problems. A return of industrial unrest is much more probable than a new depression. If such a reappearance of internal disputes should turn out to have destructive consequences for German industry, this would be the result of the almost deliberate neglect of a modern and liberal system of industrial relations. As industrial utopia, industrial democracy destroys even its admittedly modest possibilities.

Our analysis must not be misunderstood as an argument against industrial democracy. The concept can certainly have a reasonable meaning. It may signify, for example, the right of industrial citizenship, that is, the institutional and factual creation of equal chances of participation for all involved in industry. In this respect, the constitution of industry has come a long way in Germany; indeed the very reforms we criticized so harshly have had their most beneficial effects in the creation of a general status of quasi citizenship in industry. The path from the authoritarian enterprise of the Wilhelminian era to the large enterprise of modern German industry is one of a nearly continuous destruction of traditional dependencies and authoritarian structures. Much as the voters may be disappointed by their representatives in works councils, boards of directors, and executive boards, they are, after all, able to elect them, and in this manner substitute active participation for passive acceptance. That there are relics of old dependencies, especially in smaller enterprises, and that here and there a new "industrial feudalism" with a new type of tie to particular firms is developing, does not alter the fact that industrial democracy in the sense of a condition of quasi citizenship is quite firmly established in Germany.

But chances of participation for citizens are of little use if they are not expressed in lively conflicts of interest. Even the effective equality of citizens loses its consequence if institutions of controlled conflict are missing. And they are missing in German society, outside as well as inside industry. Industrial relations are most fruitful for those concerned, and most effectively regulated, on the level of autonomous disputes between organized employees and organized employers. Tendencies toward such rationality are, however, still rare and atypical in the Federal Republic, and they meet with little understanding. Employers and workers alike prefer the utopian authoritarianism of union leaders like Georg Leber to the radical liberalism of Otto Brenner. As a result, the system of negotiation and conciliation has remained underdeveloped and dependent on intelligent ad hoc decisions; mediation by non-authorized persons with authority is an exception rather than the rule; the system of arbitration is barely developed and, where it does exist, works according to "legalistic" principles, which David Lockwood has shown are authoritarian by contrast to the more adequate principle of balancing interests (cf. 133). Where industrial democracy should prove itself, we find little more than improvisations in Germany.

The attempt to explain such deficiencies leads us back to our central thesis. In many areas of German society the institutions reveal a strangely rigid attitude, shifting between unreserved retention of the status quo and a grasp for the stars. But reality is always in movement; it requires more lively and liberal attitudes if its movement is not to gain power over us. This is particularly true for the economy. But the economy does not exist by itself. What happens in it, shapes in manifold ways the total structure of societies, including their political form. That an industrial utopia has taken the place of industrial relations in Germany is of more than symptomatic significance politically: the perfect constitution is preferred to lively disputes. Instead of the recognition of an uncomfortable, but free, reality, we find the search for the Grail whose motives are as noble as its effects are illiberal. This illiberalism recurs in the persistent neglect of the level of autonomous negotiations between the extremes of government authority and the individual enterprise. Industrial relations may be a source of inspiration for democratic methods, an illustration of their difficulties and shortcomings, but also of their adequacy and fruitfulness. They are not that in Germany. Instead they have become a model of the cost and error of the institutionalized fear of social conflict.

12. THE TRAGEDY OF THE
GERMAN LABOR MOVEMENT

The constitution of industrial relations in Germany may be traced back to the state socialism of the Imperial era. But its development received new and lasting impulses in the Weimar Republic, especially during its early years, from 1918 to 1920. These are the only years in which the labor movement was directly responsible for shaping the course of German history. Free trade unions and Social Democratic parties took up the thread of state socialism and tried, here as elsewhere, to recast tradition in their own mold, that is, to dye the thread new colors and, above all, to prevent it from breaking. This was an undertaking in which many eminent men, disappointed lovers of the German Empire, took part with new hope; it was also an undertaking that stimulated the enthusiasm of young intellectuals.

The emergent labor law offered open frontiers to some gifted young lawyers; it is not surprising that many of them had to leave the country after 1933, among them Ernst Fraenkel, Otto Kahn-Freund, Franz Neumann, Max Wolff, and others who were to make a mark, often as political scientists, in England or the United States. But even before their involuntary exile most of their enthusiasm for the social order of Weimar had cooled off; long before 1933 some of these men were disappointed by their own work. Franz Neumann, who re-examined the economic democracy of Weimar in a new light after the Second World War, fell into open self-criticism in the process:

> In pursuit of this goal [of economic democracy], trade-unions indeed became part and parcel of the administrative machine of the state. Their representatives were in labor courts, social insurance bodies, the national coal council, etc., without resigning their union position, thus maintaining a dual role of trade-union functionary and, in some way, official of the state. The question is whether this whole approach of transforming the trade-unions into semi-administrative bodies is beneficial to the interests of the working classes. What I

say is a kind of self-criticism, because I am in part responsible for the 1928 program of the trade-unions and drafted many of the laws the trade-unions put through.

It is therefore only consistent if Neumann observes of the postwar period:

It has become increasingly doubtful to me that any program of co-determination is viable and desirable, and I have become more and more convinced that in reality the program, far from achieving anything, may actually destroy the little militancy that is left in the German labor movement. (156, pp. 102 f.)

The trade unions did not listen to Neumann's warnings. But then, Neumann is discussing in personal and political terms a problem that has a social and historical dimension as well. We have seen that the unions were and still are among the main motors of a policy that distributes the weight of industrial democracy among two institutions, the state and the individual enterprise. This is a curious policy of self-denial; for where is the place of free unions if not between these two institutions, in the open country of economic and social divisions?

To be sure, the union's self-denial did not prevent them from securing a place for themselves in the two main regions of industrial utopia; formally and informally, they play an important part in the relevant agencies of the state as well as in individual enterprises. But even if one ignores the problematic consequences of such a policy for the regulation of industrial relations and for the maneuverability of the union movement, their attitude remains absurd: an organization founded to represent solidary interests within an institutional order deliberately pursues a policy that renders this very representation of interests pointless. It might be argued that if those points of their program dearest to German trade unions were realized, this would mean a decisive weakening of their own internal organization and the destruction of the only system of rules within which trade unions can act effectively. Put in a brief, and probably somewhat exaggerated polemical formula: In a country in which industrial relations are largely settled by the state or within the individual enterprise, it is relatively easy to nationalize the unions, or to abolish them. In the recent history of the country, German unions have had to suffer both these fates.

This is a harsh statement. Yet it holds in its basic figure (which one might be tempted to describe as a political death wish, and which must in any case be located beyond the pleasure principle) not only for trade unions, but for the German labor movement in general. German Social Democracy, too, has had a disturbing inclination to advance, with the best of intentions, political conceptions and methods that make the realization of these conceptions impossible. Thus there can be no doubt that the Social Democrats have needed political democracy at all times, and that they have desired and defended it at almost all times too; but the conception of state and society favored by them has, in fact, contributed to weakening the constitution of liberty whose weakness they have so persistently deplored. As driven by invisible demons, Social Democracy has time and again sought the goal of a free society with means that led in the opposite direction, and yet held on to both goals and means with equal and constant intensity of conviction. This is the tragedy of the German labor movement.

Before we elaborate and document this thesis, two reservations are needed to avoid misunderstandings. Here, as throughout this study, we are concerned with German phenomena. But I am not unaware of the fact that some of the things that exist in Germany may be found elsewhere as well. The fear of conflict and nostalgia for synthesis, for an authority above the troubled waters of political strife, for example, is a French problem too (indeed, a study of democracy in France would yield many common conclusions apart from some rather important differences). The tragedy of the labor movement, that is, its tendency to destroy by its choice of means its own goals and yet to hold firmly to both means and ends, is probably a German problem only in its specific expression, its language so to speak. In principle the indicated death wish governs at least all democratic socialist parties and, in a modified form, Communist parties as well. Thus in its polemical aspects our analysis is an attack on German Social Democracy only in the sense that it is an attack on the context in which the Social Democratic drama took its tragic course.

This leads to a second remark. It is almost suspicious by now to refer once again to the "tragedy" of a political movement; moreover, it is hardly fair to add yet another to the

increasingly numerous polemics against German Social Democracy. It sometimes appears that the German labor movement, in principle too fond of rather than averse to self-
criticism, has merely official friends and independent critics
left, for all its friends are also its members, whereas all who
are not members criticize it. But the German labor movement
is too diverse to deserve such uniform criticism; Lassalle's
Workers' Association and the Social Democratic Party (SPD)
whose representatives in 1933 opposed Hitler's Enabling
Law; the West German SPD and the East German Socialist
Unity Party (SED) have few features in common.

And the German labor movement has too many achievements to its credit to justify a critique as intense as this; it
was a mainstay of resistance against dictatorial tendencies in
Imperial Germany, against Nazi rule, and against the arbitrary rule of the SED. In addition, of course, an entire chapter could be written describing the labor movement's contribution to the establishment of citizenship rights in Germany;
these did not come about by themselves but required the concerted action of many groups, among which trade unions and
socialist parties occupy the most prominent place. Yet we
have to join the ranks of the many critics who have left no
phase of the development of the German labor movement
untouched by often relentless attacks. The critics range from
Guenther Roth (*The Social Democrats in Imperial Germany*)
by way of Erich Matthias ("Der Untergang der alten Sozialdemokratie, 1933" [The Downfall of the Old Social Democracy, 1933], and *Sozialdemokratie und Nation* [Social Democracy and Nation, On the History of Ideas of the Social
Democratic Emigration 1933–1938]) to Theo Pirker (*Die
SPD nach Hitler* [The SPD after Hitler]).

This list could easily be made ten and, with some effort, a
hundred times as long, for few subjects of recent German history have been studied and discussed as extensively as the
history of the labor movement. We will not be able to add
any evidence to these studies; but by drawing their findings
into our own context of analysis we may be able to gain a
new critical vantage point.

The path of the German labor movement may be described
as a series of misconceived necessities (which were perhaps
necessary misconceptions as well). These all follow the same
pattern: the labor movement needed the right, but sought

the false. The formula obviously involves a value judgment; but it is more than that. Any fruitful activity, if not the survival itself of trade unions requires a working system of industrial relations, but by their policies German unions have helped to prevent the emergence of such a system; analogously the labor movement as a whole showed a fatal tendency to prevent, unwillingly and sometimes willingly, the emergence of the only conditions under which it might become effective. There can be little doubt about the good intentions of the labor movement and its leaders. But even good intentions are apt to lead astray, as will become evident if we discuss the first of four significant contradictions in the history of unions and socialist parties: The German labor movement needed liberty, but it sought morals. This is an ambiguous formulation. It appears today that socialism has taken over the heritage of puritanism all over the world, whereas liberalism is sometimes confused with libertinism; but I mean neither one nor the other here. It may be clearer, therefore, to say that while the German labor movement always needed liberalism, it sought morality.

The combination of socialism and liberalism is surprising for at least two reasons. The first and more obvious one is that socialist organizations originate in the protest against the liberalism of a capitalist bourgeoisie. This is the self-interpretation of German Social Democracy too; we have yet to explore the reality corresponding to it in a country without either a classical bourgeoisie or a classical liberalism. It is nevertheless clear that socialist parties and trade unions in Germany (as elsewhere) never intended to be liberal in the sense of adopting an economic policy of non-interference, a domestic policy of support of autonomous social forces, or a constitutional policy of keeping the state weak; the "night-watchman's state" has remained a word of abuse in the dictionaries of socialists right down to the Godesberg Program of the SPD, and the same holds for many other fundamentals of a liberal view of society such as those of interests, competition, profit, private capital, and the like: "The interest of the whole must take precedence over the interest of the individual. In a society determined by the striving for profit and power, democracy, social security, and the freedom of the personality are threatened. Democratic socialism, therefore, aims at a new economic and social order" (19, p. 81).

The other reason why the combination of socialism and liberalism sounds improbable may be a little less obvious. We know today that the intellectual belief in the proletariat as a guardian of liberty is wishful thinking, clearly contradicted by reality. In fact, the lower strata are a seat of extremism rather than liberalism. S. M. Lipset summarizes the complex picture emerging from a large number of empirical studies: "The poorer strata everywhere are more liberal or leftist on economic issues; they favor more welfare-state measures, higher wages, graduated income taxes, support of trade unions, and so forth. But when liberalism is defined in non-economic terms —as support of civil liberties, internationalism, etc.—the correlation is reversed. The more well-to-do are more liberal, the poorer are more intolerant" (131, pp. 101 f.).

A concept of liberalism in which the welfare state appears as a liberal invention, is rather remarkable. It would seem far more plausible to attribute all the attitudes described by Lipset to a single syndrome, which Lipset himself has given the name "working-class authoritarianism." In their basic attitudes many workers are authoritarian; they have little respect for minorities and dislike political parties, they tend toward extremist organizations in politics and religion more pronouncedly than other groups, and many of them display character traits of the "authoritarian personality." In so far as the labor movement represents the lower strata, it can hardly be liberal.

Once again, representation need not mean representativeness; the labor movement might well have been liberal despite the preferences of its members. There are other arguments for such a course. Liberalism as we are using the word here has little to do with party politics and almost nothing with traditional liberal parties. Indeed, this liberalism may well be described as a necessary condition of social democratic politics; it is the principle that provides reason and rationale for the struggles of parties as such and that defines human liberty as the maintenance of alternative chances.

But in practice at least the German labor movement never accepted this principle. The Marxian denunciation of the liberal concept of freedom as "merely formal" and the demand for a more substantive notion of freedom, which promises more than chances, has remained a cornerstone of social democratic programs. Social Democracy has turned away from Marx only in that it has replaced historical necessity, that is, a blind law of development, by social justice, that is, a moral demand for human action.

To say that it has "only" done this may appear somewhat unfair; it certainly minimizes a great ideological and practical difference, but it also serves to emphasize a common feature, which may well be as significant as all differences. Liberty is not enough, it must be supplemented by justice; democracy is not enough, it must be filled with substance by socialism; liberalism is not enough, it must be replaced by morality—these are common convictions of the German labor movement in all its phases of development, and they are in practice convictions with at least a dangerous potential.

Liberalism and morality may become opposites. Whoever is not satisfied with the form of liberty, soon finds himself prescribing to people a substance that restricts and, in the limiting case, abolishes their choices. Whoever regards the form of democracy as merely an instrument for the realization of a definite political substance, runs the risk of destroying the form by dogmatizing the substance. There is an element of paternalism in every policy of morality, an element of dogmatism and of rigidity, of the grasp for substantively final solutions, for justice itself, which must yet remain uncertain. To that extent a policy of morality is always in danger of becoming authoritarian, that is, of appointing some the guardians of the morals of others and regarding truth or justice as the privilege of the few. In this way it can happen that those who set out to do good manage to do much harm to the cause of liberty.

In paradoxical contrast to many of its claims, the German labor movement bore and to some extent still bears authoritarian traits. A second contradiction may help us to explain this fact: The labor movement needed society, but it sought the state. Quoting Lassalle as the crown witness of the labor movement is no more just than quoting Marx, Kautsky, or Bernstein as such. But he certainly is a material witness:

The fourth estate has not merely another formal political principle than the bourgeoisie . . . but it also has . . . quite another, entirely different conception of the moral purpose of the state than the bourgeoisie.

It is the moral idea of the bourgeoisie that nothing but the unhampered self-activation of his forces has to be guaranteed to every individual. . . . By contrast it is the moral idea of the workers' estate that the unhampered and free activation of individual forces by the individual does not yet suffice, but that in a morally ordered community there has to be added: solidarity of interests, community and mutuality in the development.

Corresponding to this difference, the bourgeoisie regards the moral purpose of the state thus: it consists exclusively of protecting the personal freedom of the individual and his property.

This, gentlemen, is a nightwatchman's idea, because it can conceive the state itself only in the image of a nightwatchman whose whole function it is to prevent robbery and theft. Unfortunately this nightwatchman's idea is not merely at home with the true liberals, but may often enough be encountered even with many alleged democrats, as a consequence of lacking intellectual formation. . . .

The fourth estate, gentlemen, conceives the purpose of the state entirely differently, and it conceives it as its nature is in truth. . . .

It is the state that has the function of accomplishing [the] development of liberty, [the] development of humankind to liberty. . . .

Thus it is not the purpose of the state merely to protect personal freedom and property for the individual, with which he supposedly, according to the idea of the bourgeoisie, enters the state; it is rather the purpose of the state to enable individuals by their union to achieve such purposes, a level of existence such as they could never achieve as individuals. . . .

Thus it is the purpose of the state to bring human nature to its positive unfolding and progressive development, in other words to form the human destiny, that is, to realize the true design of the culture of which the human race is capable; it is the education and development of mankind to liberty.

This is the real and moral nature of the state, gentlemen, its true and higher task. It is so much this that it was more or less realized by the state at all times, by the force of things themselves, even without its will, even unconsciously, even against the will of its leaders." (124, pp. 167 ff.)

If only there had been in Germany a bourgeoisie as strong, confident, and liberal as Lassalle describes! Unfortunately, this was not the case; Lassalle's bourgeoisie is that of Great Britain, or perhaps merely of theory, although his error has the excuse that it was committed in 1862, when the fate of the liberal bourgeoisie in Germany was not yet completely decided. When it was decided, German society acquired a labor movement that fit its bourgeoisie, not least because it assimilated many features of Lassalle's *Workers' Program* (from which our quotation is taken). These were fundamentally illiberal features—dogmatism in place of an experimental attitude: the fourth estate conceives the purpose of the state "as its nature is in truth"; rejection of the plurality of political interests and designs: the persistent singular in talking about a substantively conceived "purpose of the state"; nostalgia for political institutions removed from all control: the state as the reality of the moral idea.

In fact, Lassalle has formulated the political theory of the authoritarian state, with one small difference from its official version: in his opinion it is not the traditional elites who have found the secret of politics, but the new elites of the working class, or rather, the "workers' estate." It therefore sounds like applied Lassalle when the social democratic historian Friedrich Stampfer writes about Friedrich Ebert's achievements in the early years of the Weimar Republic: "Where emperors and kings, princes and *Junker* had failed, the former saddler's apprentice had to create order" (206, p. 439). The order is the same, it is still order and not change; and the "saddler's apprentice" has to prove his right to govern by not differing from his predecessors—what a pathetic mixture of lack of self-confidence and authoritarianism!

Obviously, German Social Democracy was not simply authoritarian in outlook. But out of an unfortunate attitude of illiberalism it developed a fatal love for the state, while it was from the structures of society and their change that it drew its raison d'être. Here the behavior of Social Democrats as the first ruling party of the Weimar Republic is especially telling. It was to be expected, of course, that the SPD would expand the welfare-state socialism of Imperial Germany, much as such policies might favor the survival of authoritarian dependencies. But more surprisingly, the Social Democrats "saved the state" by joining forces with military and paramilitary groups of the right against the extremism of the left and thus continued a conservative policy that repressed social forces in the name of the state. Indeed, nowhere did the predictive justice of Lassalle's praise of the state become as apparent as in Prussia, the largest province of Germany and governed by Social Democrats throughout the Weimar Republic: the nature of the state is always moral; not even the hated "princes and *Junker*" of Imperial Germany could alter this basic fact; this higher truth shone through even their worst errors. Now, by its better administration in new hands, the moral nature of the state comes to its full right. In a way, German Social Democracy turned out to be the protestantism of the Prussian state. Although protesting against the alienation of its original values in the hands of false priests, it stayed within the world of these values. This made possible even the final insult that Bismarck and Ebert were held up together as models for the nation by anti-democratic groups of the right. The Imperial labor movement had saved the state; what remained by the wayside was its own ability to stimulate a more liberal social development. In other words, German society fell by the wayside.

Apart from Ebert, two names stand out in the history of the German labor movement, August Bebel and Kurt Schumacher. They remind us of a third contradiction in the German labor movement's politics, the road from August 4, 1914 (on which the first war credits were voted), to the "Chancellor of the Allies" (as Schumacher called Adenauer in a debate in the Federal Parliament in 1950). It needed the alliance of reformers and the peaceful union of peoples, but it sought the nation. This oldest trauma of the German movement is, despite related difficulties in other countries, what reveals most clearly its national affiliation. Nothing has hurt its leaders more deeply than the charge of being "fellows without fatherland"; nothing made them fight more intensely, therefore, than the attempt to refute this arrogant piece of malice.

As it happens, "How do you feel about the nation?" is still the question by which Germans like to test each other. What is more, whoever does not answer it spontaneously to the satisfaction of the small group of right-wing extremists who continue to intimidate everyone else in this respect—even after they have destroyed and divided the country they pretend to love and brought shame to its name everywhere—soon finds himself in a disgrace from which he never recovers. The Social Democrats knew this when they voted the war appropriations; and the masses, always not merely authoritarian but also national in their inclinations, thanked them with the enthusiasm of the early days of the First World War.

An old Social Democratic editor probably summarized widespread sentiments when he wrote in 1916: "In this war we have learned once again what we had almost completely forgotten: that apart from all class conflicts something is common to all classes of this nation. We German Social Democrats have learned in this war to regard ourselves as a part, and certainly not the worst part, of the German nation. Never again do we want to be robbed, by anybody of the right or the left, of the feeling of belonging to the German people."

Once again one is tempted to add: society fell by the way-side. The traumatic relationship of the German labor movement to the nation has ramifications for the whole of German society. Guenther Roth has followed the process of how socialist radicalism was domesticated by the "isolation" of the working class—as he calls it—by stages (cf. 186). What was missing was the inner "democratization" of society that alone might have led to the calm integration of the working class into society. Calm integration was replaced—so we might follow up Roth's analysis—by an excited, erratic, and thus precarious if not necessarily merely temporary integration, as shown by the enthusiasm for national unity in the early days of the First World War.

Since national unity is never the whole truth and as a rule does not solve or even alter social problems, but merely suspends them, this integration had to be an interlude, followed by new divisions. They began, in political terms, with the secession from the SPD of the Independent Social Democrats in 1916 and later with the formation of a strong Communist Party (KPD). More significantly, however, the following decades remained characterized by the alternation of enthusiastic national integration and evident social disintegration, popular unity and social division. Nothing has promoted and cemented the dismal state of German society more effectively than the suicidal primacy of the national.

It is not the fault of the German labor movement that it had to act before this background. That it, by and large, accepted this background and allowed itself to be used by others against the background, documents one of its misconceived necessities. The expectation that by its own nationalism it could help labor to social acceptance and its organizations to political recognition had to be vain. Both these goals were to be reached not by a policy of embraces (which was not an invention of contemporary West German Social Democrats), but by a militant policy of self-assertion. The contrast between the radicalism of Social Democratic proclamations and the meekness of their political practice has often been remarked. There is nothing very radical about the Godesberg Program; but even here the disproportion between the programmatic promises of socialism and the practical policies of the SPD is striking. It is here that we encounter, in the practical activities of the labor movement, a fourth contradiction, which summarizes all others: the German labor movement needed conflict, but it sought order.

It would seem obvious that a political party of protest against the ruling powers and the social order supported by them needs a political system that permits it to fight. As the bourgeoisie needed political democracy in order to carry through its claims against older established leadership groups —the theoretical bourgeoisie, to be sure; for the actual German bourgeoisie never advanced such claims—the labor movement needed the constitution of government by conflict in order to be heard and make its influence felt.

The Social Democrats in Imperial Germany clearly knew this; they fought therefore for equal suffrage and fair representation, for the abolition of all political privileges and disadvantages. Even in Imperial Germany, however, and more strikingly in the Weimar Republic, it became evident that the labor movement did not like the conflict that it needed. Its leaders (and probably its adherents as well) looked upon the political class struggle as a regrettable corollary of every capitalism that had to be overcome rather than as a permanent condition of the constitution of liberty. Not conflict, but order has been the guiding thread of its policies.

Even in the 1959 Godesberg Program of West Germany's Social Democrats, "order" is one of the most frequent words: the "new and better order," the "order of the state," the "liberal-democratic basic order," the "economic and social order," the "order that is based on the fundamental values of democratic socialism." Although one finds an occasional reference in this program to "competition on an equal footing" between parties for "the majority of the people," the Social Democratic concept of democracy has little to do with the lively disputes of antagonistic interests:

> The Social Democratic Party of Germany professes democracy, in which the power of the state derived from the people

and government is at all times responsible to parliament and aware that it permanently needs its confidence. In democracy the rights of the minority must be safeguarded as well as the rights of the majority. Government and opposition have different tasks of equal rank; both carry responsibility for the state. (19, p. 82.)

The Rousseauian illusion of sovereignty emanating from the people, which J. L. Talmon has shown could become a source of totalitarian democracy, is followed by a reference to the relationship between government and parliament, the grammatical subject of which is government. Then a telling statement ensues. Not antagonistic parties but "majority" and "minority" encounter each other in parliament; rather, they do not encounter, but sit next to each other; they do not fight each other, but have "rights" which "have to be safeguarded." Almost apologetically government and opposition, the theoretical protagonists of political conflict, are ascribed "different tasks," so that the notion of contradictions and tensions may be avoided at all cost; and immediately, "responsibility"—another favorite word of the labor movement—has to be pulled in and with it the state. It is true that 8 per cent of all adult Germans charged the SPD even in 1959 with "permanent opposition at all costs," which "prevents reasonable work"; but the fact that there are people who dislike social and political conflicts even more than the Social Democrats do hardly justifies the aversion of those who, after all, need them.

Making the nostalgia for synthesis the pivot of our analysis is not an idiosyncratic whim. Conflict keeps societies open to change and prevents the dogmatization of error. Aversion to conflict is a basic trait of authoritarian political thought, which means in effect that government loses control of change, and the citizens lose their freedom. This is why we have criticized the German Social Democrats' consistent dislike of conflict, their suspicious longing for responsibility, for the unity of the nation, for the state, and for order. Since the Godesberg Program, the West German SPD has driven its policy of embrace to new extremes; even before it joined government, the "great coalition" seemed a fact; and the price was paid by German society in terms of the vitality of its democratic institutions.

And, of course, the Godesberg Program was only a temporary end point of a long chain of similar policies. It was preceded by the many measures of industrial utopia, from the Works Council Law of 1920 to the Co-Determination Law of 1951, that derive from Social Democratic initiative and aim at ultimate solutions. Erich Matthias has shown how Social Democratic émigrés during the Third Reich sought ways of abandoning the notion of class struggle and replacing it by less antagonistic notions, such as those of the people and the nation. This, too, had in fact happened long before; Ebert and Müller, Braun and Severing can hardly be understood apart from the theory that prefers even the suspicious calm of the old order to the discomfort of permanent class struggle.

The intellectual error underlying such aversion to conflict is not confined to the labor movement. One way of describing it is to say that it consists of a dangerous confusion between social integration and social harmony. The confusion is dangerous because it suggests that creating harmony is the first task of politics; but this can never be accomplished except by repression. The confusion is erroneous because there may be well-integrated communities in which lively conflicts take place; indeed, the less the common membership of antagonists is doubted, the more creative are their antagonisms likely to be; a quarrel between friends is both more probable and more fruitful than one between strangers. Admittedly, this argument leads us into the vicious circle in which the German labor movement also found itself: If social integration is a condition of lively and fruitful conflict, who then accomplishes integration?

The history of the German labor movement is a history of painful self-appraisals resulting in courageous, if not always encouraging changes. It is remarkable in itself that any party should have survived a hundred years of German historical discontinuity; the German Social Democrats, however, have truly suffered this history: they have been outlawed and suppressed, reduced to a secret movement in exile, but they have been government and opposition party as well. There is obviously no single formula to describe all these experiences. What is more, it has long been very problematic to speak of a single labor movement. The general notion includes such incompatible organizations as the West German SPD, the East German SED, the SPD and KPD of the Weimar period, the diverse trade unions before 1933, the government-controlled trade-union council of the DDR, and the West German trade-union council. Does it make any sense at all to try to find common features in all these forms?

For all specific purposes of political history the differences between the distant offshoots of the common root of the labor movement are greater than the similarities. And yet they have, at least in negative terms, certain common features. The labor movement was illiberal in all its manifestations, not only protesting the consequences of a class-bound notion of liberalism embodied in bourgeois society, but also in its aversion to the color and diversity, the contradictions and confusions of a civil society that does not promise the individual more than the chance of liberty. The nostalgia for a synthesis that supersedes the antithetics of reality, a propensity for utopia, live on in the labor movement. In the process of translating such distant dreams into day-to-day politics, utopia quickly reveals its poverty. If utopianism becomes militant, it leads to terror, to the suppression of every stirring of liberty, as in the DDR. If utopianism is but a mild light of order, it still leads to the rejection of emphatically liberal action, as in the West German SPD. In no case does the grasp for the stars help the constitution of liberty.

Whenever its policies were policies of protest, the German labor movement contributed to the establishment of the institutions and habits of liberal democracy. But in its positive, "responsible" aspects the policies of the labor movement have been a contribution to the persistence, if not the strengthening, of social structures in which liberal democracy could hardly gain a hold. This is why the German labor movement stands, by and large, like the Imperial era in which it was born, on the debit side of the liberal balance in Germany.

Could one really expect the German labor movement to be any different considering its social context? Are we not turning the labor movement into a scapegoat, which distracts us from the responsibility of the really guilty? The labor movement is certainly not the cause of the pathology of democracy in Germany. Its fault is that it remained tied to its social context although its goals would have permitted, if not forced, it to break this context. This is a guilt by omission, which invariably requires somewhat problematic constructions to be proved. But if we ask for the causes of the German nostalgia for synthesis, the tragedy of German liberalism becomes more important than that of the labor movement. The question of causes takes us back to the faults of German society and their political expressions, and to those who profited from these faults. If culprits have to be found, they are certainly among not the victims but the profiteers of the German inability to stand contradiction.

13. THE MYTH OF THE STATE

Ferdinand Lassalle is not representative of the German labor movement; although West Germany's SPD related its hundredth anniversary to Lassalle's foundation of the General German Workers' Association in 1863, many other impulses entered into its history. Lassalle is not representative of the German bourgeoisie either; although his father was a wealthy silk merchant and his rather bourgeois flirt with aristocracy cost him his life in a duel, he was a Jew and thus, from the outset, a marginal man. Lassalle is not representative of Bismarck's Germany; although his conversations with Bismarck in 1863 and 1864 may well have influenced the Chancellor's reasonably tolerant attitude to the labor movement before the attempts on the Emperor's life, Lassalle did not himself live to see the German Empire. Lassalle is not representative of German science, or of any school of Hegelian thought. But as one enumerates the groups at whose margin this sensitive and highly explosive man was placed, one begins to suspect that his ideas are more than the expression of a precarious private existence; they represent a dominant theme of German thought on the threshold of political action.

The grandfather of this theme, which has shaped German history in more than one version before and after Imperial times, was Hegel; its fetish and most important subject matter is The State. Nowhere is the figure of thought we are imputing to the institutions of German society as their implicit rationale as evident as in the dialectics of "morality" in Hegel's *Philosophy of Right* of 1821. "Morality" crowns the development of what Hegel calls liberty in both history and theory. It supersedes the positions of "abstract law" and its negation, "practical ethics," that is, Roman law and Kantian philosophy, in a higher unity (if we accept for the time being the disastrous ambiguities of Hegel's formulations). However, this highest stage of the idea of freedom, the "concept of freedom which has become the existing world" is complex in itself; it is a process. The process is worth following in some detail.

To begin with, that is, in its historically earliest and intellectually simplest version, morality is manifest in the family; this is the thesis, or position of the process. In its description we encounter some familiar ideas: "The family, as the immediate substantiality of mind, has its felt unity, love, as its condition, so that the disposition is the awareness of its individuality in this unity as the essentiality in and for itself in order not to exist as a person by itself, but as a member" (95, §158, p. 149). If one is unimpressed by Hegel's art of linguistic camouflage and translates what he has to say into reasonable language, this simply means that the family is a world of community, not of society; of love, not of right, to which the individual belongs not as a person, but as a "member" devoid of the capacity for rational decision. Hegel is, however, not as simple-minded as some of his latter-day followers. "Children are in themselves free"; their education leads them "out of the natural immediacy in which they originally find themselves, to independence and free personality" (95, §175, p. 158). Thus the family has an inherent tendency to abolish itself; it points beyond itself to the second step of the process of morality, civil society.

Hegel's presentation of civil society as a system of needs, as a process of the legal development of formal rules of the game and as a neutral administration of things has become justly famous. It testifies to his insight into social structures as well as to his familiarity with liberal ideas. But civil society is, in Hegel's process of morality, merely the antithesis or negation; and Hegel did not like opposition. "One can regard this system to begin with as the external state,—the state of emergency and of intellect" (95, §183, p. 165).

Here, too, there is no lack of value-laden dichotomies; the bad "external state" is confronted with a better "internal state," the limited "intellect" is followed by the limitless, indefinite "reason," the "objective mind." Nothing implies, for Hegel, a more relentless criticism of civil society than its description in words of unlyrical rationality. By contrast, even his language rises to a dull poetry of enthusiasm as he reaches the third step of the dialectical process of morality, and thus its completion: The State. "The state is the reality of the moral idea—the moral spirit as the revealed will, apparent to itself, substantial, which thinks and knows itself and accomplishes that which it knows and in so far as it knows it" (95, §257, pp. 207 f.). And further:

The state is, as the reality of the substantial will which it has in its generalized self-awareness, the reasonable in and for itself. This substantial unity is absolutely unmoved purpose for itself, in which freedom comes to its highest right, just as this ultimate purpose has the highest right against the individual whose highest duty it is to be a member of the state.

If the state is confused with civil society and is defined by security, the protection of property, and personal liberty, the interest of individuals as such becomes the ultimate purpose for which they are united, and it would follow that it is something random to a member of the state. But the state has a very different relation to the individual; the state is objective spirit itself, and the individual has objectivity, truth, and morality only in so far as he is a member of it. The union as such is true substance and purpose, and it is the definition of individuals to lead a general life; their further specific satisfaction, activity, mode of behavior has this substance and general validity as its starting point and result. (95, §258, p. 208.)

It might be tempting and would not be difficult to pour irony and polemics over these much-quoted sentences. But this would help us little. They are sentences full of substance; they are above all—and this is why we are discussing them here— German sentences, which provide us with a key to many traits of German society.

Let us remember first of all the formal figure of the dialectical process. The undeveloped beginning, thesis or position, is followed by the step into the complexities of history, the antithesis, opposition, or negation. But for Hegel's arrogant ambition, antinomy is not enough; its indecisiveness seems to him a symptom of insufficient development; he wants not only to suspect or postulate, hope or long for the thing in itself, but to grasp it fully. Thesis and antithesis are therefore *aufgehoben* in the synthesis with the triple meaning of the German word: abolished, conserved, elevated to a higher level. But the triple meaning of the synthesis is not merely deliberate ambiguity on Hegel's part. The synthesis abolishes, with the antinomy of thesis and antithesis, the antithesis, the negation; it is no accident that Hegel prefers to call the antithesis, negation of the negation. Thus it is above all civil society, with its right of individual interests, its classes and parties, that is abolished in the state. On the other hand, many a feature of the thesis is conserved in it. In the state, as in the family, the individual participates as a "member" rather than a person.

Finally, elevation to a higher level of analysis clearly implies a value judgment.

This, then, is the decisive implication of Hegel's synthesis, that civil society is insufficient historically as well as morally. It is profoundly lacking. Because it is constructed out of many individuals each with his own interests, out of their combinations in classes and parties, the competition of interests, the struggle of classes, and the clashes of parties, it is incapable in principle of bringing about a satisfactory constitution of human society. Even the contract of the individuals, their agreement on certain rules of the game of conflict cannot accomplish this. Hegel attacks Rousseau in whom he recognizes a fellow illiberal (". . . Rousseau did have the merit of having established a principle which is idealist not merely formally . . . but substantively, which is thinking itself, that is, the will, as the basis of the state . . ."), but who in his opinion did not go far enough in the right direction:

> However, by comprehending the will only in the definite form of the individual will (as Fichte did later too) and the general will not as the rationale of the will in and for itself, but merely in terms of the common features emerging from the individual will as a conscious one: thus the union of the individuals in the state becomes a contract, which has their choice, opinion, and arbitrary explicit agreement as its basis, and all the other merely intellectual consequences destroying the divine, which is in and for itself and its absolute authority and majesty, follow. (95, §258, pp. 209 f.)

Thus the state is in no way a product of civil society; as such it would be bound to remain "artificial," merely "intellectual," "arbitrary," based only on the agreement of those concerned. Rather, the state transcends the structures of civil society altogether. The state constitutes a new political principle not derived from anything else, justice itself on earth, which (as Plato described so tellingly) is not induced by men but descends on winged horses from the heavens of ideas to the pathetic intellectual reality of earth.

It is well not to lose sight of the lyrical, or, more precisely, the dismally metaphorical quality of such reflections. "The state is the reality of the moral idea." What is being said here? Who is "the state"? And who or what is the "reality of the moral idea"? Perhaps "the state" is government in the sense of all governments of world history; perhaps the "reality of the moral idea" refers to actions that may, by some standard, be called ethically good. Thus, all governments of world history act (always?) morally good. It is a peculiarity of Hegel's metaphors that the attempt to render them precise by translation regularly yields evident nonsense. Unfortunately, this fact has not prevented the metaphors from becoming effective, although it is probably the reason why Hegel's adepts are at such pains to denounce any attempt to translate the master's metaphors into clear language as falsification.

But we are not engaged in philosophical exegesis here. Our first interest is not a critique of Hegel. Our starting point is, rather, that the Hegelian notion of the state has influenced political thought and practical politics in Germany to the present day. By way of Lassalle it slipped, as we have seen, into the baggage of the labor movement. But Lassalle was an avowed Hegelian. The significance for German thought of the notion of a state suspended above the struggles of parties becomes even more apparent if we examine some non-Hegelian views of the matter.

Heinrich von Treitschke, the Prussian national historian sometimes described as liberal, explicitly rejected Hegel's "deification of the state" in his lectures on *Politics* (219, p. 32). But only a moment later all the metaphors and spirits return. The people is not a plurality of individuals or indeed citizens, but of families (219, p. 13), and one "has to hold the original family to be the original state" (219, p. 16). Between family and state, however, civil society intervenes, which Treitschke, too, describes in lively colors as a world of interests and of conflicts, only to add immediately: "This concept of civil society does not describe any subject in reality, but is an abstraction of scholars. Where is there a common organ of civil society?" (219, p. 54.) The next steps are taken more and more rapidly:

> Law and peace and order cannot accrue to the plurality of interests in their eternal struggle from inside, but only from that power that stands above society, equipped with a force that is capable of taming wild social passion. Here one begins to get a clear conception of what one might call the moral sanctity of the state. It is the state that introduces justice and mutual care into the world of social struggles. (219, p. 56.)

The state is an "independent force" which "stands above the social antagonisms," is "just" and "non-partisan," has a "character," "is a personality, originally in the legal and further in a moral-historical sense." And practice follows theory: "On principle, it does not ask for good intentions; it demands obedience." In this respect Treitschke is much more cynical —or merely frank?—than Hegel: "The state says: I do not care what you think, but you must obey" (219, pp. 32 f.).

And so the world is turned upside down so that the myth of the state becomes reality and the tangible reality of society a kind of ground fog above which one has to rise. Cui bono? We will have to ask this question again. But what such theories mean in practice is already apparent. "The state," that is, those who hide behind the protective shield of this name, has rights against the individual; its "member" has obligations, among them that of obeying without protest. There are individual rights as well, but these may, indeed must, be "abolished" in the superior rights of the state.

Here, the constitution of Imperial Germany begins to shine through the metaphor as its historical substance; in its reality Hegel has found an application. The Imperial parliament, the "chatterbox," symbolizes a civil society of interests and conflicts. Underneath it, social reality is a world of families who are all minors; and above it rises the state in its majesty. In this way, party struggles never reach the center of authority; they remain confined to a lower level and have to be superseded by the certainty of an authority that is no longer partisan itself. It is almost as if Hegel had anticipated, in the incompatible blend of his enthusiasm for the events of 1789 and his embrace of the Prussian state of his time, those faulted structures of the industrial feudal society and the authoritarian welfare state that Lassalle and Treitschke both document and describe and that became real in Imperial Germany.

The dream of a synthesis above the antinomies of reality was not confined to Imperial Germany, however. In ever new versions it has become a kind of leitmotiv of the ways and byways of German politics. Many turns of the Weimar Republic can be understood in terms of the search for the lost synthesis. It was promised by the Social Democrats who continued Imperial traditions; the saddler's apprentice who turned out to be a better emperor than his exalted predecessor comes to mind. But not even the saddler's apprentice succeeded in covering his actions with the cloak of non-partisanship that his predecessors had inherited. The problematic office of president in Weimar—Max Weber's charismatic creation—evidently did not suffice by itself. If Hindenburg later succeeded where

Ebert failed, this testifies to the growing aversion to the "system," that is, to a political order that by its very principle does not transcend civil society:

> When after the First World War the front against the "Western democracies" was made a dogma, and it became a requirement of "national" intentions to reject in principle the "chatterbox" of parliament, the romantic nostalgia for a "true state" found expression in the simultaneous demand for re-establishing the estate order and for creating a leader-state representing the people's community in an authoritarian fashion, without people minding the contradictory character of these postulates too much at first. (73, p. 40.)

The postulates described as contradictory by Ernst Fraenkel, however, can be thus called only in their specific consequences (although the National Socialists managed to accommodate even such specific contradictions in the hodgepodge of their ideology); but they have in common the search for synthesis, for the "abolition" of the conflicts of social and political reality in authorities that are placed above the parties. Hitler made careful use of this particular weakness of German political attitudes for his own purposes; the "leader" who is allied with "providence" once again has the certainty of the moral idea on his side. Compared with the Weimar Republic, the principle of government by conflict seems firmly established in the Federal Republic. Indeed there are encouraging trends. Four times a representative sample of West Germans was asked by an institute of opinion research:

> Two men talk about how a country should be governed. Which of the two opinions comes closest to your own—the first or the second?
> One says: "I like it best if the whole people places the best politician at the top and confers on him the entire power of government. Together with a few selected experts he can then make clear decisions. There is not much talk, and things really get done."
> The other says: "I prefer it if several people have a say in the state. Sometimes there is some hither and thither before things are done, but it is not so easy to abuse the power of government."

In 1955, 55 per cent agreed with the second (31 per cent with the first, 14 per cent remained undecided); by 1957 the proportion of democrats in terms of opinion research had risen to 60 per cent (26 per cent, 14 per cent), by 1960 to 62 per cent (21 per cent, 17 per cent), and by 1962 to 66 per cent (18 per cent, 16 per cent).

A very similar trend can be observed in respect to the question: "Do you believe that it is better for a country to have several parties so that different opinions may be represented freely, or only one party, so that there is as much unity as possible?" Between 1951 and 1961 the multiparty system consistently gained in support from 61 to 73 per cent (cf. 104). Thus more than two thirds of all Germans accept the principle of government by conflict today. But unfortunately things are not as simple as that. In drawing up their questionnaires, opinion-research institutes have overlooked one possibility, which appears absurd in theory but constitutes in practice the resigned and second-best modern equivalent of the state as the reality of the moral idea; they have failed to include the question: "Do you believe that it is good for a country to have several parties so that there is as much unity as possible?"

This question would have struck a chord in the political subconscious of many Germans. In October 1961, 28 per cent of all West Germans favored an all-party coalition, and a further 23 per cent a so-called "great coalition" between CDU and SPD (104, p. 443). (Among adherents of the SPD the corresponding proportions were, incidentally, 38 and 39 per cent.) A great coalition, however, means the end of party conflict as an instrument of democratic government almost as much as the creation of an authority "above the parties."

There are other symptoms of a lasting German dislike of the uncomfortable world of conflicts. The notion of persons or institutions being "above parties" has been mentioned; it is regarded as very much of an *epitheton ornans* in Germany and is sought even by the "people's party" in a paradoxical combination of terms. The "people's chancellor" has already found it; in the place of party programs there are "communal tasks"; the sting is taken out of election campaigns by an agreement not to differ; a common aversion is directed against "the rule of interest groups"; all groups try to turn the still present nostalgia for a lost authority above the troubled waters of conflict to their own uses.

Possibly the most absurd and at the same time disturbing testimony to such nostalgia for synthesis in contemporary Germany is the widespread lament by indubitable opponents of communism (including many refugees from East Germany) that while in the DDR at least some sense of the higher purposes of the state has been kept alive, in the Federal Republic everything has been drawn into the whirlpool of personal interests and all sense of the majesty of community has been lost. Thus even the victory of the constitution of liberty is secretly bemoaned as defeat.

Illustrations do not prove anything. This is also true of two symptoms of the German aversion to political conflict that have survived almost without modification all changes of the last hundred years. Nevertheless, their discussion may advance our analysis by guiding us to the contested boundaries of our thesis. One of these symptoms issues from the Prussian heritage; its phenomenology is characterized primarily by the German idea of the rule of law (*Rechtsstaat*). Since Robert von Mohl and before, down to the Basic Law of the Federal Republic and beyond, the concept and reality of the rule of law have remained one of the fetishes of German politics.

There are many definitions of this principle—that "the power of the state is subject to the idea of law, and all its manifestations are legitimized by the law" (3a, p. 685), that "the state . . . provides its citizens with a certain area of liberty and commits itself to interfering in this area only under certain, legally regulated preconditions" (21, p. 176), that certain formal principles of legislation (in relation to "fundamental rights"), the legal order ("continuous court system"), and jurisdiction (*nulla poena sine lege*) are maintained.

All these definitions, however, refer away from the rule of law to the "general estate" of those who administer it: "The struggle for the rule of law presents itself primarily as the endeavor to realize concretely the principles of an abstract constitutional law with the assistance of an effective administrative law in the political, economic, and social sphere" (27, p. 243). Fraenkel states this with an air of detachment; the statement (in a dictionary article) is followed by a reference to the article on "administration."

The rule of law means first of all that all political actions have to follow certain rules; as such, it is politically indifferent. This is why Otto Mayer's much-quoted dictum that while constitutional law passes, administrative law persists, is not merely cynical, but also terrifyingly correct. There is little reason to doubt the observation by a liberal lawyer: "The German Empire under Bismarck's auspices was, as a whole and in its member states, a state embodying the rule of law, although its constitution did not contain any clause about the granting of fundamental rights" (21, p. 178). It would be even harder to dispute that the rule of law characterized the Weimar Republic. Interestingly, Roland Freisler retained the word, although he went his own way in substance as well as language, in the National Socialist *Handbook of Legal Science:*

> The rule of law is the organized form of life of a people, which combines the entire vitality of the people to secure the right of the people to life on the inside as well as the outside. . . . For only this concentrated popular force will do, as only a concentrated charge was capable of taming the tank threatening the front. This organized bringing to action of the concentrated charge of the people's force for the protection of the people's life is our concept of the rule of law. (cf. 27, p. 247.)

Obviously, Article 28 of the Basic Law of the Federal Republic with its reference to the "social rule of law" means something utterly different; but neither this article nor the frequent ceremonious invocation of the "principles of democracy and the rule of law" should deceive us about the fact that a moral administration does not guarantee liberalism, nor political actions domesticated by the rules of valid laws, democracy. Ultimately, the exaggerated faith in the rule of law as an institution beyond all conflicts of interest betrays the same aversion to discord, and thus the same evasion of the uncomfortable diversity of uncertainty, that is inherent in the German idea of the state. The conclusion risks misinterpretation, but leads in the right direction: the rule of law is less important for the constitution of liberty than the vitality of conflict. Liberal democracy is less endangered by a politician acting somewhat outside legality than by the search for authorities allegedly above parties as this is expressed institutionally in an overestimation of emperor and president, national unity and all-party coalition, administration and the law. Or, put in a way less likely to be misunderstood: without the basis of the rule of law the constitution of liberty cannot really work; but the basis alone does not guarantee the constitution of liberty. Taken by itself, it may become an abstract formal standard, which not only submits to any master for use but continues to have authoritarian effects even if nobody wants to be master any more. In any case, democracy needs liberalism more urgently than morality.

We have distinguished here for the first time a "basis" of the constitution of liberty from its proper patterns. What this basis means may become clearer if we turn to a second significant symptom of the German aversion to political conflict, the national-social ideology. It has probably not passed unnoticed that so far I have suppressed one—and not the better —half of the theses of my crown witnesses for the German myth of the state. This is what this half looks like to Hegel:

> The people to which such moment is due as its natural principle is charged with the execution of same in the progress of the developing self-awareness of the world spirit. This people is, for this epoch in world history—and it can make the epoch but once—the ruling one. Against this, its absolute right to be the bearer of the current stage of development, the spirits of the other peoples are without rights, and they, like those whose epoch is past, no longer count in world history. . . .
>
> [The three empires of the past, the Oriental, the Greek and Roman, are now followed by the last epoch of world history in which] the spirit repressed to itself in the extreme of its absolute negativity, the turning point in and for itself, [grasps] the infinite positivity of this its inside, the principle of unity of human and divine nature, the conciliation as the objective truth and liberty appearing within self-awareness and subjectivity, all of which the Nordic principle of the Germanic peoples is charged with accomplishing. (95, §§347 and 358, pp. 291 and 296.)

Here, too, the labor leader Lassalle was a faithful disciple of Hegel's: "All the old nations have taken the world ahead by a stage of the road, that is, exercised free development. But in antiquity every people has developed but one moment, one natural definition. . . . The very definition of the Germanic spirit consists in combining the whole cultural idea into one unity; and thus the previous deficiency of the nationality of the Germans is their very strength in future" (124, p. 129).

Finally, Treitschke, in dealing with this question, translates the boundless arrogance of ideas on the part of Hegel and his disciples into the simpler Prussian-German blend of sentimentality and the demand for power:

> Here the high moral value of national honor plays a part, which is handed on from generation to generation, has something absolutely sacred, and forces the individual to sacrifice himself for it. . . . Thus every people has the right to believe

that certain forces of divine reason present themselves most beautifully within it; without overestimating itself a people does not come to an awareness of itself at all. . . . For the state to deny its own power is truly the sin against the Holy Ghost. . . . In the distribution of the non-European world among the European powers Germany has so far always done badly, and yet the question of whether we can become a power beyond the seas as well merely concerns our existence as a great power. Otherwise there arises the horrible prospect that England and Russia divide the world among themselves, in which case one really does not know which would be more immoral or disgusting, the Russian whip or the English money bag. (219, pp. 24, 29, 42 f.)

German nationalism, too, is a testimony to the nostalgia for synthesis in all its versions, from the desire for unity through megalomania back to a more modest desire for unity. Time and again the demands of the nation had to serve, in German history, to suspend civil society and with it the vital questions of men: "In this hour of emergency we all have to stand together." There are indeed situations in which the survival of groups demands the expensive sacrifice of the suspension of all internal divisions; but if these become as frequent and as lasting as they were in German history, that is, if nationalism has to serve as an ideology of a permanent state of emergency, the rank order that consistently prefers the national to the social becomes both suspicious and dangerous. The suspicion concerns those who might profit by the absence of conflict; we will try in a moment to disperse the mist of the state ideology in order to move them into the light. But the danger involves all citizens living in this condition. For if conflict is suspended, stability as well as liberalism is in jeopardy. A society that persistently prefers the national to the social is bound to pass through an unending chain of internal upheavals, for by its "abolition" civil society disappears at most from the field of vision, but not from reality. The simple fact remains that while one may deny and hate, camouflage and suppress conflict, one cannot get rid of it.

Despite this conclusion, we have in fact reached the contested boundary of our analysis now. Discussing the rule of law and the nation finally makes inescapable a question that has been apparent for some time: Conflict may be an unavoidable, indeed a fruitful social force, but it cannot constitute the whole of social life. Do not all contradictions need a frame of agreement? Does not conflict become a destructive force if it affects the common basis of the contestants? Is not one of the lessons to be drawn from the downfall of the Weimar Republic that a country has to be concerned about the foundations of its constitution and keep these out of party strife?

There are good arguments for each of these suggestive questions. Even apart from the basis of the formal rule of law, there is in the notion of the common good an old name for the general foundation of party conflict: "A fundamental limitation of the power struggle is accomplished only if one can count on the interested parties recognizing that there is a common good above our private good and that of groups, to which we have to adapt" (78, p. 175). And who would doubt the liberalism of Theodor Heuss who did not need the nation to say: "The state is not merely an apparatus, it is also the subject of inborn dignity, and as the bearer of the ordering community it is for man, and man is for it, no abstraction" (32, p. 19). Is it really so mistaken to look for a common bond of the contestants above all conflicts?

This attitude is far too widespread to be called mistaken. Yet it is likely to be misunderstood, to say the least, if not prone to give rise to the very authoritarianism that lies at the basis of the German Question. Since it is possible to settle the problem of the common basis of conflicts and yet not abandon the liberal approach underlying our own formulation of the German Question, it may be well to summarize the steps of our argument:

1. There is no work of man that does not display the imperfection of his hand and that thus may not be wrong. There is no political program, no party, no particular decision, and no institution that may not be partisan. Put more carefully and more correctly: it is impossible to demonstrate that any authority is wholly removed from the conflict of opinions and parties. To this extent the political process takes place throughout in a horizon of uncertainty, of incomplete information.

2. If this is the case, the permanent conflict of parties is the only protection against the dogmatization of error. Conflict is not a second-best solution, much less a mechanism in order to find the one, ultimately right solution—the one leader—but is by itself the goal of the political process that provides the

chance of progress. For the constitution of liberty, formal principles are sufficient substance; conflict is liberty, that is to say, what liberty political institutions are able to grant, consists in conflict. (Within this framework, specific programs of great diversity, among them liberal ones in a partisan sense not intended in this study, may and must, of course, be advanced.)

3. There is no conflict between Peruvian chess players and German housewives. In this sense, it is true that the notion of conflict presupposes a common context of the contestants. It is also true that this context includes more than a physical territory; it means two things: agreed-upon rules of the game of conflict and a structure of authority within which this takes place. Thus conflict implies both social contracts: the contract of association to domesticate the war of all against all by accepted rules of the game, and the contract of government to tie together the common context by an authority invested with power. By referring to contract theory, we have clarified that we are not concerned here with more or less decorative additions to social life, with common will or common weal, but with the survival of all involved.

4. Both rules of the game and governmental authority are in some ways located apart from, but certainly not above, parties. Government has representative tasks apart from repressive ones; in so far as it has to translate interests into valid norms it acts on behalf of the whole of society; but at all times it remains a party regarded as the whole and thus subject to debate, criticism, and opposition. So far as the rules of the game are concerned, they must neither privilege nor put at a disadvantage either of the conflicting groups; the courts that watch over their observation are, like mediators and arbitrators, powers recognized as neutral in dispute; but they, too, are by no means wholly removed from party strife, for even rules of the game lose their neutral character and require review; above all they do not hover above the parties as a superior truth, for the conflict of parties alone contains the chance of truth, or—since we are moving here in the realm of politics—of justice.

But it requires melancholy reservations to say all this for Germany. The constitution of liberty has considerable power of self-perpetuation, since it is adapted to the persistent forces of social change. But change cannot be brought about without the rational organization of these forces; and thus one easily gets into the vicious circle of demanding from politicians what their society cannot yield, and criticizing in society what its politicians do not want. If the conflict of political groups works, the rules of the game are discussed and modified at times, but generally remain an undisputed common property.

Among these rules of the game are the constitutional rules pertaining to the control of power, and also citizenship rights and possibly the accepted territorial framework. If these rules are deficient, or if they are themselves the permanent theme of political conflict, the common context is put in jeopardy, and the understandable hope for stability is translated into the mistaken nostalgia for synthesis. Germany's curse is not that she did not become a nation, but that she did not become a society. As a result, the social contract itself is permanently at issue—or so one is tempted to say, only to add immediately that here, too, a vicious circle becomes apparent.

Like the social contract, the contract of government is problematical in Germany. The state is nothing but the man-made authority that permits some to exercise power over others, that is, convert interests into valid norms. One characteristic of liberal democracy is that it domesticates this authority—by effective control and the institutionalized exchange of those in power. Thus democracy is not community or association, as German political theorists keep on demanding, because they, too, do not like conflict.

In a democratic context, Bismarck and Adenauer would have been two great liberals, for both of them exposed considered political conceptions to conflict, both loved debate; and one can hardly accuse them of not having produced their own opposition as well but having increasingly accepted the more comfortable existence of unopposed rule. Many Germans do not like power any more than conflict, at least not for themselves; they are inclined to leave this unpleasant reality to others. Thus the aversion to conflict and power creates patriarchal authoritarianism in the favorable case, and total submission in the less favorable one; German society has paid both these prices. But here again it is not enough to distribute personal guilt and thus try to escape the vicious circle easily.

I am well aware that I have failed to offer an explanation of the German propensity for synthesis. That this propensity exists, so that all institutions of German society are characterized by the attempt to evade conflict or to abolish it in superior authorities and institutions, I hope to have shown sufficiently. What the consequences of such an approach are, German history of the last hundred years has demonstrated. But where does the attitude itself come from? Are we supposed to bring in national psychology after all? "The German 'people's character' has been characterized for some two hundred years by a problematized, unsure and particularly tense sense of self with occasionally strong inclination to sthenic reactions of defense and attempts at stabilization" (14, p. 32). That would certainly be an explanation—for the individual who is trying to evade the conflicts of his existence, but only in metaphorical transposition for an entire society as well.

Or are we supposed to embark on the road into history? Certainly *The Belated Nation* and *The German Idea of Freedom* and many other factors have contributed to the nostalgia for synthesis. But where does the road of explanation end as we go back into history? And what is the status of the statements to which it leads? If there is any explanation that concerns German society and avoids the bottomlessness of the individual soul as well as that of national history, it must be found in the answer to the long delayed question of who profits from the utopia of social harmony and, above all, who has profited from it in the last hundred years. Even if this question has no other merit, it does lead us back from myth to reality.

DIVERSITY *OR*

ELITES BETWEEN

MONOPOLY AND CARTEL

14. CHANGES OF THE
GERMAN ELITE

As a political community, society is founded on the contract of government. Society implies the agreement that some are given the right to provide social norms with the binding force of validity. These "some" are, to be sociologically more precise, in the first place roles and positions, positions of leadership. There are times—as we shall soon discover—when these positions are vacant; but in general, social leadership groups correspond to the positions of leadership. One may, with Pareto, call these governing elites, or, with Mosca, a political class—at the peak of the mountain of social power there is no name that has not acquired suspicious connotations. Here we will speak mostly of elites, occasionally of power elites and the political class as well. Thus the contract of government has given human societies, along with the certainty of valid norms, power elites, and with these, resistance against them, conflict (though it should be clear that we are not referring here to an historical fall from paradise, but to a theoretical principle, which is intended to hold for all societies).

Most of the time it is not very comfortable to be at the top, and not only because of the opposition of those who aspire to such eminence. Nevertheless, there is no political class in history that has willingly and happily abdicated its possession of authority. For those who have, or once had it, power holds a strange fascination. For that very reason power makes men inventive. It is almost invariably surrounded by ideologies of legitimacy, which adduce tradition, divine grace, or the law in order to support the establishment of those at the top. These ideologies are, strictly speaking, instruments of mystification; yet they are permissible weapons so long as they do not prevent the other side from returning them in kind. In Germany, even this rule leads us into trouble, but let us bypass this question for the time being.

The remarkable inventiveness of those older leadership groups, which established a German national state under auspices that enabled them to retain their position despite all

resistance and the onslaught of modernity, is striking. Some
of the inventions were not very original, among them, force,
or rather, in its own language, "repression." But many other,
more skillful and original means contributed as much to the
state's survival: the reserve officer corps and the large enterprise, the formalization of social status and the disciplining
of industrial work, the national state of emergency (even if
it had to be prompted a little at times) and the idea of the
majesty of the state. The very fact that German language permits so many sentences whose grammatical subject is "the
state" may be called a success of the old elite concerned about
its power.

This success assumes almost frightening dimensions if we
consider that the traditional elite not only took the sting out
of the aspiring bourgeoisie, but even managed to bind the
growing labor movement by the spell of its ideology of legitimacy. To be sure, each of its victories led German society
further away from liberalism, rationality, modernity, stability,
although, if one does not accept the claim that in the elite of
Imperial Germany the moral idea found its historical incarnation, one may derive from this a charge against the leadership
group as well as against those who should have opposed it.
Who was the mysterious and remarkable political class?

Let us stay for another moment with the abstractions of sociology: What were or are the social positions whose incumbents may be described as the German political class? We are
not concerned here with the rich as such, or the famous as
such, but with the powerful. Among them there may be rich
and famous people as well—power may be followed or preceded by money and fame—but they include in the first place
those who are able, by virtue of their positions, to make laws
(to paraphrase John Locke's definition of power). Among
them are the incumbents of the more narrowly political positions of leadership: members of the executive, the legisla-
tive, the judiciary. In their immediate vicinity we find the
leaders of parties and interest associations and the top of the
service class, that is, the highest civil servants including the
military. Certain social groups influence those in power so
systematically that they must be regarded as part of the power
elite. Among these are: leaders of interest groups, captains
of industry, church leaders, and, increasingly, those who direct the mass media. Other groups provide the reservoir
from which the powerful are regularly recruited: in Ger-

many, these are lawyers, state officials, and university-trained people generally.

This catalogue describes the circle in which we have to seek the power elite. If we select now, from the inclusive groups listed, merely the most important positions, there remains a set of perhaps two or three thousand men (for there are few women among them), which, while it is stratified considerably within itself—nowhere is the drop of power as steep as near its peaks—represents as a whole what may be called the German power elite. To return then to our question: Who were the incumbents of these two thousand positions who managed to play their roles with such disastrous skill?

It is appealing to approach this question by a journey into a distant country (so to speak), that is, by means of a man from Mars, almost entirely unirritated by historical knowledge. This is precisely what, unintentionally no doubt, Maxwell Knight has done in his study of the German executive (cf. 114). Knight examined the social biographies of fifty-four chancellors and secretaries of state of Imperial Germany—a rather small group to express results in percentage figures—but we can enjoy his findings for the time before 1914 quite apart from such professional criticism.

Maxwell Knight discovered that: a particularly large proportion of the executive of Imperial Germany (53 per cent) came from Old Prussia and Berlin; comparatively as many (53 per cent) were born in villages and small towns; their church affiliations were overwhelmingly Protestant; almost two thirds (64.5 per cent) were titled, two fifths by descent; almost three quarters of the Imperial secretaries of state came from families of civil servants, landlords, military officers, or lawyers, but only a small proportion from those of entrepreneurs and merchants (10.4 per cent), and not one from a worker's family; nearly all of them had a secondary-school education, almost two thirds an academic degree as well, and a further 16 per cent had attended a military academy; by their "non-political occupation" (as Knight calls it), civil servants, lawyers and officers dominated, whereas entrepreneurs were extremely rare (1.3 per cent, or one person); more than two thirds of all secretaries of state had held other non-elective political positions before their appointment, most of them (65.8 per cent) as members of the Federal or Imperial Council; no less than 62 per cent did not belong to any political party. "Government under the Kaiser," Knight concludes, "was regarded as not only above parties, but also above 'commercialism'" (114, p. 42).

This is, putting it mildly, a minimal result. Even from Knight's data one can compose stone by stone the mosaic of the Prussian-German elite, often described as feudal, of the Imperial era; and it can do no harm to follow this inductive path for once, even if the pattern of the finished mosaic comes as no surprise.

The executive is not the whole power elite, although Wolfgang Zapf has found that in Germany it is representative of the elite in more respects than one would assume. Other groups display a slightly different picture made up of the same colors. Studies of future university lecturers (Eulenburg), of law graduates in Baden (Mombert) and of higher civil servants in the Düsseldorf district (Most) before 1914 concern its reservoir rather than the power elite itself; even for these wider upper-class groups, however, a pronounced tendency of self-recruitment emerges (232, p. 42). A study of "famous contemporaries," that is, of persons mentioned in the German Who's Who of 1921, straddles, with the decade from 1910 to 1920, two political regimes; even so its result is that the majority of the "intellectual upper class" of "intellectuals and officials" (56.1 per cent) belong to it by descent, and those who do not, have generally come no further than from the "economic upper class."

The only avenue of mobility is to be found in political positions, notably those that, because they represent civil society, are far removed from the center of authority. Joachim Knoll, who studied liberal members of the Imperial parliaments from 1871 to 1912, finds it "striking that most of the time more than half the parliamentarians had an academic education and only a small proportion had attended primary school only" (115, p. 171); moreover, at least one third of the liberal members were lawyers and nearly 20 per cent agrarians. But these findings might be interpreted very differently. Compared with the executive, for example, it is far more striking that there are so many lawyers, independent businessmen, and factory owners in this group, and that it includes any members at all (about 10 per cent) who have a primary-school education only. Such results qualify but do not invalidate the conclusion that Zapf states in a brief sentence: *"Junker* and bourgeoisie supply themselves and each other" (232, p. 48).

At the top of the society of Imperial Germany, self-recruitment was high; in so far as there was any circulation at all, it followed two patterns in particular: "Thus one can say that in Imperial Germany the economic upper class (bourgeoisie by wealth) like the intellectual upper class (bourgeoisie by education) were not only endeavoring to blend with the aristocracy, but that they continuously attracted if not many, at any rate the most gifted, representatives from the middle classes" (232, p. 43). Homogeneity and dominance of the ruling class were not affected by such processes.

But we really do not need necessarily incomplete and late studies of partial groups where the design of the mosaic is concerned. The idea of the state provided a very welcome myth for the leadership groups of Imperial Germany whose only basis was, after all, the apparatus of government. To be sure, agriculture, too, went through a period of prosperity in the early phase of industrialization, and there were also numerous relations between the governing elite and industry; but fundamentally the power elite of Imperial Germany had lost its social basis, its *Hinterland* or constituency. The elite was the state: its civil service, its military, its teachers and professors, judges and registrars. Because this elite had no basis in civil society, it had to try to sever the ties that connected society with government and instead to force both into a synthetic rank order.

Perhaps a situation of this kind permits the prediction ex post facto that the rule of the elite was drawing to a close. In the long run the thin air of the state severed from the forces of society could not suffice for survival. But there is always something dismal about such references to the "long run." The elite of *Junker* and civil servants maintained its power long enough to shape not only German politics of the time but German society of the following epochs as well. The success of its unchecked self-interest—for this it was, although in the end the elite itself began to confuse its interest with "the state" and the "common good," probably by habit rather than malice—proved a Pyrrhic victory, whose astronomical cost had to be paid by German society.

Our own interest in the power elite of Imperial Germany is not confined to the search for the real substance in the mythical fog of the state. German elites express certain traits of

German society that, like underdeveloped citizenship and unwanted conflict, are a structural obstacle to the establishment
of liberal democracy.

It has often been said and is probably true that democracy,
being a competitive system, presupposes the competition of
social forces as well. In a monolithic society organized by
military standards there is neither competition nor democracy.
But who or what in any society are the competing social
forces? It might be said that churches and interest groups,
industry and agriculture, the legal system and the military,
in other words, the great institutional orders of society should
compete with one another in order to fill political democracy
with social life. Such formulations are however hardly less
abstract and metaphorical than the German idea of the state.
Who are the "interest groups"? Who is "agriculture," or "the
military"? In observable social reality at least, the competition
of social forces generally takes place between their leaders,
that is, within the elites. In them the diverse forces of society
are represented; their shape and actions tell us how the lively
diversity of social structure is doing. In this sense, German
elites may be taken as pars pro toto, as the head for the whole
person, so to speak, if we are concerned with the question of
how social diversity is doing in German society.

Competition implies diversity in the sense of the existence
of several elements with approximately equal rank and
chances that are struggling for advantages on this basis. Translated into the language of elite analysis, this is the problem of
the democratic elite. But since we are speaking here of German society, and of Imperial Germany at that, we had better
begin with the counterpart of competition. There are indeed
several such counterparts, each of which has—as we shall see
—shaped the pattern of German society at one time or other.
Even monopoly, the clearest counterpart to competition, may
take on two forms at least. The first, simpler, and more mechanical one consists in one single elite filling all positions of
power with its members and thus keeping the administration
of society entirely under its own, homogeneous management.
In Imperial Germany, this was already largely a bygone type
of elite monopoly; it reappeared in different versions in National Socialist Germany and again in Communist East Germany, and is perhaps characteristic of absolutist political
structures. In Imperial Germany, on the other hand, we encounter another, milder, cleverer, and more interesting ver-

sion of monopoly. Here, one homogeneous social group does indeed rule without restriction, but it does not insist on managing its rule itself. Instead it uses other groups, which are not part of it, to exercise power in its name and according to its directions; in other areas there are "public enterprises," "production under license," and "profit-sharing" among the monopolists. In place of uniform totality we find the hierarchy of authoritarian rule. The appearance of diversity is upheld, only to be permanently abolished in the unambiguousness of a small dominant group: a new turn in the dialectics of state and civil society.

The power elite of Imperial Germany was monopolistic in that its ancient core of Prussian *Junker* and officials clearly set the tone by which all others tuned their instruments. Until the First World War this core elite managed more or less to maintain its dominant position. Then the monopoly was shattered. Following some of the relevant changes of German elites in the ensuing decades will provide both a framework for the detailed analysis of specific elite groups and the data for developing the model of democratic elite.

Let us begin once again with our visitor from Mars, Maxwell Knight, who not only studied the symptomatic group of Imperial secretaries of state, but also compared them with their colleagues in the Weimar Republic and the Nazi regime. This comparison has been extended to the Federal Republic by Hannelore Gerstein and Hartmut Schellhoss (cf. 231). What significant differences are there between the executives of these four epochs of German constitutional history?

So far as regional origin is concerned, Prussia and Berlin have systematically lost in importance since 1918, although the proportion of South Germans was not always as great as under the Nazis (Bavaria: 18.2 per cent, Württemberg and Baden: 15.2 per cent, Berlin: 0 per cent); the proportion of ministers coming from large cities has increased considerably; the same holds, at least for the two democratic periods, for the proportion of Roman Catholics; in National Socialist Germany the proportion of titled former aristocrats once again rose considerably (27.3 per cent), but otherwise it decreased in favor of middle- and working-class men; similarly, the military academy as a place of training rose to an importance comparable to that in Imperial Germany only for the National Socialist executive, whereas in the other two periods there was a slight increase in the proportion of university-trained men;

on the whole, although not consistently, the proportion of ministers whose occupation by training was to be found in business has risen (Weimar: 16.4 per cent, Nazi Germany: 27.3 per cent, Federal Republic: 19 per cent), although civil servants and lawyers, and in the Nazi regime military officers as well, continue to have a peculiar proximity to top political positions. Similar conclusions hold for the social origin of members of the executive; with "commercialism," civil society has invaded cabinets in the form of party membership so that the number of non-partisan ministers had declined almost consistently, interrupted only by a brief period after 1933.

This juxtaposition of epochs shows that changes have in fact taken place. But while even Martian eyes cannot fail to grasp the nature of the Imperial elite, the confrontation of executives of different periods fails to reveal the direction of the changes that Germany's political class underwent. Here, Wolfgang Zapf is more helpful; he has gathered and interpreted a wide range of data about German elites from 1919 to 1961, combining comparisons of periods with analyses of processes. It will be useful, however, to translate his findings immediately into the language of our own analysis.

That the revolution of 1918 did not take place, has been said so often that one hesitates to repeat it. "The revolution of 1918 was a re-formation of elite groups" (232, p. 140). This means that in many areas the old leaders remained in top positions, but the positions themselves appeared in new structural contexts. Above all "the administrative elites survived the revolution unbroken" (232, p. 139); with reservations this also holds for the elites of the economy, the military, the churches, the legal system, and in part even politics. Yet this continuity is not the whole truth of the development of German elites after 1918:

> The nobility was first of all politically finished, even if individual representatives of it survived the inflation relatively well. In any case the mechanism had broken down which had brought about, in the select co-optation of nobility by birth, feudal-capitalist aristocracy of wealth and aristocracy of learning, a firmly structured master caste, which had worked well even on the next lower step in that it had guaranteed the regular replenishment of the bourgeoisie as well without threatening the class structure as a whole. However, the new masters led in the economic sphere only. They were not able to take over social and cultural leadership. The new republi-

can [political-R.D.] leaders on the other hand, who had carried the main burden in abolishing aristocracy, were defamed time and again by the "new masters"; referring to the "trade-union state" of Weimar was a slogan of the times. Many were more easily prepared to re-enthrone the abdicated *Junker*—and this happened consistently to the end of the Weimar Republic—than to allow the "politicians of the system" to interfere with their own realm of power. (232, p. 49.)

I have quoted Zapf so extensively here because his statements are informed and informative on the one hand, but reflect on the other—and perhaps not wholly intentionally—by their slight confusion a characteristic of German society at the time of the Weimar Republic. After 1918, the simple and comparatively transparent picture of a monopolistic elite had been shattered. The year 1918 may not have meant a revolution, but the events of that year have ticked on as a time bomb in the cellar of German society. Unusually high rates of elite circulation—both a reflection and a cause of political instability—bear witness to this fact. The monopoly was disbanded; but as yet nothing new had stepped into its place. If there was diversity, it did not become effective in competition. As public affairs began to slip out of control, the new masters, unsure of themselves, remembered the bygone elite, whereupon that elite marshaled the energy for its last-but-one historical deed.

The time bomb exploded in 1933. "The National Socialist revolution has done away with the representatives of the Weimar system in the course of rebuilding the state with admirable speed, and replaced them by men of the new spirit." An unknown author said this in 1933 in an official catalogue of ministerial positions on both the national and the provincial levels. The first half of his statement at least is correct; the unwilling masters of the Weimar Republic disappeared even from seemingly remote positions, such as Protestant bishoprics. They were replaced, however, not by one but by two groups in an evil misalliance: a sizable number of survivors of Imperial Germany, representatives of the nobility and officer corps, civil service and law on the one hand; and on the other, those marginal petty bourgeois who have led Daniel Lerner to describe the Nazi elite as a "rise of the plebeians" (cf. 129).

In its claims and its effects this elite was monopolistic too; but in a strange turnabout it was now the monopolists of the past (or at least the more pathetic half of its remainder) who took directions from a new elite and acted under strange management. The Nazi elite was stable, indeed stagnant; an almost complete absence of circulation proves that it never got to the point of providing for its inner renewal. "The most immobile political elite group Germany has seen in this century was the central committee of the NSDAP. In the course of twelve years there were but five changes in all," the nature of which Zapf rightly regards as typical of a "leadership clique in the center of totalitarian power": Röhm is murdered, von Schirach is sent off to Vienna, Hess flies off for private peace negotiations to England and is discarded as mentally ill, Bormann moves into his place, Lutze dies (cf. 232).

If it did not appear to be an attempt to minimize its crimes, one might be tempted to say that the internal stagnation of its elites characterizes National Socialism as a short-lived historical phenomenon; it is as if its leaders were never prepared for a regime that extended beyond the span of their lives. In any case, the Nazi elite—if we include in it, as we are doing here, merely the two or three thousand top positions of power —disappeared almost completely after 1945, so that one may say that "the most decisive change in the German elite occurred after the defeat of the Hitler regime, and not in 1918 or 1933" (232, p. 137).

We shall have to return to the question of what this change means, and whether it has led to the formation of a competitively diverse democratic elite. On the negative side this at least may be said: in East Germany, one monopoly has been replaced by another in a deliberate process of transformation. In West Germany, on the other hand, the monopolistic structure of elites has been shattered even more irretrievably than it was in the Weimar Republic; in contrast to Weimar, even the memory of bygone monopolistic claims has become increasingly pointless, if not impossible.

The image of German history on which our study is based so far suggests that the striking discontinuities of its political development have developed on a social foundation of discouraging continuity of non-liberal patterns. It is almost encouraging, therefore, to discover that the important group of elites has undergone profound changes. It would be unwarranted to try to destroy this impression again. But in order to evaluate it and formulate the thesis underlying this part of our study, two further presuppositions are needed, one empirical, the other theoretical.

Empirically, it is useful to reverse the perspective for a moment and look for those continuities of the German political class that have remained unaffected by change, for these exist, and they are not confined to directors of the President's chancery or permanent secretaries in the Chancellor's office. For one thing, not all elite groups were involved to the same extent in the changes described so far. Obviously, the more narrowly political elites have changed with the constitutions; on the other hand, certain elites, such as bishops of the Roman Catholic church, have proved relatively immune to politically induced changes.

But more important than these are continuities in the development of other groups, especially the administrative and the economic elites. Lewis Edinger, a student of the social biographies of the West German political elite after the war, found two extreme career types: 100 per cent of all generals, and 0 per cent of all members of cabinet were in the same position in 1955 that they had been between 1940 and 1944, or between 1933 and 1940 (cf. 62). Administrative and economic elites (represented in this study by sixty-six and forty-seven top positions respectively) can be found between these two extremes; thus every other top-level civil servant and one out of three economic leaders was in a similar position in Nazi Germany. Zapf has shown that the chances of survival were similarly great for these groups in 1918 and 1933; the average period of office of their members is much longer than that of political elites. Zapf believes that he can observe certain tendencies of change here too: "Careers become more and more similar" (232, p. 136). But so far these are merely incipient tendencies.

The same groups that have proved relatively immune to the changes of the last decades have also—not surprisingly—undergone the least social transformation. While the social profile of the political elite has changed very considerably since 1925 (especially by the rise and fall of the Nazi elite) there has been little change with respect to the administrative and economic elites, to top lawyers, generals, and leading entrepreneurs in particular (232, p. 195).

Moreover, these groups are in a sense merely a special case of a general phenomenon. Despite the breakup of the old monopoly and the consequent dwindling significance of nobility, German elite groups from 1918 to the present have been consistently recruited to a disproportionately great extent from middle and higher groups of the service class and the middle class as well as from their own predecessors in elite positions. This general phenomenon has been noted before in our description of German social stratification. Among two hundred and fifty selected incumbents of top positions in Germany, there were in 1925 thirteen, in 1940 five, and in 1955 twenty-four who came from families of the lower half of the hierarchy of social status (in Janowitz's terms), that is, from the "upper" or "lower lower class"; the thirteen in the Weimar Republic were exclusively party and trade-union leaders, the five in the Third Reich were in analogous positions, and the same holds true for nineteen of the twenty-four of the Federal Republic (232, p. 180). The social origin, based on their fathers' occupations, of ten undersecretaries of state in the Federal Republic selected at random (in 1955) is in principle characteristic of the origin of the entire German elite throughout all changes—historian (Dr. phil.), cloth merchant, editor in chief, higher civil servant (architect), professor, civil servant, mayor, physician (professor), physician, professor.

Short of a more thorough analysis, we can only suspect the significance for German society of such constants in its political class. The economic elite, unaffected by the winds of political change, may signify the persistent separation of state and civil society; the economy as the epitome of civil society remains far removed from the centers of political decision. At the same time, the continuity of administrative elites has robbed government, especially in the Weimar Republic, of its properly political character. "All officials are servants of the whole, not of a party," Article 130 of the Weimar Constitution decreed—a principle not upheld by the Basic Law of the Federal Republic and probably utopian in any case.

We have referred to Germany's divided society before; its persistence does not promote lively diversity in German social structure. Thus one is led to conclude that the enduring structures of Germany's political class more than the changing ones are the guide to its illiberal traits. So far, however, the basis for this conclusion is far from sufficient.

In order to provide this basis, we need inter alia the second, theoretical presupposition. What is a democratic elite? I should like to evade a direct answer to this question for the time being and instead do something sociologists are fond of doing if they do not know how to go on, that is, construct a fourfold table.

Power elites may be described in terms of two independent dimensions: that of their social position and type, and that of their political interests and attitudes. There are elites whose social type is characterized by intimate cohesion. Its members are united not merely by similar positions of leadership, but also, for example, by the ways in which they are recruited, the course of their social biographies, significant common experiences, and the other things that we mean when we say that people speak a common language. The number of common subjects of conversation and the degree to which these extend from the sphere of shoptalk to that of small talk, might indeed provide a good index for variations in the social type of elites. If the degree of coherence is high, we will call it an *established elite* (a concept into which the English notion of the Establishment has entered). On the other hand, there are elites that are not "real phenomena" in any sense, but mere "phenomena of order," units constructed by sociologists whose members have neither an intensive sense of belonging together nor many common experiences, biographies, or subjects of conversation. Here the elite is not a group or stratum (in the stricter sense), but at best a category or quasi group. In these cases we will call it an *abstract elite*.

Since we have already referred to the political attitudes of elites at several points, the relevant distinction may be introduced briefly. There are political classes that are largely *uniform* in their political behavior, that profess unitary political ideologies, represent common interests, display little internal conflict or diversity of apparent conviction. Other elites are, on the contrary, politically *multiform*, not to say pluralistic. They have an internal diversity of opinions and interests, which make them appear politically varied and at least potentially contradictory, and they are not motivated by the will to submit to one ruling group and opinion.

The game of crossing such dichotomies (see below) does not yield a theory. In principle it is as arbitrary to cross-classify the concepts as to form them in the first place. But the game provides us with a useful if somewhat involved language to formulate the thesis of this part of our study a little more subtly than has been possible so far. German society began its journey to modernity with an elite that may be described as politically uniform and socially established, at least in its dominant core. This elite corresponded to a political

FOUR IDEAL TYPES OF POWER ELITES

Social type	Political Attitude	
	Uniform	Multiform
Established	Authoritarian elite	Liberal elite
Abstract	Totalitarian elite	?

authoritarianism characterized by the benevolent repression of semicitizens. Traces of this authoritarian elite have survived to the present; they were re-enforced time and again by significant continuities in the development of German elites. Otherwise, however, German elites have experienced the gradual and parallel destruction of their established social type and their uniform political attitude. Twice, in National Socialist Germany and in the Communist DDR, this process was diverted to illiberal purposes by the creation of socially abstract but politically uniform elites. In the Federal Republic, on the other hand, it is proceeding rapidly. The destructive process has not, however, led to the construction of a political class that gives expression to the competing diversity of social forces and is capable of supporting a liberal democracy.

This is but the beginning of the questions to which we shall have to address ourselves: In what sense did the dissolution of established uniformity not lead to liberal diversity? Why did it not? What does the assertion that liberal elites must be politically multiform but socially established mean? And what is hidden behind the question mark in the lower right quadrant of our box game? We will not try to answer these questions in the abstract here; they are the subject matter of the following three chapters, in which the categories introduced here rather rapidly and without much explanation will gain color. This much may be anticipated, however: the development of German elites has produced a dangerous possibility of illiberal structures, which deserves a question mark if only because today it is threatening liberal democracy everywhere.

15. LAWYERS OF THE MONOPOLY

As civil servants belong to the state of Hegelian phantasy and Wilhelminian reality, lawyers are the "general estate" securing the rule of law. It is worth noting therefore that the two estates are largely congruent: more than one half of all German lawyers are civil servants; more than one half of all higher civil servants are lawyers. Indeed, German lawyers have accompanied the rule of law in every version and perversion of its interpretation in the last hundred years.

Perhaps this was their duty, or at least their social role. The general estate, being committed to neutrality, cannot take sides in political matters, so it remains untainted by the struggles of civil society. This means, however, that such an estate is always dependent on masters who give it directives; if we look at it as a social reality rather than a fiction of metaphysics, the general estate is invariably a service class. It is really subject to the demand of unquestioned obedience that the theorists of authoritarian tradition would like to prescribe for us all.

If obedient service of the powerful were the whole reality of German jurisprudence, this might provide a reason for some melancholy reflections about the byways of the relation between power and justice, but it would hardly justify examining the position of lawyers as part of the analysis of the power elite. But obedient service is by no means the whole reality of German law. Just as the rule of law could, in the German political tradition, turn from a formal condition of liberal politics to the substance of the political order itself, its service class was transformed into a master class, a power elite. The general estate alongside and at the service of the parties has become a general estate above the parties; the referee, an authority. It is as if the procedures of the criminal trial were extended here to the whole of society: the experts of law are transformed from advisers and mediators into an agency of inquisition, of attribution of guilt, and of punishment; they remain throughout "masters of the trial" without whom nothing happens. The fallacy of certainty clothes them in dubious authority.

Discussion of the social position of lawyers, like that of the rule of law, gives rise to questions rather than criticism in the first place. There were two periods in German history when the number of lawyers in elite groups decreased significantly —National Socialist Germany and the Communist DDR. Among the incumbents of 250 selected top positions, there were 83 lawyers in 1925, but merely 49 in 1940 (1955: 74) (232, p. 178). While on the average at least 20 per cent of the members of German parliaments were lawyers, only 14 of 466 delegates of the East German People's Chamber (1958) had a law degree, 7 of whom had moreover acquired their degree by correspondence course (cf. 231).

It could be added here that the proportion of lawyers in parliaments is much higher in Great Britain and the United States than it ever was in German history; but this, while a statement of fact, also confuses matters unless we add an analysis of the different social and economic positions of these lawyers, the different legal systems, and the much smaller proportion of lawyers in other British and American elite groups. Thus we can at the most conclude negatively that wherever the proportion of lawyers in leadership groups drop below a certain threshold, this indicates a crisis of the rule of law, and perhaps even of the legitimacy of the regime. This conclusion cannot be reversed without considerable reservations for the rule of law, and not at all for the constitution of liberty. An elite of lawyers may guarantee some version of the rule of law, but certainly does not guarantee a liberal state. There is a specific significance to the fact, therefore, that the German political class may be described, in its central elements, as an elite of lawyers. If we sketch the portrait of the lawyers, we can hope to trace some of the peculiarities of German leadership groups at the same time. It is helpful that for this group (whose members dislike, as Walter Weyrauch reports, social research for its "dissecting" quality) a fairly wide specter of data is today available.

If we take the power elite of German society to consist of the, say, two thousand incumbents of top positions, it is safe to assume that about one half of them are lawyers by training. This is true for the republics of Bonn and of Weimar, with modifications for the Imperial era, and with considerable reservations for the DDR and the Third Reich. In any case, lawyers are, within the German political class, the largest single group characterized by a common feature of social and political significance. Moreover, a hike across the peaks of power in German society shows that lawyers occupy the top everywhere, if in slightly different concentrations.

Let us begin with the "typical" elite category of German society, the political executive. In all regimes, including the Nazi, more than one half of all cabinet members were lawyers. It is not very remarkable perhaps that—to take the example of the Federal Republic—all eight ministers of justice were (until 1965) lawyers; but one of the two chancellors, both foreign secretaries, all four home secretaries, and all three ministers of finance had the same qualification. In the legislature, the proportion of lawyers is lower (22 per cent of the members of the Fourth Bundestag), but still considerable. Among leading members the proportion is higher; 10 of 28 parliamentary and party leaders were lawyers in 1955. Incidentally, and by way of illustrating the general uses of law in German society, these lawyers came to politics from a variety of occupations; of the 114 lawyers of the Fourth Bundestag, 44 were solicitors and barristers in private practice, 21 higher civil servants, 7 judges or public prosecutors, while the remaining 42 were recruited from a colorful mixture of positions in politics and business. If one takes the more narrowly political segment of Germany's power elite as a whole, about two fifths of it are lawyers by training.

In view of the long legal and persistent factual force of the "lawyers' monopoly" on admission to higher civil service, it is not surprising that their share is considerably higher in the administrative elites. Leaving generals aside, more than two thirds of all top administrative positions, including those of "political" (that is, non-career) civil servants were held by lawyers in the Weimar Republic, the Third Reich, and the Federal Republic (232, p. 178); in the wider reservoir of the higher civil servants of all ministries of the interior on the federal and state levels this proportion amounted to 85 per cent in 1962 (cf. 231). Filling top positions of administration with lawyers of the German kind, that is, experts in codified law, is certainly adequate in many cases; but we also have to remember how boundless the range of public administration is in the authoritarian welfare state, where it includes schools and universities as well as opera houses and museums, authorities for the supervision of churches, enterprises in public property, railways and telephone companies, and many other institutions.

Needless to say, lawyers comprise all of the third power, the judiciary. But it is worth emphasizing how prominent the position of lawyers is in those fields that may be called political only in an extended sense, among them associations of many kinds and business. In the past decades, lawyers have increasingly emerged as leaders of interest groups of all descriptions, a phenomenon that may well reflect the growing political significance of these groups. But lawyers also play an important part among business leaders, executives, and managers of large enterprises. Of two thousand German entrepreneurs whose biographies Heinz Hartmann examined in 1954, 19 per cent had the title of Doctor of Laws; the number of fully trained lawyers without a doctorate could not be established, but might well be as high again. In addition, Hartmann observed a tendency in business that is present in other fields as well. His findings show, "that the degree-holders of a law faculty are preferred in young years for promotion into top management by comparison to those from other disciplines. . . . Moreover the lawyers have, among the entrepreneurs with academic training, relatively the best chance to be called into one or more boards of directors. More than one half of all doctors of law have a seat in both management and the board of directors. . . . [This group] includes relatively the largest number of members who are simultaneously engaged in one or two executive boards of enterprises and four or more positions of directors" (91, pp. 161 f.).

In all divisions of the German political class, lawyers play a considerable part. Where they have to compete with other groups, it further appears that they tend to gravitate to the top. The more important the positions of leadership, the greater the probability that they are held by a lawyer. What do these observations mean? What do they mean for German lawyers, for German elites, and, finally, for the society shaped by these elites?

One of the first questions in elite research is which road has led its members to their exalted positions. By actual occupation, the lawyers in Germany's elites can hardly be called one profession; even their relation to the legal system by which they are named differs greatly and is frequently rather tenuous; but they all have in common a few student years in the law faculty of a university. Upon closer inspection this banality proves quite remarkable. In Germany, everybody with a secondary-school final degree has free access to a university.

But if he registers in a faculty of theology or medicine, science or philosophy, this seems to involve a decision of a different order than registering in a faculty of law. In schools there is a quip for this difference, passed on from generation to generation: Whoever does not know what he wants to be, studies law. The sarcasm of this quip is premature. The embarrassment that makes many decide to study law certainly has the negative (although not necessarily bad or evil) side of a lack of specific interest in any subject; but this very deficiency may become the starting point of that journey to the top on which every lawyer has embarked. His unspecific interest proves an admission ticket to the leadership positions of society. Precisely because the student of law is not committed to any specific subject, he can become an expert on general matters, a man at the top. This is the remarkable aspect of the banality that all lawyers have their training in common: in principle, the law faculties of German universities accomplish for German society what the exclusive Public Schools do for the English, and the *grandes écoles* for the French. In them an elite receives its training.

The implications of these statements are many, and we may as well sort out some. In doing so we will assume for the time being that the political class of Germany shares the fate, or perhaps the privilege, of its core of lawyers; so that everybody's journey to the top would start in a faculty of law. What is this journey like? What experience does it involve? What is the character of those who have completed this journey?

There is, to begin with, the decision to take up law. I have quoted the school quip that this decision is unspecific in contrast to the choice of other professions. This is, of course, right only with reservations. Although school provides little basis for a reasonably precise notion of what legal studies are about, many law students have lawyers as fathers, quite apart from the fact that specific legal knowledge does, of course, exist. Nevertheless, the decision to take up law means for many a renunciation of specialized knowledge. However, it is generally not indecisiveness or lack of ability that motivates such resignation, but the very consistent desire for an elite education. Elite positions always require interchangeability; at the top the specialized qualification counts for less than the general qualification for leadership. Thus an apparent deficiency, the renunciation of a specialized field of study, proves an effective sieve for school graduates, which holds those back who never intended to become experts of the general.

The next sieve is the course of study itself; in it, a similarly subtle social mechanism is at work. There is probably no other discipline in German universities in which one hears as many complaints about the "barrenness" and "boredom" of the courses as legal science. The complaints may have two results, both of which are probably equally widespread. One is a change of subject, if not early leaving; after a miserable semester of law the undecided school graduate opts after all for a specialized discipline, unless he takes up a job somewhere. He thereby abandons—unconsciously, of course, and mostly implicitly—the claim to a position of leadership as well. Here, even the arrogant description of economists as "narrow-gauge lawyers" reveals some social justice; there are indeed many who set out to study law and then shift to economics. The other, and in our context more important, result of the "boredom" of study is not a change of subject, but one of attitude, involving among other things a re-evaluation of academic work. As a result, the demands of the university are satisfied with a minimum of energy and in the shortest possible time, often by cramming. At the same time, the non-academic aspects of university life step into the foreground, among them, membership in a student corporation, the pursuit of a rather formal type of social relation, possibly offices in student politics, and other activities that look like fun but in fact make their own demands. This is the education of an elite.

Definite and peculiar capacities are needed to escape the double sieve. Working-class children, for example, do not as a rule display these. Only in faculties of medicine is the proportion of children from working-class families lower than in law; but here too it is, with (1958/59) 3.5 per cent, significantly below the average. On the other hand, nearly 10 per cent of all students of law are the children of lawyers, and know therefore what to expect. Every other future lawyer comes from a civil-service home; it appears that this, too, provides the motivation required to pass the filters that make the journey to the top hazardous. In view of the social stratification of the German people, it is not very surprising that working-class children do not get very far in this journey. But the distance of the future elite from business groups deserves special note.

Among the students of German law faculties, the children of peasants, of independent craftsmen, businessmen, and white-collar workers are heavily underrepresented. If these find their way through the first sieve, the second is still before them. H. and W. Kaupen found that (1958/59) "of male students of law in their first semester, 21 per cent [intended] to go into the administration of law later, whereas 31 per cent wanted to go into business; among students in the eighth semester exactly twice as high a proportion (42 per cent) wanted to be lawyers or public prosecutors, while only 9 per cent (!) gave business-oriented occupations as their goal" (112, p. 134). And the others? It is tempting to suspect that they followed one of our two ways, that is, either changed their field of study or adapted to the evidently less business-prone values of the legal road to the top.

These formal data merely sketch the silhouette of the portrait we intend to paint. Although it may be said that the subject matter of the study of law provides, in Germany, merely an occasion for a very different social process—the education of an elite—this is not the whole truth of jurisprudence; indeed, it would be a great mistake to underestimate the effects of its theoretical and methodical substance. Not every subject of training could be taken, by social decision, as an occasion for elite selection and formation. But there is a choice, and evidently an elite educated in German law faculties differs from one that has passed through English Public Schools or French *grandes écoles,* or indeed one that has fought its way to the top in the competitive market of the occupational world. The differences may be made explicit.

"The conserving attitude is," Rudolf Wassermann, himself a German judge, says, "while not inborn in German judges, yet as natural to many as if it was a 'second skin'" (cf. 222). It is indeed a second skin, namely, a social role, and this not only for judges but for lawyers everywhere. The law epitomizes the norms that hold, and thus, in a society; it is the incarnation of the status quo. Whoever administers it in whatever position is, in that capacity, chained to the status quo of social and political conditions. A certain conservatism is therefore not idiosyncrasy, much less personal default on the part of lawyers, but a necessary attribute of their role in society.

Such statements are obviously too simple to describe the complicated and variegated roles of lawyers fully. Lawyers occupy many different positions; as interpreters of law, they contribute to its development as well, and their self-image places them in a field of tension between law and justice, right and might. But the lawyer can never leave what exists and holds through such openings. His role remains one in which criticism counts for less than loyalty, originality for less than sense of tradition, imagination for less than knowledge of the existing legal order. The conservatism of lawyers is the heteronomous conservatism of the service class, which does not create norms, but administers them and acts by social position rather than free decision.

There is another dichotomy of the lawyer's role that might be added to these. In it, the lively competition of the economy counts for less than the more rigid order of the state. Walter Weyrauch, a German lawyer who emigrated to the United States, reports his surprise when he first heard the economic metaphor of the "market place of ideas" used by Justice Holmes: "The metaphor may sound strangely materialistic to many non-Americans" (226, p. 207). Weyrauch quotes two famous statements of this kind, one by Justice Holmes, the other by Justice Douglas: "The best test of truth is the power of the thought to get itself accepted in the competition of the market. When ideas compete in the market for acceptance, full and free discussion exposes the false and they gain few adherents."

These are liberal sounds indeed from a lawyer's mouth. They are, as Weyrauch emphasizes, not the rule in the United States either—both are taken from dissenting opinions; but such economic metaphors are more unlikely still in German law (which rarely permits the publication of dissenting opinions). The distance of lawyers from business occupations does not hold everywhere either. "The weight of the recruitment of American lawyers rests with the families of independent businessmen and leading salaried people in the economy" (189, p. 129). It can then be maintained as a minimal conclusion that the German elite is not brought any closer to the more liberal reality of the economy by its education in law faculties.

If the conservatism of their roles is a general feature of lawyers in all countries, and the distance between law and business is not confined to Germany, we may still find a German peculiarity, and a relevant one, in the legal system that Imperial Germany bequeathed to the whole country. Corresponding to the markedly hierarchical, at times authoritarian structure of legal institutions there is, not surprisingly, a codified and generally rigid law:

> An initial insight into the German theory of legal sources can be acquired by examining the validity of the following principles:
> 1. German law is statutory law.
> 2. In Germany the attempt is made to treat substantively unitary legal categories together and in a single statute. Legislation is governed, in other words, by the so-called Principle of Codification.
> 3. Sources of law exist in a hierarchy, in which the law of the "preferred" form of social organization has precedence over that of the subordinate form. The constitution takes precedence over a statute, the latter over an administrative regulation and an internal administrative regulation. (15, p. 9.)

As so often in this study, we have to cut a long story very short in order not to lose the thread of our analysis. There are entirely different legal systems and, more particularly, much less systematic ones that are based on different principles of legal knowledge. "There is always only one answer under the law, and sociology has nothing to do with it," a German judge decreed in an interview, only to add a moment later, in comparing German and American law: "I wonder whether it is wise to put so much emphasis on problems instead of results. I feel that the underlying skepticism may lead to pessimistic outlooks on the part of the American people. Doubts will invade every sphere of life" (226, pp. 76 f.).

Doubts—or the test of ideas on the market place of discussion. Justice Holmes and "Judge X" (as Weyrauch calls the gentleman just quoted) speak of the same things; but they differ in more than their language. Whoever does not have or need certainty may have confidence in discussion and criticism; but German law is governed by an unbounded nostalgia for a certainty, by whose standards all discussion drags truth into the dust of everyday life and desecrates it. For German lawyers, with all their love of "cases," it is an insult to be called "casuistic," and an ambition to be "dogmatic." As legal institutions, and, even more, the practice of legal relations, exclude the conflict of parties wherever possible, the legal order is designed to free the lawyer from the disturbing variety of precedents without hierarchical articulation. The science in which the lawyer is trained is not experimental, but hermeneutic; here, the interpretation of texts is far more important than an independent relation to the relevant realities of past and present. Such science engenders attitudes that must be called subordinate, if not servile, rather than polemical; the certainty of German lawyers is based on unmovable givens, not on their own insights.

It is well to remember that all this is not the primer of just any, even if important, estate of German society, but that of its political class in so far as it has been educated in faculties of law. Clearly, all that has been said holds for lawyers engaged in specifically legal positions as well, and perhaps a fortiori. In fact, the dual task of law faculties to serve as specialized schools for judges, prosecutors, and solicitors on the one hand, and as institutions for educating the elite on the other, has this consequence among others, that specialized legal knowledge is depreciated and the prestige of the legal profession in the narrower sense is damaged. Those who remain in the legal profession have somehow failed to make the grade. Possibly one out of every fifty young men with a law degree finds his way to the peak of those two thousand whom we have here described as the power elite; but many of the best lawyers are climbing about on the mountains of power and end up in the legal profession because they failed to get on, or for other motives unrelated to the application of law. Under these conditions, it is obviously justified to look at all holders of law degrees as the well-defined reservoir of Germany's power elite, in which many of its traits may be found.

The social profile and attitudes of this reservoir of the German political class confirm the picture of its social role. Earlier, we discussed the social origin of German lawyers; the fact that the overwhelming majority of them come from families of similar social status. Legal occupations are not avenues of mobility, except perhaps for the children of state officials. The status of legal occupations themselves supplements this conclusion. Of about 45,000 German lawyers 40 per cent are directly in the service of the state. A further 40 per cent are solicitors; but of these only a minority may be described as members of a "liberal profession" while most are business lawyers attached to firms or in other functions. And this is true of the remaining 20 per cent as well. Lawyers are immobile not only socially, but geographically too. They share the love of the German for the familiar and shy away from those breaks with inherited ties that cast doubt on traditional attitudes and may well be a condition of a liberal sense of competition. Studies of the social biography of German lawyers regularly yield a profile of conservatism and traditionalism, which far transcends the demands of their roles.

Corresponding to the social profile is an image of society. Dietrich Rüschemeyer has tried to sketch this image in a comparison of German and American lawyers:

> It would be our hypothesis that beyond a bourgeois conservatism, which may be found in both groups of lawyers, education and the dominant groups of social origin favor the following attitude among German lawyers: a relatively narrow and unpolitical understanding of their own role in society, an image of society as a leveled-in middle-class society, and a view of politics that is shaped by implicit elitist notions, by emphasis on legal correctness and administrative order and by leftovers of a belief in objectively "right" political solutions. American lawyers frequently define their roles less narrowly and less unpolitically. Their political attitudes would vary more in general. Interests and forces standing behind the legal and political forms and developments find a more realistic interpretation, and politics is understood more in the sense of pluralistic clash of divergent goals of equal right. (189, p. 136.)

Their social origin shuts German lawyers off from large parts of the society in which they are living. Their education does not contribute to their closing such gaps, at least by way of acquired knowledge. It does not open the horizon of the children of state officials for the peculiar or, despite Hegel, neither immoral nor anarchical values of civil society. It is hardly possible to conclude from all this that openness, flexibility, preparedness for new and surprising situations, tolerance for self-steering market situations in many regions of social life, skepticism toward the claim of the state to embody the moral ideal, belong to the equipment of the German lawyer.

Such images of society are clearly still very general attitudes; between them and people's actual behavior several links are missing. However, they can all be found on one straight road, which leads us to a syndrome, the description of which brings us somewhat nearer to an understanding of the German elite. At its psychological end, findings may be relevant, as Walter Weyrauch derives them from interviews with more than one hundred, somewhat prominent German lawyers: "In summary, lawyers as a group, contrary to com-

mon beliefs and formal resolutions, may have personality
traits that counteract or retard a wide distribution of democratic values among all persons" (226, p. 279).

Weyrauch is trying hard not to single out the German lawyers interviewed by him too much from the circle of their
colleagues in other countries; he therefore formulates in general terms what obviously, judging by the course of his own
investigation, applies to German lawyers above all:

> It is doubtful that the activities of lawyers all over the world
> will effectively bar the recurrence of any of the more disturb-
> ing past events, such as antidemocratic movements, war and
> other forms of violence, extreme nationalism, race hate and
> other prejudices, suppression of minorities, general suspicious-
> ness, jealousies, and resentments. Some of the personality fea-
> tures of lawyers even seem to encourage antidemocratic de-
> velopments. Lawyers may cling to ultraconservative groups
> rather than to more permissive ones.
>
> Although in every power process lawyers will be found on
> both sides of the fence, it is likely that the more highly
> qualified will adhere to the side holding and defending an
> already existing power position. Minority groups, mere aspir-
> ants to power, and the indigent will continue to find it dif-
> ficult to retain the services of qualified legal talent. Lawyers
> will feel discomfort in situations in which power is unsettled
> or in flux. The resulting uncertainty is incompatible with the
> personality structure of many lawyers, and they may not feel
> secure until a dominating power center has been established.
> (226, pp. 280 f.)

Weyrauch combines his jurisprudence with empirical social
research and psychological interpretation in an impressive, if
not always fully convincing manner. One of the unambiguous
results of his study of German lawyers is, however, the cited
contrast between external formalism and dogmatism and inner
fears and insecurities in many of those interviewed. This conflict gives an indication of the strange condition of German
elites after 1918, which may be supplemented by other, more
sociological considerations.

The behavior of lawyers in the more narrowly legal sphere
has for decades been a focus of public discussion, especially
in connection with decisions in criminal-law cases of political
relevance. There are certain constants in this discussion. One
of these found its clearest expression in Ernst Fraenkel's study
Zur Soziologie der Klassenjustiz [on the Sociology of Class
Justice]. Even in 1927, when Fraenkel wrote his book, the

term "class justice" was not very popular with those concerned; today it is entirely taboo. Yet the question of the extent to which legal decisions reveal a bias that can be explained only in terms of the peculiar social profile of those who make them, and that in any case serves the powers that be, has not lost its urgency. The other constant in the discussion of jurisdiction concerns its more or less explicit attitude to the state. Johannes Feest plausibly refers, in his study of the social origin of Federal Court judges, to a sentence of the Federal High Court against a conscientious objector of 1939, in the argument of which it is said that the defendant should not be preferred to those "who regarded it—possibly also because of an unambiguous rejection of the National Socialist rule of terror—on the basis of an equally conscientious consideration of all circumstances as their duty not to evade military service as it was demanded from them by the authority of the state. . . ."

The "authority of the state" provides the decisive argument here, and it is quite consistent therefore if a legal journal comments on this sentence: "Even the state of injustice, which scoffs the idea of justice daily, still fulfills, in so far as it continues to exist as a territorial community, as an emergency roof a demand of legal security, because this emergency roof makes possible the physical survival of the community" (231, p. 144). This is Lassalle's interpretation of Hegel's state in a new version: Just as Imperial Germany at the time of the Socialists' Law provided an "emergency roof" for the socialist, the Nazi empire of injustice did this for the lawyer. In any case, the state remains an authority whose commands are under all circumstances sufficiently close to justice to relieve the lawyer from the necessity of contrasting law and morality.

So far, we have presented our case in an unduly static manner. The relation of lawyers to the state was by no means the same under all constitutions. It is a familiar fact that in the Weimar Republic German judges at times openly scorned the constitution in their arguments; on the other hand, there is no evidence that German judges showed a similar independence of judgment toward the constitutional reality of the Nazi regime. Kübler's summary of the practice of judges and the theories of law is scathing but unrefuted: "The more authoritarian the German State was, the more faithful to law the judge was; to the extent to which the community became more democratic, the binding force of the law became problematic to the judge" (122, p. 106).

If we assume that judges are symptomatic of that wider reservoir of elites that consists of all lawyers, a peculiar attitude to law and politics becomes recognizable. There is an authoritarian bent in the attitude of German lawyers, but the authority to which this is directed is not just that of any ruling group. Although lawyers accept any state at least as an emergency roof of order, they make more or less subtle distinctions in their behavior. If the regime is democratic in tendency, they do not hesitate to adduce natural law to remind it of its lack of authority; if the authority of the state is absolute, lawyers become its obedient servants. Thus the political attitude of many lawyers is not authoritarian in a formal sense, that is, an attitude of service to any state, but in a substantive sense, that is, related to one definite regime. This regime is that of Imperial Germany.

For the administrative elite of the Federal Republic, two authors have reached similar conclusions on the basis of interview studies. John Herz remarks that the higher civil servants survived the Nazi period virtually unimpaired, but have nevertheless changed their political attitude somewhat. Gradually the attitude of the Prussian civil service, directed against democracy but for the rule of law, is giving way to a fundamental opportunism of political and moral indifference (cf. 202). Wolfgang Zapf may be wise to formulate his conclusions a little more cautiously, but he too remarks that "the postwar years with denazification and dismissals" have "dissolved to some considerable extent the ideological putty, the autocratic-authoritarian orientation of the German civil service" (232, p. 122). Civil servants are predominantly lawyers too. If one adds such findings to the features of the social character of lawyers sketched so far, a picture of the politics of this German elite emerges.

German lawyers began their journey into modern society as lawyers of the monopoly, that is, as part of the service class of the monopolistic power elite of Imperial Germany. After 1918, the monopoly broke; but the lawyers remained and continued to orient themselves to its authority. This resulted in a grotesque, but consequential outlook; a social group insisted on serving a master who no longer existed. Relations of power had—to paraphrase Weyrauch—got into a state of flux, were certainly put in question; but the lawyers tried to stabilize them by firmly closing their eyes and ritually serving the passed-away certainty of power. They also closed their eyes to the fact that in the new, more uncertain conditions of power, what appeared to them as service was in fact an exercise of power. They turned into an elite malgré lui. The disgusting pronouncements by prominent German lawyers in 1933 and 1934 can be understood only if we assume that many of them hoped to regain the long-lost authority at last. One of the esteemed law professors of the Federal Republic expressed this feeling in 1934 in an unfortunately characteristic way:

> . . . despite this we have to be clear about the fact that speaking of the exclusive commitment of the judge to the law means something different today from what it did before . . . because by the identity of the legislator with government, an authoritarian direction of the judge by the guiding principles of the leadership of the state is today guaranteed and gives him a firm hold even in the sphere of his discretion. By this very fact it is guaranteed that every act of the Führer's will is expressed in the form of law and thus satisfies the need for legal security that is present in the people. In this sense, the National Socialist state is a rule of law as well. . . . (178, p. 173.)

The price was high; but at least National Socialism managed to make clear even to lawyers the fictitious quality of their nostalgia for a bygone authority. So far, however, the confidence of those who enjoy the market place of ideas and therefore need the liberal state has not yet been established. For the time being, nothing has come about but great insecurity, which may (as Herz suspects) lead to indifference and opportunism, or perhaps (as Weyrauch believes he has found out) to a frightening tendency for psychical and psychosomatic disturbances, or simply an endless disorientation.

Thus our elite has dissolved under our hands. Out of the lawyers of the monopoly, after its breakup, has developed not a successful monopoly, but a reservoir for a power elite against its own will, without confidence. We have assumed that lawyers are the entire political class, but, in fact, they form merely a part. Besides them there are other leadership groups, whose profile we will try to draw in a moment. What remains, then, of the general estate that administers the adaptable rule of law?

The fact remains that there are lawyers in many leadership

positions in German society. The observation, therefore, remains that the law faculties of German universities are the only institutions in which a considerable part of the German political class spends a part of its path through life together. There also remains the statement that this path promotes, for a number of reasons, a nostalgia for certainty, authority, and synthesis. We have to conclude, therefore, that the most important reservoir of the German elite is by origin, education, position, and behavior unprepared for the constitution of liberty. Neither the more inclusive category of holders of law degrees, nor the narrower group of those who have climbed the peaks of the two thousand, is a self-confident elite, or part of such. Their anxiety is greater than their political will; their desire for security, greater than that for power. Thus German lawyers have become an unwilling elite.

16. SERVICE, WEALTH,
AND POWER

If one half of the upper two thousand of German society are lawyers, who are the other thousand? We will put this question somewhat differently. Lawyers share, as we have seen, an educational qualification which, by virtue of the experiences it involves and the attitudes that follow from it, is relevant for the political sociology of Germany. For the other member groups of the German political class, however, with the single exception of the military, such tangible ties of social biography are lacking. Here we have to look first at less immediately relevant features, such as the common tasks of these elites, and speak of officers and officials, elites of churches and of mass media, leaders of interest groups and of business. All these groups include lawyers in varying numbers; but this overlap supplements rather than disturbs our analysis.

We have tried to paint a portrait of the lawyers; with the other elites of the German political class we will confine ourselves to more modest sketches. This is not because there are no data about these elites. Thanks above all to the research of American social scientists (among them Gabriel Almond, Gordon Craig, Karl Deutsch, Lewis Edinger, John Herz, Morris Janowitz, and several others), which has since been supplemented by some German authors (such as Heinz Hartmann, Helge Pross, Wolfgang Zapf), there is today a rather broad basis of data about German leadership groups. But for the progress of our own analysis, selecting some conspicuous or telling pieces from these data, is sufficient. Here, as elsewhere in this study, the presentation of data serves the purpose—partisan, if one wants to call it that—of finding a sociological response to the German Question.

The following sketches are to begin with unconnected. Characteristically, general statements about features of all German elites are hard to make—with one significant exception. Data may be assembled from many studies that suggest the silhouette of a profile of the social origin of German elites; one such attempt has been made here (see following page).

Social Origin of German Elites

	1 West Germany—Population	2 Upper middle class	3 Elite (Zapf)	4 Elite (Zapf)	5 Elite (Zapf)	6 Students	7 Members of 4th Federal Parliament	8 Federal Ministers 1949-63	9 Political elite (Deutsch-Edinger)	10 Political elite (Zapf)	11 Higher civil servants, ministries of interior	12 Judges on high courts	13 Attachés, Foreign Office	14 Generals	15 Administrative elite (Deutsch-Edinger)
	1955	1955	1925	1940	1955	1955/6	1963	1964	1956	1955	1962	1959	1962	1963	1956/7
Upper middle class	4.6	27.7	46.9	31.7	42.9	47.2	15	30	62.9	36.7	50	60.1	73	91	95.1
Lower middle class	38.6	55.5	18.0	30.1	22.4	47.4	20	50	—	36.7	44	35.0	25	9	—
Upper lower class	13.3	9.7	4.1	1.6	7.5	5.0	4	4	23.7	11.7	5	2.7	2	—	4.9
Lower lower class	38.6	5.8	1.2	0.4	2.0	—	3	6	13.4	3.2	—	0.1	—	—	—
Unclassifiable	4.9	1.3	29.8	36.2	25.2	0.4	57	11	—	11.7	1	2.1	—	—	—
n	3385	155	244	259	251	110,688	544	54	186	60	738	856	389	57	163

	16 Administrative elite (Zapf)	17 Economic leaders	18 Entrepreneurs (Deutsch-Edinger)	19 Economic elite (Zapf)	20 Church leaders (Deutsch-Edinger)	21 Church leaders (Zapf)	22 Editors in chief (Zapf)	23 Communications elite (Deutsch-Edinger)	24 Writers	25 Professors	26 3rd People's Chamber, DDR	27 Government, DDR	28 DDR "State apparatus"	29 Generals, DDR	30 Managers, DDR
	1955	1955	1956	1955	1956	1955	1955	1956	1960	1963	1959	1962	1963	1963	1960
Upper middle class	61.7	74	81	44.4	63	42.8	36.3	75	73.2	65.8	8	—	?	15	25.3
Lower middle class	16.6	26	—	15.2	—	38.2	4.6	2	24.4	31.8	34	27	27	7	36.8
Upper lower class	—	—	—	—	6	9.5	9.1	23	2.4	2.4	11	58	73	78	20.8
Lower lower class	—	—	19	—	31	—	—	—	—	—	45	15	—	—	17.1
Unclassifiable	21.7	—	—	40.4	38	9.5	50.0	—	—	—	3	26	?	—	—
n	60	52	47	52	38	12	22	79	127	4155	474	26	?	28	991

(Stratification according to Janowitz, Sources 49, 57, 105, 110, 130, 231, 232. All figures are percentages.)

If one were to pursue such social profiles into the past, certain differences would emerge—as columns 3 to 5 of our table intimate—but the differences would remain comparatively minor. German elites have not changed very much in characteristics of social origin and position since Imperial times.

Unambiguous as this finding is, it is also misleading, as our analysis of changes of the German elite has shown. We see here how crude the screen of superficial data on social mobility is if one wants to grasp the image of society and political behavior of groups. By changes in the context, for example, within which German elites had to act, even similar preconditions have acquired a completely different meaning. This may be also true for seemingly similar modes of behavior. The German lawyers' love of authority has a very different significance in the Empire, in the state of Weimar, under Nazi rule, and in the Federal Republic. For that, if for no other reason, we will have to pass time and again—possibly a little too rapidly at times—from the concrete insignificances of social research to the more relevant hypotheses of sociological analysis.

Closest to the lawyers is the *administrative elite* of civil servants in top positions. The formulation may seem misleading. Did we not find earlier that two thirds of all higher civil servants of ministries of the interior are lawyers by training? Nevertheless, the distinction has its meaning. "For a common legal profession, the administrative lawyers have undoubtedly done least of all branches of legal activity. Most of them forgot as quickly as possible, that they were 'by descent' lawyers . . ." (13, p. 19).

Fortunately we do not have to examine such charges here; but whether they are right or wrong, they document that the higher civil servant has his own social role. What is more, he fills it in his own way. So far as the proportion of members recruited from upper-class families and trained in universities is concerned, there is little difference between the administrative elite and other German elites. However, the administrative elite is, in the Federal Republic, a little more heterogeneous than others; the proportion of refugees is above average among higher civil servants; there are comparatively many officials coming from petty bourgeois families of the "lower middle class"; there is a growing number of higher civil servants by promotion in the upper ranks of ministries of the interior. These, however, may well be marginal phenomena in contrast to the overwhelming fact that in Imperial Germany, the Weimar Republic, and the Federal Republic about one half of all higher civil servants were recruited from the families of civil servants. This is the real inner continuity of German officialdom.

There has been much discussion of this continuity. The Prussian values of discipline, exactness, legality, incorruptibility have often been praised or condemned, and usually in connection with the civil service. Herz, Deutsch and Edinger, Zapf, and others have emphasized the immobility of the administrative elites in the winds of political change. But it holds for higher civil servants, too, that the same people are not the same at different times. If it is true that German officials have "traditionally considered themselves the faithful servants, not of the public, but of the state—an abstraction that has always played a great role in German political theory," the very abstractness of the point of reference has permitted very different political effects. For service always meant influence as well, and—to quote Deutsch and Edinger once again—"the extent of [the] influence [of the administrative elite] over policy making has varied more or less inversely with the power of the political elite" (57, p. 81).

This influence was considerable in the Weimar Republic, but small in the Empire and the Third Reich. In substance it meant the support of that authoritarian tradition to which Prussian officialdom owed its origin and peculiar character. This may be said today in the perfect tense. In our analysis of legal attitudes we have cited administrative lawyers as a prime example of the gradual breakup of this love for a fading authority. Opportunism, pragmatism, disorientation are the new attitudes that top bureaucrats display in the Federal Republic. In this alone they have remained akin to their predecessors in that they, too, have power without really wanting it.

The other, social continuity indicated by the high degree of self-recruitment on the part of civil servants, has remained effective throughout. Traditional Prussian virtues probably no longer describe West German bureaucrats. But hierarchical thinking, an orientation to individual competition rather than collective solidarities, a service-class mentality combined with a certain formalism, an acute sense of competences and regularities—these are traits that are propagated in officialdom.

Even the dependent minority the feudal lord was able to uphold by comprehensive "paternal" care for his officials survives in the excessive claims for security on the part of civil servants in the welfare state. Even if this must be attributed as much to its inescapable social role as to its historically specific social character, the fact remains that the administrative elite shows few traits that could permit describing it as liberal.

By officials we have so far understood the higher civil servants of public administration. But officialdom extends much further in Germany. There is hardly an institutional order in which there are no *Beamte;* and even where this is the case, their perquisites are simulated: in the theological "service examination," for example, or in the notions of banking or mining "officials." It does not seem too daring to infer from such symptoms that civil-service attitudes have spread to many non-governmental elites. This is obvious for one group that, in fact, provided the model of bureaucratic status rigidity, the *military elite.*

Much scorned, much praised—and both often for the wrong reasons—the military elite has survived the changes of the decades since the First World War remarkably unimpaired. Even in the Federal Republic, military leaders are the elite with the highest proportion of men born in Central and East Germany (41 per cent) and the highest proportion of Protestants (83 per cent). There are two other records for which military leaders compete with top diplomats: the proportion of titled members of the former aristocracy is, with 15 per cent, still extraordinarily high; the proportion of children from upper-class families is also above average. A West German general from a working-class family does not exist. Self-recruitment in the narrower sense is also notoriously high with the military: "In 1925, 52 per cent, in 1933, 51 per cent, and in 1944, 29 per cent of the military leadership group had themselves officers as fathers. Of the forty-nine Federal Army generals or admirals, for whom the father's occupation could be found out, eighteen, or 37 per cent are the sons of officers" (231, pp. 172 f.). The military is an intact elite then—or so it might appear, especially if we added the important common features of social biography both in the formal sense of career and the more specific one of historical experiences.

There can be little doubt that the double rupture in the

history of the German military, 1918 and 1945, has left its traces in the career patterns and social outlook of its elite. After 1918, the Imperial officer corps was reduced to almost one tenth of its former size; what the other 90 per cent did, was investigated by Nothaas in 1930. Most of them, especially former generals, had characteristically not acquired a new occupation; only about 8 per cent had migrated to business leadership positions. An alienated group of this size and quality had to represent a political potential as well. After 1945, the rupture was even more radical, and the prospect of rearmament much more remote. Even generals had to take up civil occupations. What this meant will become evident from an impressive confrontation. These are the occupations of the fathers of ten generals of 1955 chosen at random (namely, by alphabetical sequence): grammar school director, professor, secondary-school director, primary-school director, farmer, general, higher civil servant, higher civil servant general, officer (232, p. 182). And these are the occupations held by a corresponding group of generals themselves in the years after 1945: physician, textile representative, artistic potter, building laborer (later industry), head clerk, commander of a mine-sweeping unit, position in industry, farmer, sales manager on a pleasure steamer, employee in a travel agency (cf. 232). To be sure, nearly all these occupations are in the nature of temporary and half-hearted solutions; but even so they involve a contact of two worlds that was bound to have a lasting impact above all on the military leaders.

In the final part of this study we will discuss the role of the military in the dissolution of the Weimar Republic. In this connection, another aspect is relevant, which raises further doubts about the intactness of the military elite even in Weimar, to say nothing of the Federal Republic. Otto Heinrich von der Gablentz has a plausible concept to characterize the peculiar relation of loyalty of leading military men toward their originally royal master: "I am tempted to say that here a subalternity or subservience of an elite has developed, a position sub alterno, below another one, which involves looking up to the other as a superordinate, and this in a group that otherwise always claimed to be an elite before itself as well as others" (78, p. 208). Von der Gablentz shows that, even in Weimar, this elite subservience remained (like the service of officials) without a master to serve; an observation underlined rather than contradicted by the pathetic example of Hindenburg who, before he accepted the candidacy for Reich President, asked the exiled emperor for his permission (78, p. 216).

Officers, too, found their search for the majesty of the state apparently satisfied in National Socialist Germany; as we examine the German opposition against Hitler we shall look more closely at the nearly unbearable ambivalence of recognition and detachment that resulted from the combination of such satisfaction with the retention of traditional values. In the Federal Republic the elite subservience of the military is at last without any majesty. Two possibilities of development remain, one of which may be described as the conquest of the army by the citizen (and the bourgeois), the other as a defensive insecurity in relation to society. This career elite does not advance a general demand for power either, much as its passing traditions may contradict liberal values.

As we have seen, most generals are Protestants. Werner Baur has investigated this fact and found that in other countries with several denominations military leaders are also largely Protestants, and that even among generals originating from predominantly Catholic regions of the country, the majority are Protestants. "The explanation would have to be sought in the area of ethical-religious values. An affinity obviously exists between certain Protestant values and the ethos of service to the state" (231, p. 176).

The affinity is certain, although authoritarian political structures have not remained confined to Protestant countries and are clearly more characteristic of the internal organization of the Roman Catholic church than of Protestant churches and sects. Bismarck's struggle against Catholicism and the specific traditions of Prussian Protestantism have, however, given the two churches greatly different relations to secular authority in Germany, which is reflected in the history of *church elites*. The principle of the Catholic attitude was withdrawal; of the Protestant, surrender. Thus the Catholic bishops present the image of a highly eccentric German elite. Among them, the proportion of children from lower-class families is comparatively high, education is uniform and separate, terms of office are particularly long, and the effect of political changes is almost zero.

The Catholic church, including its leadership groups, preserved itself as a society within society with its own rhythms of change, which were almost imperceptible from outside. By contrast, the Protestant elites offer, at least since the Weimar Republic, an almost dramatically exact reflection of the political changes in the country. Within a year, in 1933, nine of the twelve leading men of the Evangelical church had been exchanged; a similar turnabout took place after 1945, and the comparison between Protestant leaders in West and East Germany confirms this picture (cf. 232). But even so radical a circulation of the Protestant elite has not led to any great changes in its social composition, if we leave the DDR aside for the time being. In this respect, it may be worth noting that only five per cent of all Catholic bishops, but one quarter of all Protestant church leaders come from regions beyond the Iron Curtain (57, pp. 106 ff.). Here too there are striking parallels between the leadership groups of the Evangelical church and the Social Democratic Party.

"Withdrawal" and "surrender" no longer describe the attitude of church elites in the Federal Republic. Today, the Catholic church has got little reason for withdrawal, and the Evangelical church is painfully aware of its own history of surrender. Deutsch and Edinger impute to the Catholic elite a special interest in the Federal Republic and its West and South European ties, which the Protestant elites do not share; these by contrast would have to be counted among the main advocates of reunification as well as a more flexible attitude to the East (57, pp. 106 ff.). Both are attitudes that do not directly concern the approach to domestic affairs, and thus the constitution of liberty. This is a condition that is as far removed from the Catholic fondness for the traditional ties of men as it is from the preference of Prussian Protestantism for order and authority. Public statements by church leaders about foreign and military policy, economic and educational policy, the "economic miracle," the "decay of morality," and "materialism" make it clear that modernity and liberalism are still alien to the churches. However, there can be little doubt that in the religious elites, conditions of change are more favorable than with the groups discussed before.

The *cultural elites* of German society consist largely of those who, as intellectuals, are the subject matter of a special analysis in this study (Chapter 18). To be sure, not all professors or artists are intellectuals, and many a civil servant who is not a professor may belong to this elusive social category—the concept is no less disputed than that of a cultural elite. But however this matter of definition is settled, we can anticipate the conclusion of later analyses and say that the social profile of these elites differs surprisingly little from that of other upper-class groups. The resemblance extends far into observable behavior. The spread of a service-class mentality has not by-passed these groups; they, too, have a defensive social self-image and are far from being a confident elite. As part of the political class, the position of the cultural elites of German society is made even more precarious by the fact that cultural policy is one of the stepchildren of politics in a country whose values define culture and politics as two contradictory worlds.

"The control of the mass media lies in the hands of a somewhat amorphous group, which includes members of most of the elites we have discussed." We can take over this sentence by Deutsch and Edinger without qualification and add to it the observation: "Radio and television networks are government-owned, but their control is shared between government officials and representatives of party and interest group elites who sit on the boards of these public corporations. Newspapers and periodicals frequently represent the views of some other elite, even when they call themselves 'independent' " (57, p. 117). But all this does not tell us very much yet about the *communications elites,* about whom our information is, in fact, comparatively scanty.

Outstanding editors and directors of broadcasting stations in the Federal Republic are on average younger than other elites; this suggests that they at least are not yet a career elite. Apart from the important but untypical interlude when the press was licensed by military government immediately after 1945, the communications elites are as exclusive in their social origin as other leadership groups; their members, too, are mostly university-trained. Peculiar features of this group are unusually short average terms of holding "office," a strong representation of members born in Central and East Germany, and the large number of those who were in active opposition to Hitler.

But these are disconnected observations, which, as such, do not even add up to a sketch. More than with other groups, we need other data than those of social origin and biography here. For many German editors, directors of broadcasting stations, department heads, and administrative managers of

mass media—the language of the service class has not stopped
short of their world!—it would seem that, despite traditionally
strong government influence, especially on broadcasting and
television, they form a relatively independent elite, which
supports the constitution of liberty with a melancholy sense
of being a losing minority. Where the German press becomes
aggressive on the other hand, its language is less liberal than
national, and only nuances of nationalism distinguish the
empire of Axel Springer from most of his opponents in Hamburg's Press House. Perhaps a thorough study of the *Spiegel*
affair of 1963 and the spontaneous reaction of German public opinion to the government measures against the Hamburg
newsmagazine might bring out the intensity and limitations
of the liberalism of German communications elites.

We know rather more, however, about the two main competitors—if that is what they are—of the postmonopolistic
political class in Germany, the elites of business and politics.
The *business elite* in particular has long been the focus of
controversies and analyses. In terms of social biography, it
also offers a picture of remarkable continuity since the turn
of the century. At the top of German enterprises, self-made
men and first-generation entrepreneurs have become the exception; the overwhelming number of leading entrepreneurs
were born into the upper class, grew up in families of entrepreneurs of professional people, and studied in universities,
generally law or technical disciplines. Circulation is almost
as rare in entrepreneurial positions as it is in the Catholic
church; despite certain changes in their patterns of mobility
they are not yet a career elite. Changes of political regime do
not immediately reverberate in the occupation of top entrepreneurial positions. There are still relatively few Catholics
among the captains of industry; at the same time, a considerable part of this group comes from Central and East Germany. In their social profile, entrepreneurs are, so to speak,
the denominational and regional counterpart to Catholic bishops; both appear as elites of great continuity.

But here again external data are a very insufficient guide
to understanding. Entrepreneurs realize, in contrast to judges
and permanent undersecretaries, editors and professors, that
they are masters. Even if they cultivate ideologies of partnership or of the community of the enterprise, they are well
aware of their positions of leadership at least "at home," that
is, in business. They like the word "leadership" and prefer it—

as Heinz Hartmann has shown—to the less ambitious concepts of "organization" or "administration" (92, pp. 56 f.).

In view of the peculiar German form of industrialization,
it is not unlikely that they conceive this leadership by
analogy to the German political tradition. Thus employers
are, even if they are "only" managers in top positions, a
strong and confident elite in their own sphere. But it is beyond this sphere that the crucial questions in any analysis
of the business elite arise. Is this group a general social and
political eilte as well? What is the politics of German business? Those who have concerned themselves with entrepreneurs and their political attitude in Germany and elsewhere
came to divergent, often incompatible conclusions. There is
no doubt that business leaders have advanced claims for
political influence, and still do so, usually by way of employers' or industrial associations. Furthermore, it is probable
that, in the Federal Republic, such claims have gained in
frequency and intensity, if only because many employers look
upon themselves and their fellows as the hidden manufac-
turers of the economic miracle.

An attitude Hartmann found time and again in interviews
with entrepreneurs is clearly not uncharacteristic: ". . .
finally, politics offers a very important field of action outside
the company, particularly for larger enterprises. Management
can replace the old political elite. Somebody who has run a
combine for twenty years and has always had a positive balance should be able to cope with leadership tasks in other
fields" (92, p. 232). But opinions differ greatly as to whether
this describes the aspirations of the active few or the reality of
German society. Following Franz Neumann's and others'
analyses of the connection between entrepreneurial politics
and National Socialism, authors such as Kurt Pritzkoleit, or
Deutsch and Edinger, have concluded that once again—or
still?—Germany belongs to its business elite: "Today, as in
the Weimar Republic, the leaders of the major interest associations of German business are determined to assert to the
fullest their actual and potential influence over public opinion, parties, legislatures, and governments" (57, p. 99).

Deutsch and Edinger believe that the business elites succeed in realizing this intention. Hartmann starts off with the
same conviction, but in the end prefers a more moderate attitude. He reports that the employers interviewed by him—
some two hundred selected men—"themselves displayed a

relatively high rate of interest in political and community action but simultaneously complained to the author about political apathy in management at large" (92, p. 231). It would seem at least possible that this complaint is based on a correct observation, and that not Deutsch and Edinger, but Almond is right in rejecting, on the basis of interviews with leaders of German business, the label of "employers' state" for West Germany and ascribing on the contrary the "tenderness of democratic institutions in contemporary Germany" to the "intellectual poverty of the German academic and business classes" and the lack of "political commitment and responsibility" among them (202, pp. 24 and 103).

There is many an indication that the image of society espoused by German entrepreneurs is characterized by a peculiar mixture of confidence and defensiveness. In their own sphere, their confidence is pronounced and clearly in evidence. But this sphere of theirs is narrow; it ends with the trade unions, toward whom even top entrepreneurs in Germany often display a curiously defensive attitude intermingled with inexplicable feelings of guilt (which, incidentally, the unions return in kind). Employers expect from government the protection of their own, in view of Germany's economic history as a rule not very liberal interests; Almond is presumably right in interpreting the call for the state, widespread among employers as among other groups, as a call for state protection (cf. 202). But otherwise a tendency is evident among business leaders not to leave their own sphere, and thus not to advance any claim to recognition as a general social and political elite. There are times when it appears that employers regard themselves as unloved by everybody and feel that they have to fight against a world of resistance—a (subjective) condition, which they then try to escape by retreating to their own sphere.

Even so, the proper sphere of the business elite is obviously large enough; protection of their interests comprises matters of economic, financial, and social policy as well as many questions of foreign relations. There can thus be no doubt about the political influence of business leaders, especially since Deutsch and Edinger found that almost two thirds of the members of the (First) Federal Parliament "were identified at least informally with one or more economic interest groups" (57, p. 91). Here, the farmers' association and trade unions are included as economic interest groups. Economic associations are less uniform than those in other areas; moreover the solidarity of employers is an old problem arising from their political minority, even in the narrower sphere of employers' associations. Once again, this is not to deny the political weight of business. It is probably greater in the Federal Republic than at any other time in German history. Possibly for the first time, the business elite has become a serious competitor on the market of political decisions; indeed, I shall try to show a little later that this fact provides one of the hopeful signs of the second experiment of democracy in Germany. But despite such more or less obvious effects of business, a question mark has to be appended to the assertion, which Hartmann borrows from others, and which many have borrowed since, that there was or is in German society a "strategic contest between business and the state over one's relative predominance over the other" (92, p. 217). At least in so far as business is concerned, there is little indication of such a contest.

The *political elite*, in the narrow sense of the word "political," continues to demand our attention. At this point, we can confine ourselves to giving contour to earlier intimations. As we have seen, the political elite, in the sense of the leaders of parties and parliament, has long been one of the few upwardly mobile groups in the German upper class. Between 1910 and 1920, the road from the very bottom to the very top, that is, from working-class to upper-class positions, led in more than two thirds of all cases into top political positions (followed, in this sequence, by positions in science, journalism, and art).

Our table of social origins shows that between 15 per cent (p. 238, col. 10) and 24 per cent (col. 9) of the political elite are from the lower classes; in this, politicians stand alone among the top groups. Twenty-two per cent of all members of the (Fourth) Federal Parliament had primary-school education only. Not all or even most German politicians are upwardly mobile people, however. The 22 per cent with primary-school education are more than balanced by the 50 per cent with a university degree; besides 15 per cent from lower strata we find 37 per cent from upper-class families. In politics, we find the lawyer, the civil servant, and the working man who has risen through the hierarchies of parties or unions; and one of the questions we will want to ask as we go on is what, if anything, the groups symbolized by these three types have in common.

Probably not very much. When Macmillan was Prime Minister of Britain and Gaitskell leader of the opposition, a British sociologist found that both had not only attended a similar school and the same university, but were also related to each other "by many corners" (cf. 2). This is, to be sure, not always the case even in Britain; nor is it necessarily an advantage. Yet the simultaneous contrast of Adenauer as Chancellor and Ollenhauer as leader of the opposition in Germany suggests two utterly different worlds; and although career politicians may gradually conquer all political parties, it is almost impossible still, in Germany, to refer to a political elite in the singular. The political elite of German society reflects that diversity without unity that characterizes the political class as a whole and robs it of the fruits of liberalism even after the shattering of the monopoly of a master caste. This reference leads us back to the main line of our analysis. But before we take up its thread, it may be useful to halt our climb over the peaks of the two thousand for a moment in order to view the mountain panorama as a whole from another, distant, and yet close perspective.

We have discovered many common features of German elites both in the longitudinal sense of their development as partial elites and in the simultaneous sense of the character of different elite groups at any given time. Despite many differences in detail, columns 3 to 25 of our table (p. 238) present by and large a rather uniform picture. One might almost feel inclined to conclude from such uniformity that the top of society, that is, any society, must look more or less as this picture shows it. This conclusion would be false. What is more, it would be false not only in respect to distant societies, such as those of the Trobrianders, the Somalis, or the Chinese; in our own geographical region and before the same historical background, radically different elite structures are possible, indeed real. In order to demonstrate this fact, I have included columns 26 to 30 in the table of the social origin of German elites.

It is not my intention at this point to examine in detail the changes in German society in the DDR. Once we approach this task (Chapter 26) it will become evident that one has to distinguish between largely peripheral and substantial changes, that is, those that might be reversed without great effort and others that are probably more lasting. Probably the circulation of political elites with its intense variations in German history belongs to the former category. Although in the past they were not accompanied by equally profound social reformations, one might suspect that the composition of the (Third) People's Chamber and of the government of the DDR are merely imposed phenomena of party rule. But the "state machinery" concerns the civil service. Its origin is as radically different from that of any West German elite as is the origin of DDR generals and managers, or—it could be added here—judges and university professors, diplomats and editors. In these cases, origin is evidently not a merely external and irrelevant phenomenon. Here, nearly all continuity has been broken and an entirely new political class has emerged, which, in contrast to that of National Socialist Germany, does not involve a problematic combination of old and new.

In laying out the problem for this part of our study we have distinguished between two forms of monopolistic elites, one in which a homogeneous group occupies all positions of leadership, and the other in which one partial elite dominates all others. It now becomes apparent that the political class of the DDR is on the way from the latter and unstable to the former and stable form of monopoly. But this is an anticipation of the more elaborate analysis of East German changes that we will take up in the last part of this book.

Here, the perspective of the distant country suggests another conclusion. Even where German elites of all spheres and epochs of German society, with the single exception of the DDR, do not strikingly differ from one another, they have certain characteristic features. It holds for all of them that the road from the bottom to the top is rarely taken in one leap; throughout the decades there are certain recognizable continuities of the social profile of most elites. For the two periods of the Weimar Republic and the Federal Republic, a further, less easily quantifiable common feature becomes apparent. It would seem that all elites were to a greater or lesser extent elites in spite of themselves, rulers against their will, at least in so far as general social power is concerned. If this impression is correct, it provides us with an answer to the question of whether German society has a democratic elite or not.

Imperial Germany had a monopolistic elite, which managed to establish and uphold, with the assistance of an authoritarian welfare state, the apparent paradox of an industrial feudal society. Members of this elite held many of the leading positions in German society themselves, but others they passed on to strange, if safely controlled hands. The monopoly broke along with the political system of Imperial Germany. But the memory of and, at times, nostalgia for the masters of the monopoly, whose passing turned out to be a long process, followed their surviving servants throughout the Weimar Republic. In any case, no distinct new political class emerged before that created by the National Socialist leadership clique and this was, once again, if in a more precarious version, monopolistic. East German society has followed in this tradition in its own apparently similar, although substantively peculiar, manner. Moreover, there can be no doubt that these traditions reverberate in West German society as well; not even total defeat produces a social tabula rasa. But two features characteristic of traditional German elites are now absent: first, the monopoly of one elite, or indeed the claim to it; and second, the nostalgic memory, which the leadership groups of the Weimar Republic had, of such a monopoly.

Can we infer that at last the plurality of competing groups now at the top of society is a structural guarantee of the constitution of liberty? This seems plausible. Heinz Hartmann has argued it: "If one were to sketch, then, the present balance of the principal social groups, one would probably find the political parties, business, and agriculture among the powerful first. Potential rivals are labor, the civil service and the military. The clergy is largely pledged to political neutralism; and intelligentsia is content with sporadic demonstrations of strength" (92, p. 250). Leaving aside debatable details of weight (that is, of labor) and characterization (that is, of church leaders), there remains the plausible picture of elite competition in a pluralist society. But is the picture then a little too plausible perhaps? Does it not sound too much as if it were drawn from a textbook about the political sociology of democracy? The questions raised by this picture suggest that while it is superficially correct, it will not stand up to a more searching analysis.

The conclusion is at the least ambivalent. In one sense it recalls the analysis of the American elite by C. Wright Mills. Mills clearly enjoyed drawing an idyllic picture of democratic pluralism, in order to take a blunt, if superior, stand and denounce it as a mere façade concealing a much less pleasing reality. Behind apparent pluralism Mills saw the invisible monopoly of the powerful triangle of political, economic, and military leaders. Such conspiratorial theories always have the dialectical advantage—which is a substantive disadvantage —of being irrefutable: whoever insists on a different explanation may be charged with having been bamboozled, if not bribed by the true rulers. This insinuation remains, however, rather inadequate. It is Mills's great error that he reduced all political decisions to the one great decision for or against nuclear war. This is obviously a decision that would mean the end of all politics; it is indeed placed in the hands of a small group of people. But as long as nuclear war does not turn from a threat into a reality, politics covers a wide range of decision that eludes the grasp of the allegedly all-powerful triangle. Mills's power elite cannot abolish farm subsidies or nationalize the automobile industry, it cannot forbid the Senate to hold hearings or force the Catholic church to accept divorce. Plurality remains a fact in all those spheres that concern people's everyday lives. And as one considers this fact, the power elite increasingly comes to resemble a transposition of the attitudes of German lawyers, civil servants, and generals in the Weimar Republic into the world of the intellectual: that is, the fiction of monopoly arising from nostalgia for a master (although, in the case of Mills, in contrast to the Weimar elites, not in order to serve, but in order to fight him). There is no power elite of this kind, either in American or in German society today. So we are left with the picture of a plurality that is superficially correct, but not really valid.

The alternative interpretation leads us away from the concept of the secret power elite. When Morris Janowitz asked a representative sample of West Germans to indicate their place on a scale of social stratification, 1.9 per cent described themselves as belonging to the "upper class." In the survey, these were sixty-four people. If one examines the occupations of these sixty-four, one finds among them ten peasants, five workers, eighteen clerical workers and officials of intermediate rank—thus more than half made fun of the interviewers (cf. 105). Perhaps a result of this kind may be taken, if not as proof, at least as an illustration of the fact, which has been observed elsewhere, that no one seriously wants to count himself among the upper class and least of all those who belong there. In fact, Janowitz lent his support to this self-deception by modestly calling the top stratum of his own scale of social rank "upper middle class." For those who are above, the "leveled-in middle-class society" is not merely a useful ideological veil concealing the reality of a divided society, but also the instrument of a somewhat anxious self-interpretation: We are all merely middle class. . . . But what if this self-interpretation should prove correct? The thesis that German society after 1918 no longer had an upper class is by no means new; Schumpeter formulated it explicitly in 1929 (cf. 198), and if instead of "upper class" one were to say "elite" and were to consider the evaluative associations of the word in everyday language one would be sure to find widespread agreement on this view. The picture of plurality then does not hide a conspiratorial group of men secretly pulling all the strings, but a vacuum. The place at the top of society is empty.

Such formulations are attractive and popular. And indeed, in a sense, they will be confirmed by the conclusion to which our analysis leads us. But as a starting point the idea that the upper class or elite is missing is much too imprecise. Let us try, therefore, to make it more precise. There are in contemporary German society—as in any society—top positions in various institutional orders, which carry with them the right to make authoritative decisions. Moreover, these positions are occupied. There is thus a social category of incumbents of top positions, and it is semantically entirely correct to describe this category as an upper stratum or, in more definite terms, an elite, a power elite, a political class. Of course, contemporary German society has a power elite. What is in question is not its existence, but its character.

We can state moreover that the power elite of German society is not monopolistic. It does not consist of a single closed master caste, nor is it clearly dominated by one partial elite. There are certain common features in all these partial elites, including the absence of a liberal tradition, if not a certain aversion to it; nevertheless this elite is as a political class pluralistic. In its political attitudes it is multiform (as we have called it with the sociologist's preference for abstruse terms). The "multiformity" or internal plurality of the German political class does not, however, show itself effectively in a lively competition between its elements. The dissolution of the monopoly has led to plurality, but not to competition. Instead, a cartel has taken the place of the monopoly. This feature denotes the peculiarity of the German political class in spite of itself.

Wherever several groupings, institutions, units of approximately equal rank meet, their encounter may assume two very different forms, one of them productive, the other defensive, one adventurous and dynamic, the other designed to reduce risk and maintain the status quo, one lively and the other rigid—one is *competition* and the other is *cartel*. American liberals seem to have assumed the existence of a "natural" trend toward cartels, at least in the economy ("Man wants concord . . ."); thus they devised legislation to maintain competition. Possibly there is a general gravitation toward agreement without risk, which secures every partner his share in the cartel and is paid for by the consumer. There certainly was and is this gravitation in Germany. It is about to paralyze the creative potential of political decentralization; the individual states do not compete with each other but agree on the smallest common denominator, which means as a rule that nothing is done. The same force of gravity has caught and domesticated German elites as well. Instead of utilizing their plurality for a lively competition on the market of political decision, they have joined forces in an agreement not to hurt one another, but to administer public affairs together.

The economic metaphor may be misleading. By the cartel of elites I do not mean any explicit, much less written agreement between generals, entrepreneurs, bishops, and party chairmen; the idea would be as absurd as the social contract certified by a notary public. What I mean is that elites behave as if they had a greed to cease from all initiative, to distribute social power according to a certain rule and not to dispute this rule. The "cartel" in this social-political sense is a conceptual implication, not a real institution, nor is its background necessarily the same as that of economic cartels. The "elite cartel" is the result of a generally defensive attitude on the part of its members. The plurality of German leadership groups has proved to be a plurality of men who awoke one day with a shock to the awareness that they were at the top, and that there was nobody above them. The shock was more than their self-confidence could stand, they were unprepared for their eminence, and as a result they decided not to put forward the claims that might be derived from their new positions but to withdraw each to his own sphere. Thus, not only do the elites as such lack self-confidence; a political class whose internal contradictions and competing claims to the same power would keep society alive and move it along is also lacking. The traditional monopoly has been replaced by a cartel of anxiety. There is yet another difference between this cartel and the cartels in certain branches of the economy. The "cartel of elites" can hardly be dissolved by legislation, nor is there a court of law before which its members might be forced to appear, although both would be beneficial, if not necessary. For like other cartels, the cartel of elites succeeds only at the expense of the consumers, at the expense of society in the constitution of liberty.

Before we look at the consequences of such developments, we must try to turn the metaphor of the cartel into more definite formulations. In doing so, we can at last replace the question mark we left in the fourth box of our typology of elites (cf. p. 220) by a description. German elites have become potentially pluralistic in that they no longer form a monolithic political class. But the potential is made ineffective by another, possibly unexpected deficiency. The elites lack the confidence needed for leadership or for conflict. If we ask why this is so, the answer must be that they are not, as a social group, established, but abstract. They do not in fact form a group, but remain a mere category. The German power elite is not an established elite; it is for that reason incapable of that self-confidence which is a necessary condition of lively competition.

One index of such confidence and establishment is subjects of conversation. What, indeed, were Konrad Adenauer, Erich Ollenhauer, and Erich Mende, at one time leaders of three parties represented in the Federal Parliament, to talk about when they met? About species of roses? About proposals to change the rules of card games? About problems of embarking on an academic career in the field of law? When one of them won the Knight's Cross in battle during the war, the other was in hiding in the seclusion of a Benedictine monastery, while the third was acting as secretary of an émigré party in London. And these are differences found within the political elite in the narrowest sense. If we add Undersecretary Globke, the commentator of Hitler's Nuremberg laws, General Speidel, a soldier from the resistance groups with a philosophical education, Berthold Beitz, an intelligent, independent manager of a new type, Bishop Lilje, the widely traveled exponent of the liberal branch of the Protestant church, and Rudolf Augstein, the national- and military-minded editor of the most influential German newsmagazine, we encounter a set of people united at best by their common membership in the German elite. Presumably, this tie would be their only subject of conversation; they might find some common ground in a faintly amused discussion of the absurdity of sociological analysis. But leaving irony aside, apart from politics, in which every one of these men is involved in one way or another, there would probably not be a common subject of conversation for all or indeed, any three of them; the restriction of their conversations to shoptalk, on the other hand, betrays the absence of any kind of social coherence. There is no school that they might all have attended; not even law faculties unite this elite; it is hard to imagine a club in which they might all be members; it is unlikely that they would all meet sailing or watching football; in so far as they are married, a ladies' tea of their wives would be likely to produce rather strained conversation; even their children probably live in different worlds. Those at the top of German society are essentially strangers to each other.

Wolfgang Zapf has used data about age, geographical origin, education, social origin, religious affiliation and position in the Third Reich for West German leadership groups in 1955 to construct an index of social distances. This enables us to tell how close or far the social profiles of these groups are in relation to each other (232, pp. 196 f.). The index suggests a special proximity of members of the executive to all other groups (which may, of course, be explained by the fact that many of the other groups are represented in it). Other elites, on the other hand, are quite eccentric; this is markedly true for trade-union leaders, communications elites, and church leaders, but to a lesser extent it is also true for captains of industry and heads of influential associations. The

conclusion to which Zapf is led by his analysis of distances
warrants extensive quotation because it is immediately relevant for our context:

Is there a German Establishment? Is there a German Power
Elite? The two questions concern different aspects of the internal structure of a social elite. The former refers to the social surroundings in which the members of individual elites
move, at social distance in a wider sense which includes style
of life and images of society. The second aspect is that of
power and relates to the ways in which the various elites,
when important decisions must be made, co-operate or compete with each other. Now both questions cannot be answered
in the affirmative, and a negative answer to the first question
may be documented fairly well with the data of this study. In
Germany after the Second World War, the individual sectors: politics, administration, economy, trade union, church,
communications are fairly homogeneous internally. But between them there are marked distances. Exchange between the
sectors is frequent in some parts, but it decreases clearly "to
the outside." There is no free interchange within the entire
elite; in West Germany the elite is, if not split, at least subdivided into firmly structured units of long traditions and
largely similar histories. This fact may perhaps render some
characteristics of postwar society more understandable: the
insecurity and heterogeneity at the top, the lack of a "society"
which sets the tone, or the relative separation of power, income, and prestige. At the same time, rudiments of a
pluralistic competition may be recognized in this situation
which differs considerably from both Weimar antagonisms
and Nazi totalitarianism. (232, pp. 199 f.)

Whether Zapf is right in this final remark remains to be
seen. But his presentation contains an indication of a further
index of established elites, which may be more serious and is
certainly more easily measurable than an index of subjects of
conversation. Zapf refers to the interchangeability in principle, and the actual exchange of people at the top across the
borders of various sectors of the elites. That in the course of
a lifetime, one man should become successively a professor
of classics, a brigadier general, a member of parliament, a
director of an investment trust, and minister of health is, to
be sure, the exception even in Britain. But the possibility of
an interchange of this kind throughout the top positions of
very different spheres documents the cohesion of a confident
political class, while on the other hand the insistence on the

expert, on the "professional" professor, general, parliamentarian, businessman, and minister means that an elite is a mere category of sociology without social reality.

Comparing Germany with Britain leads, however, to a question we have been evading for some time. Is not the English "Establishment" a persistent source of concern to liberals? Does it not represent the characteristically English survival of preindustrial and authoritarian social structures? Are not the powerful decisions of this so-called Establishment removed from public control in a manner unbearable for the constitution of liberty? Here, to begin with, a conceptual clarification is necessary. By an established elite I do not mean an Establishment in the narrow sense that includes the Archbishop of Canterbury, the editor of the *Times,* the head of the House of Cecil, the Master of Trinity College, and a handful of other secretly powerful people. What I am referring to is, rather, a property of the official elite, that is, of the incumbents of visible positions of leadership, namely, their common social belonging and connection in so far as this transcends their common positions of leadership. Thus our established elite has little to do with the concerns of English liberals. This exercise in definition does not settle the question, however. It is my thesis that the German political class has developed from unity without plurality to plurality without unity, and that both these states are highly detrimental for the constitution of liberty. But what is this unity? Is it not of necessity in itself an oligarchic and thereby authoritarian element? Does it not describe a political class separated from the masses and endowed with a will of its own?

This study is only peripherally and implicitly a study in political theory. But at some central points explicitness is inevitable, and this is such a point. The doubts and objections raised against the assumption that liberal democracy demands an established political class probably involve a misunderstanding of the relation between civic equality and social differentiation, and thereby a misconception of the idea of representation. Social homogeneity on the part of those who sit at the levers of power must by no means interfere with the principle of equal chances of participation for all citizens. For those who do not hold such positions of power, participation means above all control, that is resistance against authority; and it is certainly a condition of the constitution of liberty that the institutions of control and resistance against the political class and its parts should remain powerful and effective.

We have persistently criticized the "divided society" of Germany and the social bias in the origin of German elites; but this does not imply a demand for heterogeneity. Education is a case in point. It would not be at all bad for a political class to be established by the fact that all its members had passed through similar educational institutions. The demand for equality of citizenship merely means that access to these institutions has to be open for all. Given equal opportunities of access, even an elite consisting entirely of university-trained people—or indeed, if it has to be, of lawyers—would display more varied features than the contemporary German elite of civil servants and lawyers could possibly do. If homogeneity is acquired and not ascribed, that is, if it is to be found in the social biographies of its members and not in their cradles, then the existence of an internally homogeneous leading social stratum is compatible with equality of rights as citizens. Here we find the crucial difference between classes established in the traditional-authoritarian sense, which includes the Establishment, and those established in a modern liberal sense, even though it may be impossible for the time being to give a single clear example of the latter type.

This is, so to speak, the negative side of our thesis: the establishment of a socially homogeneous leading stratum cannot do harm to the constitution of liberty; but we do not need to be so defensive in our stipulations. Social homogeneity of the leading stratum may help the constitution of liberty, indeed it may well be thought of as a condition of its survival. Let us look at one central political phenomenon, that of conflict, to see what this means. If the political class is an abstract entity, if it lacks those ties that transcend the common share in the exercise of power, then political conflict always involves the fear and the danger of jeopardizing the system of the constitution itself. Under these conditions, it tends to assume either of two forms, apparently divergent, yet pointing in the same direction socially and politically. Either conflict is suspended altogether on the grounds of the allegedly destructive effects of strife, and thereby repressed and transformed into a dangerous potential of revolution; or it takes the form of a fundamental skepticism concerning the rules of the game of what is often called "the system"—both conditions that are clearly not very helpful for the constitution of liberty. It is striking how much more intense, indeed, in the German sense of the word, more "personal," political clashes are in both Britain and the United States, without destroying close, or at any rate reasonable, social relations of the combatants. Social homogeneity promotes fruitful conflict, because it excludes the rules of the game from the range of issues as a matter of course; by the same token social homogeneity by no means excludes the representation of divergent interests. Representative government in a liberal constitution not only may but must have an established political class.

The examples lead us back to German society. It is the lack, not of a strong sense of nationhood, but of a cohesive and confident society in Germany that weighs so heavily on her recent history and explains the "cartel of anxiety" in her political class. Lewis Edinger used the German example to refute the general assumption that a counterelite is emerging in every totalitarian regime, permanently on the verge of taking over. No such counterelite emerged in Germany after 1945. The theory refuted here is only a special version of the more general one that holds that in all authoritarian and traditional societies there can be found a liberal and modern elite prepared to transform society according to its own image of the future. This has not happened in Germany either. In this sense, one can say that the society of Imperial Germany has been followed by an "unsociety" with a persistent trend toward anomia, which is reflected in the fact that the elites failed to produce the establishment, and which has not been overcome to the present day. Since in reality there is no such thing as an unsociety, this condition actually means instability. The abstract elite thus assembled around a fiction was always on the verge of retreat rather than ready to step forward to confident rule. Nevertheless, the "cartel of anxiety" cannot be dismissed as an impermanent state marking a period of transition. Such theoretical transitions should, generally speaking, be accepted with the greatest caution, if only because they involve the lives of millions of men who can have little interest in their role as passive agents of historical transition.

The abstract, though at least potentially multiform power elite is a specific political form of society. What is this form? What is meant by the expression "cartel of anxiety"? In a very simplified form it means an agreement by the elites to alter as little as possible the present structures. Indeed, one of the most significant effects of this cartel is stagnation.

Whereas inherited rights remain guaranteed, for the function of the state everywhere is to protect existing rights and possessions, all changes of social structure are suspended in favor of an overruling concern for the precarious balance of forces. The cartel of the elites renders impossible a policy of radical realization of citizenship rights, as well as a radical-liberal economic policy applied even to mining and agriculture. It also renders impossible a constitutional policy of strengthening autonomous social forces, as well as a foreign policy aimed at the increased welfare of the majority, rather than at the greatness of the nation at the expense of its citizens. Again, this is not all maliciousness on the part of those concerned, but a result of the sense of insecurity resulting from their deficient social self-confidence. But at this point we are interested in effects rather than causes. With the strengthening of the state and the cementing of existing power relations goes a decline in the opportunity of the individual to influence the direction of things by his participation in the political process. Since the process has no direction, participation becomes almost superfluous except in terms simply of membership in one of the elites. Politics become boring, and it is understandable that the individual loses interest in them. The cartel of elites reminds one once again of the condition described in Holland as *verzuiling,* pillarization. Here, too, we encounter a condition of political stagnation. If one wants to give this form of politics a name, one would have to describe it as an unintentional authoritarianism, an authoritarianism of effect, but not of intention.

The political regime that emerges from this condition is odd. It is, paradoxically, an authoritarianism without authority. Society is ruled in an authoritarian manner, yet nobody rules in such a way. The prevailing mixture of a concentrated potential of power on the one hand, and renunciation of participation on the other, is not based on a massive claim to power or a prohibition to participate; but its consequences are not unlike those of the authoritarian state. This means above all that though competition can exist, conflict slackens. Thus, society loses its dynamics and falls back into a precarious state, which for a long time gives the appearance of stability, until in the end it turns out to be stagnation and explodes in unexpected directions. An economic cartel may function even in the long run; but the cartel of elites is a structure without permanence in the sense that it restrains the inevitable dynamics of social forces until these forge their way out regardless of the cartel. Such a cartel is weak, because it is defensive and because it camouflages rather than abolishes the divisions of social structure.

Power is an instrument for the realization of interests. When movement is brought into a stagnant political situation it must have a direction. But what should the direction be in which a dynamic modern society aims to move? What is the object of a competition of elites in the modern world? This raises the problem of the character of a democratic elite in our time. It is difficult to answer, because there is not as yet a single model of an elite of this kind anywhere. To be sure, we can draw purely formal conclusions from our analysis: a democratic elite has to be united in its status, and divided in its politics. But what are the political divergences about? Those historical elites, whose competition for power expressed the struggle for the conservation or abolition of inherited privilege, had a structural reason for competition and for conflict. Where do we find this reason today? The answer probably rests with that "democratic class struggle" Lipset has in mind as a successor to older conflicts. The competition of elites no longer in fact produces any overwhelming issues which draw everybody into their spell; it is not a duopoly. The multiformity of elites transcends past experience by far; individual political decisions take the place of comprehensive political programs of revolution or conservation. Indeed one could even argue that the dissolution of the great ideological fronts is one of the goals of the constitution of liberty. But the problem remains of how the notion of competition can be maintained against the much more comfortable possibilities of "cartelization" and "pillarization." It is the problem of a liberal elite in a modern society with equal citizenship rights for all that West German society, rather unexpectedly, shares today with those very Western democratic societies from which it differed so persistently in the past.

Who then governs Germany? Let us approach our question once again step by step. As elsewhere, there are in the society of the German Federal Republic some two thousand top positions which may be described as those of the power elite. The positions are occupied. Their incumbents, however, constitute a social category with several peculiar features. While they are pluralistic and multiform in terms of their interests and thus of their political attitudes, they are largely lacking in all wider social ties. In fact, they are not a real group, stratum, or class, but a mere category, what might be called an abstract elite. The lack of social ties further weakens the self-confidence of German elites, which was debilitated in any case by a long history of dependence on leadership, produced by a dominant leadership group. Thus political multiformity does not become effective by means of a competition of interests and persons; instead, elites of divergent interests combine in what we described as the cartel of anxiety. Each interest seeks security and protection for the position it has already acquired, and together they rob political conflict of its dynamics. Germany's political class governs its society against its own will.

This situation has a number of consequences. One of them is that nobody wants to consider himself a member of the elite of the powerful. Another is that nobody is in fact regarded as belonging to this elite. Thus the public image of those politically at the top corresponds to their own self-image. This does not alter the position of the powerful, of course, but it underlines the suspicion that actually there is no elite, because the elites lack self-confidence and a sense of social cohesion. Government must be referred to in the passive voice; to put it epigrammatically, "Nobody governs Germany; Germany is governed."

The epigram has a second, possibly unexpected meaning. A country that is "being governed" is definitely not being governed liberally. Liberal and, in this sense, well meaning as individual elites may be—which unfortunately cannot be assumed for all of them in Germany—the effect of the agreement to stand still is bound to be illiberal. At least in its consequences the cartel of elites creates a species of modern authoritarianism, which shares all the disadvantages of its historical predecessors and is, if anything, more insidious in that now it has become impossible to identify (and thus oppose) the center of authority. This leads to a pathetic condition of the political community. For all we know, it may last for some time. Like any authoritarianism that despite itself is well intentioned it permits the free play of forces so long as they neither seek nor are able to upset the existing balance. However, this headless authoritarianism may easily be misunderstood as an invitation to more active groups of pretenders; it accentuates the permanent danger of a modern totalitarianism in the European sense.

Of course, authoritarianism without authority may also lead to the development of a liberal elite and a democratic class struggle. I have dwelled for a long time in the shady corners of German society in terms of the prospects of the constitution of liberty. But I do not enjoy doing so. It is thus all the more gratifying to conclude that the cartel of anxiety offers a better hope for liberal development than the monopoly of tradition. The predominance of a monolithic political class can be transformed into the competition of self-confident elites only by revolutionary changes; but it is the path of reform that leads from cartel to competition. One might summarize this analysis in a wish, if not a demand. If one assumes that giving political expression to the internal plurality of modern society would both enliven conflict and strengthen the elites' fruitfulness, then one of the main tasks of a German society that wanted to be liberal would be the formation of a democratic elite. Many structural conditions for such an elite are present; what is lacking is its social cohesion. To create, on the basis of equal chances of access, a political class homogeneous in the social biographies of its members and, in that sense, established, is a task whose fulfillment might give democracy in Germany new and effective impulses.

18. GERMAN INTELLECTUALS, POLITICS, AND STATUS

Those who govern are not rulers all the time, nor are the governed always subjects; both are also fathers, breeders of roses, drivers of cars, men or women in their best years, believers and perhaps creditors in manifold combinations of their roles as well. But even when the rulers rule and their subjects obey them, this contrast does not bind everyone by its spell. There remains between, or perhaps besides, a "third type," as Bertrand Russell puts it, of "those who withdraw." Russell appears unduly timid about this type, and forgets the active quality of his own withdrawal:

> There are men who have the courage to refuse submission without having the imperiousness that causes the wish to command. Such men do not fit readily into social structure, and in one way or another they seek a refuge where they can enjoy a more or less solitary freedom. At times, men with this temperament have been of great historical importance. . . . Sometimes the refuge is mental, sometimes physical; sometimes it demands the complete solitude of a hermitage, sometimes the social solitude of a monastery. . . . Something of the hermit's temper is an essential element in many forms of excellence, since it enables men to resist the lure of popularity, to pursue important work in spite of general indifference or hostility, and to arrive at opinions which are opposed to prevalent errors. (190, pp. 18 f.)

It is a very ascetic type of intellectual who leaves the powerful and the powerless to their own resources. Russell himself has clearly never been a hermit. Not "retreat" from the imperious dichotomy of Above and Below, but detachment from its claims has enabled him to remain the uncomfortable sage that his country and the world know. There are men who are able to detach themselves from the vis-à-visness of power and obedience and to look at its play and effects from outside. Because of this freedom they sometimes think that, in contrast to those others in chains, they do not play a social role at all. Here their detachment fails them, for they, too, have their exits, and their entrances, namely, those of the intellectual.

Who are the intellectuals? It is easy to misunderstand this question and look for the professions of those who act the part. The misunderstanding is unfortunate because it anticipates in the definition what is a fruitful subject of investigation, that is, the status of intellectuals. It is a misunderstanding because the definition is bound to miss one feature of the intellectual, which might well be regarded as decisive. "I have considered," says Lipset, "as intellectuals all those who create, distribute, and apply culture, that is, the symbolic world of man, including art, science, and religion" (131, p. 311). I have selected this one from hundreds of definitions because it comes closest to the meaning intended here. The social role of the intellectual is characterized above all by the independent and deliberate use of the word. We all use words; man is a creature who has the power of the word. But where this possession and use becomes "independent" and "deliberate," the word is no longer simply an instrument of communication, but a means of expressing realities and convictions in that open realm that Lipset, following philosophical traditions widespread in the Anglo-Saxon world, calls the symbolic world of man. The poet, the movie critic, the teacher, the philosopher all regularly use the word independently and deliberately in this sense; the physician and the judge, the painter and the publisher may do so; in principle every man may do so, whatever his occupation may be. To be sure, certain occupations put their incumbents on the road to the role of the intellectual, others render it rather improbable; but basically it is not a role in the order of occupations at all; it is more nearly one in that of power, but most likely one sui generis.

The independent and deliberate use of words always implies some detachment from the reality symbolized in the word. Whoever acts, does not speak; and the conservative is well advised never to pronounce the names of things threatening the status quo. Burke realized this when he found himself facing the dilemma of wanting to write about the French Revolution when its very name had to be anathema for him. This is why even conservative intellectuals always have some distance between them and the vested interests of the status quo. They have removed themselves from the things of which they are speaking—and usually these are not things, but, say, relations of authority or valid notions of value or existing institutions—at least for the moment required to translate them deliberately and independently into words. The topology of the stereotypes of everyday language defines the borderline of the symbolic world, which is at best touched by the non-intellectual, whereas the intellectual traverses it freely.

Let me emphasize again that it is not a profession to be an intellectual. Politicians, too, even conservative politicians, may play this role in parts of their lives, or even their days; Bismarck and Churchill are merely outstanding examples of a species that is more promising by far than Plato's philosopher-kings. Thus it is the condition of detachment and not a status with tenure guarantees that liberates people from the prison of power and subjection. Detachment does not help one to be popular with those who act. When one begins to look at things from a distance, resistance to them is often close; it is telling that in politics the government has to act, and the opposition has to talk, that is, that the government may not talk, and the opposition may not act much.

The United States offers throughout its history examples of the tension between the anti-intellectualism of the actors and the longing of intellectuals for action. This tension is universal, but perhaps it is most pronounced in a culture whose dominant traits are painted in economic colors; moreover, the particular and certainly vexing problem that Richard Hofstadter pursued in his study of *Anti-Intellectualism in American Life* (98) may not be as damaging to the constitution of liberty as its victims believe in the heat of debate. It may be, in other words, that embrace is more dismal than rejection. In Germany, the "spiritual," and at times "intellectual upper class" has long been regarded more highly than the "economic upper class"; and all civil servants like to include themselves in this spirited group. In such a context, anti-intellectualism is an attitude of the intellectuals themselves, who warn the world of their dangerousness and who—like Martin Heidegger in his Freiburg rectoral address of 1933— would like to organize the banal catalogue of the three Platonic estates of teachers, soldiers, and peasants in a rank order that accepts even the precedence of soldiers as a form of the "self-assertion" of teachers.

But it is too early yet to elaborate these examples. They show that the intellectuals of a society not only live in a world of symbolic forms, but themselves symbolize the structure of their society in an especial manner. In the course of this study, we have encountered many a group and institution that bears witness to peculiarities of German society. This may well be even more clearly true for the political attitude and social status of intellectuals than for officials and lawyers, industrial relations or the organization of universities, attitudes to minorities or to children. This is no accident, for intellectuals talk. The deliberate and independent use of words requires a special sensitivity, which admits the context of social reality to the spoken word. Our particular interest in intellectuals and their political attitudes is part of the analysis of the diversity and uniformity of elites. A critique of the notion of an "intellectual upper class" is not meant to imply that intellectuals are not part of the upper class. But let us leave aside the status of the German intelligentsia for the moment and begin with a glance at their political attitudes. It is clearly wrong to believe that all intellectuals are politically more or less alike; "intellectual" and "leftist intellectual" is the same only for those whose social perspective has slipped altogether. In any case, this would not apply to the three attitudes that I want to assert have been above all characteristic of German intellectuals in the past and the present. Their distinction is, like that of types of elites, classification rather than theory; but it, too, may advance our argument.

The first attitude characteristic of intellectuals in German society—perhaps the most frequent of all—has little to do with the picture of the leftist intellectual; indeed, it is almost its opposite. I want to call it the *classical attitude*. The allusion to the classical period of German literature is intended; one might cite Goethe as a witness to this attitude, were it not for the fact that many of its lesser representatives under different conditions discredited this pattern beyond repair. The intellectual displaying the classical attitude has made his peace with the ruling powers and social conditions of his times. We have seen that by definition he, too, does not lack a modicum of detachment; but he uses this detachment to return, in an elegant loop, to the very things from which he had to detach himself in order to gain the word. His relation to reality remains by necessity tense; but it rests on the fundamental and explicit acceptance of a given social and political order. In this sense we are concerned here (which it may be necessary to emphasize) with a clearly political attitude.

Before we mention names to illustrate the classical attitude, a little more differentiation is in order. One version of this intellectual attitude is that of the Weimar minister of state,

Goethe: the intellectual becomes part of the existing order of authority; he becomes an actor without therefore giving up talking altogether. Germany has had professors' and doctors' parliaments; at the top of the executive there has been many a man to whom the role of intellectual was not unfamiliar. Yet this is not the typical version of the classical intellectual attitude; indeed, it comes close to abandoning intellectual activity altogether. In any case, it is more appropriate to the role of the intellectual to use the word in order to justify, embellish, and praise what exists. This is the work of the intellectual as ideologist. With his proper tool of the word he bestows on reality the appearance of necessity, or at least of rectitude; he may make reservations, combine justification with minor demands for change, interpret in a partisan manner, include criticism of details, take daring detours of argument before he returns to what is—but there remains as a hard core of all efforts of ideological imagination the attempt to prove that what is real is reasonable too.

As soon as names are mentioned, it becomes clear that this approach, too, may assume many forms. It becomes evident also how much the effect of this attitude depends on the prevailing social and political context. Obviously, there are also great differences of quality among classical intellectuals so that allocation to this category does not by itself imply a judgment of worth. Treitschke displayed the classical attitude when he wanted the Empire to be even more Prussian than it was; but the intellectual preparation of Bismarck's social legislation by Schmoller and his friends in the Association for Social Policy belongs in the same chapter. The thoughtlessly inhuman confessions of German professors at the outbreak of the First World War and the even more consequential utterings of the same kind in the early years of the Third Reich belong there, too. One cannot avoid calling Baldur von Schirach's pseudo-religious Hitler worship ("This is in him the greatest that he is not our Leader alone . . .") an expression of the classical intellectual attitude as much as the discovery of the "leader principle" in the structure of the cell by German biologists, or of the people's community in modern society by German social scientists.

Again we have to remember that our classification does not as such imply any value judgments. Public law and its practitioners are forced by their subject to assume the classical intellectual attitude; they use the word to interpret what exists in its own light. The discipline of pedagogics is in an essentially similar position; just as teaching cannot lead beyond what exists, the teaching of teaching cannot either. That sociology joins the company of these more classical disciplines, is perhaps rather rare; but I have tried earlier to expose the ideological aspects of Schelsky's theory of the "leveled-in middle-class society."

It is easy also to find examples for a second, hardly less widespread attitude of German intellectuals which I want to call—to remain within the same conceptual world for the time being—the *romantic attitude*. "What do I care about the shipwreck of the world, I know of nothing but my blessed island." Even so, Hölderlin was not entirely unpolitical; in Tübingen's Protestant seminary he shared in 1789 Hegel's and Schelling's enthusiasm for the Paris events and helped to plant a "liberty tree"; but perhaps the attitude meant here is not as unpolitical as it may appear at first sight. In order to describe it, the vexing term "inner emigration" was coined after the Second World War (in a public debate between Thomas Mann and Frank Thiess). Here, we encounter a political attitude of retreat from politics. In its hierarchy of values, not only civil society but the state as well is superseded by the "true" virtues of inner perfection, of profundity, of the world of the mind. The role of the intellectual is defined by contrast to that of the actor, until it is safely removed from any contact with the dirty sphere of action. The intellectual thus understood can—at least in the self-interpretation of inner emigrants—conduct his affairs under all political conditions without recognizable restrictions.

We are approaching here the unpolitical German of whom more will have to be said later. This is an attitude that has often been described, rightly been condemned, and yet been declared somewhat too easily a cause, or at least partial cause of National Socialist success. Once again, classical quotations come to mind: "To form yourself into a nation, you hope, Germans, in vain! Form yourselves therefore the more freely into human beings for that you can."

When the nation was formed, the romantic attitude of intellectuals found its most general expression in cultural pessimism. This is the place of the dismal dichotomies—culture and civilization, community and society, nature and culture —which, absurd as they may be individually, have a cumulative effect by invariably confronting something "true" and something "untrue," with the latter incidentally proving to be reality. Although it sentimentally deprecates reality, there is no serious evaluation of the world involved in this approach; the inner emigrant is not a fighting man but likes to leave reality to its own resources in order to withdraw himself to the refuge of "truth."

The persistence of what Theodor W. Adorno exposed to public ridicule as the "jargon of the true" also proves the persistence of the romantic attitude. While, during the Nazi regime, withdrawal to the ebony tower or the Black Forest hut remains invisible, the same motive tends to assume, under more liberal conditions, the form of a conspicuous imprecision of talking, which manages to make reality, whenever one is about to grasp it, glide off again in order to make way for the "true." Scholars and artists, the much-praised "quiet man of the country," latter-day cultural pessimists, and many others see to it that the romantic attitude remains a German interpretation of the role of the intellectual.

It is probably at least partly the fault of the inner emigrants that in discussions of German intellectuals the attitudes of the "outer" emigrants are all too easily forgotten. It is easy not to mention them; they are, after all, no longer there, and if one cannot forget them altogether, one can at least repress the memory. Yet this is a third widespread attitude of German intellectuals, the *tragic attitude* of those who cannot sleep when they think of their country, until in the end they have to leave it in order to survive. Like the other two, this is obviously not an exclusively German attitude either; every country has its intellectuals in exile. But Germany's intellectual emigration in the last century and a half would probably fill more cemeteries under the Cestius pyramid than that of any other country including Russia. From Heinrich Heine and Karl Marx to Thomas Mann and Albert Einstein and further to the young scientists who have moved to America and the young poets who prefer to live in Ischia, Ireland, and Norway, there is a distinguished and unbroken stream of German intellectuals who have parted company with their society.

One might divide them into two groups: those who had to go, and those who wanted to go. But the division would be misleading. Among the emigrants from National Socialist Germany there were some who would never have emigrated by their own free will, not a few national Jews whose Iron Cross from the First World War helped them as little as their readiness to accept the National Socialist state. In so far as these were intellectuals, they belonged to the classical rather than the tragic type (although their fate must be described as tragic in a different, if possible even more definite sense). Apart from them, however, the borderline between force and free will is too fleeting to be sustained; those who bought themselves a ticket without a word did not really leave of their own free will, and the force of illiberal ministers of the interior frequently met with melancholy agreement among those who had to go.

A more relevant distinction might be between those who have broken entirely with their country, and those who cannot find sleep in exile either, that is, between the physicist who has become an American and follows the German malaise with pity from the confidence of his new association, and the poet who is chained by his language and his audience to the country in which he nevertheless cannot live. But this distinction does not touch the core of the problem either. Here it is more relevant to observe that evidently German society throughout the past hundred years was independent of its political constitution, constructed in such a way that it could not tolerate those who used the word to express detachment from its dominant values. Whoever begins to question this society, eventually questions himself out of it. He no longer finds a vantage point that permits him to distinguish the acceptable from the unacceptable; rather, every hold on this society gives way for him. The society on its part is only too ready to question the membership of those who have begun to doubt it for themselves. The result is evidently not a very happy position or attitude on the part of the intellectuals involved, but one whose significance has not decreased much even in the democratic periods of Weimar and Bonn.

It is doubtful whether it makes sense to speak of a democratic intelligentsia, that is, of a specifically democratic or even, in our sense, liberal attitude of intellectuals. Clearly, the constitution of liberty permits, and has to permit, a plurality of intellectual attitudes to society and politics. German social structure may be peculiar in its specific blend of such attitudes, but we have no way of testing the relative weights asserted here. Two other observations, however, are more easily documented and put us on the track of a possible analysis of the relation between politics and the status of intellectuals, elite patterns and liberal democracy. The first of these derives from our discussion of the political effect of the three attitudes described.

Upon closer inspection, this effect turns out, despite considerable differences in other respects between the attitudes and those who represent them, to be surprisingly similar, at least in a general and formal sense. All three attitudes serve to stabilize, not to say cement existing conditions of power. For the representatives of the classical attitude, this consequence is in keeping with their intentions. There is little reason to doubt that they achieve their goal, although many versions of the ideological justification of existing conditions should deter rather than convince those gifted with a minimum of political or indeed esthetic sense.

The romantic attitude abstains from political decisions. Its advocates have, in a country of uncertain political constitutions, the not inconsiderable advantage of being able to declare at will and as required that they had been for or against certain regimes, institutions, or persons. In fact this, like abstention from voting, invariably means the support of the stronger, that is, of the powers that be. The inner emigrants do not threaten or make life difficult for any government. In this respect, too, the third attitude has to be called tragic. It is a decidedly political attitude, and it is certainly not one of accepting existing social and political conditions; but since its critical detachment transcends even the outer boundary of membership and lacks all realistic hope of a turn for the better, it also fails to effect any change. This absolute, often utopian vein of the tragic attitude is its great deficiency, even if it is in good part the deficiency of the society that produces such an attitude and not merely of its advocates. If emigrant intellectuals leave their country forever, they renounce all impact in any case; if they continue their criticism from a distance, this as a rule, following social-psychological laws of group solidarity, merely has the effect of gathering those attacked the more solidly around the flag of the powers that be. Thus none of the three attitudes described so far is capable of changing a reality in need of change. Instead, all three lead, in varying degrees but with equal clarity, to a strengthening of what is in all its splendor and misery.

The second observation follows from the first. Do intellectuals have to be like this? Distinguishing the three attitudes has a classificatory character, and classifications of this kind are notoriously incomplete. There is furthermore no way of determining definitely by how many classes they should be supplemented. But it is evident that one attitude is missing in our catalogue, which, if one were to believe sociological literature, is the really "classical," that is, typical attitude. With an ambiguous but still valid word I shall call it the *critical attitude*. The intellectual—or so the sociology of his social position, which I have invoked once before, in the Preface, would claim—differs from other people by having broken with many or all the primary ties of his life. He must buy the liberation from the topology of stereotypes to the freedom of independent and deliberate use of words by a chain of sad ruptures with primary groupings and intimate ties. This is how he becomes "free-floating," that is, freed from the role requirements of family and social stratum, church, and perhaps occupation too. Thus he develops the "dynamic synthesis" (to quote Karl Mannheim) of detachment and belonging, alienation and participation, criticism and agreement, which determines his role.

There is no need to test this genetic theory here. While it would be wrong to try to generalize the critical attitude of "dynamic synthesis" into a definition of intellectuals, it does indicate a fourth possibility of their attitude. Here we encounter the real "leftist intellectual," or, more precisely perhaps, intellectuals with a political orientation "left of center." The critical intellectual stands at the margin of his society but remains part of it. His criticism never questions his membership, which implies the hope of accomplishing something by it. The critical intellectual does not, as such, become an active agent of change; his detachment involves not only that given by the symbolic world of the word, but also a deliberate detachment from the existing social and political conditions. But there are many roles in which he remains on the heels of the actors: as expert, commentator, critic, adviser, analyst, exhorter.

Intellectuals, including those of the critical species, do not like to hear this, but it seems to me that there is no denigration in the statement that the inellectual of this type is the successor to the court jester, the classical fool. No longer enveloped in the discipline of power and obedience, he circles around it with biting and always significant wit, and likes to do so. He is a nuisance, but one that remains just about within the limits of the bearable—at least for the powerful of a society in which this type of intellectual thrives.

This reservation is important; for the reason why the fourth intellectual type has been introduced so late is that it does not seem to thrive in German society. There were and are critical intellectuals in Germany. Social scientists provide many an example here. To be sure, there were ideologues among them too; National Socialism forced the majority of them to emigrate; empirical social research even permits a new version of inner emigration; but nevertheless we find a variety of critics in social science: Max Weber, Georg Simmel, Theodor Geiger, Karl Mannheim, Joseph Schumpeter, and many others. However, social science did not prosper in Germany any more than the critical intelligentsia. Both grew up at the margin and were the first to be stamped out when their criticism began to bother those in power. That German intellectuals do not like to hear themselves described as fools merely documents an attitude they share with the society that accepts the fool merely in the beer-drunken solemnity of carnival.

Perhaps this defense is understandable. That *Magnifizenz* or *Herr Intendant, Exzellenz* or *Herr Direktor* is a fool—"are a fool," one is tempted to say—does not exactly appear to add to their official dignity. It is the status of German intellectuals that provides us with the causes of their politics. At this point, the question is in order: What are the occupations of German intellectuals? German intellectuals display political attitudes that, in effect, all serve to strengthen what exists; a critical intelligentsia that combines detachment and belonging is missing. Why is this so? The answer may be found in the social position of intellectuals in Germany, and this in turn leads us back to the main thread of our argument.

Lipset has described a characteristic contradiction in the attitudes of American intellectuals. On the one hand, they are the main advocates of a policy of egalitarianism, which involves criticism of the reality of their society; on the other hand, they are full of envy for their European counterparts and frequently complain about their lack of social position and recognition in the United States. What they fail to see is that the position of European intellectuals, which they desire, is possible only in an inegalitarian social context: "Ironically some of the reasons why American intellectuals do not get the signs of respect which they crave spring from the strength of the egalitarian standards which they espouse" (131, p. 320). Lipset, too, is an American intellectual: "It is certainly true that there is a difference between the European and American treatment of the intellectual. This difference is no more or less than the difference between a fairly rigid class society and a society which emphasizes equality. In Europe, open deference is given to *all* those with higher status, whether engineers, factory owners, or professors, while in this country it is not given to *any* to the degree that it is abroad" (131, p. 327).

It is wrong to believe, however, that European intellectuals are more content than their American colleagues. Indeed many of them dream, individually and in common, of the incomes and standard of living of American intellectuals. Perhaps such embarrassment is also part of this excentric role. But let us consider social status to begin with. In so far as it is true that the status of intellectuals is high in Europe, and thus in Germany, this is not due to their being intellectuals. Even the private scholar draws his status from his fortune and not his scholarship. The decisive factor in the status of German intellectuals in society is the extent to which they have other, "legitimate" occupations. This extent is, however, no less remarkable than the kind of "legitimacy" of the occupations.

If one seeks out German intellectuals at their normal, everyday places of work, one is likely to find oneself in one of three areas: the institutions of the educational system, artistic institutions, and the media of mass communication. Educational institutions are, in Germany, almost exclusively public, government-controlled. Whoever works in them finds himself in prescribed career patterns and formalized status systems, which are borrowed from the administrative bureaucracy; indeed, teachers and professors are technically civil servants. That this involves more than an oath upon taking office is evident from the secular contest between secondary- and primary-school teachers for their relative status, and the persistent comparisons of professors with higher civil servants. In Weyrauch's interviews the remark recurred "that the German university professor rates about equal to or 'perhaps a little higher than' a *Ministerialrat*" (226, p. 125), and here status is evidently well under way to becoming a mentality. But many artistic institutions in Germany are public and government-controlled too, and those that are not tend to imitate this pattern. Thus there are "state actors," civil-servant producers, and general music directors, and at the age of sixty the honorary title of "professor" from the government.

Compared with education and art, the traditional mass media are government-free, but for the incomes of German intellectuals, at least after the Second World War, broadcasting and television have become far more important than publishing and the press, and these are again public and government-controlled. Here, too, there is no shortage of patterns and symbols of status, or of civil-service type security provisions for the heads of departments, administrative managers, directors-general, and co-ordinators. The structure of public honors supplements this system of occupational security by a plurality of academies into which intellectuals may be called, and by orders and decorations in fine gradations up to the peace class of the Pour le Mérite.

Not all intellectuals are employed in such official-looking occupations. Correspondingly, the picture of the social origin of intellectuals shows a little more variability than that of generals and diplomats. Of all artists among the "famous contemporaries" of the years 1910 to 1920, almost one third came from "middle and lower classes of the people"; not only politics, but scholarship, writing, and journalism have long been avenues of upward mobility in German society (232, pp. 44 ff.). This, of course, has to be seen in the context of a rigid and divided society; by other standards one might well reach the opposite conclusion. In terms of their social origin, professors in Germany differ little from judges and show a greater exclusivity than higher civil servants in ministries of the interior (see above, p. 238). For prominent literary figures in the Federal Republic, that is, the two hundred members of academies, Gertraud Linz has shown that they are recruited as generally from upper status groups as other leadership groups (cf. 130). Not merely by their function, but by the status of their occupations and the profile of their social biographies as well, intellectuals are part of the elite in Germany.

Under such conditions—or so one would suspect—the double detachment created by the free use of the word and by criticism of existing realities must be difficult. When American state universities, under the pressure of McCarthyism, demanded the loyalty oath from their professors, the existence of private universities with independent views made resistance much easier; the unambiguousness of intellectual positions fashioned on the civil-service model is one reason for the pathetic display of German universities after 1933. But this is no more than an example, which may be translated from universities to nearly all spheres of intellectual activity. German intellectuals are by no means free-floating; instead, the state pays for most of them the curtain supplement for civil servants, if they move into a larger flat or house. That the same state may, under favorable political conditions, grant them a considerable freedom of action and thought, may slacken the leash on which they are held, but cannot make it disappear. Above all, the secure, dignified, recognized, regulated status of most intellectuals penetrates into their mentality and conditions them for a classical or romantic attitude.

This is not a plea for the poor poet in his attic. A reasonable, recognized status does not exclude critical detachment. Conversely, the German example shows that civil-service security does not necessarily strengthen the self-confidence or even the contentedness of intellectuals. German professors usually wear a flattered, shy smile when they are told that, according to surveys, their social prestige is above that of all other occupations. Other intellectuals are no different in this respect. They prefer to see themselves as "middle class," most happily if they can console themselves about this rank by invoking the leveled-in middle-class society. This is a mechanism of defense, but one clearly different from the sense of deprivation among English and American intellectuals. The German approach is less a protest coupled with solid demands for improvement than a service-class reluctance to see one's own elevated social position emphasized as such. This may be why the defense does not result in the historic orientation of intellectuals "left of center," but in a loyalist, not to say state-conservative attitude instead. We know this mentality; it unites German intellectuals with the other elites of German society. Intellectuals, too, stand where they are against their will, and in any case do not form a part of a socially established elite.

German intellectuals lack social establishment in yet another sense, which may concern them even more immediately than contact with the powerful. Those who use the word need their own cohesion in order to do so in a lively and fruitful way; they need what one might call the intellectual community. This may be an abstract community: a system of discussion and mutual criticism, standards of judgment, a free flow of all relevant information. But it helps if the intellectual community assumes concrete forms as well: a capital city with publishers and newspapers, academies and cafés. That Germany has never, or at best only for a short time in the twenties, had a capital in this sense, is certainly not the only reason for the conspicuous lack of a functioning community of intellectuals. Here, too, the civil-service type status of its members is significant; it dissolves them as a group and relates them to disconnected centers. The intellectuals remain enveloped in occupational worlds that are accidental for their roles as fools until the official desk, the name plate on the door, the title, and the pension become more important than the word. They are not oriented to the community of intellectuals, but to the organization to which they belong—the university, the opera house, the broadcasting station. The intellectuals themselves suffer from all this, but so does the whole society.

I have claimed that there is no democratic intelligentsia, no specifically liberal intellectual attitude. The constitution of liberty permits and demands many different attitudes. Even a liberal preference for the concept of a critical intelligentsia cannot involve the prohibition of intellectual actors and ideologues, the quiet in the country, and even the voluntary exiles. But there is a non-democratic intelligentsia. If intellectuals as a group and in their diversity fail to provide the sting and doubt that accompany every form of distribution of power, every single political decision, but either embrace the powerful or sever all ties to them, then their effect is not democratic. German intellectuals have had this effect. Neither individually nor in combination did the attitudes to society and politics prevalent among them lead beyond existing German conditions; and these were not liberal. Even in the Federal Republic the intellectuals, by lacking self-confidence, strengthen the cartel of the unhappy powerful that must have authoritarian consequences despite good intentions.

Is it guilt? Is it omission? Is it the unavoidable consequence of a society even intellectuals cannot escape? It is evident that the author himself is involved at this point; I have quoted the Preface once before. Thus it may be permissible to leave for a moment the detached role of the analyst and open the imagination to wishes. German intellectuals are certainly a symptom, and possibly a symbol of the structure of German society. Their politics may be derived from their status. But if any social group is capable of breaking the evil circle of social condition and political effect and making new beginnings, it is the intellectuals. Here lies the chance for their detachment. The Federal Republic shows hopeful beginnings of the emergence of a critical and thus uncomfortable intelligentsia. To continue along this line, make it the rule, spread and develop it, is the political task of the intellectual elite among which I count myself. To loosen rigid political conditions, disseminate impatience with reality, strew about, blow away the fog of ideologies of justification, are necessities on the road to the constitution of liberty, which intellectuals have to accept. But I cannot state this without immediately returning to the observer's detachment: If the intellectuals succeed in accomplishing this critical—fool's—task of theirs, this will at the same time be a symptom of the progress of German society on the road to the constitution of liberty.

PUBLICNESS *OR*

THE MISERY OF PRETTY VIRTUES

19. THE PUBLIC AND THE PRIVATE VIRTUES

The social structure of the constitution of liberty has four elements. The building of social stratification may have many floors and corridors, so long as its foundation grants effective equality of citizenship to all. The institutions of law and education, science and religion, economy and politics each have their own conditions of internal order, but liberal democracy demands the same established pattern of a rational regulation of social conflicts in all of them. The variety of interests and convictions in social groups can find adequate expression only in a political class that is diverse in itself but united by a common bond of social cohesion. German society has failed to satisfy any of these demands. In the course of the decades since the foundation of the German Empire many inequalities of the status of citizenship have been abolished, a more rational attitude to conflict has become established here and there, and the traditional monopoly of a small political class has been broken; but even today the distance to the goal is greater than that to its starting point. Much of the social basis of the constitution of liberty is still missing.

If the three pillars of the precarious basis of the social structure of liberty we have examined so far were relatively concrete and related to identifiable, at times even quantifiable features of German social structure, the fourth element can hardly be described as a pillar. We are moving here from the solid world of institutions to the thin air of values, and we have to guard our statements even more carefully against the arbitrariness of unbounded speculation.

One can discuss values splendidly without stating anything at all. Let us note at the outset, therefore, that we are here concerned with valid values only. Our interest is not with the private convictions of individuals or even respectable groups, not with a philosophy of value or political morality, but with value attitudes that have the binding quality of role expectations because they are sustained by the sanctioning power of an elite. In this sense, membership in any society involves certain demands on the standards of value judgments, which probably find their expression in the behavior of people. I say "probably" here, because there is fortunately always deviant behavior also, and perhaps this alone makes a society ripe for future developments; but conformity to ruling demands remains the rule. There are many—logically, infinitely many—ways of classifying the ruling values in human societies by form, function, and substance. Here, Parsons' pattern variables are no better than the miserable dichotomies of German intellectual history or the (I hope, less miserable) couple of concepts we will add to them here. The ensuing analysis alone can demonstrate whether it is fruitful in our context to distinguish public and private virtues.

I want to suggest certain terms here as a guide. There are societies whose ruling values aim at the frictionless mastery of relations between men. These relations are by no means necessarily political in kind; they involve behavior at the family dining table no less than in school, in the streets, at work, on the sports' ground, and in political debate. If I call the values related to this behavior of men toward one another and its frictionless progress, "public virtues," I do not intend to draw the intimate sphere of the family into the public limelight, at least as yet. "Public," as a property of social values, is supposed to describe their character as a model of general intercourse between men. The "private virtues" are not a general model in the same sense; "private" regions are unfilled spaces that imply a degree of resistance to anything public. Thus private values provide the individual with standards for his own perfection, which is conceived as being devoid of society. Patterns of intercourse between men that are virtuous in a private sense correspond to this notion: they are immediate, not domesticated by general rules, intent on honesty and profoundness rather than ease and lack of friction. One might even ask in what sense private virtues can be described as social values at all.

Only the analyses of the following chapters can give body to the value syndromes envisaged here. A few further indications are therefore hardly less preliminary in nature. The predominance of public virtues may be described in terms of the values of sport, particularly of team sport. He who is virtuous in this sense is "a good sport"; he is "fair." He thus adheres to those rules whose rationale is to promote and at the same time domesticate the competitive effort of sports.

In this process the individual with his worries and dreams, flights of nostalgia and of desperation, retreats. Getting along with others becomes more important than these concerns; and this can be accomplished only if one does not burden one's relation to others with one's own inner person. Frictionless relations are also unburdened relations. Perhaps the single maxim that best characterizes public virtues is "Keep smiling": make things easy for the others, even if this is hard for you! Do not burden others with matters that make it difficult to get along; keep what is private to yourself! There is a strong element of the contractual in public virtues; they copy, so to speak, the articles of the social contract for all spheres of life. Since the personal sphere is left out, men are evaluated by their visible ability to get on with others. All society is role play, but the public virtues turn role play into a moral maxim.

A society in which the private virtues prevail is soon described by a stereotyped set of adjectives: it is dishonest, unnatural, and, above all, hypocritical. It is my intention to describe here with what I call public virtues precisely the attitudes that Germans like to decry in Englishmen as hypocritical, that is, the smiling role behavior in accordance with structured interests in every condition. If one were to look for the countermaxim in the world of private virtues to "Keep smiling" in the public, one might think of something like, "Be truthful!" This "proper" concept of what is truthful regards it, in contrast to the demands of society, as a search for an invisible truth. Frequent reference to "natural" behavior also documents the departure from all "merely external" things. Indeed, the personality of man proves itself by not requiring others at all. But where men meet, truthfulness involves burdensome relations: How are you? Ah, well, I have a toothache, and moreover I had a fight with my wife. . . . The gain in depth is a loss in contractual reliability. If the "external" world of social norms is devalued, the unexpected, which springs so much more easily from the intimate, emotional, and reinless than from the rational, gains in strength.

It is no accident that it is difficult to describe the private virtues as social values; they are in no sense virtues of participation. If, in a society of private virtues, the individual takes part in the social and political process, this remains "external" to him and he reserves the chance of retreat. This is why the prevalence of private virtues may become an instrument of authoritarian rule. It keeps subjects in that state of minority that allows the masters to maintain their benevolent-strict regime. The masters themselves, of course, do not adhere to the virtues they promote; in their own circle the aristocrats of history have always cultivated public virtues. It is therefore not my intention to claim that the prevalence of public virtues is a sufficient condition of the constitution of liberty. Such prevalence may have many consequences, but it is ambivalent in a specific modern sense: it unites liberal and totalitarian democracy. However, I do want to claim that the prevalence of the contractual values of public virtues is a necessary condition of liberal democracy; without it, liberal institutions cannot flourish.

I am not unaware of the dubious methodological status of such descriptions of "virtues" and "values." Indeed, this brings us close to the borderline of the traditional myth of national character that we rejected at the outset of this study. What is more, we will continue to straddle this border for some time. It is small consolation that we will try throughout to keep in mind the binding force and institutional consequence of the values in question. But perhaps the best way to demonstrate both the potential and the limitation of this kind of analysis is to let our imagination loose for a little longer.

An analysis of language, which is, after all, part of the system of norms valid at a given time, may possibly make more precise the difference between private and public virtues. Untranslatable words and idioms are often quoted, among them (to continue the confrontation of German and English virtues) *Schadenfreude* and *Weltgeist,* cant and common sense. Seemingly translatable expressions that nevertheless undergo subtle transmutations in the process are even more telling. There is an especially consequential example of this in the word for collective guilt, *Kollektivschuld,* which loomed large in public debate of German affairs after the Second World War. The notion of a German collective guilt was, to be sure, promoted by German emigrants as well, who were presumably familiar with the linguistic contexts. But the fact remains that collective guilt has a very different, much more "external" connotation for Anglo-Saxon ears schooled in public virtues than it has for Germans. "Guilt" (*Schuld*) in German always has an undertone of the irremediable, incapable of being canceled by metaphysical torment; *Kollektivschuld* binds every individual as such for all time. On the other hand, one of the corollaries of collective guilt is the notion of reparations or, more generally, of making up for past failures; what is meant is a collective responsibility that forces those responsible to answer by common effort, that is, in political and economic ways, for the damage they have brought about. Such guilt does not really involve the individual as a person, as a human being —as one would say in the language of private virtues—but in his membership role, thus as a German national. In principle, one can cast off the guilt with the role.

Peter Hofstätter has pursued another problem of this kind. Although he may well have underestimated the difficulties of translation that he set out to study, his investigation of German and American loneliness is nevertheless a useful illustration in our context. Hofstätter's question was, "Whether an American who would describe himself as lonely, would find himself in a comparable state of experience with a German who makes the same statement," and in order to find out he interviewed Americans and Germans (100, pp. 63 ff.).

His investigation led Hofstätter to unambiguous conclusions: "If we want to reproduce the condition of the American feeling lonely in German, we have to think of the condition of anxiety as it is known to us rather than of our own experience of loneliness (*Einsamkeit*). . . . Without formulating it *expressis verbis*, the lonely American describes himself as unloved, unsuccessful, and unmanly. The lonely German does not; he, however, experiences himself as tragic, which is hardly the case with the American. . . ." These are some of the words the Americans interviewed associated with "loneliness": "small," "weak," "sick," "cowardly," "empty," "sad," "shallow," "obscure," "bad," "ugly." And these are some of the associations of Germans: "big," "strong," "healthy," "courageous," "deep." To Americans the dictator appears lonely; to Germans, the hero. Hofstätter adds: "One is naturally tempted to go on speculating from here, and to consider, for example, that the lonely American might feel in need of psychotherapy whereas the lonely German would be able to see positive sides in this state of his" (100, p. 66).

The temptation to go on speculating about German and American loneliness is great indeed; but it seems to me that

Hofstätter's own speculation falls short. As he approaches his data, it must surprise him that a parallel study, which he conducted among English students, belies the implied confrontation of European and American attitudes: "It is significant for us . . . that English 'loneliness' is more similar to American . . . than to German. . . . In England, too, loneliness stands in a relation of contrast to love and success . . . ; it, too, resembles the German *Angst* . . ." (100, p. 70).

If one speculates in the direction indicated here, this result is not at all unexpected. To begin with, Americans and Englishmen have, despite everything, a common language in which the same words have as a rule the same connotations. Furthermore, the valid values in both countries are dominated by public virtues. Where public virtues prevail, loneliness is necessarily a sign of failure, subjected to the sanctions of society and therefore experienced with anxiety. Among the private virtues, on the other hand, loneliness occupies an eminent place. Not everyone can bear it (there is certainly much to be said for the objection raised against Hofstätter that German loneliness indicates largely only a verbal tradition), but whoever can is a hero; he is strong and healthy.

The application of the theoretical thesis of this part of our study—that the predominance of public virtues among the valid social values is a necessary condition of the working of the constitution of liberty—has already emerged too clearly for us to be able to postpone its explicit formulation any longer. Throughout the period in which we are interested here, the standards prevailing in German society were provided by other, more private virtues in terms of which people oriented their actions. But this thesis must not pass without immediate reservations. Here we are decidedly no longer concerned with the peculiarities of German society; with significant variations in substance, the same dominance of private virtues might be asserted for French and Russian, Italian and Mexican society, and many others as well. Another reservation is even more important. The last decades have brought about profound social changes, in German as well as English society. While the former discovered public good, the latter found privacy, and each regarded the values of the other as attractive. This is understandable, for both are—if for once we relate them not to the constitution of liberty, but to general moral or anthropological considerations—virtues. Both may well be thought of as ideals of the individual. The condition we encounter here reveals, in fact, a peculiar ambiguity of the constitution of liberty.

While our presentation of the two groups of virtues has been (and will continue to be) informed by a value judgment—an option for the public virtues—one might well opt the other way, and the result would be at least as impressive. What, after all, does concentration on getting along with others mean? Does it not lead straight to that lust for adaptation in which Americans are said to indulge? Is it not the road to uniform social behavior and thus to the "lonely crowd," which Riesman has described as vividly as critically and which Hofstätter would prefer to call the "anxious crowd"?

Such questions are not easily discarded. The literature, sociological and otherwise, is full of examples of the vagaries of over-socialized man, especially in the United States, and these provide many a successful party joke in Europe. Yet this is a rather simple reaction, for such examples show two things at least. On the one hand, they illustrate the education for the public virtues of getting along with others with which we are here concerned. At the same time, they are examples of the loss of inner-direction, of personal self-determination, of the surrender of the individual in favor of the uniform claims of a democracy without liberty. Perhaps this deviation is not necessary, yet even the English visitor remembers the impression of a certain uniformity of behavior oriented to the belief in the common man, and doubts soon mingle with the attraction of the different. However, the inner-direction of those oriented to private virtues is incomplete. It is inner-direction without its liberal element, the carrying over of interest to the market of politics and the economy. To be sure, even in its perversion one recognizes the misguided liberal motive. Protest against society, against the claims of authority, may be liberal or utopian; for the liberal, too, seeks detachment from valid norms in order to explore their better potential. The utopian is the unsociety; its effect stabilizes what exists, if indeed it does not freeze and thereby deteriorate it. The virtues of the inner emigrant, and at times those of the despairing on their way to exile, are also private—the liberalism of illiberalism. That this attitude has its virtues becomes evident if one considers the dimensions it opens for the individual's personal existence. The inclinations many Germans are said to have for the fundamental and the romantic, for lyrics and metaphysics, for profundity and even imprecision, mere divination, are disastrous in their political consequences; but there are many other standards by which they could by no means be condemned.

Many people have described the ambivalence and political danger of private virtues in Germany, among them such eminent authors as Fritz Stern and Harry Pross, Hans Kohn and Jürgen Habermas. But no one has given it a more pertinent name than Eliza Marian Butler in her book, *The Tyranny of Greece over Germany* (37), first published in 1935. The book was soon put on the index in Germany, although it dealt in a scholarly manner with the timeless beauty of the world of Winckelmann and Herder, Goethe and Hölderlin, and the possibly no-longer-quite-so-timeless world of Nietzsche and George; thus the destiny of the book proved the explosiveness of its harmless-sounding thesis.

E. M. Butler emphasizes that the Germans since Winckelmann were moved not by the polis of Greek reality, but by the sterile purity of a beautiful Hellas; that is, by an imagined esthetic ideal world, which lacks any admixture of civil society. She shows this in terms of the great Germans' conception of Laocoon and Prometheus, Iphigenia and Diotima, and also in terms of a strange metaphor, which betrays her own sense of politics and poetry:

> I imagine the world of men as a race of children marooned on an island of hard facts, most of them with their backs to the sea busily digging or building in the sand. They squabble a good deal; they achieve considerably less, and the little they accomplish is often wholly or partly obliterated by the waves, so that they have to move their pitch and begin all over again. The more adventurous gather by the water's genious, make primitive crafts to which the bravest of all entrust themselves, struggling back to land if they can when the boats ship water or capsize. From this scene of activity and endeavour some few hold themselves aloof, motionlessly staring out over the ocean as if absorbed by its wonder, mystery and menace. Taken as a whole they are less prepossessing than the others; something brooding in their looks and strained in their posture seems to indicate that they are less fit for life on the island than those around them; but as long as they are occupied with their dreams they will remain unnoticed.

These are the Germans, of course; and when E. M. Butler wrote she already knew that they had not stuck to their dreams. Therefore the chapter that begins with the tender colors of the idyll, closes in much stronger tones:

> Those solitary children on the imaginary island drew together at last and rose in a body to play with the others. They dug deeper, but built less securely; they swam faster but not so far; they made larger boats which capsized sooner; they grew angry and created confusion and uproar; they either could not or would not assimilate the rules of the various games. And yet they knew something the others did not, something about the nature of the sea. (37, pp. 3 and 8.)

Here, the ambiguity of German roles has been cast in a strong metaphor; E. M. Butler is much impressed by her subject, which she wants to warn her readers of. The beautiful world of the private freedom of imagined Greeks is also an ugly world of minority: "If the Greeks are tyrants, the Germans are predestined slaves" (37, p. 6). But the ambiguity remains. Perhaps young Germans are today becoming a little "skeptical" toward this dimension of beautiful imprecision, thinking more calmly, calculating more rationally, and choosing the reliability of contract to the enthusiasm of emotion; at the same time, young Englishmen are discovering the rhetoric of privacy, life in the false but effective feeling of detachment from social claims, the secret of the sea. Both directions are potentials of human existence with their own peculiar values.

Since we have already begun to admit immediate impression and speculative imagination without any claim to serious science, we may as well take a final step to uncertainty. Let us assume that private and public virtues exclude each other, so that a society can choose either, but not both, as a standard of behavior for its members—what would follow from this assumption? We know what follows in the case of private virtues. Where they prevail, public matters remain underdeveloped. Here man, the human personality, becomes a creature without a public life, and the formation of the nation is left behind. Many may well be quite content with this state of affairs. Their greatest happiness is found in private life, in the heights and depths of friendship and familial harmony, in the satisfaction of imprecise reveries, perhaps even in the nearly metasocial bonds with others in unstructured collectivities. The dismal state of public affairs normally does not worry such men because it does not affect their values, which are wholly geared to privacy.

The opposite choice opens up more unexpected perspectives. It would mean that people pay a private price for the success of their public affairs. Because they concentrate on getting along with others in an unburdened and frictionless manner, they no longer get on with themselves. I do not want to add speculative psychology to speculative sociology, but it is at least conceivable that human impulses, never wholly domesticated, take by unpleasant surprise a rational existence fashioned even in the most intimate spheres on the model of the contract. There would have to be observable signs of this failure of rationality: divorces, for example (or in England, where the law makes divorce very difficult, legal separations), certain forms of delinquency, symptoms of sexual repression, psychic disturbances of diverse kinds. Possibly the significance of psychoanalysis, the incidence of neuroses and psychoses, rates of divorce and separation in the Anglo-Saxon countries are pertinent facts in this connection. However, it is always both easier and less fruitful to document assumptions than to refute them.

It might nevertheless well be true—and this is why we embarked on this excursion into speculation—that the constitution of liberty demands a price, a human price. It might therefore be true that the price of a full private life in the narrow sense is political disorganization or loss of liberty, whereas political liberty forces the individual into the public at the expense of his apolitical dimensions. Whoever wants liberal democracy must renounce metaphysics, although this, too, is a path to knowledge; he must exchange romanticism for sentimentality and depth for definiteness; his *Freunde* become transformed into friends, and his *Glück* into happiness. In this sense, the rational world of public virtues is a little less comfortable. Worse still, once one has created it, the constitution of liberty is not even certain. The same uncomfortable rule of public virtues may lead to democracy without liberty, in its harmless version of the social tyranny of the majority (in the sense of John Stuart Mill), and also in its perfidious version of a totalitarianism that has to forbid the privacy of its citizens in order to uphold its power. Modernity is disquieteningly ambiguous.

At this point, if not earlier, the unsatisfactory character of this speculative excursion becomes fully apparent. The rule of public virtues is another expression of what we have called modernity in the context of our discussion of citizenship. To want it means, of course, not to want certain other things. That the individual bee is happy and the individual Papuan also claims to be, is not a very strong argument against a world of adult, free men. Public virtues mean respect for the other and his sphere. Rules of the game secure the players against the spoilsport. Men who are trying to get on with one another are probably spared the extreme evilness that makes it possible simply to rule some people out of the world of men in order to expedite them out of it afterwards. The very fact that they remain formal makes public virtues a condition of the possibility of liberty. That they do not create liberty is not a deficiency of theirs, but follows from the nature of liberty as we understand it. Freedom is always a possibility—"merely" a possibility, if one chooses—and it is therefore always threatened. "Modernity is," as Jenny puts it, "no utopia in which everything is solved" (cf. 108).

We are concerned here with German society in which the predominance of private virtues has proved a notable obstacle to the establishment of liberal institutions. In our discussion of social conflict, we saw that what may reasonably be understood by "democratization" does not consist of a simple copy of democratic ideas or institutions in other areas of society. Our present subject rests on an analogous thesis. A functioning democracy demands neither voting rates of 99 per cent nor the permanent politicization of the entire population; rather, both of these conditions characterize an emergency state of liberty, if not its total abolition in a totalitarian utopia. A functioning liberal democracy does, however, require a sense of public life, of the market of men and its rules, which is lacking in those who have fallen in love with private virtues.

In a modern society, which no longer consists of small cantons, public virtues have their place in the family, the classroom, in road traffic, on the sports ground, at work, in shops, in passing encounters with strangers rather than in the immediately political realm. Habermas is without doubt right; here, where it began, public commitment is no longer alive (cf. 87). But mourning the death of public commitment is, like bemoaning the leveled-in middle-class society, an ideology of the loss of structure that overlooks the fact that old institutions are usually transformed rather than abolished. There is sufficient room for public virtues both concretely at the places where men meet and abstractly in the institutions in which the roles of men are bound. "Democratization" in the sense of a spread of the rules that govern a functioning public in the older liberal sense becomes more complicated, but no less real, and certainly not less useful; what matters are not the institutions in which it takes place, but the virtues by which it is governed.

It is easy to see for us by now why these virtues have had a hard time in German society up to the present day. The mere possibility that they might prove to be the virtues of free citizens necessarily made the values of getting along with others suspect to a power elite eager to found its rule on tradition and divine grace and not to be exposed to the bothersome control of its subjects' institutionalized resistance. When the monopolistic political class of Imperial Germany was broken, it was not replaced by a group interested in the spread of public virtues.

Probably the National Socialists, in their own interests and yet against their explicit will, did more for the spread of public virtues in Germany than any other group. They did it by negating the old private values, thus providing them, after the end of the Third Reich, with a new and wholly undeserved splendor. Whether political education can eliminate this false splendor is one of the questions with which we have to deal. But it is doubtful that the cartel of anxiety at the top of German society has any particular interest in destroying Germans' love for the intimate and the private, for those things removed from all contract and thus from the public domain. A measure of emphasis on public virtues may follow from the realization of citizenship rights—the cartel of elites in any case is in spite of itself too worried to prevent this development—but the tyranny of Greece over Germany is still not broken. The country is still governed by the pretty virtues of privacy, to the detriment of the constitution of liberty.

The discussion of values leads us into thinner air than the discussion of institutions. But we are concerned with valid, ruling values, and these are not suspended in mid-air. By being chained to the social roles of men, they have left their stamp on the institutions of society. Here, their consequences for the social structure of politics become fully apparent. It is our aim in this part of our study to discover and discuss them in the organization of social institutions.

20. IN THE PEDAGOGICAL
PROVINCE

If the claim that the distinction between private and public virtues opens up a new access to the social structure of the constitution of liberty is more than pure speculation, it must have observable consequences for social institutions and the behavior of men within them. We have assumed that the prevalence of private virtues renders the establishment of liberal democracy difficult; we have further assumed that this prevalence is generally maintained at the expense of public virtues; we have claimed moreover that both the prevalence of the private and the neglect of the public are characteristic of German society. In stating this, our intention was not a literary description of the German character, but the formulation of testable statements about German society. Such statements may indeed be derived from the considerations of the preceding chapter, if we relate them now to social institutions.

Impressive as it may sound to speak of values and roles as valid or ruling, such statements remain mere promises so long as we do not identify the links between values and the people whose actions are supposed to be guided by them. For ruling values to be valid, it is not sufficient to write them into party programs, laws, or even constitutions. Men must get to know the values by which they are supposed to act; they must learn them. In a general sense we can say that the validity of the values in question is mediated by the process described by sociologists and social psychologists as the socialization of the individual. The rule of these values is established only by their transfer from the constitution and by way of education into the behavior-steering centers in the individual. We must look therefore for the consequences of our theses in those institutions that are devoted to the education of men, the family and the school.

In doing so, we will ignore the theoretical question of whether family and school are sufficiently characterized by the task of "socializing" those in their charge, that is, in René

König's words, assisting them in their "second, socio-cultural birth." Here, we simply assume that one of the purposes of these institutions is to mediate between valid values and individuals. We need one additional assumption, however. In history and at present, family and school display great variations in their structure and substance. Some characteristic patterns of their formulation will be the subject matter of our analysis in this chapter. But in all variations a core remains that makes it possible to allocate the two groups of values with which we are here concerned: under all social conditions it is more likely that the family is the place at which the private, and the school the place at which the public virtues are mediated, than vice versa. There are colorful mixtures and many overlaps; but the presupposition that the family has a special proximity to the virtues of privacy, and the school to those of publicness, does not lead us entirely astray.

On this basis, our speculations can now be translated into testable statements. The prevalence of private over public virtues must mean that, in Germany, family and school stand in a rank order in which the family has precedence over the school. That only the prevalence of public virtues may provide a social basis for the constitution of liberty, must mean that in a liberal democracy the educational institutions have to occupy a special place. To the extent to which the family is given precedence over the school, the prevalence of both private virtues and authoritarian political institutions are institutionalized; conversely, authoritarianism is ruled out by social structure to the extent to which the school is preferred over the family and public virtues are thus cultivated. In this way the confrontation of continental European and Anglo-Saxon countries might be removed from the vague sphere of unreflected impressions to the comparative analysis of the organization of family and education. But this is only one possible gain from the crystallization of social values into their institutions as we propose it.

There can be little doubt that, in German society, the family has precedence over the school. Many observations confirm this assertion. The formation of a separate system of schools and, at least in Prussia, the introduction of compulsory schooling are older than industrialization in Germany; but Hegel's claims for the family were a cornerstone of more than merely his own dialectical structure of state morality; its distant effects may be sensed even in the notion of parental prerogative as it is embodied in the Basic Law of 1949. The paradox of this parental prerogative has been demonstrated before; by removing important decisions about education from the light of public attention, it often not only harms those immediately concerned, the children, but indirectly the whole country, whose political community must continue to lack citizens and, along with them, liberty. Here, the connection between an institutionalized preference for the family and the persistence of authoritarian political patterns is particularly striking; but it exists in many less evident forms as well.

All we need to do is follow the German child from its first day of school, if not from its first day of life. Entering school is the axis around which the relation of school and family turns. When German children get their bag of sweets on the first school day they have to be six years old and are therefore usually six and a half or more. School physicians, teachers, and parents are moreover agreed that children should enter school later rather than earlier; it is much easier to effect a postponement by a year than earlier acceptance. The word *kindergarten* has found its way into the English language; but the institution itself has remained the exception in Germany, and in any case *kindergarten* are not regarded as educational institutions. There is no preschool system of any kind in Germany; indeed, schooling at the age of four—with a playful kind of school, to be sure—appears to German parents, teachers, politicians uniformly as a monstrous infraction of the rights of the family.

When the child has at last been allowed to enter school, the rights of the family continue to determine the course of the school day. As a rule, German schools finish at midday. This is a seemingly small fact of great consequences; nothing determines the status of women in Germany more decisively than the necessity of cooking lunch for the children, which makes "housewife" a full-time occupation. Nevertheless, the day school is not popular in Germany. In a survey of fifteen hundred parents in Hamburg (to which we will refer frequently in this chapter), Janpeter Kob found that only one third favored the day school, whereas 56 per cent rejected it. Moreover, those who favor the day school regard it as a means to "keep the children under good supervision" whereas the opponents fear "a disturbance of family life and family education" (116, p. 42). It is not surprising under these conditions that one third of all parents interviewed by Kob regard any extension of the influence of the school beyond the hours of formal lessons as an "infraction of parental rights" (116, p. 43). These are results that would probably emerge even more clearly in other, that is South German, more rural, more Catholic regions. While in England and the United States the child is at times almost given up by the family upon entering school, and the family turns into a kind of holiday institution, the school in Germany remains a mere supplement to the family as the main educator, and the assumption is that its range should be kept as narrow as possible in favor of the family.

In another representative sample survey, people were asked: "Why does one educate children?" Among the answers, the "cultivation of human values" on the one hand (48 per cent) and the "preconditions for success in life" on the other (45 per cent) were dominant. It takes little daring to suppose that the "human values" have to be understood in the sense of private virtues; when a list of possible goals of education was presented, "My child is supposed to be a good German at all times who feels committed to our liberal order" (admittedly not a very intelligent formulation), took last place (58, pp. 568 f.). Kob's findings confirm this conclusion; among the parents interviewed in Hamburg the goals of "education for citizenship" and "social education for the community" met with the least enthusiasm (116, p. 77). Probably not only the "human values," but the "preconditions for success in life" as well are private virtues, that is, capacities and skills that refer the individual to his own resources and not to others. This is as true for "general education" as for "required basic knowledge," to quote the two tasks of the school regarded as most important by Hamburg parents.

Thus the legal rights of parents seem well founded in people's actual desires and behavior; indeed, the actual wishes seem to go beyond the legal guarantees of the constitution. No less than one third of all Germans believes that the state should not take part in the education of children (58, p. 572). Bernhard Linke suggests a Schelsky-like trend to explain this: "One can suspect here an increasing appreciation of family education and the private sphere in education" (58, p. 558). However, there are some doubts about the prestabilized harmony of the rights and wishes of parents, and these are raised by more than the striking contrast between parental preferences and the insistence on public denominational schools in some parts of the country. It is significant that Kob in his typology of "educational self-confidence," that is, of parental insistence on the privilege of educating their children, found this markedly more pronounced in the higher than in the lower strata (116, p. 55). Here, too, the motif of class bias in education is evident.

If we pass now in this survey of the conditions of the German educational system (which will presently be supplemented by a somewhat more thorough examination of its substance), from the first to the last day of school, an analogous picture emerges. The ninth year of compulsory schooling has been thoroughly discussed by now, and is already established in large parts of the Federal Republic, so that a majority (if a narrow one of 52 per cent) accepts it. But the tenth year of school, attended voluntarily by up to two thirds of all children in other countries, if not compulsory in any case, meets with little enthusiasm. One quarter of all Germans at the most is in favor of it; the others believe: "Young people grow too old for apprenticeship." "The children earn nothing for too long." "The eighth, or ninth year of school is sufficient" (104, pp. 350 f.).

At first sight, a new motive seems to become apparent here. "Practice," the world of work, is as a rule no longer identical with the world of the family, at least not the family of origin. But we have seen earlier that the individual family by necessity tends toward its own abolition. So far as the appreciation of educational institutions by parents is concerned, the two worlds—family and practice—belong together: the family is sacred, and practice is inevitable; the educational institutions are stuck between the two. Not without a surprising sense of triumph Kob insists that it would be wrong to suppose that the school has robbed the family of its educational tasks. Theoretical considerations and empirical studies lead him to the same conclusion "that an ambiguous and linear development in this sense [of an increasing diminution of familial educational functions] can by no means be observed, but exactly the opposite trend may be demonstrated in important respects" (116, p. 40).

The author's delight about this conclusion confirms the taboo on the subject, which with many Germans touches upon profound resistance and extensive ideological clouds. Taboos must not be taken lightly, even if one believes that they should be broken. Whether the strong position of the family and the correspondingly weak one of educational institutions might not have its value, too, whether it is not, in particular, a fortress of resistance against totalitarian assaults, is a question to which we shall have to return. This much may be said in anticipation, however, that we are not advocating here a program of abolishing the family and its educative influence. But in our context the conclusion that Germany's educational institutions fulfill at best subsidiary tasks is relevant. On the one hand, they are understood as servants of the family, and therefore not merely support, but all essential impulses of education come from the family. Parents and teachers are entirely agreed that the "chances of the school to influence the attitudes of contemporary youth in a favorable manner" are, and should be, small (116, p. 43). On the other hand, the general schools (though not the secondary schools of which we shall speak presently) are roads to practice; they provide the individual with some of the basic skills he needs for his occupation. The harmony of family and occupational practice is complete; they complement each other in this direct relation, and in both spheres the emphasis is on values that direct the individual less to getting along with others than to his own personality and its development. Both are also characterized by a certain amount of dissatisfaction with the school, in so far as this interferes with their harmony by its own claims and ideologies.

We shall presently turn to the peculiar laws of the German school tradition. But even if, in terms of time and substance, they intervene between family and practice, they do not, in Germany, become a vehicle of the formation of public virtues. Indeed, the German school fails to render even what little contribution is left to it to the strengthening of public virtues; it remains within the dominant world of the private values of the family. Thus it is not only the general rank order of the two institutions in German society, but their substantive patterns as well that explain the weakness of public virtues in Germany. Even where the school rules, its regiment is one of private orientations, of a polished education and individual skills, in which other people fall by the wayside.

This may be applied to the family analogously. Under all circumstances, the family is an institution in which private virtues are implanted and expressed. Modes of behavior that guide the individual in his more intimate spheres, his relation to mother and father, wife and children, and to himself, are as a rule shaped in the family, even if their expressions are no less socially structured than economic or political behavior. But the family shapes the individual above and beyond this core of its activity as well; and here, the varieties of history are great.

Dietrich Claessens summarizes international research correctly, but overlooks the fact that it is largely Anglo-Saxon in origin when he describes one of the effects of the nuclear family on the individual thus: "The experience of the necessity of confidence and solidarity in a framework of co-operation may thus be found also as an inner experience of the individual: as an invitation for confidence and solidarity toward the components of one's own personality structure in its process of differentiation" (39, p. 93). Claessens justly adds in a footnote: "The eminent significance of this matter for education as a political task must be strongly emphasized in this study!"

The reason for this significance is, however, precisely that Claessens' summary does not hold for all societies. For if a society does not recognize, or regard as important, "confidence and solidarity in a framework of co-operation," then these public virtues may be replaced by more private ones such as truthfulness and faithfulness, more intimate ones such as friendship and community, less social ones such as the self-sufficient personality. Conversely, in societies in which the public virtues dominate, their seemingly non-familial contractual aspects may pervade even the private sphere. A clearly contractual understanding of marriage (as being capable of dissolution by agreement), the payment of children for helping at home, the translation of love into respect or indeed tolerance, and of family sense into co-operation are some examples of such forms of familial society.

All these examples are pertinent to the German case. There have been obvious changes in recent years, so that many today regard the notion of partnership as characteristic of marriage in Germany, and the intrusion of economic rationality into family life is evident. Here, too, a pointed thesis must not be taken without reservation. Only by comparison to other societies can we say that the family in Germany still favors privacy above all. There is no "return" to more modern patterns involved in the observations by Schelsky and his disciples that the German family, even after the Second World

War, provides for many a refuge of intimacy and privacy and remains untouched by civil society. It is unlikely that there are many countries in which people would mention, in response to the question of their best properties, after conscientiousness and dutifulness (49 per cent) and industriousness (46 per cent) that they have "much family sense" (43 per cent), with men and women not differing very much in this respect (104, p. 190).

Almost against its principles, the family can not only impart public virtues, but anchor them in its own structure. In some countries this is its hallmark, but not in Germany. We have also assumed that the institutions of the educational system are quite analogously capable of communicating, contrary to their public character, the private virtues, or at least of rejecting the public beyond an inevitable minimum. That this is true of the German school, further confirms our thesis of the dominance of the private in German society.

One possible misinterpretation of this thesis should be cleared up at this point. Connecting the school with public virtues might give rise to the assumption that I am trying to advocate an extension of political education. This may be a good thing, but it is in no sense my intention here. A school does not become democratic by devoting twelve or even twenty-four hours a week to political education. Where there is an emphasis on public virtues, this reaches deeply into the substance and methods of teaching. One might reflect here about the narrow space given to sport and its rules in German educational institutions, or about the minor importance of discussions and work groups; one might point to the lack of interest on the part of parents and pupils in the school as an institution and its administration, or cite studies according to which even peer group structures remain underdeveloped in German grammar school classes, and are, where they exist, motivated by scholastic interests, without at the same time having any relation to the formal organization of schools (136, pp. 129 f.).

Instead of a catalogue of such symptomatic details, however, it seems more rewarding to look somewhat more closely at two basic pillars of the German school, particularly the secondary school (on the assumption that it is, while not typical, significant as a leading model). In the terms of German educators these pillars of wisdom involve the relation between "formation" and "education" on the one hand, "formation" and "training" on the other. In order to avoid useless terminological discussion, both these issues will be dealt with in terms of concrete instances; one of these is a general phenomenon—early leaving from secondary schools, while the other one is a specific event—the "basic plan" of educational reform submitted by an official commission and the relation between education and society implied by its arguments.

Stuck between family and practice, the school in Germany fulfills largely subsidiary tasks. To make the education of children by its own standards its concern, is neither the school's commission nor its intention; this is true above all of the secondary school and the parents of its children. German grammar schools supplement the educational effort of the family by those elements the family itself cannot provide; they may at times advise the family, but they otherwise leave it its most precious property, the children. There are other ways of putting this: The school renounces the active education of children, leaving them instead to their own resources, and ascribes even its greatest failures to the children or their parents. Robert Burger's study of early leaving from secondary schools was not written in a critical vein so far as the schools are concerned; thus it reveals involuntarily the individual and social drama of a phenomenon that involves one out of every six Germans. Although 22 per cent of all West Germans have attended a grammar school for some time, five per cent at the most succeeded in finishing it with the final degree (104, p. 357). Why? The reasons are complex, and obviously not all of them should be sought in the school. But it is worth looking a little more closely at the destiny of twelve children who left a large grammar school in Munich (taken as exemplary by Burger) after the fourth form, at the age of fourteen, and to consider the educational approach of the school in their case:

Lothar K., who was judged "able," with normal grades, for unknown reasons.

Helmut M. had not reached the goal of the second form, had then fallen ill and interrupted school for two years. After taking up his studies again, he had failed to reach the goal of the fourth form as well, although at seventeen he had a considerable age advantage over his classmates. Because of exceeding the age limit he had to be sent down. In his form he was, as it says in the last evaluation by the teacher, "in no way a model." His suitability had appeared questionable from the beginning.

Werner F. had similarly been described as "still suitable" only with considerable reservations. He did not reach the goal of the fourth form and achieved nothing but bad results in the repeat year as well. Teacher's judgment: "Logical thinking creates difficulties."

Helmut M. had passed through the third form only by "reprieve," but no longer managed to reach the goal of the fourth form. He left for some occupational training. "Moderate talent, little energy," was the judgment of the teacher in his last year. Even in the test of ability four years earlier he had been judged "not suitable."

Manfred S. on the other hand had been judged "well suited." He, too, did not reach the goal of the fourth form and left in order to take up an apprenticeship. In the last evaluation of his teacher it is noted: "Father overly strict. Manfred has given up upon first failure. Is stubborn, rows much in class." Cause of failure despite undoubtedly good talent: educational faults of parents.

Karl T. had also been judged "suited" upon entering secondary school. Even in the second form he was regarded by teachers as gifted above average. In the fourth form his good intellectual talents are also emphasized. On school excursions "he vibrates with ideas." Nevertheless, he has not reached the goal of the third form, and since he would have had to repeat the fourth form as well, he was excluded by the rules of the school statutes. As cause of his failure the pupil's file states: lack of ability to concentrate. . . .

Rudolf A. was also excluded on the basis of the school statutes. He, too, did not reach the goal of the third, and again of the fourth form. The test of ability had described him as "suited in terms of talent," but emphasized even at the time that his working habits could not guarantee success.

Dieter D. had been judged "well suited." The teachers of the first form also mention good gifts, but a lack of concentration as well. In the third form it is reported that the parents are traveling a lot and do not look after the boy. In the fourth form the teacher observes that Dieter is frequently ill, does not feel understood and is treated with loveless strictness by his mother. Result: Dieter does not reach the goal of the third form, would have to repeat the fourth form as well, is therefore excluded and leaves for an intermediate-level school. Here conclusions similar to those in the case of Karl T. are indicated. The talent of the boy has never been doubted by the school either.

Günther K. by contrast has been judged "not suited" from

the beginning. He did not reach the goal of the first form and would have had to repeat the fourth form as well. Since in doing so he would have transgressed the age limit (he had completed his seventeenth year), he is excluded by the rules of the school statutes. Apart from his achievements he was not a pleasant character otherwise either. Even at the time the test of ability was taken it had to be noted that he was noticeably neurotic. Although the son of a simple laborer, he boasts in class about his pocket money. He has a conspicuous amount of it at his disposal, without the origin of it ever having been cleared up. On the occasion of an excursion he spends 12 DM—for his lunch alone.

Heinrich M. leaves the fourth form for an occupation without having been forced to do so by bad grades. Reasons of early leaving are not definitely known. . . .

Werner Fl., judged "suited," leaves for an intermediate-level school after not reaching the goal of the fourth form. Even in the first form he was known to be sensitive, anxious, and industrious, and he has probably taken his failure in the fourth form harder than would have been necessary.

Dieter B., also judged "suitable," took up an apprenticeship after he had barely reached the goal of the third, and no longer that of the fourth form. The pupil, who had shown slightly introvert tendencies even in the test of ability at the beginning of his secondary-school time, had difficulties only in the two foreign languages. . . . (36, pp. 66 ff.)

It is hard not to begin the analysis of this report about a piece of German reality by looking at it as a document of inhumanity, the inhumanity of institutions and of persons. There is the catalogue of charges: pupils are "slightly introvert," "neurotic," "give up upon first failure," and indeed it can work to their disadvantage that they are not only "sensitive" and "anxious," but "industrious" as well. The loving understanding of the educator for the children in his trust becomes particularly evident in the cases of Karl T., Dieter D., Günther K., and Werner Fl. Everywhere one is tempted to add exclamation marks to the text: "unknown reasons" (!), "age advantage" (!), "reprieve" (!), "working habits" (!), "result: Dieter does not reach the goal of the third form" (!).

But anger alone does not help our analysis here. What Burger describes and how he describes it is not a matter of individuals and their personal guilt, but of institutions and their dismal structure. Burger, who is very much part of this structure, not surprisingly has an ambiguous explanation of the fates of the children described by him: "Thus twelve pupils leave secondary school in the fourth form. With five of them, suitability was questionable or uncertain from the beginning. But the pupils judged suitable, too, tend to leave school after one, in some cases repeated, failure. Only two of twelve leave with normal grades. For those children whose talent is adequate the educational failure of the parents must be regarded as the cause of failure in school" (36, p. 68).

This conclusion is the reason we have quoted Burger so extensively here. The parents can fail educationally, but the school cannot as a rule, since it never even attempts to succeed in its educational task. It is true that Burger comments on the case of Karl T. that, apart from the "strict application of school statutes," it shows a "lack of an effective pedagogical assistance" (36, p. 67); but the total picture remains one of a frightening distance of the school from the children in its care. The school, and the secondary school especially, is an abstract world, which takes all that might be changed and formed as unalterably given: the "suitability" or "talent" of the child, the "educational faults of the parents," the child's temperament, the "ability to concentrate" and "working habits," the "neuroses," the good and the bad "properties." The German school is indeed not in a position to render its own contribution to the education of children; and this is not because it is short of teachers or classrooms, but because of its structure as a subsidiary institution, a prolonged arm of the ultimately responsible family. The position of the school in society, the children's time conceded to it, its rank by comparison to the family, the general appreciation of it, its character as a place to learn rather than to be educated, makes it virtually impossible for the school in Germany to bring its own formative force, informed by public virtues, to bear on the education of children. A school that is little more than a place to impart knowledge that the family cannot give not only has to be cruel, being all but forbidden any serious concern about people; it must also fail in its task to educate in public virtues.

To make matters worse, it appears that the German school does not even want to fulfill this task; and it is an open question whether its theory provides the ideology of justification for its dismal position, or whether this position is at least in part a result of its theory. If the tyranny of Greece over Germany has become effective anywhere, it is in the German Gymnasium; this in turn has provided a model for all other schools and their teachers. By that I do not mean the teaching of Greek in the so-called humanistic Gymnasia, although this rarely suffices to read Aristotle's *Politics,* while every attempt to reduce its importance ensues with teachers and professors, in grotesque attempts to defend allegedly threatened heart pieces of "occidental culture." Here I mean the fact that (as Charlotte Lütkens has put it) the idea of higher education in Germany has to be sought "beyond things social" (136, p. 33), so that public virtue seems suspect to the only institution that might have been capable of implanting it in people. At this point, political education, the role of legal, economic, and social knowledge in school curricula, become relevant too, but less for the conspicuous underdevelopment of these fields than because of the reasons given for it. Rather than continue the vague and fruitless discussion of the libraries that have been written in Germany about the concept of education, let us look at a "case," which may serve to illustrate the point.

When the German Committee for Education presented in 1959 its outline of reform, called the Basic Plan, it met with legitimate criticism from many sides for its "sociologism," that is, the noticeable tendency to confuse facts and norms, social realities and political maxims. The way teachers misused this legitimate criticism for telling declarations of principle is, however, characteristic. Karlheinz Heunheuser quotes the sentence from the Basic Plan, "The technical civilization has made a new higher education emerge" and remarks:

> In this sentence there is, if one takes the word "education" in its fundamental meaning, that is, as education itself [?], nearly everything false or falsified. For technical development or civilization as such can never make an education emerge, much less a new one and under no condition a higher education. In terms of the essence of education the quoted sentence is really a barbarism. . . . If by "education" is meant training, then the sentence has its justification, but then this sentence cannot provide a basis for demanding a reform of the educational system, but only for a reform of the training system, which leads in a very different direction. (196, p. 105.)

The voice of but one man? Let us hear two teachers' associations, the German Classical Philologists Association and the German Philologists Association, in official statements: "We have the impression that the terms education and training have not been meticulously separated. We cannot admit that 'the technical civilization has made a new higher education emerge' . . ." (196, p. 129). The Basic Plan with its "dogmatic concept of society involves the danger that the man suited for the technical world and planned away for immanent purposes steps in the place of a man called upon to decide freely and to think for himself and able to do scholarly work. Evidently, for the authors of the 'Basic Plan' education is adaptation to the passing conditions of a technical civilization. In this way education becomes nothing but training. We on the contrary understand by education three things: specialized knowledge, an ability to organize and use this knowledge with meaning, and a moral responsibility toward the values that sustain our lives" (196, p. 27).

Fortunately, the last sentence dispels the worst suspicions. Nevertheless, one has to conclude that "our lives" have nothing to do with "technical civilization" and that therefore the "values that sustain our lives" are exclusively private virtues. In all this, the concept of education has the strange quality of tending to evaporate into a cloud. Formation is not education. To consider the welfare of the pupil first, to guide him in his growth, prepare him for social and economic competence in school, family, and community and help him in his development to become a happy, responsible member of society—these are elements of the code of honor of the Californian (cf. 108), and not the German teacher. Education is not training. To make the pupil familiar with the skills he needs in order to stand his ground in a technical civilization is below the dignity of the German secondary school. Unfortunately, there is no shortage of esthetic metaphors for what remains when everything necessary has been deducted. But if one turns these into more definite statements, a conception appears that even in its most harmless aspects would have to be called the ideology of an unpolitical bourgeoisie. The other reality, civil society, cannot be denied; thus it may intrude in the educational system as well or, more precisely, in the "training system." There may therefore be a special final degree for those interested in economics, there may be vocational schools, technical colleges, and specialized training courses, so long as the basic rank order in which "education itself" holds first place remains undisturbed. Prestige grows with distance from reality—in this principle, school and family agree with those who do not care whether their power over reality is decorated with prestige as well.

This is evidently a very partisan analysis, and we have to face a number of obvious objections: Is the attitude criticized here really as bad as we have made it appear? Do German schools not have their indisputable merits? Was not the humanistic Gymnasium held to be a model for the whole world? Does not the German educational system in its variety combine the claims of education and training? Have not the schools already moved a long way from the somewhat historical picture sketched here? Is not the tradition of the German concept of education, leading back to Humboldt, at the same time a tradition of German liberalism? Did not American schools, which rested on different and, by the implication of our analysis, better principles, fail miserably in their tasks? Does not the much-praised "democratization" of education prove insufficient in view of the demands of modern society? And does not the German family have its great values? Is not its resistance against the assault of modern technics and politics a sign of inner strength? Does it not protect the individual in a way in which no other institution could? Is it not a symbol and instrument of integrity in the modern world, which is imitated rather than criticized elsewhere? Are not the polemics and recommendations contained in this chapter of our study totalitarian rather than liberal, devoted to society or the state and their power rather than the individual and his welfare?

These questions are suggestive, but legitimate, and we shall have to answer them. But before we do, it may help to reformulate our thesis. The prevalence of private virtues cannot provide a social basis for the constitution of liberty; this requires public virtues, which commit the individual to getting along with others. In so far as the virtues of valid values are implanted in men by education, and in so far as the family may be regarded as the seat of private, the school as that of public virtues, the thesis may be translated into institutional terms. One of the reasons for the pathology of liberal democracy in Germany is the precedence given to the family over the school. This finds its expression in the social perception of both, in the definition of their respective educational tasks, in the claims to the time and personality of the child granted to both, but above all in self-interpretation and reality of the didactics of the school. The German school has assumed a restricted function, differentiated from the family, and the way a phantom of education is used as an ideology documents the non-public character and effect of its activity. This is a condition that serves to perpetuate authoritarian structures, if only because it strengthens a subservience in people's attitude to public affairs.

This is our thesis. Its two ambiguities serve to strengthen rather than weaken its weight. The first hinges on the fact that one may certainly approve of both school and family as they exist in Germany. The notion of a "subsidiary task" that is carried out by the educational institutions is borrowed from serious discussions of the problem. And after all, just as Schelsky does not criticize the intact German family, Kob does not dissociate himself from the restricted German school. The teachers and teachers associations quoted are certainly by and large satisfied with the substance as well as the relative position of school and family in Germany.

It would be unjust to couch such remarks in merely ironical terms; many an argument may be advanced for a strong family and a weak, subsidiary school system. Among these are, as we shall presently see, political arguments; but they are negative in kind. For what follows from our considerations, and is the hard core of what I want to assert, is: One can approve of family and school as they are in Germany, but one cannot want them as they are and want the constitution of liberty at the same time. Whoever supports a family with a comprehensive claim to education and an esthetic school of humanistic values has by the same token made a decision against the political structures of liberal democracy.

Words have to be weighed carefully here. Whoever wants to restrict the family to its intimate sphere and give the school a wider range of education for more public goals has not automatically decided in favor of the constitution of liberty. Here we encounter the second, possibly more important ambivalence of our discussion. Modern liberal as well as totalitarian democracies emphasize the public institutions of education; in England children spend as little time at home as in the DDR. The family, in resisting by its comprehensive claim for education liberal political forms, constitutes at the same time a powerful means of defense against totalitarian patterns. Nowhere does the motif of the ambivalence of modernity and liberality, which pervades our study, become quite so apparent. There can be no doubt, of course, about the differences in detail between family and school in the United States and the Soviet Union, or Great Britain and the DDR. In order to identify these differences, we might return to our notion of a liberal market rationality, or public values as a market of interested individuals on the one hand, and a totalitarian plan rationality, or a thoroughly organized public under central direction, on the other hand. But the fact remains that these two, market rationality and plan rationality, are so to speak more easily convertible into each other than either of them is into traditionalism and traditionalism is into both. Whoever wants the constitution of liberty also wants its specific and extraordinary dangers.

Thus the connection between ruling values and political patterns is in the first place negative. Certain values exclude certain patterns. It is understandable that the National Socialist struggle against the family and the unlimited public nature of educational values in the Communist DDR make many people in West Germany hesitant to accept the risk of a change that must remain ambivalent. In addition, the cartel of anxious masters of this society has little interest in such a change; it would disturb the suspicious quiet of an authoritarianism malgré lui. But it is unlikely that the reaction to the totalitarian errors will be able to hold up the slow realization of more strongly public virtues. The mixture of intensity of tone and deficiency of substance among the defenders of the old order is just another sign of their fading power.

21. THE UNPOLITICAL GERMAN

Authoritarian rule combines the dominance of an exclusive group of leaders with the non-participation of the many. It is the political version of minority, and as such it is both easier to bear and harder to shake than totalitarian rule. "The greater the changes in the structure of the society or organization that a governing group is attempting to introduce, the more likely the leadership is to desire and even require a high level of participation by its citizens or members" (131, p. 180). Lipset's hypothesis remains plausible if we apply it to our distinction. Totalitarian masters intend to change their societies fundamentally; they need the permanent and controlled participation of all men. Liberal democracy, too, is a form of institutionalized change. Not everybody has to participate in its political process, and few have to do so all the time; but in order for it to remain lively, political participation is indispensable. The authoritarian state on the other hand is a constitution of stagnation. Non-participation belongs to its structure, if only because change has to seem objectionable to its permanent masters. Authoritarian rulers need the many merely as objects of their decisions.

That the German—meaning presumably: Germans in their majority, or the social role of the German—is unpolitical and by this deficiency facilitates authoritarian rule, is one of the stereotypes of the literature on democracy in Germany. Occasionally, especially in the past, saluted as a liberation for higher purposes, more frequently and especially in the present scorned as an obstacle to liberty, the thesis comes up in ever new versions: "The *animal politicum,* so characteristic of the countries of the West and so immeasurably important for them, has never flourished in Germany, and politics never became a national passion or a respected part of national culture. Indeed, when German liberalism stumbled from defeat to defeat in the nineteenth century, the exact antithesis of the political being emerged, the deliberately unpolitical German." And many conclude from such observations with Fritz Stern: "I regard the unpolitical German as both cause and effect of Germany's divergence from the West and her persistent political failure" (cf. 209).

But who is the unpolitical German? Where do we find him at work? The questions are less easily answered than might appear at first sight.

The man who places the private virtues of withdrawal from others above the public virtues of contract and co-operation, is certainly a version of the unpolitical German. We can thus see him at work in the rank order of valid values as well as the hierarchy and structure of the institutions of socialization. But in our discussion of these values and institutions we have left out, almost too obviously, the area in which one would first suspect the effects of the relative appreciation of public and private virtues, the area of politics. In this manner, we have almost become a little unpolitical ourselves. How then does the unpolitical German conduct himself, when he conducts himself politically?

The question sounds paradoxical, but the sound is deceptive. For even Germans are not so unpolitical as not to act politically; indeed, if we regard the external signs of political participation in Germany, it seems strange that the German could ever acquire the attribute "unpolitical." Earlier, we have surveyed the history of suffrage in Germany by comparison to other, more liberal countries. If we compare the history of actual participation in elections, we encounter essentially the same picture. Since the 1880s, participation in national elections in Germany has nearly always been high, with moderate fluctuations between 70 and 90 per cent; throughout the period under discussion it was much higher than that of many other countries, notable among them Britain and the United States. Is that the picture of an unpolitical people?

But we have also found that there is no linear relation between a liberal motivation for political participation and the level of voting. Research on the factors that move the individual to cast his vote or hold him back, has led to complicated catalogues in which social status appears next to actual government policy, economic privilege or disadvantage, the presence of cross-pressures, and many other forces. Even in a greatly simplified conception we have to distinguish at least three incongruent rhythms of participation. One is the rhythm of the growth of effective citizenship; its effects can probably be observed in the general tendency toward increasing participation in Imperial Germany (see table below). The second is the rhythm of the legitimacy of a political regime in the sense of its support by those living under it; this may be observed, for example, in the increase in participation during the early years of the Federal Republic. The third rhythm is more complicated. It marks the cycles of stability and crisis and is caused by the fact that as a rule participation increases in times of crisis; the end of the Imperial era, the beginning,

Participation in National Elections in Germany, 1871–1961
(Percentage of actual voters in parentheses)

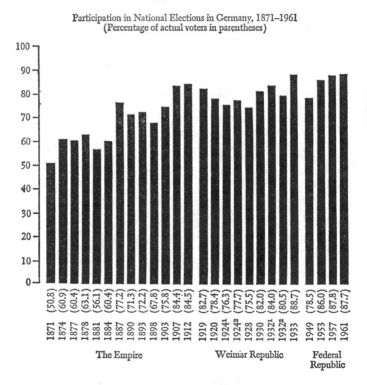

and above all the end of the Weimar Republic might be adduced here. In these crisis peaks of participation it becomes apparent that voting is not necessarily an expression of confident political interest. There were not a few people who voted only once during the whole period of the Weimar Republic, namely, for the National Socialists on March 5, 1933; and they hardly showed themselves as very political Germans by this act.

Such arguments, however, have the unpleasant flavor of an attempt to save a lost theory. Is not voting a form of political participation, even if one is tempted to describe its substance as a public vice rather than virtue? We can pursue our question a little further by viewing political participation in Germany in its less obvious expressions as well. In doing so, we profit from the fact that publications of opinion research institutes and the analyses of Renate Mayntz, Wolfgang Hartenstein and Klaus Liepelt, and above all Erich Reigrotzki (whose broad empirical material has been further analyzed in the United States by Juan Linz) provide a basis of information for the Federal Republic from which we learn how many people are members of political parties, how many talked to whom about political matters last week, and who has heard the name of Konrad Adenauer. The result is a panorama of the political German.

Even a first view of the panorama yields results that are surprising in many respects:

In the Federal Republic there are approximately
      1,600 members of parliament and *Land* diets
   220,000 members of district councils, city councils, etc.
 1,200,000 members of political parties
 5,000,000 participants in political or economic meetings
 6,000,000 trade-union members
10,000,000 television viewers
11,000,000 people who talk about politics in primary groups
11,000,000 readers of the popular press
13,000,000 regular church attenders (10 million Catholics, 3 million Protestants)
15,000,000 members of voluntary associations
25,000,000 readers of regional newspapers
27,000,000 regular voters in *Land* elections
32,000,000 regular voters in federal elections
37,000,000 voters. (89, p. 44.)

This is how Hartenstein and Liepelt in 1962 summarized a condition that, while it continuously shifts in detail, changes its general proportion rarely if at all. But is this really a "condition"? More particularly, is it a political condition? Is reading the popular press or attending church regularly a political activity? Hartenstein and Liepelt think that the memberships gathered by them "are all, to a greater or lesser extent, connected with political participation"; but until that is proved their catalogue remains a rag bag of incompatibles.

A few years earlier, Erich Reigrotzki tried to sort out this rag bag:

> More than four fifths of the adult population of the Federal Republic take part in elections; but only 3 per cent are members of political parties. With this we have evidently grasped the two cornerstones of political activity, assuming that party membership constitutes the most intensive form of political integration, and voting the weakest. But this inference from quantity to intensity may be made only with great reservations. It is hardly conceivable that between these two corner positions there is a political vacuum. It is our task, therefore, to search for the forms of political integration that fill it. (180, p. 71.)

Reigrotzki believes that these forms may be found in a multitude of "subsidiary social activities," which, while not directly political themselves, have political consequences. He continues to specify what these look like, and how widespread they are in Germany, in terms of three indices constructed on the basis of a representative sample survey of West Germans. This is first of all the "index of small political activities" which combines the frequency of political conversations, the frequency of participation in election meetings, and interest in political radio commentaries. According to this index, a group of "higher activity" (22 per cent), another one of "medium activity" (28 per cent), and a third one of "low activity" (50 per cent) may be distinguished.

A second "index of political information" on the basis of four test questions ("Do you know whether parliament has adopted or rejected the European Defense Community treaty?," etc.) also results in three groups, a well-informed one of 61 per cent, a medium one of 29 per cent, and an ill-informed one of 10 per cent. On the basis of his third feature, the "index of political judgment," which measures the readiness to take a stand in current problems ("Are you yourself for or against the European Defense Community?," etc.), Reigrotzki distinguishes four groups of 26, 26, 24, and 24 per cent respectively. Reigrotzki is aware of the fact that the immediate information value of such indices is small: "If we have found out here 30 per cent of the population belong to the best-informed group, it is impossible to tell whether this is a good or a bad result" (180, p. 95). The indices are not certificates of political achievement, but in principle arbitrary constructions. All they show conclusively is that the apparent "vacuum" between the 3 per cent party members and the 80 per cent reliable voters is in fact filled by a multitude of politically relevant activities, and that different groups fill it in different ways. Reigrotzki takes this result as a point of departure for his analysis of political integration.

Out of this analysis, the question of which groups prove to be particularly "unpolitical" in terms of the indices and further data is of particular interest in our context. Among the "unpolitical" are, in the first place, many women. While men are approximately evenly distributed over the three groups of higher, medium, and lower activity (36–34–30 per cent), no less than 68 per cent of all women belong to the third, inactive group.

The result is even more striking in respect to the index of political judgment where the sequence of a decreasing readiness to take a stand is 45–29–18–8 per cent with men, as against a nearly converse one of 12–23–29–36 per cent with women. A second comparatively unpolitical group emerges in terms of social stratification; it consists of workers, especially those with low skills, low income, and low educational achievement. Younger people constitute a third group that tends to be unpolitical, with (in 1954) the generation of twenty-five- to twenty-nine-year-olds, that is, those who grew up under the Nazis, showing a particularly striking lack of activity. Furthermore, the same three groups display the most pronounced anti-democratic inclinations, in so far as this can be told in terms of the answer to the question: "Do you believe that it is better if there is one party, several parties, or no party?" While 50 per cent of those interviewed pleaded for several parties, this was true for but 36 per cent of all women and 40 per cent of all unskilled workers, while no less than 28 per cent of all twenty-five- to twenty-nine-year-olds said they would be content with a single party. "Integration into the existing political order increases with education, with income, with information about political affairs; it is correlated with political activity and with participation in the political life of the nation in general" (180, p. 111).

Reigrotzki's analysis of the relation between "mental political activities" and political organization, or the general readiness for social participation ("sociability") and its significance for political participation, has been carried out carefully and convincingly. Nevertheless, his entire investigation has a strangely unspecific air in respect to our problem. Only occasionally do more relevant questions arise, and then from the reader more often than from the author: Who are the 50 per cent who have no "small political activities" to show? What does it mean that only 50 per cent regard "several parties" as necessary? What light is thrown on political participation by the fact that it appears especially high among practicing Catholics? How can we explain the high proportion of those who have expressed "no opinion" or given "no answer" to many questions? Reigrotzki answers these questions in his own way, and yet one is left with the impression that, in respect to political participation, Germany is very nearly the best of all possible worlds. Participation is, if one includes the subsidiary activities, remarkably high, and it is democratic, for the only undemocratic group is that "with a particularly small proportion of informed, active, intelligent people" (180, p. 118). Actually, this impression is not only a result of Reigrotzki's analyses, but one that generally gains in currency under comparatively normal political conditions. But is the impression correct? Is it not merely the truth, but the whole truth?

"Speaking very generally, are you interested in politics?" A representative sample of West Germans was asked this question seven times since 1952 by a leading opinion research institute. Between 27 (1952) and 34 per cent (1962) answered "Yes," between 24 (1962) and 35 per cent (1959), "Not at all," and between 36 and 41 per cent were "Not particularly" interested in politics. But this finding does not help us much either. We want to trace specific political modes of behavior in Germany, and we want to do so a little more thoroughly than opinion research and the correlation of its results would permit. It is conceivable after all that those who are interested in politics have merely added this interest superficially to their personality, whereas many a natural political temperament does not profess any particular interest. It might be that in the forms of participation themselves an authoritarian defense against politics continues to be at work. Participation could be opportunist or goal-directed, illiberal or liberal in its substance. In order to decide such questions we have to reach behind the findings of survey research without surrendering their content of controllable observation to the arbitrariness of mere assertions.

Fortunately, Jürgen Habermas, Ludwig von Friedeburg, Christoph Oehler, and Friedrich Weltz have done precisely this in their study of *Student und Politik* [Student and Politics]. The path of the analysis by Habermas and his colleagues constitutes a notable contribution to our subject. Even the objects of their investigation, a reservoir of the German elite of tomorrow, are of special interest. Moreover, their first findings seem consoling; they confirm Reigrotzki's conclusion strikingly:

> The majority of students develop, on a high level, an understanding of the formal rules of the democratic machinery of government; they are largely free of occupational interests and not used to judging political matters in a "prepolitical" way in terms of the occupational sphere (and that of the family); and finally they are subject to a permanent appeal of education and therefore display, by contrast to their age-fellows elsewhere, a certain sense of obligation to participate in political life, even and perhaps particularly where they in fact withdraw. (86, p. 71.)

But these early observations are merely the beginning of analysis. Which is the position of politics in the life budget of students? How does the physiognomy of things political appear to them? To what extent are they themselves prepared to become active politically? On the basis of extensive interviews of the admittedly limited and statistically not representative number of 170 university students, Habermas and his colleagues distinguished six types of "political habitus" in respect to such questions: the "unpolitical" (13 per cent), the "irrationally detached" (11 per cent), the "rationally detached" (19 per cent), the "naïve citizens" (19 per cent), the "sophisticated citizens" (29 per cent) and the "committed" (9 per cent). Thus nearly two fifths of the students seem to have a conscious commitment to politics; but it is more telling in our context to look at the other three fifths, the majority.

Here we find the deliberately disinterested, many girls among them, and "the interviewed of this type overwhelmingly report an integrated family life" (86, p. 75). "All the unpolitical [students] answer the question of the 'decent' life in the horizon of their private sphere" (86, p. 78). "The experience is that a paternalistic regime meets the needs of the unpolitical" (86, p. 83). The "irrationally detached" behave similarly, but with them antipathy against things political takes the place of unpolitical apathy. The "rationally detached" turn away from the apparent disorganization of liberal political conditions; they would prefer to leave politics to experts; "in essence, politics is reduced [for them] to the schema of scientific management" (86, p. 101). "A future teacher finds the formula for the habitus of rational detachment: 'Neutral is still the most ideal' " (86, p. 106). Strictly speaking, one has to add to these the fourth group of "naïve citizens." "In truth there is not much to their integration as citizens. Their political interest is a little artificial" (86, p. 111).

Here, too, the consequences of the habitus are decisive, and they unite the naïve with the unpolitical and the detached: "To the naïve citizen the political sphere appears rather like a statesmanlike order in which great men direct history with dignity and strength" (86, p. 109). The consequences of all these attitudes are authoritarian; their style is private: once again we encounter the syndrome of private virtues.

Habermas and his colleagues have added to this course of their analysis two others in order to amplify and test their findings. The first of these concerns what they call, rather ambiguously, "the political tendency," or the "judgment about democratic institutions" (formed in terms of three questions). This approach confirms the suspicion of widespread latent authoritarian inclinations. Although in these terms, too, nearly one third appear as "genuine democrats" who grasp the democratic system with all its difficulties, the largest group consists of "formal democrats" (39 per cent). They accept the existing system, but there is no telling whether they would not accept entirely different conditions, too, if they were given.

"On the whole these students often give rise to the impression of a contradictory consciousness. Democratic and authoritarian perspectives are innocently juxtaposed: 'So far we have experienced only a bad dictatorship. If there was another one—(then, after some hesitation) we may as well stick to democracy with its disadvantages' (student of economics, 9th semester)" (86, p. 139). Thus the "formal democrats" are not all that far removed from the explicitly authoritarian persons (22 per cent): "In principle dictatorship is the ideal solution, if the man sits at the top who is 100 per cent right, who can enjoy full confidence, has the well-being of all on his mind, and that would have to be an extraordinary man. That is why this is, then, again utopian, that is clear. But in any case it would be better than all the interfering and talking about things and making each other unsure (student of economics, 5th semester)" (86, p. 140). And promptly the private virtues appear: "Freedom, real freedom that one has, one can only have in one's own four walls (student of mathematics, 7th semester)" (86, p. 141).

Such remarks refer to the substratum of political motivation that Habermas, following Popitz, calls "image of society." How do the students see their own German society and themselves in it? Only a small proportion of them has "classical" images of society in terms of sociological literature, that is, images derived from their own class position (10 per cent). A much larger proportion has a highly individual, occasionally abstruse image of society or none at all (23 per cent). But we are interested above all in those many (54 per cent) who have "modified images of society," that is, combinations of diverse elements. There we find the "model of inner values" (10 per cent): "Differences are largely based on education; I categorize people not by position, much less by money, but by education. There is an educated stratum and an uneducated stratum . . . the uneducated stratum endeavors to display its favorable material sides (student of economics, 7th semester)" (86, p. 174).

An even more widespread model is that of the "intellectual elite" (23 per cent): "I believe the worker has to be led by the academic. But if the emperor stoops to the level of his subject, he has lost the right to be emperor. The academic must not stoop to that level. He must assert the position that is his due with dignity, he must have the courage to rule (student of philology, 2nd semester)" (86, p. 185). Then there is the "model of social equality" (14 per cent): "I only see human beings, not specific groups (student of philology, 1st semester)" (86, p. 186). Finally we find in the circle of these images of society the "model of the leveled-in middle class" (7 per cent): "There no longer is any stratification in the traditional sense really. . . . The strata of the past are like water on an oil skin, on which they form small islands. They try to pretend that there are strata (student of psychology, 8th semester)" (86, p. 194).

There are obviously differences of considerable importance between these images of society displayed by German students. But if we examine their political potential, such differences rapidly disappear. The notions of social equality and of the leveled-in middle class betray the same fundamental withdrawal from the realities of society which finds its theoretical expression in the model of inner values and its political application in that of the intellectual elite. Under given political conditions one may conclude with Christoph Oehler that this attitude "seems to be determined equally by retreat into the sphere of inner values and by a pragmatic adaptation to the so-called external necessities" (86, p. 150). But what is going to happen if and when the "external necessities" change? Habermas has put this question, and in answering it he has joined together the three courses of the analysis of his data. The answer is not very encouraging (86, p. 232):

Students with		
definitely democratic potential		9%
indefinitely democratic potential		66%
but more democratic	20%	
wholly indefinite	26%	
but more authoritarian	20%	
definitely authoritarian potential		16%
disparate potential		9%

The "potential" is supposed to indicate how firmly rooted people's political attitudes are. Let us remember once again that in the study under discussion quantitative statements can give indications only. The impression nevertheless remains that the great majority of students has no really definite political consciousness—and that of those who have there are fewer liberals than supporters of authoritarianism. Political behavior is not integrated into the social personality of students. Since it is stuck on, it is subject to incalculable shifts, or rather to shifts that may be calculated from the changes in objective social and political conditions. Only a small part of the students is likely to promote authoritarian tendencies actively; but if these tendencies prevail, most students will evidently feel more at home than they would with the uncomfortable constitution of liberty. These students are a very appropriate reservoir for the cartel of anxious lovers of authority at the top of German society.

Yet another finding of the study by Habermas and his colleagues should be noted because it helps to tie together some loose ends of our own argument. Habermas has correlated images of society with other characteristics of the students and found that the "image of inner values" (and, with variations, the other "modified images of society" as well) are most frequent among children of clerical workers and officials; the fathers of these apostles of an authoritarianism of inner values are mostly university-trained, one quarter of them are academics in the second or third generation; the children themselves prefer to study in a faculty of philosophy and have generally received their school education in a humanistic Gymnasium. One could go on extrapolating to the intact home, the education in the family, the school in a subsidiary function for the purpose of learning—to the normal case, in other words. For if anything is frightening in this mixture of inner values, ritual adaptation to given political conditions, and authoritarian potential, it is the fact that it is not at all eccentric in Germany, but an implication of the official ideals of education and therefore representative of ruling social norms.

We have used the study by Habermas and others extensively, because the way in which it proceeds from opinion research data to effective centers of political motivation seems exemplary. Habermas himself tends to place his findings into a nationally unspecific context of fading liberalism. Thus he takes the road of all sociology to which we have added here at least an ironical reservation: generalization means theory; it does not mean that statements must be valid for all societies of an epoch. It seems to me that the findings of Habermas may be generalized for one area only, that is, German society, which is thereby distinguished from others and which for that reason, too, fails to support the constitution of liberty. With this notion in mind, let us retrace the steps of analysis from election participation to the unpolitical German once again.

We have seen that participation in elections is notoriously high in Germany, and there is no lack of other forms of apparent political participation either. Even here we are not really speaking of all citizens, of course; a group of totally unpolitical people, among them many women, can be identified by the statistical analysis of participation. There is much to be said for the suspicion that many of the others really dissociate themselves from politics, or at best fulfill their duties as citizens naïvely. This means that the political sphere of life remains alien to people, stuck on like political education in the classical grammar school. So far as the habitus of people is concerned, the area below the ritual act of voting is empty after all, that is, not filled with activities of immediate political relevance experienced as significant by the individual. The political socialization of the German is incomplete. While opinion research rarely makes the resulting gap widely visible, its permanent effect is considerable.

This effect is expressed above all in the quality of political behavior. Democratic institutions are accepted; but they remain external, distant, ultimately irrelevant. The individual is not committed to these institutions with his person, and is therefore hardly seriously prepared to defend them. Democratic behavior becomes ritualized, a mere observance of external demands, a "duty" of citizenship. If one scratches this ritualism but a little, there often appears one of the many versions of active and passive authoritarianism, or a complete lack of orientation, the political effect of which is probably no less authoritarian. This authoritarianism is not malicious; like that of the German elite it is an authoritarianism against itself, a consequence of non-commitment, a form of incomplete modernity and citizenship. As long as it is not activated by authoritarian structures or elites, it can slumber and even pass away. For we should not exclude the possibility that what was stuck on does at last grow on and that ritual adaptation becomes intelligent and independent practice at last.

However, for the time being, widespread images of society make such developments unlikely; the evaluative rank order of private and public virtues prevents people from giving even faintly political matters a secure place in world orientation and social structure. Even today, the lonely—or anxious—crowd does not describe German society. As a phenomenon of other-directed overadjustment it is symptomatic of a country lacking in private virtues rather than one lacking in public. The further one pursues the images of society of many Germans, the more the motives of public virtues disappear. Along with the "real" values, the personality appears as a self-sufficient construction. Indeed there hardly remains an "image of society" at all; instead this evaporates into a "world image," a "world view."

The unpolitical German is thus a rather complicated creature. Whoever observes him from the distance is unlikely to regard him as unpolitical at all. He faithfully complies with his duties as citizen, reads newspapers and listens to news, talks to his colleagues at work about reunification, nuclear armament, and high prices, occasionally even attends a campaign meeting, and in any case casts his vote regularly. Except on the local level, he is rather more hesitant to join a party himself, stand as candidate or desire this for his children; moreover, "he" differs from "she" and both are not as homogeneous as the singular suggests; but all this the German shares with the Englishman, the American, the Frenchman, and many others. That the appearance of political behavior is nevertheless deceptive, becomes evident only when one gets to know him more closely. Then one discovers that political activity belongs, for the German, to the outer ring of those duties that are bothersome but inevitable under the circumstances. Like, say, paying rent, not to say taxes. Political activity remains an activity in quotation marks, from which one dissociates oneself in one's heart and therefore, if external circumstances demand it, in fact as well. The German is unpolitical because the political is deeply unimportant for him; he is authoritarian because he would really much prefer not to be drawn out of the "freedom" of his four walls. Whether he is the cause of the German Question seems uncertain; but he is certainly a consequence of its social form.

It would be unfair to conclude this chapter without mentioning the democratic and highly political minority that even Habermas (who does not usually tend to optimistic analyses) found. There is this minority, and there is something to be said for the assumption that it is growing. The indicated syndrome of ritual participation, private virtues, and authoritarian consequences was certainly more symptomatic of Imperial Germany than it is of the Federal Republic. It is less consoling that at the same time the public virtues are in retreat in the older democracies, except that it underlines the possibility of change in this area and thereby raises hopes for Germany, where almost any change must involve a strengthening of political commitment.

22. HUMANISTIC THEORY AND PRACTICAL INHUMANITY: AN EXCURSUS

The constitution of liberty is founded on civic equality, the rational regulation of conflict, a liberal elite, and the predominance of public virtues. Where these social structures are absent, distorted, or perverted, liberal democracy cannot gain a hold. This was the theoretical starting point of our analysis, and it will, enriched by manifold observations, stand at its end as well. But our subject is the German Question, and the further we proceed, the less possible it is to ignore the objection that we have evaded the very issues that make the German Question disturbing: How was Auschwitz possible?

I want to try to maintain the emotional detachment of analysis even in the face of the horrors invoked by this question, at least as long as possible. It is no accident that our theoretical perspective fails to bring into focus the worst face of the German Question; in fact, we have known this from the outset. The reason is an uncomfortable fact, which is often concealed by imprecise references to Germany's recent past: if we succeed in explaining the events of 1933, this does not by itself explain those of 1940; the National Socialist seizure of power does not itself imply the "final solution" of the Jewish question. This may be put in even more general terms. Liberal democracy and humanity are two matters; there is inhumanity in democracies and humanity in non-liberal political communities. In this sense it is, so to speak, an evil accident that both humanity and democracy suffered harm in Germany. Thus, liberal democracy is no patent medicine for all the potential troubles of man's social life, and, accordingly, an analysis of the pathology of liberty is not, as such, also an analysis of the cruelties for which, above all, the name of Germany will be remembered in the world. Thus we must interrupt the course of our argument unless we want to miss the inescapable question altogether: How was Auschwitz possible?

The name of the camp in which the SS-state found its evil perfection symbolizes for many the horrible face of National Socialist Germany. But let us remain exact and not be satisfied with symbols. We are dealing with human beings here who, clinging to one another, were pushed into gas chambers, poisoned, robbed even as corpses, and burned—and with those who did this. There is little to be gained by the sweet metaphor that helps such realities to evaporate into the language of psychoanalysis or of intellectual history. Thus we are not concerned with national neuroses or historical burdens, but with the facts that hundreds of German lawyers knowingly took part in judicial murder; hundreds of German doctors knowingly killed, at times in cruel experiments, human beings; hundreds of German officers knowingly murdered women and children, or ordered and supervised their murder. More than elsewhere, one should be cautious with figures here. But such caution does not alter the fact that thousands of alumni of German Gymnasia did not let the cultivated humanism of their intellectual formation prevent them from stamping out people like ants whom one may not even notice because one is so busy looking up to the stars that one does not watch the streets. The social image of inner values? What we have to explain is not simply "Auschwitz," but how it was possible that, in National Socialist Germany, thousands of members of a small elite became licensed murderers.

This is neither the first time that this question has been asked, nor will it be the last. The answer, moreover, will probably be long in coming. For neither the military oath nor the banality of evil, neither an "emergency-roof" theory nor one of early childhood repressions, provides this answer, or so it seems to me. I will not be able to provide it either. This is a negative balance; but there are small steps one can take to trace what men have done to men in Germany.

One can observe certain things in German society of the day before yesterday, yesterday, and even today, which raise the suspicion that they are somehow connected with a mentality that turned doctors and judges and officers into murderers. There are corners of this society in which an often-thoughtless inhumanity survives systematically. There is the shocking contrast of humanistic ideology and the factual indifference to life. In this excursus I want to focus the searchlight of analysis on some of these dark corners of German society. In doing so, I am throughout concerned with the integrity of human life, with that "respect for life" that is so easily praised in Germany. And throughout there hangs above the realities of the present, dark as they may be, the much darker cloud of memory. I will not always succeed, therefore, in maintaining that calmness of analysis that, in combination with definite value decisions, describes the virtues of the sociological imagination. Even words, to say nothing of the deeds they depict, are too painful here.

Most of those who were killed by Germans during the war were not German citizens, "normal people." They were Poles and Russians, or people otherwise defined out of the comparatively narrow circle of things German: Jews, gypsies, the mentally ill. We have seen earlier how narrow the circle of those who enjoy full citizenship rights is in Germany—and how those fare who are left outside this circle. Yet their number is not small, and their destiny is no leaf of fame for the others who have in no way earned their membership and whose spiteful conformity is therefore entirely arbitrary.

The role of the non-member has many facets, ranging from the depressive to the sex killer, from the deaf-mute to the foreign laborer. They are all strangers with whom one does not want to be burdened and who have to pay the price therefore of the German pressure to conformity. This price increases the longer the stranger stays and the more indispensable his services become for the members. His indispensability makes it impossible to dispense with the foreign laborer altogether. The separation is thus realized in symbolic ways; he is put in a ghetto, an "institution." Even more effectively than the fences around its huts—barbed-wire once, and plain-wire today—a world of prejudice divides the ghetto from its environment, above all the prejudice of the criminal propensity of the stranger. Those who belong fail to notice the evil circle of this attitude, its self-fulfilling prophecy, as they ignore the documented fact that, despite this circle, delinquency is generally no greater among strangers than among natives. In the stranger, many suspect the attack on their own security, as symbolized in the attack on "their own" immaculate girls. Nobody speaks of crimes committed by Germans on foreign workers, men and women; and the number of accidents in which foreign workers are injured for life and not seldom killed while their work helps to establish the prosperity of Germany, provides hardly a notice in the German press. There are after all "only" Italians, Spaniards, Turks involved.

Of course, every society has its own conformism, and thus its members and its strangers, whether these are called Negroes, Jamaicans, or Chinese. I think it could probably be shown that countries are distinguished by more than nuances in their treatment of these strangers; but the German disease, the virus of inhumanity, is so evident that subtle distinctions of this kind are hardly necessary. Let us proceed, then, to a further group, the strangers found at home, the abnormal. For men and women in eccentric dress, people turn around with grimaces in Germany; if there were German Beatles, their appearances would be more likely to be forbidden by an "Action Clean Stage" than rewarded by an order of merit. He who espouses unorthodox opinions is threatened in word and deed, not only from official places; even mild left-of-center intellectuals permanently risk being forbidden to speak publicly. People turn away from those who are sick through no fault of their own; the kindergarten remains closed to the thalidomide child, and the mentally ill are locked up by the uninformed decisions of young trainee lawyers.

All these reactions—grimaces, prohibitions, threats, the turning-away, and the enforced *apartheid*—are modes of an abandonment that in the end makes it possible to adumbrate even murder as beneficent for the victim: "euthanasia." The behavior of many Germans toward other people is characterized not by conformity alone, but by the extreme narrowness of the range of permitted actions. Most people would much prefer to shake off the different, the abnormal, and not be bothered by it. The human defeatism that characterizes the absence of any attempt to help those at a disadvantage through no fault of their own, easily turns into indifference. The question of what it is like in those "institutions" into which, in Germany, one might so easily be put, is never asked. Since the question is not asked, nobody knows the answer either. People get worked up about the "snake pit" of others without even knowing their own, and above all without realizing that it was the others themselves who opened theirs to the light of publicity. It is certainly true that most Germans "did not know anything" about National Socialist crimes of violence: nothing precise that is, because they did not ask any questions in the country in which "one" does not bother about things outside the narrow frame of normalcy.

What holds for the concentration camps of the Nazis, is basically true for today's prisons as well: Who knows after all what is going on in them? And who wants to know? And yet the alienation from social life that any conflict with valid laws brings about is so close to everybody "normal" that this alone would be a sufficient reason to deal with it rather more humanely.

Der Spiegel calculated on the basis of scanty data published by the German states in 1964 that, in the Federal Republic, about 50,000 orders of arrest are carried out every year. For those under arrest, however, the much-praised values of society are suspended. This is also true for those 15,000 per year, for whom warrants of arrest later—often much later—prove to be entirely or partially unjustified: one out of three prisoners on trial is either acquitted or sentenced to terms shorter than the time of remand before trial; with many of the others an astonishing pre-stabilized harmony between the duration of remand and the terms of sentence emerges. The average duration of arrest before trial is seventy-one days; but the average conceals the fact that many have spent one, indeed two years in prison by the time their trial is opened: "In at least 90 per cent of all cases of arrest, the police arrests first, and then it begins, now rather slowly, to gather evidence. Public prosecutors, whose interests are identical, allow themselves to be drawn along" (204, p. 38).

That this is a procedure that—inevitably perhaps with "the most objective authority in the world"—puts the accused at a disadvantage, is but one, namely, the legal, side of its scandal; here we are concerned with the question of humanity. Arrest awaiting trial is not pleasant. It involves the entire routine of regulations which must humiliate and affect in their human integrity those concerned. The 1250 years annually which people in Germany spend in prison by mistake —"the breakage rate of German criminal-legal care," as *Der Spiegel* expressed it with a metaphor which characterizes the inhumanity of the matter—are not merely lost for those concerned but leave lasting traces in them: "I was kept in solitary confinement for three weeks. . . . While I used to be harmless in every way, I am now full of cynical views and look at things with the eyes of one suppressed and full of inner wrath. . . . Often I am shaken by crises of crying which last for hours . . ." (204, p. 45). Whoever has been in prison him-self, and in solitary confinement at that, knows what this woman teacher is talking about.

Humanity, of course, does not end with those arrested by mistake; at least it should not end there. But in Germany it would be more true to say that it does not begin at the end of the trial either. In the Federal Republic today the accused, when he comes to trial, need no longer fear the style of Judge Freisler in the National Socialist People's Court who shouted at the accused ("You swine! You low liar!") and whose hoarse voice dominated the whole trial. However, was not Freisler perhaps in some respects but the excess of a rule that at any rate did not make him impossible? Does the judge as "inquisitor" always treat the accused with that special respect that a human being in his difficult position deserves? Are there no longer any judges in Germany who shout at the ac-cused ("Will you immediately take your hands out of your pockets and stop standing there like a question mark?") and impute things to them that, having no connection with the case, should not be mentioned in court at all? Can the accused in Germany, even if he is not an army doctor or a higher civil servant, be quite sure that in case of doubt the deci-sion will be in his favor?

When, after trial, the political prisoners of the German re-sistance against Hitler were able to exchange the cells of concentration camps, or of the Gestapo house in Berlin's Prinz Albrecht Street, for those of ordinary prisons, they knew that their chances of survival had multiplied. Tradi-tionally, German prison officials display the humorless cor-rectness of their Prussian tradition, and this often meant, be-fore a background of SS and Gestapo arbitrariness, that one's life was saved. Even this, however, does not turn German penal institutions into welfare institutions.

Welfare institutions? one may ask. Is that what they are supposed to be? There are many theories of punishment, but only one of them can justify the conditions that obtain in German prisons, that is, the primitive theory of "an eye for an eye, a tooth for a tooth." And even apart from the dubious rationality of this theory, there remains the more damning question of why so many have to give two eyes in German prisons for one that they took. It has little to do with isolation from society, to say nothing of resocialization and thus humanity, if young people after a first default, and contrary to the separation of juvenile prisons demanded by the law, are locked up for years with notorious criminals under conditions that can hardly be called humane—and this after the court in which they were tried had uttered the pious wish that they would soon find their way back into society. If they return to court a few years later (which under these conditions is more than likely), they are sure to be treated with a formula that Hans Göppinger rightly calls "almost grotesque": "The execution of the last sentence was evidently not sufficient to deter him from committing new crimes. A rigorous sentence was therefore indicated now in order to warn the accused urgently and meet the development of an inclination to theft" (85, p. 20).

Like other institutions, those of the penal system are secluded in obscurity. Visiting them is not one of the regular duties of the student of law, the trainee lawyer, or the judge; as yet no parliamentary commission has studied them in order to present an honest report; and the science of criminology is kept away from its proper subject matter by being defined as an appendix to criminal law.

Foreign workers, mentally ill, prison inmates—are they really the adequate witnesses for humanity in Germany? I think they are. Numbers apart, for where people's treatment of one another is concerned, counting is no answer, those at the margin document what is happening in a society. The deficiencies described are not the result of a failure of individuals. Abandoning others is a social rule in Germany and is thus internalized by the individual along with other prevailing values. He who is humane cannot expect to be liked: the accusing criminologist by his lawyer colleagues, the self-critical judge in his profession, the friend of the mentally ill with his friends, the proprietor who opens his restaurant to strangers with his clients. That the virus of inhumanity has caught so many follows from the weakening of their resistance by social structures. Its effect is therefore not limited to marginal groups. The infection spreads; disrespect for life and for the integrity of the individual is applied to those who belong as well. This begins at times and points where they cannot defend themselves and are therefore also pushed to the margin of an increasingly narrow normality: as children, as sick people, as old people. Here we encounter one of the bitterest, most evil sides of German reality; its core is the theory and practice of German medicine.

Abortion is punished by prison in Germany. The law, the courts, the churches, many organizations and individuals are agreed in their denunciation of this "crime committed on growing life." But is it not best to fight evil by doing good? There is a myth of the "naturalness" of childbirth which gives all the civilized precautions that accompany pregnancy and birth elsewhere an undertone of weakness, indeed cowardice in Germany. There one simply is not as queasy with human life; as a result, a developed system of prenatal care is still missing, and is indeed declared, even by university professors of medicine, a psychological luxury.

It is not a luxury—but what if it were? What could be held against it then? There is a shortage of hospital places for births; there are hospitals that announce at almost predictable intervals that they have closed their doors altogether to expectant mothers. If possible, childbirth itself, since it is a "natural" process and "no illness," must be experienced painfully in every phase by the mother, whether she wants this or not; anesthetics are scorned. And all this is not merely unfortunate reality, but accepted theory. When a large South German hospital had once again closed its gates because of overcrowding, the Medical Press Office of the region reacted not with a public expression of regret, but with an article under the title "Why Always in the Hospital?" (12) in which it says: ". . . nobody has as yet had the idea, which is not new but has merely slipped into oblivion, that childbirth can take place at home as well, indeed that one can get well in one's own home with the help of the family doctor and the loving care of one's family and friends."

What an idyllic picture, of which the Medical Press Office rightly remarks that "until a decade ago it was the normal and usual." The apostles of Hippocrates did not bother to look at the figures of maternal and infant mortality that belong to such practices; they were busy with things other than their oath: "No—childbirth is one of the healthiest expressions of life that there are in the life of a woman." And in this circle of sanctification by tradition, "naturalness," and "health," "community" must, of course, not be missing: "For care in childbed after childbirth at home, use has to be made of the love of close ones—and this should and must come from those who are close, for this is most natural. Great praise has to be sung of our grandmothers here. . . ." And so on, with medical advice to the expectant mother who is supposed to have her child "secure with her own." Perhaps she will die in the process, or her child will; perhaps they "merely" suffer a little more than under the slightly better conditions of a hospital—but all this concerns civilization and not culture, for the latter has its place at the springs: "But does it not really belong to the most archaic being of a mother to prepare her 'nest'?"

We are not pursuing intellectual history here. Even where we are dealing with ideologies, their consequences are directly murderous. Comparative statistics of infant mortality document the seriousness of the question which no irony can obscure. In 1961, 319 out of every 10,000 children born in the Federal Republic died during the first year of their lives, as against 155 in Sweden and the Netherlands, 195 in Australia, 208 in Switzerland, 221 in Great Britain, 252 in the United States, 258 in France. A "breakage rate of German medical care"? That the corresponding figures are 401 for Italy and 888 for Portugal further darkens the picture of Germany rather than blanching its sinister colors (208, p. 32 †).

A variety of causes is responsible for these high rates of infant mortality; some believe today that the comparability of figures for various countries is doubtful; moreover, infant mortality has declined rapidly ever since 1950 (when 552 out of every 10,000 babies had to die in their first year of life). But a few unanswered questions remain. Could not better medical care before childbirth prevent many a deadly improvisation at birth? Is not the relatively large number of births at home, which doctors so warmly recommend, one of the reasons for higher infant mortality? Is really everything necessary (to say nothing of everything possible) being done for babies of all "classes" in the hospitals of the "leveled-in middle-class society"?

Here again, the biggest question would seem to be why the figures published every year by the Federal Statistical Office worry the public, including the mass media, so much less than, say, the statistics of passenger cars and television sets. Once again, we see what we have called the virus of inhumanity at work. Neglect of the weak at home, of mothers and babies, is not the work of malevolent individuals either. It is unfortunately not that: malevolent individuals might be educated or, if there is no other way, locked up. But here inhumanity is systematic, it is thoughtlessness become structure; and in this manner even what is regarded as human is shifted somewhat to stand out from the background of inhumanity: the doctor tries to console the desperate mother for the loss of her child, but he, too, acts in a system in which much remains undone that might have been done to prevent the loss. It is painful to pass through the darkest corners of German society; but we have to continue it, for knowledge alone makes insight and change possible.

The expectant mother is weak, and so is the baby; but children, too, count among the weak who fall victim to the virus. It has been said that the Germans treat their cupboards like children and their children like cupboards; presumably this refers to the ways in which both are kept in order. In the place of cupboards one might well put cars today, which are cleaned and cared for, on which every scratch upsets the owner, whereas children are treated more like tolerated things.

Heddy Neumeister has put the role of the child in Germany in such drastic and penetrating words that the quotations need no comment. She begins with an apparently harmless observation, the child in the baker's shop who gets many a kindly look from the women around him, but is nevertheless pushed back time and again, although his turn has come. He is merely a child after all. . . . But the scene is by no means harmless. Heddy Neumeister shows that little less than life and death is involved here:

> The little scene that occurred in the baker's shop may be observed every day in hundreds of shops. One can see it, in slightly different form, in the streetcar where children are nearly pushed to death at entrances and exits—in so far as they have not, having grown a little older, copied the behavior of adults and begun to use elbows and feet themselves. One can watch it in the frightening indifference with which the public takes notice of the murders of children—and old people—who are run over. Supposing the child or the old person had behaved contrary to traffic rules in every single one of these cases: since when does the infraction of traffic rules justify death?

Then Mrs. Neumeister adds the sentence:

> Yet these are the more harmless brutalities that one sees often enough in Germany and that cause the older contemporary to

have unpleasant thoughts about the question of how far the National Socialist attitude with its contempt of the weak has really been overcome in our people. (cf. 164.)

It soon transpires that the examples cited so far are really the more harmless ones. Maltreatment of children, deliberate brutality of parents toward children, become ever more frequent in the country of the most intact of families. Sometimes they are indeed approved publicly; as when a father, who beat up his twelve-year-old son in ire about his unruliness, threw him out of the window, and thus broke both his legs, gets away in court with a token penalty of two hundred marks. "A dishonest family policy, which uses the sanctity of marriage and the child in order to make it the basis of massive financial demands on the state, contrasts strangely with what actually happens to children, to far too many children, in Germany." Furthermore, it not only happens to children in the baker's shop and the streetcar, but in school as well; and here, too, the contrast between the reality of the classroom and the flowery speeches at the school graduation celebrations could not be worse.

That schools, too, are "no welfare institutions" has been said in many teachers' conferences. But why are they not that? Are they not entrusted with the welfare of children as much as with their ability to learn Latin words by heart? We have seen how the German school defines its task, and that it confirms in this way—how could it be otherwise?—the ruling values of society. It became clear, then, that one cannot but call the attitude of the school to those who leave it early, inhuman. The worker's child Günther K. is "not suited." He is moreover "noticeably neurotic." But psychological wisdom remains as ineffective with the teachers as all other knowledge about the soul of the children: "Although the son of a simple laborer, he boasts in class about his pocket money."

Possibly we are no longer directly concerned with human life here; but the integrity of the human person is at stake here too, as the next sentence shows in which the poor chap, instead of being pitied for the silly actions forced upon him by the middle-class school, is implicitly suspected of having stolen his money (see above, p. 307).

We are faced here with three different levels of the reality of the school, which seem disconnected and yet belong together. The first is that of flowery speeches, in this case about the educational calling of the Gymnasium and the like. The second is that of thoughtless teaching and crude achievement marking, which takes the pupil as a thing, equipped with certain talents, unchangeable, without right or claim to understanding. The third level is the unknown human reality, what goes on inside the pupils who are weak and therefore require special care. Who knows this reality?

"I was glad on the one hand and thought, now you have left the misery behind. (Why?) Well, at the time the school was, generally speaking, not much fun for me. (And why?) That is hard to tell really, why. I suppose, if I had had perhaps better marks, it would be possible that it would then have been more fun for me. We were just from the country, inhibited toward the others. They were better dressed than the sons of workers and peasants. One example: If one had to go up to the blackboard . . . some do not care, others were inhibited. If I had been the son of a doctor, I might perhaps not have felt inhibited. I do not know, but I just felt set back a little" (cf. 227).

Thus he left school early, a living witness of the "breakage rate of German educational care." And increasingly it becomes clear that German society is abundantly full of such "breakage rates," and this especially at points where it should "care" for people and allow them to get their human rights.

This is the temperature so to speak, which indicates the fever that accompanies the infection. But we are now in a position to describe the symptoms of the disease a little more fully. Wherever people are weak in Germany, in need of care and help, there is a tendency to abandon them which is murderous in its effect. Weakness is dealt with as if it were an inescapable and disagreeable fate from which one turns away in concealed anxiety, which is in any case not taken as a challenge to one's activity. It is tempting to use here the metaphors of psychoanalysis; the more so since the inactivity of abandonment that produces the breakage rates of German society is often beclouded with great words; but I am deliberately avoiding these metaphors. For once again we are not concerned with upset or sick individuals, but with social demands with a dangerous potential. The inhumanity of letting the weak and those in need of care suffer, coupled with empty humanistic talk, is the recognizable beginning of a chain that does not exclude the mass murder of defenseless people.

Whoever thinks that these conclusions attempt to construct

rather too long a bridge, which is bound to break, should follow us back from the suffering of children in streetcars and schools to the place where life and death are immediately at stake. It is not one of the bright sides of human existence that we are able to sense pain. Pain reveals men in their suffering need; it reduces our persons and makes us a shadow of ourselves. Perhaps pain is inevitable. Yet one would think that one of the great tasks of medicine is to alleviate pain. In many countries, doctors indeed regard this as their duty, but only with reservations in Germany, where unhewn, deadly "nature" is often held in higher regard than a "culture" formed, created, and controlled by men. Here the statement still holds that pain is a necessary indicator of disease, and thus a healthy reaction of the body. Dentists spread the lore that an anesthetic is impossible because they have to realize by the pain of their patients when they have hit the nerve—a German tale. We have mentioned pain at childbirth before. It is regarded as heroic in Germany to stand pain, that is, to suffer the avoidable, as if there were not enough to be suffered in this world after its alleviation. Thus brutality and stupidity are glorified even in medical theory. The limits of the inevitable are drawn too narrowly, the attempt to extend them is given up too soon.

The imperialism of rationality, of the control of the world, and of respect for human beings is unfortunately not nearly as strongly developed in Germany as the imperialism of the nation; if it were, things would be better. The attitude of doctors is symptomatic here—although once again not of individual guilt, but of social norms; the doctor's attitude is faithfully reflected in the protestless expectations of patients.

This is true in a final, awful respect as well. Many Germans feel inclined to laugh about "death in Hollywood." This is understandable. But it would be tolerable only if the same people felt inclined to protest against death in Germany. In many old hospitals the dying are wheeled, from the often overcrowded wards of the lower classes, to the lavatories to die. That this is not merely a terrible emergency, but in a sense systematic, emerges when the traditional procedure is maintained even in sparkling modern steel and glass buildings. The dying no longer count; they do not notice anything. . . .

While it is hard for the outsider to bear the professional cynicism of doctors, he can sympathize with it. It may be a beautiful calling to help human beings, but it is surely overwhelming to see human suffering every day, every hour, and to be unable all too often to help. But it is hard to take that the understandable cynicism can kill every sense of human dignity to such an extent that the dying are refused that minimum of respect for which, admittedly, the living have to fight in Germany and that is found easily only by those who are privileged.

Germans need not fear becoming like foreign workers, at least not in their own country. Possibly most need not worry that they themselves might have to share the fate of the abnormal one day. Nature has restricted the number of those who bear children, and generally adults suppress what happened to them as babies and children. Most men rarely think of death and know nothing about how it happens. Pain is an occasional evil, which in any case does not dominate life. In this manner of reduction, a "normal role" gradually emerges: the non-foreign worker, the non-abnormal, the grown man who is neither too young nor too old, who has no disease and loves the natural, in other words, the unworriedly strong young man between twenty-five and forty, or perhaps twenty and thirty-five years of age.

The narrowness of social perspective this institutionalized image of man betrays, the reduction of human diversity to the soldierly, accounts for the brutal quality in the pressure to conformity in German society. The "normal role" excludes four fifths of the population at the outset from the blessings of an existence in conformity with expectations. It creates millions of weak people, as if this supplementation of a vexatious nature by the barbarism of deliberate unculture was needed.

But there is no immunity against the virus of inhumanity. Designed for the weak, it has repercussions for the strong, the normal. Their lives, too, everywhere bear the traces of that murderous lack of fiber in the face of life and the person that may well be connected with the possibility of organized mass murder. Once again we have to collect examples, only now they are such that nobody is immune any longer on the grounds of age or sex, youthful strength or lucky health. The question now is how inhumanity penetrates into the houses of all and pollutes the air that Germans breathe every day.

When one talks about dangers to human life, including the life of the soldierly "normal," the example of road traffic immediately comes to mind. Much has been written about the mass murder on German roads without public opinion having been shaken to awareness in any way. Erich Kuby is but the last in a long line of authors who noticed this:

> These busy machines and their drivers produce at present 16,400 so-called traffic deaths every year, and these are plainly deaths. Dead people. The uneasiness about this figure is comparatively small in our public, not to say zero.
>
> 16,400 people—that is a sizable small town with a mayor, churches, a county office, a prison, and a sports' stadium.
>
> What would the reaction be if a town like that were destroyed overnight by an earthquake, for example, and nobody stayed alive? What was the reaction to a German who wanted to leave his state across the Berlin Wall and was shot dead in the process? There seem to be gradations of quality among the dead in public opinion, and the least valuable seem to be the victims of a traffic which increasingly takes on the character of a collective murder performance.

And further:

> In Germany, 10,000 cars and thus 10,000 drivers kill 14 people every year. In America the same number merely accomplishes the death of 5.2 people. This key figure of 5.2 does not let the American public and the American government rest. A 40-billion-dollar program for the construction of long distance roads was inaugurated, and it is already being realized. In lapidary words, the Bureau of Public Roads describes the success of this program as follows: "At this time we prevent about 2,000 deaths a year; in 1972 there will be 9,000 deaths a year less." Thus the United States seems to be a country in which traffic deaths are not merely a statistical figure, but dead people. (cf. 123.)

And Germany is not such a country. It is probable that here, too, the causes are more varied than all-too-simple theories might suggest. From the psychology of drivers to the state of the roads there is a long chain of reasons. But once again, the worst aspect of murder is to be found in the readiness to give up before trying, the fact that the death of people is accepted as unavoidable instead of the cause of restless worry about possibilities of avoiding or at least postponing it. When a leading German daily paper took up the subject of traffic in Germany under the title "11,000 Traffic Deaths too Many Every Year," the press officer of the Federal Ministry of Transport wrote a long letter to the editor in which he did not explain what the ministry intended to do to stop the mass murder on the roads, but tried to obscure the obvious reality with statistical tricks: "The author has evidently drawn a number of false conclusions from the statistical data at his disposal . . ." (cf. 159). How press officers resemble one another!

Even in the world of the normal, the virus of inhumanity is not always as visible as on the roads. Rather, its effects are most vicious in little things, where the infected can barely perceive it. There are great human rights like the integrity of the person, or freedom of speech and writing, which can be guaranteed by the constitution and guarded by a constitutional court. There are rights derived from these such as adequate, not to say humane treatment by the police, which are already much harder to secure, even though they, too, are guaranteed by law in Germany today. But then there are the little, though by no means less important rights, which can be threatened every day, but whose formal guarantee meets with difficulties. Perhaps this very fact makes them all the more symptomatic of the state of civilization in a country. If they are threatened, this betrays a deficiency in the social substratum of formal law, and thus a condition that is much harder to repair.

I am thinking of the city technicians who enter one's own garden without asking; the building masters who are allowed to work their noisy machines (muted in other countries) from six o'clock in the morning; the bank clerks who shout the accounts of their clients to each other in the crowded hall; the switching-off of electricity or water or telephone for building work of some kind without previous warning; the thoughtlessness of sending people from one room to another in public offices; the institutional atmosphere of mass X-ray examinations where people have to queue half-naked until they are called. All this and much more need not be as it is, for it is not like that elsewhere. Perhaps it should not be as it is either; for in every single case a contravention of rights could be demonstrated. But it nevertheless happens in Germany, and it happens not merely in the exceptional case but is regarded as bearable. Whoever complains about such infractions must expect to be ridiculed. It is obviously part of living in Germany that one either becomes a grumbling nuisance (which is bothersome not only for those around) or grows accustomed to accepting, like everyone else, the permanent infractions of the integrity of one's own sphere, which means putting up with the fact that in many sensitive little areas one is not allowed to be a sovereign citizen and respected person.

Since even rights are threatened in Germany, one hardly dares speak of amenities. And yet they, too, are no mere extras, but, as a testimony to civilized existence, at the same time a symptom for the way in which human beings are treated in a country. It is an amenity, and in this sense pleasant, if rubbish is collected every day and even unwieldy rubbish more than three times a year. It is an amenity if mail is delivered and forwarded reliably and larger postal orders do not land with a neighbor. It is an amenity if the telephone operator does not try to inform one that Birmingham is in Alabama and not in England, or the shop assistant, that red vermouth or black olives "do not exist." It is an amenity, and useful in addition, if children do not have to pass through the bustle of city streets or adapt to country timetables designed for others in order to get to school, but have school buses for the purpose. It makes life easier if one is treated politely even when one is in error, or has stepped on someone else's feet by mistake. Alas, there are many examples that underline the melancholy question of why it should be impossible to enjoy these amenities of life in Germany, since they are, after all, not fiction, a play of utopian phantasy, but accomplished facts elsewhere.

What is more, with prosperity, even the much-praised German sense of orderliness has proved a merely external discipline, which breaks down as soon as it is no longer upheld by force or need. In this way the lack of civilization becomes coupled with disorder, uncleanliness, unpunctuality, unreliability—and the suspicion arises again that the social contract has by-passed this country in a strange way. What remains is the ideology of the *aurea aetas,* but the reality of the *bellum omnium contra omnes.*

This is where the inclination that—with an admittedly problematic metaphor—I have called the virus of inhumanity links up with the absence of public virtues. Both document the same retarded development of civilization. The unreflected readiness to accept as "nature" or "fate" even what is capable of being changed by man, indeed to taboo many changes of "nature" as well as the struggle against "fate," leads to the abandonment of the weak as it does to the humble acceptance of suffering and the renunciation of the rights and amenities of a civilized existence. If this retarded development were a purely passive phenomenon, one might shrug one's shoulders and turn away. But it is virulent. Omission is a crime by itself, and this frequently in a very literal sense; but above all the tolerated crime may rely on omission, that is, on the absence of protest.

Nothing is more nauseating than the combination of this retarded development of civilization, evident at a hundred places, and a hypocritical cultural allure, which proves thin even on superficial inspection. The country is very proud of its educated men—but even to them, features that are elsewhere regarded as part of education are alien. People in Germany, and particularly so-called educated people, read little. The book, at least potentially an important access to civilized consciousness and to the association of men with men, remains strangely external and distant to a cruder, less polished consciousness. This may be surprising at first sight: only 20 per cent of all Germans have no book in their home, and these are by the wisdom of opinion research almost entirely "primary-school attenders" (104, p. 149). But 62 per cent of all people, and even 24 per cent of all secondary-school attenders "never, almost never" enter a book shop, and a further 31 per cent only "every now and again," which probably also means "almost never" for many whose response is dictated by status concerns rather than honesty. More than one half of all Germans have never bought a book, and this still holds for 11 per cent of all secondary-school attenders. More than two thirds of all people, and of all secondary-school attenders never borrow a book from a lending library (104, pp. 150 ff.); public libraries frequently reflect this.

The picture is even more striking with students. I do not think that the average student in Germany reads more than five books a year, whether in his subject or not, and I know for certain that many a young academic has not read more during his whole university career. At the same time I am sure that one has to multiply these figures for American students by ten, if not by one hundred. As a result, the contact with national and world literature is missing in Germany; the educated are full of beautiful words, but without binding knowledge. They are, as they like to say, "educated at heart." That they "prefer to read one book thoroughly to ten diagonally" (as a widespread recommendation of German teachers and university professors would have it), that they make fun of American rapid reading techniques and thus lose all sense of the development of book production, excludes the educated German from a civilized world, among whose human traits is an intimacy with books that forbids burning them as much as burning living people.

Enough of examples. A last observation may conclude this catalogue of German vexations that converge in an evil syndrome. In Germany, if anywhere, protest is the citizen's first obligation. In Germany, if anywhere, however, a great quiet rules among the citizens. It is "not done" to get worked up, and definitely not about the inhumanities in one's own world. They are hardly even noticed; people close their eyes and do not see them.

The first aspect of the great quiet is the difficulty of getting precise information about the matters of which I have spoken in this chapter, often on the basis of impressions or individual examples. For Britain, for the United States, even for France, which is in other respects so similar to Germany, at least one book might be mentioned for every one of the observations cited that has stirred the public to change conditions. That these books do not exist, that there are no parliaments that force governments to replace their hypocritical generalities by precise information where crimes of police and courts, hospitals and schools are concerned, that even statistics are officially used in Germany to obscure rather than light up issues, does in itself not speak very well for German humanity.

The second aspect of the great quiet, however, is the capacity of the German public not to react even to published social ills. While one can win elections in Germany with a few reunification phrases, one cannot do so with serious attempts to overcome the human malaise of medical or legal care, education or road traffic. Humanity does not sell.

One need only say this to recognize that it is imprecise. For this is the third aspect of the great quiet in the face of inhumanity in Germany, that it appears coupled with an unbounded waffle about humanism and humanity as no other country knows it. In the end, it is probably this blend of humanistic theory and practical inhumanity that makes Germany so unbearable at times: the holy family and the deadly childbirth at home, the sacred rule of law and the reality of arrest before trial, the idea of education and the illiteracy of the mentally handicapped, the SS man who recovers from a hard day outside the gas chamber by playing the violin.

I know that these are harsh statements. At this point, however, I want to accuse, not explain. Possibly some of the arguments mentioned against Germany are applicable in other countries too. Perhaps there is a country in which they all hold; in that case, this country is as hard to bear as Germany. There are recurrent motives in these arguments: the pressure to conformity, the defeatism of practical humanity, the suggestion to put up with things rather than to protest and to act, disrespect for the weak and defenseless, scorn for a civilization that makes life more humane in favor of a culture of trees where mothers build their nests. I believe that this is a syndrome of murder; this is why I accuse. But who is accused here? I remember having reflected even as a boy of barely sixteen in a concentration camp about the chain of apparent accidents that had brought me to the inner and not the outer side of the camp fence. Thus I do not mean the others, but myself with them, since I belong to this country without feeling at rest about its worst sides. This means that there is hope for a change. I have this hope, although I confess that in respect to the nauseating combination of the humanism of words and the inhumanity of deeds it is pure hope, that is, hope without a definite basis for or even knowledge of the starting points of change. Here we are no longer concerned with social institutions, but with what we make of them; every one of us.

23. THE GERMAN CHARACTER

Now that we are about to close the inner and more narrowly sociological circle of this study, it might appear that the final piece of argument is to be an old, though hardly a good acquaintance: the national character of the Germans. Having tried at the outset to pulverize the phantom of national character, it has now—or so one might think—condensed and returned. Equality may be described as an orientation, conflict as an attitude, diversity as a competition of behaviors, and public values as virtues. Do these pieces not make up their own social character of the Germans? Is the final product, quite apart from its human traits, methodically so much more attractive and safely founded than that of Willy Hellpach or Wilhelm Röpke? It is a worthwhile task to pursue these questions a little, describe the German character in the process, and crystallize it at the same time into more tangible structures of society. In doing so we will incidentally be able to summarize our analysis of German society in terms of the four social bases of political democracy.

One of the obvious deficiencies of all quasi-literary accounts of the German character—of which Hellpach and Röpke provide two outstanding examples, which are not easily discounted—is that they make a principle of the bias of perspective to which even exceptional individuals are subject in their observations. Opinion research is no more true than the well-considered judgment of an intelligent person; what is more, it is bound to miss some of the things that Thomas Mann could state out of passionate insight in his Washington speech on *Germany and the Germans* in 1945; but it does provide a welcome corrective to flights of intuition. This is why there is a point in turning briefly to some of the findings of opinion research about the Germans' image of themselves.

Put in terms of virtues, the German self-image may be expressed in a brief formula. Germans regard themselves above all as "industrious, hard-working, able, and ambitious" (cf. 104). In this respect, there has been little change in the decade from 1952 to 1962, although the self-image was probably rather more appropriate in 1952 than in 1962. While in both years more than 70 per cent of a representative sample described the German character by these properties, all other traits, including the German syndrome "orderly, precise, reliable, thorough, thrifty" were left far behind. To be sure, some changes in the decade from 1952 to 1962 are brought out even by opinion research; they mostly involve a decrease in the believed significance of virtues: "good, kind, well-meaning" from 12 to 3 per cent; "loyalty, cohesion" from 11 to 4 per cent; "soldierly virtues: courageous, able as a soldier" from 7 to 3 per cent, "cleanliness" from 4 to 0 per cent. The self-image evidently does not entirely lack a sense of reality. It confirms the image of Germans that among the "good properties" of people, "conscientious, dutiful," an "industrious" appear at the top, as it possibly confirms the sense of reality that "strict against myself, self-controlled" and "imaginative, full of esprit" are found at the end of a long catalogue.

The self-image gains in interest if we hear that as many as 16 per cent of a representative sample of West German citizens think that the Germans are unpopular in the world because of their "industriousness" and "ability." Not surprisingly, therefore, more than 40 per cent regard the Germans as "more able and gifted" than other peoples (104, p. 259). This is a remarkable blend of confidence and self-consciousness, in which the element of confidence is moreover decreasing rapidly; the proportion of those who do not regard the Germans as more able and gifted has risen since 1955 from 39 to 55 per cent. Comparative studies show, however, a similar trend to place less emphasis on national peculiarities in many countries since the war.

Such comparative statements are suggested by cross-cultural surveys as they were first undertaken by Buchanan and Cantril in 1948. So-called auto- and heterosterotypes of nations come out clearly, if not always convincingly, from these studies. But something else also emerges, and this is more relevant for our discussion than any list of properties ascribed by people to themselves and others: national stereotypes change, and while they are but the subjective aspect of what might be called national character, there is no reason to think that this does not change too, if more slowly.

It is amusing and possibly informative to consider the images peoples have of themselves and of others as they are suggested by surveys, but this is clearly not the last word on our subject. The changeability of stereotypes is not the only argument here. People may also be wrong about themselves and about others. There was little congruence, for example, in the findings of Buchanan and Cantril between the Europeans' image of Americans and the Americans' image of themselves. Europeans regard Americans above all as "progressive" and as "practical," but not as particularly "peace-loving." Americans on the other hand look upon themselves as being "peace-loving" and "altruistic." Who is right here? Might it not be that neither is right? Is it not conceivable that people indeed believe of themselves the exact opposite of what they are? Elementary assumptions of psychology suggest this possibility, although the suggestion involves its own problems. Psychoanalysis has an unfortunate way at times of explaining identical modes of behavior with equal certainty by opposite causes and, vice versa, opposing modes of behavior by identical causes, so that its statements are sometimes hardly more testable than those of intellectual history. However, while such doubts should not be forgotten, they must not prevent us from pursuing the attempt of several authors who were guided by psychoanalytic theorems to discover behind the behavior of people and their self-images a social character or a basic personality. What then is hidden behind what Germans say about themselves and others, if we look in particular for the political potential of this secret force?

Industrious, hard-working, able, ambitious, conscientious, dutiful, courageous—this is a list of virtues that, if one turns it around, presents a very different picture. In a sense, every virtue is also its own vice. The vice, however, that many suspect in the German self-image is the "authoritarian personality." In this study, we have frequently spoken of authoritarian structures, or authoritarian patterns of social behavior; a terminological clarification is therefore in place before we consider the "authoritarian personality" as understood by T. W. Adorno and his colleagues. We have called a behavior authoritarian that supports the specific political constitution of authoritarianism, that is, the benevolent-strict regime of an exclusive elite often united by tradition, and without the participation of the many. By contrast, Adorno's concept of an authoritarian attitude is less specific politically, and more specific psychologically.

Let us take the social-psychological side first. Theodor W. Adorno, Else Fraenkel-Brunswik, D. J. Levinson, and R. N.

Sanford have tried to elaborate, on the basis of empirical research conducted immediately after the Second World War, the picture of a political-psychological type, and of its countertype. Their techniques were projective surveys relating to the four topics of (in the terms of the study) anti-Semitism, ethnocentrism, political-economic conservatism, and fascism. In interpreting their findings, Adorno and his colleagues worked on the assumption that people who reach high scores on all four scales—the so-called "high scorers"—generally show a syndrome of an inclination for fascism loaded with prejudice, which the authors call "authoritarian" in a sense coined earlier by Erich Fromm. The high scorers are authoritarian personalities and thus the stuff from which fascist countries are made.

The detailed description of those revealed as authoritarian by their high scores, that is, their inclination for anti-Semitism, ethnocentrism, political-economic conservatism and fascism, betrays the psychoanalytic bent the authors of *The Authoritarian Personality* share with Fromm. The character of the high scorers is sado-masochistic; according to Fromm, he who has it "admires authority and tends to submit to it, but at the same time he wants to be an authority himself, and have others submit to him" (76, p. 141). Other traits of the authoritarian are his propensity for painting everything in black and white, the brutal division into friend and foe, a pronounced rigidity of thinking, and at the same time a tendency for projections as they are common in anti-Semitism.

The authoritarian personality cannot bear ambiguity but clings to solid values, as Else Fraenkel-Brunswik expresses it; time and again he tries to escape from freedom, as Erich Fromm puts it. Rigidity of behavior makes the authoritarian dogmatic and unable to adapt or change. Although he is active, all his activity is embedded in an ultimate feeling of impotence, and thus in the invocation of abstract agencies like "fate" or "providence," which are supposed to confirm the inevitability of the real. That this is more than theoretical social psychology need hardly be emphasized. "By the term 'authoritarian character' we imply that it represents the personality structure that is the human basis of fascism" (76, p. 141). Thus it is Germany and the character of the Germans that are at issue. But let us suspend this application for another moment.

The construction of an authoritarian character and especially its incarnation in the "authoritarian personality" have met with much criticism. Even apart from more technical objections, it is relevant in our context to ask whether it makes any sense at all to develop such typologies, considering that they always involve an undemonstrable statement ("The German has an authoritarian personality"). There is another question, and that is, whether anti-Semitism, ethnocentrism, conservatism, and fascism really vary together, or whether there cannot be—as Hofstätter claims to be able to prove—conservatives who are not anti-Semites, and anti-Semites who are not conservatives. In addition to such objections, we have to see that a typology of constructed characters really tells us very little about the world. It may be striking, but it remains strangely devoid of substance. One can give it literary dignity, but this does not raise its empirical significance either. The question remains, so what? And this question can be answered only if the "pseudo-individual" of the type (to quote Klaus Eyferth) is dissolved into the statement of the "functional relations" between personality traits and modes of behavior, experiences and decisions (cf. 14).

It would be unfair to Adorno to imply that he has not done this. By simultaneously reducing the authoritarian personality to psychoanalytic and sociological categories, Adorno and his collaborators have done in their way what two other great psychoanalysts, Erich Fromm and Erik Erikson, have tried without an elaborate typology, that is, to produce a psychology of German politics. In the literary imagination of authors like Hellpach and Röpke the German character remains both socially unfounded and historically unchanging. The empirical foundation by survey-born self-images does not alter the primitive and at bottom unhistorical characterology, to say nothing of the lack of subtlety and coherence in such descriptions. With the socio-psychoanalysts—as I shall call them—we find an attempt to avoid both mistakes—lack of empirical data as well as lack of historicity. The attempt is exciting even in its weakness; and in trying to correct its deficiencies we come close to not only an acceptable notion of the notion character, but also a summary of the four central parts of this study. That the resulting notion is sociological rather than social-psychological is the point of our critique of the approaches of Adorno, Erikson, Fromm, and others.

At the beginning of all socio-psychoanalytic studies of the German character there are two statements:

There is an authoritarian character of the individual.

There is an authoritarian structure of the political community.

From what has already been said it is clear that the word "character" must not be understood in the static sense of classical characterology, but as a unit of dispositions of behavior, which is dynamic in itself. It is unnecessary to describe the syndrome of dispositions again. However, a word is needed about the other side of the theory in question, in which the word "authoritarian" appears again, and not without design. Unfortunately the socio-psychoanalysts are much less precise in their social and political terminology than in their psychology. As they speak somewhat loosely of "fascism" where they hardly mean Mussolini and certainly not Franco, their concept of authoritarianism is ambiguous too. They tend to borrow the concept from early analyses of National Socialism, notably from that by Franz Neumann, without realizing that the political systems of Nazi Germany and of Imperial Germany have hardly a single positive trait in common. There is no awareness here of the distinction between authoritarian and totalitarian patterns, and indeed the distinction would embarrass our authors. While an authoritarian system may be described as the transposition of the patriarchal family into the political realm, the totalitarian constitution is a specifically modern pattern resting on the equal, if planned and organized participation of all (even though some are more equal than others). If one wants to combine them both for certain purposes of analysis, as we, too, have done at times, only negative statements can be made, such as: There are illiberal structures of the political community.

Another objection to the socio-psychoanalysts weighs even more heavily. In their studies, they do not always, and never sufficiently, pay attention to discovering the road that leads from the first (psychological) to the second (political) statement. What are the links between certain individual dispositions and at least negatively defined political orders? Between the two statements there is a big X, an unknown area. To make this known, that is, to build the bridge from the authoritarian personality to the political constitution of illiberalism is our intention here. In realizing it, we find in our own analysis rather more solid elements for the political side of the bridge than the sociological improvisation of the socio-psychoanalysts can provide. This is true even of the initial stages of the bridge:

There is an authoritarian character of the individual.

Certain childhood experiences provide the basis of the authoritarian character.

X.

Certain social factors form the basis of illiberal political structures.

There are illiberal structures of the political community.

Naturally, the particular interest of the socio-psychoanalysts is devoted to the genesis of authoritarian behavior in the individual. Erikson and Fromm both use Hitler's *Mein Kampf* as a basis of their often free associations about the childhood and youth of the authoritarian. Erikson emphasizes most of all the experiences of youth, that is, what he calls the "strange combination of idealized revolt and obedient submission" in the "German character" (65, p. 316). In his puberty, the "critical German puberty," the young German gets into a phase of wildly roving revolt, of "aimless initiative in the direction of complete obstinacy" (65, p. 315); but it is already too late to give both a liberal direction. Revolt is accompanied by a profound sense of guilt in which the deeply rooted authority of the father makes itself felt. Thus revolt turns into submission; the boy becomes "bourgeois" in the worst German sense of the word. "For if in early youth a patriarchal superego has once been reliably established, one can let the reins loose for youth without worrying: it cannot get away" (65, p. 316).

Here the traumatic puberty refers back to early childhood, that is, as Fromm indicates, to the unsolved Oedipus situation: "However, when the parents, acting as the agents of society, start to suppress the child's spontaneity and independence, the growing child feels more and more unable to stand on its own feet; it therefore seeks the magic helper and often makes the parents the personification of 'him' " (76, p. 153). Later, then, the vacuum of authority can be filled with variable figures.

Once again the socio-psychoanalysts are much less precise

in their etiology of authoritarian political structures. Perhaps they betray themselves a little here by an oddly antiquated approach, which is not entirely absent from their psychoanalysis of society either. Thus Erich Fromm borrows from Franz Neumann and other Marxians the theory of the alliance of big business and National Socialism almost without reservation. In the following chapter, we shall see how imprecise, if not naïve, this theory is. But polemics apart, there are other elements with which to construct the bridge from the social side, and we know them already. The factors in which the constitution of liberty, and thus implicitly the constitutions of illiberalism too, are anchored, have been the subject of this study. Where the effective equality of autonomous citizens is lacking; where conflicts are not regulated rationally, but allegedly "solved" and in fact suppressed; where elites either cannot or do not want to compete with one another in cohesive diversity; where people are oriented to private rather than public virtues—the constitution of liberty cannot thrive. Thus this constitution has its own social structure.

These, too, are evidently only the beginnings of our bridge. Some further links between authoritarian character and illiberal political structures are still missing.

There is an authoritarian character of the individual.

Certain childhood experiences provide the basis of the authoritarian character.

Certain family structures make these childhood experiences probable.

X.

Certain social groups have an interest in the persistence of these factors.

Certain social factors form the basis of illiberal political structures.

There are illiberal structures of the political community.

We are speaking of a bridge, and so the first statements have to be read from top to bottom, but those following the X from bottom to top. We are trying to bring the two most distant statements toward each other.

The road from childhood to society leads through the family. And here at last we can no longer avoid the picture of the German family that we have so far pushed aside as slightly absurd. The basic conception, as formulated by Fromm, makes obvious sense; the parents "transmit to the child what we may call the psychological atmosphere or the spirit of a society just by being as they are—namely representatives of this very spirit. The family thus may be considered to be the psychological agent of society" (76, p. 245). This has since become a sociological commonplace and was our assumption, too, with respect to the mediation of private virtues. But here we are not concerned with the theoretical question of socializing agencies, but with the much more concrete one of the character of these agencies.

One might quote many of the authors of *Studien über Autorität und Familie* [Studies on Authority and the Family (102)] for the picture Erikson presents with few reservations:

> I want to try to give an impressionistic version of what I regard as one of the basic inner pictures of the German father of the time [Erikson is speaking of Hitler's youth here—R.D.]. When the father comes home, even the walls seem to "pull themselves together." The mother, although she is frequently the unofficial master of the house, behaves so differently now that even a small child must feel it. She hurries to fulfill the whims and fancies of the father and avoids everything that might annoy him. The children hold their breath, for the father tolerates no "nonsense"—that is, nothing of the female moods of the mother, of the playful ways of the children. As long as he is home, the mother has to be at his disposal; his behavior expresses his disapproval of the unity of mother and children which they have enjoyed in his absence. Often he speaks to the mother as he speaks to the children, that is, he expects obedience and cuts off any answer. The little boy gets the feeling that all the joyful ties to the mother are a thorn in the father's side, and that her love and admiration—models of so many later goals and gratifications—may be acquired only without the knowledge of the father or against his explicit wishes. . . . (65, p. 311.)

One cannot help feeling that these impressions convey experiences restricted to certain times and places, and possibly even certain social categories; and here again the suspicion is confirmed on the other side of the bridge where the socio-psychoanalysts pass over problems even more easily. For if Fromm refers to groups that have an interest in the persistence of the social bases of illiberal constitutions, he takes refuge in strange constructions. First of all he acquits from any charge of a propensity for actively illiberal attitudes "the working class" and the "liberal and Catholic bourgeoisie," in an interesting, if not easily identified combination (76, p. 182). Then he constructs for the "lower middle class" a kind of social sado-masochism that at the same time turns this stratum against big business (Fromm says, "monopoly capital"), and ties it to it. In Hitler's person and the ideology of the Nazis this conflict finds its political "solution." Here, psychoanalysis is altogether converted into an imprecise metaphor of sociology. Little is missing, and the whole of society appears, as in Plato's *Republic*, as a gigantic image of the soul of the individual. It is questionable, to say the least, whether an analysis of this kind helps us much.

There was one group in German history that may be said to have had a pronounced interest in maintaining illiberal structures, the traditional-authoritarian leading stratum of Imperial Germany. At several points we have discussed its destiny, its destructive but also benevolent effects. However, even in the Weimar Republic the situation was already much more complicated. There was no stratum there to which an active interest in illiberal structures could be imputed, until the clique of National Socialist leaders used this deficiency for its own purposes. The trouble (or part of it) was that there was no stratum which had an active liberal interest either. Authoritarian structures persisted out of embarrassment rather than conviction, that is, because of the absence of political alternatives. To be sure, many of those who had suddenly and against their will been catapulted to power, accepted this position without complaint, and possibly with a certain pleasure. But this does not alter the fact that, to be correct, we would have to reformulate the positive statement about illiberal groups negatively: No social group had an interest in the abolition of these factors.

This reformulation is necessary for Germany. Strictly speaking, there has been no reference at all to Germany yet in our process of bridge construction. For the sake of clarity at least it is therefore necessary to supplement our sequence of statements by this reference and thereby bring the problem to a head:

There is an authoritarian character of the individual.

Certain childhood experiences provide the basis of the authoritarian character.

Certain family structures make these childhood experiences probable.

These family structures are particularly frequent in Germany.

X.

These social groups are particularly strong in Germany.

Certain social groups have an interest in the persistence of these factors.

Certain social factors form the basis of illiberal political structures.

There are illiberal structures of the political community.

It is possible that the observations about German reality stated in these sentences are, or at least were, correct. For the social side of the analysis we have presented some confirmation for this, if in other terms than those borrowed here from the socio-psychoanalysts: There was indeed a monopolistic elite in Imperial Germany, which had the vested interest of its own rule in the illiberalism of society. Mutatis mutandis the same holds for National Socialist Germany and the DDR. But throughout, and as a dominant trait in the democratic periods of Weimar and Bonn, the negative fact was much more important: there were no powerful social groups that had an interest in the creation of liberal social and political conditions. This is the critical fact that challenges further attempts at explanation, whether these transcend the borders of our own study historically or systematically.

The socio-psychoanalysts on the other hand offer little proof for their assertion. Hitler's childhood is hardly a sufficient confirmation for the presence of certain family structures in German society. The social dimension of socio-psychoanalysis is often dealt with in terms of unproved, at times implicit assertions. And thus one may begin to suspect that the construction of our bridge is somehow faulty. The missing link must be very crooked and unstable indeed in order to join the two unequal parts. Like this, for example:

> I have tried to show in Hitler's writings the two trends that we have already described as fundamental for the authoritar- ian character: the craving for power over men and the longing for submission to an overwhelmingly strong outside power. Hitler's ideas are more or less identical with the ideology of the Nazi party. . . . This ideology results from his personality which, with its inferiority feeling, hatred of life, asceticism, and envy of those who enjoy life, is the soil of sado-masochistic strivings; it was addressed to people who, on account of their similar character structure, felt attracted and excited by these teachings and became ardent followers of the man who expressed what they felt. But it was not only the Nazi ideology that satisfied the lower middle class; the political practice realized what the ideology promised. A hierarchy was created in which everyone had somebody above him to sub- mit to and somebody beneath him to feel power over; the man at the top, the leader, had Fate, History, Nature above him as the power in which to submerge himself. Thus the Nazi ideology and practice satisfied the desires springing from the character structure of one part of the population. . . . (76, pp. 203 f.)

Elegantly, Fromm's nice phrases jump over an abyss of problems: In what sense, for example, are Hitler's neuroses "identical" with the double line of party and state, the de- struction of the family, the idea of "people without living space"? How many members of the "lower middle class" or any other stratum shared his psychic fate? But let us abstain here from any detailed criticism of the socio-psychoanalysis of National Socialism, all the more since we will return to the explanations of National Socialist success presently. Here we are concerned with the German character. The socio- psychoanalysts try to construct it in terms of a psychological figure, the "authoritarian personality," or the "sado-maso- chistic character." But the deficiencies of their attempt to find a social basis for the clinical figure are telling and worrisome.

It has been said that Freud's concept of superego in fact reflects only the bourgeois father of his time. Such time- bound explanations have apparently been inherited even by his critical disciples. In order to find a basis for the asserted social sado-masochism, the socio-psychoanalysts need and use a picture of the family and of society that, if it was ever real, probably never held for the whole of German society and possibly no longer described a living reality in the later years of the Weimar Republic. To this picture belong the father of Erikson's "caricature" (a word he uses himself since, unlike Adorno and Fromm, he is not deadly serious about his analyses), the romantic-socialist idealization of the working class coupled with a distorted image of the middle class, the bogey of monopoly capitalism, and the invention of absurd conspiracies between malevolent entrepreneurs, psychopathic political outsiders, and small minds shaken by inferiority feelings. Even apart from such deficiencies, a strangely unhistorical picture of the character of the Germans emerges here, from which the fundamental difference between authoritarian and totalitarian political structures could not even be described.

Such arguments exclude as useless the connecting piece of our bridge, which says: "The groups that are particularly strong in Germany also display the family structures that condition the authoritarian character." But it would be exaggerated to infer that there is no point at all in trying to connect the constitution of politics and the individual soul. It might be advisable, though, to start the bridge on the political side and—however problematic this may be in civil engineering—to wait and see where the enterprise ends on the other bank. We have already added many corrections to the socio-psychoanalytic constructions on the political side; but the X has remained open. Its solution, and possibly the most important stabilizer of the bridge, would seem to be: The German has a social role.

Analysis of the social conditions of political liberty in German society suggests the construction that concerns first of all not the individual as such, but only his social figure, or, more precisely, the modes of the behavior expected from him in his society. As the father is expected to look after his family, the German is expected, in the context of his society, to prefer the pretty private virtues to the useful public ones. By becoming a German, one enters this horizon of expectations, to which being conscientious and dutiful, industrious and hard-working, also belong. The role of the German includes other elements; we have seen that in one perspective—equality, conflict, and diversity may all be understood as expected modes of behavior. The German character is thus nothing but a role performed by German society and expected from every one of its members.

This is more than a new name for an old thing, as three brief considerations can show. The sado-masochism of one's own soul is there to stay; to shake it off is difficult even on the psychoanalyst's couch. But one can deviate from the claims of social roles. If the individual decides to do so, this is painful for him. It is no compliment for a German if he is regarded as a Frenchman or an Englishman by his compatriots; describing him thus means that others dissociate from him, and is thus a negative sanction. But one can bear sanctions too. Moreover, it is quite possible that—to adopt the bad habit we often find in the literature on the subject of making the adjective comparative—some groups are more German than others, i.e. that there are social categories in which the ruling values embodied in the role of national character are particularly well or particularly poorly developed. One may suspect, for example, that the role of the German is sanctioned especially fiercely among workers. The picture of society and a people can thus be heterogeneous even in respect to a role that one might think unites all.

While roles are—and this is the second consideration—socially defined, they do not remain external to the individual. With this, the construction of our bridge continues in the direction of the bank of the individual. The quasi-psychological side of the social role of the German is what Erich Fromm calls in the appendix to his *Fear of Freedom* the "social character" of the Germans: "The social character comprises only a selection of traits, the essential nucleus of the character structure of most members of a group, which has developed as the result of the basic experiences and mode of life common to that group" (76, p. 239).

Fromm is standing on the other bank. From our perspective the social character is the role as the object of the socialization of the individual. People learn roles, among them, if they happen to live in that country, the role of the German. By learning roles—first in the family, then in school—they change as persons. Internalizing society also determines the character of the individual. Perhaps some traits of the social role of the German promote the formation of sado-masochistic or other neurotic syndromes, a certain immaturity of the individual and the like; probably other national roles favor other aberrations from an historically somewhat simple notion of normalcy in certain psychoanalytic schools. But in so far as the resulting behavior is politically relevant, it should be described, rather than by the misleading notion of the "authoritarian," by the less ambitious, but more useful notion of a preference for private virtues.

This leaves a final consideration in this and at the same time in the entire systematic part of our study. In the last nineteen chapters, we have dealt rather generously with the dimension of time. While there have been many references to the historicity of social structures, illustrations taken from 1910, 1930, and 1950 were used almost indiscriminately. Indeed, the attempt to synchronize the diachronous has at times gone so far that one might be tempted to summarize the analysis now in terms of a German character, a social role of the German that has persisted throughout all changes of the last hundred years: averse to public virtues, preferring the rigidity of the cartel to lively competition, anxiously avoiding all conflicts, seeking a hierarchical world of fundamental inequalities. It seems to me that not only the literary, but the socio-psychoanalytic national characterologists as well, have yielded to this temptation. The understanding of the German character as a social role can, however, help us to avoid this error as well.

Roles are structures of social institutions in their individual face, that is, in the form in which they present themselves immediately to the individual. The institution of the industrial enterprise appears to the individual first of all in his capacities as turner, accountant, or labor manager. Like the institutions in which they are joined, roles are permanently subject to change. This is true for all social roles, including the German character. Thus the social role of the German was different in Berlin in 1910 from Berlin in 1925 and Berlin in 1940; in one year, say 1955, the role is different in Leipzig from what it is in Frankfurt am Main. If there have been certain persistent traits of the German at all these times and places, these were but reflections of persistent traits of German social structure. What is more, it takes no great effort to dissolve the apparently synchronous analysis of German social structure in the four central parts of our study into a diachronous sociological-historical presentation as we have used it to pose the German Question. If we do so, we find the answers German society has given to its question.

GERMAN ANSWERS

24. THE PATH TO DICTATORSHIP

Many symptoms tell of the pathology of the constitution of liberty in Germany; but the victory of National Socialism will forever remain the most striking among them. Explaining this event will therefore be the supreme proof of any general diagnosis. Moreover, a successful explanation of National Socialism not only provides the contemporary with understanding, but with the beginnings of therapy as well, or at least with the tools for testing the liberal potential of our era. It is not our intention here to describe German political developments from 1928 to 1934, or more generally from 1918 to 1945. Not only is the historian more competent to do so, a number of young German historians have already done so with remarkable skill: Karl Dietrich Bracher and Rudolf Morsey, Ernst Nolte and Gerhard Schulz, and several others. Our intention here is more general, and in the terms of some historians probably less scientific. We want to assemble the data needed for a general explanation of the failure of democracy in Germany, which includes, of course, the success of the National Socialists. If our analysis has succeeded, we should now have these data and be able to provide the explanation. The time has come to take up the chronological thread of analysis where we left it before entering the systematic parts of this study.

First of all, it should be made quite clear what it is we want to explain. "National Socialism," "the National Socialist success," and the like are rather general phrases, which invite the imprecisions of which there is no shortage in the literature. What, then, is the critical fact in the case? At least three different problems of National Socialism may be formulated.

There is first the problem to which we have devoted a bitter chapter without offering more than a few observations that may be relevant for an explanation: How was Auschwitz possible? Or, more precisely again: How was an organized mass murder possible in which thousands of "educated" Germans participated without any group protesting audibly? I believe that for the time being this question transcends the horizons of scientific explanation; it is too close and too overwhelming to be studied *sine ira et studio*.

The second problem takes us a little further back in the history of Nazi Germany: How was the almost complete absence of active resistance, thus the apparent acceptance of National Socialist rule during, and, more strikingly still, in the years immediately preceding the Second World War possible? This is an important and difficult problem of Germany's political sociology. It implies the assertion that the National Socialist regime was, at least in a technical sense, legitimate, and it will stand in the background of our analysis of National Socialist Germany and the social revolution.

There remains the third problem: How was January 30, 1933, possible? How can we explain the extraordinary gains in popular support for the National Socialists in the late years of the Weimar Republic, and the largely unresisted acceptance of Hitler's seizure of power by other parties and groups? This is a comparatively definite question which may prevent us from escaping into the clouds of generalities.

The word "explanation," if applied to historical events, is likely to be misunderstood; it is used here in a definite sense. January 30, 1933, is not explained by a description of what happened. But it is not explained by invoking other historical events such as "Versailles," "the Inflation," or "the Depression" either. Invoking such events leaves out precisely those links with which we are concerned here: What does "Versailles" mean? Does it imply that there is a natural law, according to which members of a people who had to accept a peace treaty involving territorial losses and reparations are bound to give their vote fifteen years later to a nationalist party? And are the corresponding "natural laws" with respect to inflation and depression any more plausible?

Adducing specific events as causes is only seemingly precise and concrete; upon closer reflection it turns out to evade the issue by leaving its solution implicit, and in terms of little plausibility at that. However one wants to assess the weight of specific events in the prehistory of National Socialism, there is no getting away from the social basis on which they occurred and from which the political reactions of people become understandable. However one turns the problem therefore, its solution must be sought in the structures of German society—and it is clearly preferable to analyze them explicitly rather than to rely on implied and highly problematic "natural laws."

So far as the analysis of the social structure of democracy in Germany is concerned, a chain of four statements follows from our study which relate to the four sets of factors discussed. The realization of the social role of the citizen has been slow and to the present day incomplete in Germany. For a long time, the social and political rights of participation were far from universal; but above all, people were tied by the fetters of tradition so that they could not grow into the modern citizen role. Despite all technical and economic progress, people remained tied and thus unable, and often unwilling, to carry their interests freely into the market of political decision. Pre-democratic patterns of behavior remained prescribed for large groups, and this could all too easily turn into the anti-democratic behavior of a nostalgic demand for the nest warmth of the closed society.

In the institutions of society, the aversion against the open society found its expression and permanent confirmation in the treatment of conflicts. The principles by which the inevitable antagonisms of interests were regulated in the various areas of social structure were dictated without exception by the search for certainty. Thus the settlement of contest was sought everywhere in its abolition rather than in reasonable regulation. Most social institutions favor this approach in any case, by virtue of their inherent and inevitable drop of authority; but in Germany this unfortunate condition was ideologically transferred to the political field as well, where there is in fact no such drop. In this way, the intention of "superseding" democracy as a system of government-by-conflict was built into the social structure, and the constitution of liberty discredited from the outset as the third best, if not the worst, of all possible systems. At the same time, the authoritarian mixture of benevolence and suppression favored an illiberal constitution of political things, which would be more in accordance with the pattern of their social basis.

Who was to take this illiberal course? Here, as the human agents of social change, German elites in their peculiar shape, or rather shapelessness, should prove decisive. No self-confident leadership group had followed the monopolistic elite of Imperial Germany. Remainders of the old elite stood next to the anxious cartel of those who unexpectedly found

themselves at the top and who were, for lack of social establishment, at best capable of maintaining the status quo. It
was to be expected that an elite of this kind would offer little
resistance to the assault of a coherent and militant group,
whether this came from outside, or from its midst; in a way
the cartel of the anxious always presents an invitation to the
less anxious to put an end to indecision by arbitrary definiteness. If, as increasingly happens in modern societies, such
definiteness fails to be accompanied by a program based on
structured interests, it turns into pure definiteness, political
existentialism, or at least applied decisionism. It is a nice question of historical analysis, precisely how strong this particular
element was in the National Socialist seizure of power.

But not only the elites made it easy for a militant clique
to seize power in Germany. The prevalence of private virtues kept the doors toward a world of "true things" wide
open for the semicitizens, who could thus find consolation
for the misery of public affairs. The political indifference
springing from private virtues is not as passive as it may
appear. As the small-lot peasants of France could not represent their interests themselves and therefore constituted a
welcome challenge to a usurper, Louis Bonaparte, to arrogate
their representation, so the German friends of private virtues called mutely for the dictator to satisfy their needs. The
only difference is that insulation, in the case of the French
peasants, was a geographic fact, whereas with German voters
it is a less clearly visible consequence of their social role
that forces upon them a personality unaffected by the "external world" of public matters.

These are the conclusions we can derive from our analysis
and offer by way of explanation of January 30, 1933; but they
are obviously no cause for triumph. Much as these statements
may describe characteristic traits of German social structure, it is hard to recognize their immediate relevance to the
National Socialist seizure of power. Where "Versailles" or
"the Depression" are too concrete, the quartet of structural
factors is too abstract. To be sure, the hodgepodge of ideas
the National Socialists called their program included many
points that were in line with the factors we have studied.
Speaking of "blood and soil" flatters traditions, and the "people's community" confirms the aversion to conflict, as does
the hatred of the "system period" of Weimar; promising a
new elite and a leader may have satisfied the sense of inde-

cision under a cartel of anxiety, and there are many who yielded their public responsibilities to the new leaders' definiteness, because they mistook it for certainty. But these facts do not, as such, create relations, much less causal relations. In what sense does our quartet of factors provide an explanation of National Socialist success?

Let us first consider the quartet itself once again. It is not a mere collection of isolated factors, but forms a syndrome. The four factors combine into the image of a society characterized by the explosive faultings of traditional-authoritarian and modern-democratic structures. Despite their apparent instability, the faultings must not be underestimated as a mere transitional stage on a recognizable road; they have themselves become an effective reality. Negatively speaking, they signify a widespread aversion to the constitution of liberty, which makes members of many groups respond to all concerns about real conditions on ther prevailing interpretation with the search for new fundamental solutions outside the existing political system. Thus the syndrome serves to explain the inclination of many Germans in the later years of the Weimar Republic to vote for parties that promised to put an end to government by conflict; by the same token it explains the hopes placed by many in the system and the policies favored by these parties.

While the German syndrome explains the necessity and imminence of changes, it does not by itself account for their direction, however. It was clear that this had to be anti-democratic; but the negative notion leaves open the great alternative that divides authoritarian from totalitarian rule. However insufficient our explanation may be, it is no weaker than reality itself. To the not-yet-burned children on the threshold of dictatorship (as the benevolent general term has it) the alternative could not be very clearly apparent; and it seems doubtful whether anybody knew for sure, in 1933, the direction of change. There were significant groups that tried to gather together those anti-democratic sentiments that essentially meant the revival of authoritarian government along the lines prescribed by Imperial Germany. Such groups existed within the Nazi party as well. Many may have sensed in 1933 that this party was ultimately governed by other intentions; but few can have had any clear idea of what was hidden behind the "total state" the National Socialists advocated officially in the early months of their rule.

The Fascist model meant little here; in Italian Fascism, traditional and thus authoritarian elements were clearly dominant. Only in retrospect can it be said that, in 1933, traditional anti-liberal groups with authoritarian convictions combined temporarily with the modern anti-liberals of totalitarian conviction in a mésalliance that turned out to be catastrophic for the former, but highly successful for the latter. When the combination came about, the leaders of the traditional right were deceived into regarding the National Socialists as harmless; when they discovered their potential, it was too late for them, and for the country. The representatives of those widespread anti-democratic sentiments in the population that provided a mainspring of Nazi success united very heterogeneous traditions and groupings; their internal struggles provide the leitmotiv of subsequent developments.

Among the questions left open by this analysis, one is particularly significant: Where did the totalitarian potential in National Socialism stem from? This is an historical question, so far as the genesis of totalitarian government is concerned. Hannah Arendt, Carl J. Friedrich, Ernst Nolte, Karl A. Wittfogel have, each in his own way, contributed to answering it. But it is also a sociological question, so far as the "realism" of the notion and the social basis of its adherents are concerned. Only a modern society, that is, a society in which the traditional social ties of people have been destroyed, can be totalitarian; this is why the hostility of the Nazis was directed against tradition above all. Only new social groups may provide the social basis of this new political movement. This is why the connection between the new middle class of clerical workers and officials and the rise of totalitarianism, especially in Germany, is significant. But while the history and basis of modern totalitarianism, the particular history of German National Socialism, the mésalliance of the conservative and radical opponents of democracy in 1933, and, of course, the personalities of Von Papen and Hindenburg, Von Schleicher and Hitler, the events of the Depression, and many another phenomenon link the events of January 30, 1933, with the syndrome of the faulted society, its social structures provide the starting point of any explanation of the phenomenon.

There are many explanations of National Socialism in the literature. Even apart from obviously insufficient pseudoexplanations such as those in terms of specific historical events, much in these attempts remains problematic. It constitutes both an application and a test of our own findings to confront them with some of the prevailing explanations. In presenting them, we can use Karl Dietrich Bracher's distinction of "three significant methods of explanation" offered for the National Socialist seizure of power, "an historical, a sociological, and a political one" (30, p. 154). However, Bracher's characterization of these methods needs to be supplemented.

There is, first of all, the "historical-ideological explanation in terms of intellectual history"; it "reaches far and believes that it has to explain the events of 1933 and 1934 as a kind of inevitable consequence of a German tradition, especially a prevailing tradition of nationalism and authoritarianism in German history" (30, p. 154). Bracher notes that such explanations often seek their causes in distant grounds; earlier, we have described them by the catchword "Tacitus" and connected them with the vexatious thesis of an unchangeable national character. To be sure, such derivations in terms of intellectual history are not necessarily wrong (although it is suspicious that they can neither be proved nor disproved unambiguously). But they do not provide an immediate explanation for January 30, 1933. Here again, too many links are missing, for in its general version the behavior of known groups remains unexplained. *The German Mind from Luther to Nietzsche* may give some useful indications of the horizon within which modern German society has developed, but it is too indefinite a phenomenon itself to serve as an explanation without reference to social structures.

In our analysis of German values we encountered one variant of this attempt to explain January 30, 1933, which is little more definite. The notion of a German social character may be found halfway between intellectual history and society. But this concept, too, raises as many questions as it answers: Were there really masses of authoritarian personalities in the Weimar Republic? Why were they there? Where were they to be found? Was the authoritarian personality structure of people the reason they voted for the National Socialists? Why did authoritarianism spread so quickly in the later years of the Weimar Republic? If one reduces the character of the Germans to their social role, one grasps the sum of social structures in the sense of our syndrome, and the two types of analysis meet.

Bracher is rather vague in what he calls the "sociological explanation" of the events of 1933 and 1934:

It emphasizes . . . the significance of general conditions, which the class state of industrial society has created with the process of massification and collectivization of the individual, with the complication of the economic structure and the crisis propensity of capitalism for the rise of totalitarian movements and the surrender of the individual. Thus the emphasis is here on the non-German and supra-German factors of a development for which neither the individual nor even the people of a specific country can be held fully responsible. Even the conflict-laden interdependence and deterioration of international relations, which works toward worldwide clashes, belongs to these factors; technical development and particularly that of military techniques has loaded international tensions and conflicts with catastrophic possibilities and consequences. (30, p. 155.)

There are sociologists who argue like this. Also, Bracher has brought out two deficiencies of sociological analysis: it tends to regard German society of the Weimar Republic as more modern and developed than it actually was, and it prefers explanations that hold for all other industrial countries as well as Germany. But in detail these explanations are usually much more concrete, as can be shown by looking at the two most important versions of the sociology of National Socialism.

Theodor Geiger's thesis about the middle classes and National Socialism is the first example. As we have seen in discussing the social stratification of the German people, Geiger postulated as early as 1932 a connection between the mentalities of the old and the new middle classes and the economic and political ideology of National Socialism (cf. 79). His conception was later elaborated by others. Harold Lasswell in particular made it the focal point of his analysis of the "psychology of Hitlerism" (cf. 126), and even in 1960, Lipset (in his essay on " 'Fascism'—Left, Right and Center") believes that National Socialism can be explained in terms of the political mentality of the middle classes.

A number of observations provide the starting point of such analyses, of which two are outstanding. The first concerns electoral behavior. In the parliamentary elections between 1928 and 1932, the traditional "middle-class parties," including the German People's Party (DVP), Democratic

Party (DDP), Economic Party, and a number of smaller groups, were reduced to one fifth of their initial size. While in 1928 they had still won 25 per cent of the popular vote, their share had shrunk to 5 per cent by November 1932, and was halved again in the March elections of 1933. During the same period the National Socialist share in the vote rose from 2.6 to 43.9 per cent. The second observation concerns Nazi party leaders. Lipset has related calculations by Hans Gerth about the social composition of these leadership groups in relation to the occupational structure of the German population and found that four occupational groups are significantly overrepresented among Nazi leaders: state officials (147 per cent), clerical workers (169 per cent), service personnel and members of family enterprises (178 per cent), self-employed (187 per cent). In the sources of its support as well as in its own composition the early NSDAP at least may thus be described as a middle-class party (cf. 131).

But why should the middle classes support an anti-democratic mass movement? Lipset points to the peculiar fact that as industrialization progresses, a radicalism of those who traditionally stand in the center moves alongside the radicalism of the left, carried by the proletariat, and the radicalism of the right in the interest of the large property-holders in land and capital. This third and improbable radicalism is informed by the aversion to the other two radicalisms; its advocates seek protection against the grindstone of the class struggle from left and right; they want the powerful state to offer a third way between what they experience as the two evils of capitalism on the one hand and socialism on the other.

Theodor Geiger has put this attitude into a brilliant sentence, which we have quoted before: "A class denies with disgust that it is a class and conducts a bitter class struggle against the reality and idea of the class struggle" (80, p. 168). Whether class struggle or not, the root of this extremism is insecurity of social position; its standard bearers are the least educated and intelligent groups of the middle class; its ideology is fascism.

Powerful data seem to support this theory. Lipset shows that the thesis can be upheld even against the objection that the electoral successes of the Nazis are primarily due to the participation of previous non-voters. But the crucial question is: What does this theory prove? It cannot explain January

30, 1933; there was a middle class in all industrial societies, but a National Socialist seizure of power only in Germany. Why did England and the United States not fall victim to the "extremism of the center"? The question is not as absurd as it may sound. There were notable tendencies toward anti-democratic politics on the part of the traditional center of these countries as well. Fascism had its epoch. And this is where the theory of the affinity between the middle classes and National Socialism has its significance. The theory explains the peculiar character of the National Socialist movement itself, and especially its difference from extreme nationalist parties (such as the German Nationals of the DNVP), and extreme socialist parties (such as the Communists of the KPD). It does therefore give an indication of the peculiarity of the new political phenomenon and also explains why this anti-democratic extremism could not take the authoritarian turn but had to orient itself differently, namely, in a totalitarian way. But the more specific question in which we are interested here—why this movement bred by the insecurities of middle-class position fell on such fertile ground in German society—still requires that other explanation we have sketched in this study. The middle-class theory supplements our explanation in one important respect, but it cannot replace it.

There is a second, equally old sociological theory of National Socialism for which prominent crown witnesses may also be quoted, although it clearly contradicts the middle-class theory. This is the Marxian theory of National Socialism as the highest and final stage of capitalism, or, more pointedly, of the conspiracy between big business and National Socialism as the motive force of Germany's path to dictatorship. An early version of this theory may be found in Franz Neumann's book *Behemoth*, the first edition of which described National Socialism from the perspective of 1939, which is hard to reproduce today; for this reason the book has itself become an historical document. There are a number of observations to support the theory that the victory of National Socialism rests on the combination of the Nazi party and big business (plus big agrarians). Among these there is above all the personal relationship between Nazi leaders and captains of industry ever since Hitler's much-quoted speech before the Rhine-Ruhr Club in 1931. A number of significant developments in the prehistory of Hitler's seizure of power are regarded as consequences of this personal relationship, among them the growing financial support of the NSDAP from business circles, the separation of the party from its socialist wing, the formation of the Harzburg Front, and Hitler's evident readiness to co-operate with conservative groups. At this point, however, the theory usually departs from confirmed observations and imputes to big business (at best a term used rather unspecifically in this context) the motive of wanting to use the NSDAP as a representative of its interests by the promotion of a policy of national self-sufficiency and military rearmament, from which industry could expect to profit.

The argument bears unmistakable traces of a conspiracy theory. By suggesting secret arrangements between Hitler and a few monopoly capitalists who are distorted into supermen, the theory pleases a naïve preference for "tangible" explanations of otherwise incomprehensible phenomena. Methodically it might be described as the anti-Semitism of the left. If one tries to take it seriously, the first remark to be made is that the theory cannot in any way explain at least one crucial phenomenon—the electoral gains of the National Socialists—and needs a rather complicated construction to explain another—their middle-class support. In fact, it is an attempt to save Marxist conceptions of development in the face of a phenomenon that contradicts precisely these conceptions so flagrantly that doctrinaire Marxists had to feel threatened. With National Socialism, a popular movement had emerged that could hardly be considered to the left even during the Hitler-Stalin Pact, an anti-socialist mass movement in the country that even Lenin had believed to be near the threshold of the proletarian revolution. No general strike prevented the leaders of this movement from seizing power; its echo apparently resounded even further than its call and took in even its political opponents.

There can be no doubt today that there was an alliance between some big industrialists and leading National Socialists. It is clear also that it was useful for the Nazis, who were as concerned about their economic basis as about their social recognition, to enter into this alliance. It is rather more questionable whether the uses of the alliance were equally great for those who financed it. The fact must not be overlooked that, to the end, the dwindling parties of the liberal center found more favor among businessmen than the

NSDAP; moreover, the direction of the economic policy of a National Socialist government had to be described as at least uncertain, on the basis of the confused program of the party. If one combines the materials .of Marxist theoreticians, worried trade unionists, and Nuremberg judges, the alliance of the NSDAP and big business permits a very different explanation as well. It appears at least as likely as a conspiracy for mutual benefit that the industrialists were primarily interested in reassurance. At a late date and with moderate means, they supported a party they feared would soon be in power. In fact, they behaved exactly as one would expect from members of the anxious cartel, defensively and without any positive conception, concerned about the status quo of the political order, or at least of their own position. We know today that some entrepreneurs went far beyond such contracts of reassurance; but on the whole the much-cited alliance of big business and National Socialism was little more than a worried attempt on the part of business to create goodwill among the anticipated rulers of the future.

This much may be said in favor of the Marxist theory of the National Socialist seizure of power, it hits the level on which an explanation of the phenomenon has to be sought. Bracher's own medicine against theoretical errors, that is, the "third approach to explanation," "political analysis that considers the immediate process of the seizure of power itself under the novel conditions of our time" (30, p. 155) does not seem to be very effective. To be sure, nobody can read *Die Auflösung der Weimarer Republik* [The Dissolution of the Weimar Republic] without a sense of being informed of the way it all came about. But the other question remains of how it *could* come about. This question is so urgent that not even the historian bent on description can evade it.

Germany could—and possibly had to—step on the path to National Socialist dictatorship because her society bore many traits that resisted the constitution of liberty. But at no time was German society merely a crystallized pattern. Even in the confused years of the Weimar Republic it was subject to change; it is no accident that the January 30th occurred in 1933, and not in 1923. Germany's peculiar development, the critical climax of which may be seen in the National Socialist seizure of power, has its origin in the extraordinary ability of Imperial Germany to control the industrial revolution. Neither in the sense of a society of citizens nor in that of one dominated by a confident bourgeoisie did a modern society emerge. In order to establish the political institutions of liberal democracy in the society that did emerge, a social revolution was necessary. But the Weimar Republic held up rather than realized this revolution, and this is one of the major reasons for its social explosiveness and political instability.

These categories help us to follow some of the major steps of German social and political development since 1918. In 1918 one of the most skillful elites of modern history, the authoritarian elite of Imperial Germany, lost its political basis. The state, the moral ideal of which was anchored in the claim for certainty advanced by traditional leadership groups, began to float. No counterelite emerged to fasten it. Neither bourgeois republicans nor socialists had a clear conception of the social and political future, or the confidence to realize such a conception. This was the soil on which the cartel of anxiety throve, seeming to fear nothing quite as much as revolution—and thereby almost inevitably bringing about what it feared.

In Germany, the revolution that is meant here had to be a bourgeois revolution first of all. It had to open the road to modernity for the country. Successful as the combination of traditional patterns of culture and modern modes of production was in Imperial Germany, it could not last. Nonparticipant submission to authoritarian rule is plainly more likely under pre-industrial conditions of social insulation than after industrialization, the more so since the social problem forces many to participate in order to secure the material basis of their lives. But the parties of the Weimar coalition did not want the social transformation that they needed. Instead, they adopted the catastrophic paradox of the labor movement, which consistently undermined by its politics the foundations of its success and effect. In so far as the Weimar parties had ideas of social reform at all, these were largely directed at the transformation of the authoritarian welfare state into its republican version; but most of them regarded the national question as more important than the social question.

Perhaps it is unfair to accuse the parties of the Weimar coalition of failing to carry out radical social programs in the interest of the constitution of liberty. It is probably difficult under all conditions to introduce such reforms in a democratic manner, and in any case the mandate of the Weimar coalition did not permit such radicalism. But even in the little things within their range, the governing parties of the first decade of the Weimar Republic showed few signs of a political conception inspired by radically new goals.

This is how the contradiction came about between a political system that permitted, and a social structure that forbade democracy. In theory it should have been possible to fill the Weimar Constitution with the life of social conflicts founded in cleavages of interest; but the reality of social institutions prevented or deflected these conflicts everywhere. In theory there was no reason why citizenship rights should not be fully realized; but the political class was content with formal rights and ignored their social context, to say nothing of the continued effectiveness of traditional ties. The ruling class itself, unsure of its position, both deliberately and unintentionally promoted the survival of authoritarian dreams and realities, which met with little resistance among those condemned to permanent minority, if only because their imaginations had not yet been stimulated by modernity. Thus the years of misleading stability before 1928 appear in retrospect as a period of attention for a surprise that could not surprise.

The surprise was not long in coming. Society and democracy not only remained incompatible in the Weimar Republic, social reality provided a basis for the militant protest against the political form of democracy. This was the protest in which the two unequal forces of conservatives and Nazis were united. There were those who wanted to supersede democracy by a return to the still familiar patterns of authoritarian rule. These conservatives were recruited from the traditional "governing strata" of the civil service and the military, as well as agriculture and industry. One may call Hindenburg their symbol; their means were more concrete. On the other hand, there emerged in the NSDAP a new kind of anti-democratic force, rejected with suspicion at first by the conservatives. Certain as its opposition to the constitution of liberty was, its own political goals remained uncertain for a long time. The support this party found testifies not only to specifically German developments, but to a tendency that became visible everywhere with the growth of the service class. But while this "extremism of the center" was but a passing threat to the constitution of liberty in England and the United States, it succeeded in Germany.

In negative terms, the reason for this success may be described by the absence of resistance against anti-democratic forms among people of almost all groups and strata. Almost any other constitution had to correspond more closely to the faulted structures of society than political democracy. Because the new illiberalism of the National Socialists fell on the soil of an illiberal, namely an authoritarian rather than a liberal tradition, it succeeded in seizing the power in Germany that it failed to achieve in more liberal countries. The same picture emerges if we turn from the patients to the actors of this development. In Germany, the National Socialist leadership clique could join forces with another anti-democratic and activist elite, the traditional authoritarian groups, and the alliance enabled it to seize the power that made the abolition of the Weimar Constitution possible. There was no liberal elite that might have stopped such developments.

It must be emphasized that this is nevertheless not an automatic process. Not only might it have had a different end, but significance of the conditions that set it going must also not be underestimated. Those who were hit hardest by the Depression did not rush into the arms of the National Socialists; the electoral losses of Social Democrats and Communists in the elections of 1932 remain within limits. But the indirect consequences of the crisis, and particularly its economic and psychological ramifications for a middle class enamored with order and security, certainly furthered the rapid growth of the National Socialist vote. Still, whatever the significance of these initial conditions may be, there is little indication that the defenders of the Weimar Republic realized the dimension of the task of social change required to create a social basis for the constitution of liberty. This dimension was evidently seen only by those who wanted change in order to destroy the constitution of liberty.

So Germany's most terrible answer to the German Question took its course. At its beginning stood an historical error, the short-lived alliance of the heirs of Germany's authoritarian past with the forefathers of her totalitarian future. The error may be understandable in so far as the direction of National Socialist politics was anything but clear in 1933. That it was successful was due to the illiberal structures of

German society to which the bulk of this study is devoted. That it was an error became evident soon after the composition of that apparently harmless first cabinet of Hitler's, in which the National Socialists "generously" left the numerical majority to "bourgeois" members. Now the revolution took its course, which it had not taken in 1918, which to have held up was the only and tragic success of the Weimar coalition, and which the Nazis' allies of January 30, 1933, wanted above all to avoid.

The social history of National Socialist Germany has not yet been written. Understandably, German historians have devoted their interest first of all to the dramatic events of the years from 1932 to 1934. But once the history of the subsequent period is written from a social rather than a national point of view, it will reveal many a surprise. Even in respect to the National Socialist seizure of power in 1933, historians speak of a revolution, a "revolutionizing process" (Helmut Krausnick), a "legal revolution" (Karl Friedrich Bracher). What they mean is the rapid and firm transformation of the political constitution of the country. But the concept might prove adequate even if one considers the changes in German society that followed the political revolution. Here—to use Theodor Geiger's terms—not only the "style" of an epoch, but the "epoch" itself was transformed. National Socialism completed for Germany the social revolution that was lost in the faultings of Imperial Germany and again held up by the contradictions of the Weimar Republic.

The substance of this revolution is modernity. Autonomous equality of opportunity for all men, which epitomizes modernity, does not, as we have seen, come about by itself. It is not a necessary consequence, or a condition, of industrialization. Moreover, wherever it did come about, at least the beginning of the process was violent. Entering the modern world proved painful for those involved everywhere. It required revolution and insecurity, uprooting and human sacrifice. The conclusion is hard to avoid that the road to modernity was not taken spontaneously and happily by men anywhere, that force was always required to make people embark on it. Only afterwards, if at all, did it find the agreement of men freed of the chains of minority. Breaking with the closed society hits people the harder, the later it occurs—harder in Germany than in England, harder in the new nations of our own time than in Germany. However, brutal as it was, the

break with tradition and thus a strong push toward modernity
was the substantive characteristic of the social revolution
of National Socialism.

Even the intimation of a comparison between the National
Socialist leadership clique and the Jacobins, or even the Bol-
sheviks, is bound to raise doubts and objections. While this
will not allay such doubts, it should be added that the social
revolution effected by National Socialism was an unintended,
if inevitable result of its rule. It would clearly be wrong to
say that Hitler set out to complete the revolution of modernity. On the contrary, his writings and speeches, indeed the
entire cloudy National Socialist ideology seem to demand
the recovery of the values of the past; the Nazis liked to appear Catonic where they were in fact radical innovators. For
whatever their ideology, they were compelled to revolutionize
society in order to stay in power.

The contradiction between the ideology and practice of
National Socialism is as astonishing as it is understandable.
It means, however, that the veil of ideology must not deceive
us. As such, it was little more than an episode and in its substance a horrible mixture of all the half-truths of the time; but
its social effects make the Nazi regime—quite apart from
the consequences of the war it started—far more than an
episode in German history. It gave German society an ir-
reversible push, which exposed it to totalitarian dangers and
opened it to liberal chances at the same time. The starting
point of this development may be found in the political con-
stellation of the year 1933. Hitler came to power on January
30, 1933, by virtue of the historical error of the alliance between an anti-democratic right and an anti-democratic center,
which was concluded before the background of a general
mood of hostility toward the constitution of liberty. If we
add that Hitler and his followers had no intention of giving
up their power again, much else follows almost by necessity.
The short road of the conservatives from allies to bystanders
and then to opponents of the Nazis is a symptom of this
course of events, if one that can tell a story worth recounting.
But to stick to the actors for the time being, for them maintaining power meant extending it into total power and stabilizing it as such. Hitler could find a foundation and anchor for
his rule only by demolishing parliamentary democracy. But
he was well aware that this process of destruction required
more than an enabling law or the outlawing of political par-

ties; he had to remove what social realities there were behind these methods as well, but above all he had to attack the much more pronounced patterns that, while they did not support democracy, worked even more strongly against claims to total power. Total power presupposes the destruction of the power of all partial institutions, of all even faintly autonomous secondary centers. The revolution took its course along these lines.

The social basis of German authoritarianism, thus of the resistance of German society to modernity and liberalism, consisted in a structural syndrome that held people to the social ties in which they had found themselves without their doing and that prevented them from full participation. In Germany, the constitution of liberty was jeopardized by the institutionalized minority of its people. But—and this is not always seen—the claim to total power advanced by a political clique was necessarily jeopardized by such structures too. Authoritarian leaders find the chances and outlets for their peculiar mixture of benevolence and suppression in secondary centers without a claim to comprehensive influence. But for claims to total power even private virtues, and certainly the institutions springing from them, become a source of resistance. Just as the rulers of the new nations of our time have to break the tribal loyalties of their peoples in order to establish their power, the National Socialists had to break the traditional, and in effect anti-liberal, loyalties for region and religion, family and corporation, in order to realize their claim to total power. Hitler needed modernity, little as he liked it.

Hitler's speech of February 1, 1933, was an apparent praise of tradition:

> Beginning with the family, by way of all notions of honor and faith, people and fatherland, culture and economy up to the eternal foundation of our morals and our beliefs, nothing is spared by this purely negative, universally destructive idea. Fourteen years of Marxism have ruined Germany. . . . [The national government] is going to conserve and defend the foundations on which the strength of our nation is based. It will take Christianity as the basis of our entire morality, and the family as the seed cell of the entire body of our people and state, into its safe protection. (165, p. 419.)

On this very day, however, Hitler's deeds were in fact directed to the goal he imputed to the parties of the Weimar Republic: the destruction of the traditional basis of German society in family and religion and all other spheres.

The beginning of this process was the deliberately pursued *Gleichschaltung,* co-ordination; to this extent we can agree with Krausnick when he says, " 'Co-ordination' *is* the revolution" (118, p. 181). The process of co-ordination soon and effectively put the Weimar Constitution de facto out of force and abolished the rights of parliament. This was not by itself a process of very great social consequence; but other measures were to follow in the first year of Nazi rule. The restriction and eventually abolition of the rights of the *Länder,* for example, attacked one of the characteristic traditions— and faultings—of German social structure. The blend of regional loyalty and national unity that characterized Imperial Germany and the Weimar Republic may not have been very effective politically, but it symbolized a mixture of modern requirements and binding traditions that nobody had dared touch before, while it took Hitler only three months to dissolve the mixture at the expense of traditional loyalties.

Public bureaucracy and the courts had certainly not been sources of modernity or liberalism in the Weimar Republic; we have seen how their effects were—partly unintentionally, but often quite deliberately—authoritarian throughout. This was due to some considerable extent to the traditional character of these institutions, which the Weimar parties again had not dared touch. Hitler was less hesitant. In the first months of his rule he enacted the laws and created the institutions that were needed to "co-ordinate" the bureaucracy and the legal system. This meant that he wanted to subject them to his rule; and the interventions in traditional autonomies and customs and habits required by this intention were so profound that they had to change these institutions almost out of recognition.

Co-ordination soon reached the other institutions too. It neutralized the Reich President until his office disappeared after the death of Hindenburg. It broke into the army as it had revolutionized public bureaucracy and the legal system before. It led to the abolition of the autonomous economic institutions that had amounted to a system of industrial relations however incomplete, and that were replaced by state-controlled organizational patterns. It robbed the press of its independence and subordinated it to the total purposes of the state. Later on, co-ordination began to approach those institutions that were further removed from the state, the churches and private organizations, universities and traditional associations, in order to subject all sectors of society to rigid control.

The notion of "co-ordination," which—like that of the "total state"—is not an invention of interpreting scholarship, but was introduced by the National Socialists themselves in the early years of their rule, was meant politically. But inevitably it had a social dimension as well. "Co-ordination" always means the abolition of uncontrolled autonomy. Wherever relatively self-sufficient institutions or organizations exist, they have to yield to organizations directed to the one purpose of the state and its personification in the Leader. In this process people are removed from traditional, personal, often especially close and intimate ties, and made equal in kind, if not in rank.

One can put this more metaphorically and thereby indicate once again the contradiction between the ideology and practice of National Socialism by saying that the Nazi regime tried everywhere to replace organic social structures by mechanical formations. Instead of an interdependence of a diversity of institutions with a degree of autonomy, and often with their own historical dimension, National Socialism needed the uniform orientation of all institutions to one purpose. In the place of many partial elites of limited but independent significance stepped a monopolistic clique; in the place of a multitude of binding partial roles stepped the diffuse role of the *Volksgenosse,* the compatriot, or comrade of the (same) people, with its numerous expectations.

The contrast to an ideology dominated by organic notions —if in a primitive or vulgar version—could hardly be more acute. But then a view of state and society as an organic system of interdependent elements could not be in the interest of the claim to total power. The organic theory of the state is an authoritarian notion. It concedes to the constituent elements a life of their own, so long as this does not affect the claim to certainty advanced by the leading stratum. Since the leading stratum claims merely the ultimate, and not the permanent right to decide, since its legitimacy is founded on the non-participation, and not on the permanent organization and control of the subjects, the area of autonomy remains quite large. What happens in family and school, church and community, indeed to some extent in the army and the courts, the bureaucracy and voluntary organizations, does not worry the authoritarian political class so long as its position is not threatened by it. But a totalitarian leadership group is threatened by any autonomy of institutions. It cannot afford that generosity that allowed even cartoonists and satirical writers their cat-and-mouse games with censorship in Imperial Germany. It needs that mechanical co-ordination that involves the destruction of all loyalties that support the autonomous life of the individual.

The contrast between the National Socialist ideology of the organic and the mechanical practice of co-ordination remains so striking that one is almost tempted to believe that the ideology was not simply an instrument to mislead people deliberately. Possibly the National Socialist leaders themselves believed in some of their sentimental traditionalisms, that is, they sought authoritarian rule. But even if this was so, their wishes had to remain unfulfilled. The return of Imperial Germany in any version, including modified forms, was probably impossible even in 1933; it was certainly impossible for Hitler and his adherents to bring about such a return. As a traditionless clique that could hardly be described as conservative in outlook, the Nazi leaders were inescapably doomed to the path of totalitarianism to find a basis for their power. This in turn presupposed the co-ordination of all institutions with any degree of autonomy, the destruction of all loyalties of men not devoted to the state, the unbounded extension of the social role of the *Volksgenosse*. The National Socialist leaders had the choice of either disappearing as such or setting in motion a social revolution in Germany with all brutality.

"Co-ordination" in the strict sense of the early years was only the beginning of this process. In the years before the war it was supplemented by a number of consequential measures of which only the most significant need be mentioned here. Two basic structures of social differentiation in all societies are those of regional differentiation and of social stratification. These may assume very different forms. They can both produce somewhat artificial, passing roles, which may be acquired and also shed; or they may be burdened with a long history and surrounded by far-reaching expectations. One of the aspects of German traditionalism before 1933 was that regional differentiation and social stratification were, for many, far more than systems of achievable positions. They bound the individual in a way that resounds with notions of the closed society. These were ties that introduced an element of immobilization and thus an obstacle to the development of democracy in the country.

But—this is the tragic figure of modernity at the basis of our argument—obstacles to democracy are also obstacles to totalitarianism. The National Socialist leaders had to try to weaken the binding force of ties of region and class, and they did so. Moving people away from their inherited (or even chosen) places of residence is not a Russian or Polish invention; it was a principle in National Socialist Germany as well. Even where no "resettlement" of larger groups took place, there were plenty of well-planned occasions for alienating people at least temporarily from their accustomed environment and thereby casting doubt on custom and heritage for those concerned. The mass organizations of the party and its affiliations, and later on the army, offered many an occasion of this kind. These institutions served at the same time to level social strata, the differentiation of which was ideologically reinterpreted, following the Soviet pattern, as one of "workers of the forehead" and "workers of the fist." Clearly, this would not make the differentiation itself disappear; but its halo of customs and expectations shrank in view of the expansive claim of the "comrade of the people" —a role that, not unlike the role of "citizen" in this respect, makes the unequal equal and the ascribed achievable, and in that sense has specifically modern traits.

The struggle against the loyalties of memberships, which, while they may be achievable, were often sanctified by long tradition, assumed many more pronounced forms from the early years of the Nazi regime. To many it seems contradictory today that among the victims of this struggle we find the traditional organizations of socialist trade unions as well as of student clubs. But in terms of totalitarian rule there is no contradiction here; both types of organization and others of similar kinds allocate roles to their members, the substance of which is taken away from the general, equal role of the *Volksgenosse* and thus the disposable general public. They withdraw a part of the public activity of the individual from general access and control by the state and have to abide, therefore, by the verdict of co-ordination, which is inescapable for the establishment of totalitarian power.

This is true for church membership as well. Discussion of

the question of whether the Catholic church lacked moral fiber in its attitude toward the crude and eventually murderous anti-Semitism of the Nazis has obscured our vision to the fact that the churches had to be entirely unacceptable islands of autonomy for the Nazi leaders. The struggle for the social realization of total power had therefore to be directed from the outset against the churches. This was all the more necessary since the churches were powerful in Germany and represented, at least in the case of the Catholic church—as shown by the development of the vote for the Center Party in the Weimar Republic—stable political counterweights. In the case of the Evangelical church, this struggle soon led to more than superficial successes for the regime, although decidedly anti-Nazi groups emerged almost equally soon from the midst of the co-ordinated Protestants. The adaptation of the "German Christians" was followed by the resistance of the "Professing Church." So far as the Catholic church is concerned, Nazi successes were certainly more limited. But one development affected both churches and is therefore of particular interest in our context: National Socialism made disinterest in, and even hostility to the churches socially acceptable in Germany. Before 1933, the "dissident" was recognized only in the subculture of the labor movement; but the "God believer" (a secularized non-Christian type promoted by the Nazis) became a creature clearly approved by the state. In this way more than by direct influence on the churches, that is, by inroads on religious traditionalism rather than the politicization of religious institutions, the Nazis won their successes in their struggle against the churches.

The most striking and consequential testimony to the National Socialist's struggle against traditional loyalties—and to the contradiction of ideology and practice—can probably be found in terms of the position of the family. There is no shortage of Nazi declarations in praise of the family and its crucial social significance. But in reality, the Nazis' family policies all amounted to the systematic reduction of the functions of the family to the one overwhelming task of reproduction. Where the family could not fulfill this task, or not fulfill it sufficiently by ruling standards, the masters of the regime quite consistently did not care about the institution; whether the "spring of life" (*Lebensborn*) and state-supported promiscuity for demographic purposes existed or not, there can be little doubt that the rights of the family ended where it failed to meet its alleged obligations, and this meant a reduction of its right to nearly nothing.

These obligations were conceived entirely in terms of a public aspect totally alien to the family itself. They had little to do with promoting cohesion within the family, to say nothing of the happiness of men, but were derived from goals like the military strength of the nation, which are far removed from the individual and his rights. For that reason also the rulers of National Socialist Germany took from the family the task that above all documents the prevalence of private virtues: the education of children.

National Socialist school policies, and even more strongly the significance of obligatory membership in the Hitler Youth for all children from ten years of age, involved an increasing and deliberate restriction of familial rights and tasks. The Hitler Youth emphasized even among the ten-year-olds independence from, and indeed exploiting the age-old antagonism of generations—hostility toward their parents. Total power involves at least the intention of permanent control of every person by the rulers and their organizations. Such control presupposes the extrication of people from all social spheres that are removed from the grasp of public agencies. In this sense, the family was an obstacle on the path to the establishment of total power. In this sense, the educational policies of the Nazis promoted public values—if in the form of the public vices of uniformed demonstrations, the denunciation of friends, and unquestioned activities of other kinds.

Thus the role of the *Volksgenosse* grew in substance all the time. Many other memberships and loyalties were swallowed by this equal and public role. The *Volksgenosse* participated in public affairs without influencing them; the effect of his appearance was at best a demonstration of somebody else's power; yet he had to participate because this alone enabled the powerful to control his activity as they had to. This meant, of course, that the fellow and the friend, the Christian, and the son or father, and many others had to yield their claims to the *Volksgenosse*. In addition to their immediate purposes, policies of this kind satisfied the wishes of youth; its universal aversion to ascribed loyalties appeared sanctioned by the state, and in this way the leaders of the future were tied to the leaders of the present. The *Volksgenosse* was the figurehead of the National Socialist revolution.

But we have to stop here in our account of the social history of this role; for its victory was by no means absolute. Like every revolution in history, the National Socialist revolution of modernity did not remain undisputed. This is evident in the fact that, for example, many a corner of society was never reached by the process of "co-ordination." The attitude of "inner emigration," which many German intellectuals displayed, would have been as impossible in a perfect totalitarian state as in a perfect modern society. Nevertheless not only intellectuals succeeded in the "inner emigration." Many a highly regarded and declaredly anti-Nazi politician of the Weimar Republic survived nearly unmolested until July 20, 1944, and occasionally even to the end of the war. The hold of state and party on the family did not extend into every family by any means. The churches managed in many places to avoid "co-ordination" altogether. Despite government-sponsored mobility, regional ties frequently remained as intact as patterns of social stratification. Schools and universities, courts and prisons, large sectors of the army and of the economy, and many private organizations maintained a certain autonomy. Even in 1938, National Socialist Germany bore not only the features of totalitarianism, but equally pronouncedly authoritarian traits, among which the unprotesting non-participation of many must also be counted. While "co-ordination" was the dominant tendency, it was clearly not generally realized before the beginning of the wars of conquest.

To the unplanned resistance against the social concomitants of the totalitarian seizure of power, more or less open active opposition against the regime was soon added. This opposition is generally described as "resistance." In terms of our thesis, the German resistance must indeed be understood as largely a reaction; in this we encounter one of the most difficult and tragic chapters of recent German history. If it is true that, in order to establish its total rule, the Nazi regime had to bring about a social revolution, then resistance against the regime may be described as counterrevolutionary. Given the premise, the substance of resistance is the attempt to resurrect the prerevolutionary state. Where the National Socialist revolution promoted, however reluctantly, modernity, the counterrevolution aimed at the conservation of traditional ties to family and class, region and religion. While the social revolution of National Socialism was an instrument in the establishment of totalitarian forms, by the same token it had to create the basis of liberal modernity; the counter-revolution on the other hand can be understood only as a revolt of tradition, and thus of illiberalism and of the authoritarianism of a surviving past.

Whoever, as a German, considers this phase of German history, cannot but envy a people that can despise its ancien régime and praise its revolution. For the perversions of German history are such that even the liberal has to praise the ancien régime because revolution fell upon it in such a devilish form, and the counterrevolution was so humane. German resistance against Hitler is a leaf of fame in German history; but it is not a step on the path of German society toward the constitution of liberty. Worse still, it was Hitler who effected those transformations of German society that make the constitution of liberty possible, while the resistance against his regime acted in the name of a social tradition that could provide a basis only for authoritarian rule. Nowhere did morality and liberalism part company as visibly as in Germany; nowhere is it therefore as difficult to desire the free and the good society at the same time.

It soon became evident that the alliance of National Socialists and conservatives, which destroyed the Weimar Republic, was plainly a mistake. Much as Freisler would praise the National Socialist state as a rule of a new type, the adherents of the traditional rule of law were not pacified by such transparent sophistry. Among the supporters of the institutions subjected to "co-ordination," the universal interest in maintaining the status quo was added to moral indignation. Both, however, moral indignation and resistance to all threats to vested interests, were first aroused among those conservatively inclined groups that had originally joined forces with the Nazis to destroy the Weimar Republic. From the point of view of the new rulers, these conservative groups clearly had to appear as a major threat even after the alliance was concluded. Nobility and higher bureaucracy, military leaders and some lawyers, as well as several other groups were, after all, the survivals of the society of Imperial Germany. They embodied the very traditionalism in German society that the Nazis had to destroy if they wanted to generalize their power. It was a rather late insight therefore if Ulrich von Hassell noted in his diary in 1944 that the Nazis intended to push from their position, and indeed exterminate physically "nobility and the educated classes" (cf. 93). In fact, this was the necessary policy of the party from the first day of its rule, because its hope of survival lay in the total and brutal modernization of German society.

The German resistance movement comprised many groups; but with the one exception of the Communists—remarkably weak as they were as a force of resistance—they can all be described as deliberate or unintentional defenders of the ancien régime. This claim is not refuted by the alliance of the military with the Social Democrats in preparing July 20, 1944. The explicit goals of this alliance were largely negative; understandably, they consisted in the abolition of the Nazi regime and the end of the war. In their generally vague positive conceptions, resistance groups differed greatly; even within the military, and equally within the Social Democratic Party, there were considerable disagreements. But at least by implication, if not by explicit declaration, the intention was common to all to re-establish many of the values and institutions that had shaped the Weimar period and that provide a basis for an authoritarian rather than a liberal society. The question must even be raised whether the resistance groups of July 20 did not deliberately envisage an authoritarian form of government at least for the period immediately after the success of their revolt. In view of our earlier analyses, notably that of the wisespread aversion to social conflict, the union of the military with the Social Democrats appears indeed neither surprising nor accidental in this context. It is the open continuation of a tacit coalition that had its origin in Imperial Germany.

July 20, 1944, described the tragic conclusion of the social revolution brought about by the National Socialist regime in Germany. It was clear after this that German society could never return to the structures of Imperial times. So far as their human agents are concerned, it is relevant to note that after many young members of the nobility had been killed in action during the early years of the war, German nobility lost its best representatives after July 20. Much the same may be said, at least with respect to the effects of July 20, for leading Social Democrats, and for bourgeois politicians as well. July 20 and the persecutions resulting from its failure mark the end of German political elite. Along with its human basis, the reality of an idea passed away—an idea that is symbolized for many by the name of Prussia. Prussian discipline, lawfulness, morality, but Prussian illiberalism as well, the honest directness but also the authoritarianism of Prussian tradition, the humanity but also the deliberate minority of the many in the political landscape of the Prussian tradition—all this found its last triumph on July 20, 1944. Moral values, and frequently their reality in the German past, were held up against the arbitrariness of the Nazis; the old regime was indeed a morally better world, but its revolt failed and the brutal path to modernity took its further course.

There are, to be sure, many causes of the failure of the revolt of July 20. Furthermore, nothing is further from my intention than to justify, even by innuendo, this failure. Even the liberal was forced to long for the pleasure of an authoritarian rule of law in the face of the terrors of National Socialism. But it cannot be denied that the direction of the social development the Nazis set in motion told against the politics of German resistance. This may also well be a major reason why the conclusion is unavoidable that National Socialist rule in Germany was legitimate, at least in the sense of factually recognized validity. In so far as the absence of widespread protest is by itself a testimony to legitimacy, this was clearly the case; the invisible and ineffectual forms of private protest that many claimed for themselves after the war were, in fact, subservient ways of agreement. Further than that, there was in all phases of National Socialist rule the more or less silent agreement among the large majority of men that is expressed in emergency situations as readiness to defend the regime.

We have tried earlier to answer the first of three questions about National Socialism: How was January 30, 1933, possible? Now the second of our questions becomes relevant: How was the nearly complete absence of resistance, thus the evident acceptance of the National Socialist regime by the population possible? This question, too, we can now answer, although in doing so it seems proper to differentiate between the prewar period and the war period.

In respect to the structure of society, the Weimar Republic marked a phase of hardly bearable stagnation. Moving to and fro between old regime and modernity, people found no point of orientation for their behavior; the parties with whom they sought such points of orientation usually disappointed them. In that sense the mere fact that something happened under the new rulers seemed a relief. That this involved rigid

forms of organization, strengthened the new feeling of security, although it was precisely this basis of security that
was precarious and would hardly have withstood a longer
period of peace. If the push into modernity meant a painful loss for many, others saw primarily the gain; Karl Mannheim has pointed out the special relevance of youth for the
legitimacy of National Socialist rule, which we have discussed before. If one adds that the unambiguous departure
from the uncertainties of the past was combined with a period
of economic prosperity, the legitimacy of the Nazi regime
can hardly come as a surprise. Indeed, it is almost surprising that the leaders of the regime met with any resistance at
all.

Ernst Nolte suggests that the absence of resistance to the
National Socialists must be explained above all by their
policy of "war in peace" (cf. 165). The permanent invocation of a national state of emergency may indeed lead to sus-
pending all internal divisions, so that even personal enemies
find solidarity together. There can be little doubt that their
noisy nationalism rendered a useful service to the Nazis in
this respect. But the social psychological motive that emerges
here dominated the period of the war itself much more clearly.
It was only then that absolute "co-ordination" turned from
program to reality; during the war, even the islands of inner
emigration were threatened. If resistance nevertheless did not
grow beyond all limits, this was clearly due to the handicap
of legitimacy enjoyed by every wartime government. On the
other hand, the fact that even in wartime resistance grew to
a revolt documents the precarious power position of totalitarian leaders.

All this amounts to the conclusion that National Socialism
was not merely an episode. It was not a work of seduction
by a small clique, but, by its toleration, a German phenomenon. We have to remember, of course, that factual legitimacy
does not establish moral legitimacy; what works, does not
have to be good. Our third question, how the National Socialist crimes were possible, remains unanswered, unless our
observations about humanitarianism and inhumanity in Germany are taken for an answer. Morally, the road to modernity
could hardly assume more brutal and inhuman traits than it
did in Germany.

What remains of the social revolution of National Socialism? If our thesis is correct, that is, if National Socialism was

not an historical episode but the German revolution, it must have left its traces in the subsequent phase. This is indeed the case, although these traces are obscured by that other heritage of Nazi rule, which results from total defeat. The starting points of German social development after the war consisted first of all in a number of simple, if consequential facts. By war damage and war consequences Germany's economy was thrown back to an almost pre-industrial state. By the expulsion of millions of people from the eastern territories, economy and society in Germany were faced with extraordinary additional tasks. The disappearance of the entire National Socialist leadership elite made it necessary to form a new political class. The subdivision of the country into zones of occupation and the enmity of the occupation powers, which soon became apparent, imposed many additional limitations on the situation from which Germany took off. Even a sociologically informed account of German postwar development has to start with these initial conditions, and we shall do so. But by way of summarizing this chapter, there is the more general and possibly more important question: Which was the path prescribed to German society after the war in respect to the task of mastering the problems mentioned? Which path was precluded for it? In answering these questions, the lasting result of the social revolution of National Socialist Germany becomes evident.

German society remained illiberal in its structure and authoritarian in its constitution throughout the decades of industrialization. Although many of the bases of the absurd yet effective mixtures of old and new in the politics and society of Imperial Germany had gone in 1918, the Weimar Republic departed only very partially and anxiously from the old patterns. In times of crisis the nostalgia for past experiences grew. The mistaken alliance of conservative and National Socialist opponents of parliamentary democracy in 1933 was founded on this nostalgia; but soon after the seizure of power its false assumptions became clear. In order to maintain their power, the National Socialists had to turn against all traces of the social order that provided the basis for authoritarian rule. They destroyed inherited loyalties wherever they could; they co-ordinated all traditional institutions equipped with a life of their own; they generalized the social role of the *Volksgenosse* as far as they could.

Despite the indescribable ruthlessness with which the

process took place, they did not succeed wholly. There remained corners of tradition, sources of resistance and counterrevolution. But the push into modernity succeeded sufficiently to remove the social basis for future authoritarian governments along traditional German lines. National Socialism has finally abolished the German past as it was embodied in Imperial Germany. What came after it was free of the mortgage that burdened the Weimar Republic at its beginning, thanks to the suspended revolution. There could be no return from the revolution of National Socialist times.

For the direction of postwar development itself, this by no means tells the whole story. The National Socialists demonstrated the ambiguity of modernity. Where the *Volksgenosse* prevails, the subject cannot return; this is his specifically modern face. But he may be followed by the citizen as well as the comrade, and perhaps there are other, still unknown social figures of modernity with similar problems. This is why the pathology of democracy in Germany is not completed even with the brutal revolution of the Nazi *Reich*.

26. THE TWO GERMANIES: THE GERMAN DEMOCRATIC REPUBLIC

Why did the constitution of liberty fare so badly in German society? If this is the German Question, modern German history may be understood as a chain of diverse answers to this question, all of which refer to defects in the social infrastructure of politics.

Imperial Germany brought about hitherto unknown faults of industrial and preindustrial structures which are impermissible to the present day by the standards of all accepted theories; as a result, an authoritarian political constitution managed to assimilate the new conditions of an industrial civilization. The Republic of Weimar had lost the authority that belongs to this constitution; at the same time, it delayed the revolution that might have opened its society to more liberal patterns. The achievement was not unlike that of Sisyphus, for it did not prevent the rock from rolling; in the end, revolution came after all. But revolution now showed its ugliest face; modernity entered Germany in its totalitarian dress and thus forbade the constitution of liberty once again. This was the most costly answer of German society so far to its ever more pressing question; eventually, it led to the challenges of total defeat in May 1945.

Occasionally the sociologist finds himself in the role of the surgeon or, perhaps, the pathologist of society: he is liable to become a professional cynic. It may be important, therefore, to emphasize that the following account is not a product of cynicism. I am not forgetting the human beings who are the actors, as well as the victims, of developments that are here dissected with almost clinical detachment. Rather, the appearance of cynicism serves to make the unbearable bearable: the suffering the reality of German history has brought to all too many men. With this reservation, Germany's condition in 1945 may be described as one of exciting social challenges.

How could German society master its second industrialization? Whom would it choose as its new leaders? On which values would it orient its future? Where would it seek its new centers? These are some of the major questions, besides which many smaller ones must not be forgotten: How would German society cope with its millions of refugees? How would it cope with its own past? What and how much would it assimilate from its occupation powers? And the answers to all these questions had to be given in the context defined by the conditions National Socialism had left behind for German society. Socially, this meant that a return to the authoritarian structures of the past was no longer possible; politically, the challenges of 1945 at least implied the impossibility of returning to a National Socialist regime. For these reasons, no name is as misleading for subsequent developments as that of "reconstruction." Whatever happened had to be a new construction —a new answer to the old question of democracy in Germany.

This is the starting point of a development that makes it even more interesting for the sociologist, but even more painful for the people involved, to follow Germany's postwar history: the division of the country. After 1945, German society gave not one, but two answers to the challenges of defeat. However great the differences between the parts of Germany may have been before 1945, there can be little doubt that these were differences within one society. After 1945, this one society with its one, illiberal tradition fell apart by the sociological accident of increasing enmity between its occupation powers. It fell into more than two parts; in a more detailed account it would be worth exploring the differences between regions occupied by British, American, and French forces and, more particularly, those between the Saarland and the remainder of the Federal Republic in terms of the decisions of the immediate postwar period. But today the significant dividing line runs along the former Iron Curtain, which nowadays keeps almost only the two Germanies apart. Thus, political boundary made it possible that one and the same country responded in two widely divergent ways to the same challenges.

I know of no historical example for a political and social experiment of similar dimensions—and for the comparably impressive result of such a test. For while the two Germanies may still debate the academic or, rather, diplomatic question of whether they are two states, they have already become two societies. The proof of this thesis leads us to new paradoxes of German social structure.

The spring of hope was brief for the few surviving liberals in the eastern part of what remained as Germany in 1945. It hardly lasted to the summer, and certainly not to the winter of that year. Around the turn of the years 1945/1946 it was evident to nearly everyone living in the then Soviet zone of occupation that the brief interval in which the reins of power had been held more loosely was to be followed by a development that, for many people, differed little from the National Socialist past.

If anything, this development documented how incomplete the National Socialist revolution of modernity had remained. The East German revolution went further. It attacked the same survivals of a closed past; but it did not stop short of any one of them. This time, the last farm, the last family, the last church community was drawn into the process. The success of such changes was and is remarkable. The social structures of agriculture are often an embodiment-of tradition, so that the East German land reform soon after the war may be regarded as the signal of the systematic destruction of the past. Land reform and resettlement were followed later by the creation of agricultural production co-operatives, to which even small peasants had to yield their property. The number of self-employed in agriculture declined rapidly; and the new property structure brought about entirely novel economic patterns. At the same time, the rights and immunities of the family were, in both town and country, reduced greatly even by comparison to National Socialist Germany. A much larger part of the education of children was given over to public institutions; today, almost two thirds of all three- to six-year-olds are being looked after in public nursery schools.

Even before the schools, the process of "co-ordination" for the sake of controlling everybody at all times and thus establishing total power had reached the ancient bastions of region and religion. Once again the states (*Länder*), revived but briefly after the war, disappeared in the DDR; the new central administration shows no respect for the autonomy of local communities. The church again has to exist in a world in which it accords with the ruling values to be secularized, indeed to prefer the state ceremony of "consecration of youth" to confirmation by the church.

Such examples might be amplified. They show that the *Volksgenosse* has been replaced by the comrade, the co-ordinated man whose public role absorbs ever new traditional roles. By contrast to National Socialist Germany, there are hardly any islands of tradition left in the DDR. But then, the social revolution of National Socialism was continued quite deliberately here. Already its result may be described as the total modernization of the country, that is, the general transformation of social positions that used to be quasi-ascribed into positions that the individual may in principle acquire for himself. While a few faithful churchgoers, some old people, the rare self-employed who have so far been forgotten by successive waves of nationalization may for a while resist the onslaught of co-ordination, the comrade has already won the day, and the new society is complete.

To realize what this means, we will have to apply to the German Democratic Republic and its society the four sets of factors we have used throughout as our tools of the analysis of democracy in Germany. The first of these factors, equality of citizenship rights, we are already discussing. The very expression sounds nonsensical in a country in which the equal subject, the comrade, has taken the place of the citizen. But it would be too easy by far simply to mourn people's lack of rights in the DDR. In fact, social development in Eastern Germany after the war is characterized by a double tendency. While the formal rights of citizenship shrank to a new low, the social context of these rights was, at the same time, developed to an extent unheard-of in German history. In the Weimar Republic the role of the citizen was formally guaranteed to all, but this offer was undermined by the absence of the social preconditions of its realization. In the DDR the preconditions are present, but the realization is made impossible by numerous formal restrictions on the citizenship rights that are part and parcel of the constitution of liberty. De facto, there is no universal, equal, free, and secret suffrage, no liberty of the person and of political activity, no equality before the law; but there is a society that would enable its members to make effective use of these liberties, if only they had them. Once again modernity shows its Janus face.

It is a fact of great importance that the inclusive process of social co-ordination in East Germany has involved the realization of that equality that is a precondition of effective citizenship rights; all the more since it probably constitutes the hard core of East German social changes, which can never be undone.

The process may be described on three levels. On the one

hand, civic equality includes, as we have seen, certain social rights apart from legal and political ones. These social rights comprise in particular protection in conditions of indigence, old age, and sickness, a minimum income, an equal minimum of medical treatment, and similar rights. By virtue of its welfare-state tradition, such rights have a long history in Germany; but the system of social security, too, has been greatly expanded in the DDR. A second level of social equality concerns educational opportunity. Here above all German society in the DDR has undergone profound changes. By diverse state measures which were in part—as the "50 per cent clause" by which all secondary schools were compelled to have at least 50 per cent workers' and peasants' children in every class—as absurd as they were effective, the DDR has succeeded in abolishing the inherited social stratification of educational opportunity. In 1963, more than one third of all college and university students, and one half of all students in technical colleges were children of workers in the DDR. This change tells already in the composition of occupational groups; the recruitment of professors and judges, generals and managers differs radically in the DDR from the Federal Republic. The success of these measures presupposes changes on the third and most important level of social equality, that of the traditional ties of men. By abolishing all institutions that serve to sanctify tradition, the rulers of the DDR have ruthlessly torn people out of their inherited loyalties and forced them into an equal basic status, which frequently enough contradicted their own wishes and intentions.

The political purpose of these developments is evident. For a regime bent on the establishment of total power, islands of tradition are invariably islands of resistance as well. But this open purpose of co-ordination must not deceive us about its lasting and politically quite ambiguous effects. If one interprets modernity as we have done throughout, the society of the DDR is the first modern society on German soil. In it the French Revolution has been led to its horrid extreme, unimagined as such even by the conservatives of 1789. People participate in the social and political process almost entirely as public creatures, if as comrades rather than citizens. The society of inherited status has largely given way to a society of achieved status, if one that measures achievement by curious standards. A number of questions must be raised here: Can one really want this modernity? Does it not mean the end of all human richness, indeed all freedom? We have given our answer to these questions. Whoever wants the constitution of liberty must want modernity, even if he acquires with it the very immediate danger of totalitarianism. But one can certainly answer these questions very differently too, and German history makes different answers very likely.

The social core of the constitution of liberty—to turn to our second factor—consists of the institutional recognition of social conflict in all sectors of society. It is self-evident that a party that stakes a claim for total power is not capable of such recognition, even though this documents the weakness of its political principle. Outside a narrow range defined by the state, political antagonisms are forbidden in the DDR. The same holds for industrial conflict, as it does mutatis mutandis for strife in the other areas of society. This is, after all, what we mean when we speak of totalitarian power, that one group monopolizes all decisions and claims for itself the ability to make these decisions correctly, and in any case finally. Contradiction is suppressed; the rulers rule absolutely.

However, we have also seen that in the long run the suppression of conflict cannot succeed. Social conflict is a reality that does not bow to the dictate of even the most powerful state party. In fact, the history of the DDR may be a history of internal conflicts seeking modes of expression. Where the open clash of solidary groups is forbidden, the rising energies of opposition find their expression in other ways. One of these was, up to the building of the Berlin Wall on August 13, 1961, escape. Antagonism based on internal social conditions was expressed in thousands of individual decisions to leave the country. The fever curve of refugees from the DDR since its establishment in September 1949 is an impressive document of the failure of totalitarian rule: in no month since this date did less than 7000 people leave the country, in most months the number of refugees was more than 15,000, in some more than 30,000. Besides escape, there were both more violent and less visible unplanned patterns of or substitutes for conflict. It suffices to call to mind the revolts of June 17, 1953, on the one hand, and the desperate retreat to an ever more threatened privacy by many, on the other.

But the deviation of social conflict into apparently individual decisions could not at any time suffice to domesticate the rising energies of resistance against those in power; after the building of the Berlin Wall this became fully impossible.

Like any totalitarian regime, the government of the DDR has therefore evolved a number of techniques and institutions that serve to cement its rule by canalizing conflict. Indeed, from one point of view, the state party itself may be regarded as a gigantic opinion research institute, which passes on information not only from the top downwards, but upwards as well. There are in the party, as in the various sectors of the society and the economy, ritualized forms of conflict that at times resemble even the more liberal patterns of disputes or parliamentary debate. Since these expressions of conflict are deliberately kept secret from the non-participant public, we do not know very much about their working; but it may be assumed that they play a considerable part in the social fabric of the DDR.

One of the decisive mechanisms of canalizing conflict in the DDR is the extraordinary development of the principle of steered discussion. In all their social contexts, Germans in the DDR are permanently asked to discuss matters: in school and work, army and party, mass organizations and neighborhood. These discussions are not free, nor do they have a recognizable relation to the decisions that are at issue. Nevertheless the fact that they have to take part leads many more people to express their opinions about many more things than they do in free countries, and these opinions may often be quite controversial. Targets of production, methods of housing construction, armament techniques, a new line of the party ideology, and above all a thousand apparent details of everyday life are persistently being discussed and thus provide opportunities to express the antagonisms that are inevitably present. For the political leaders this means simultaneously a source of information, a chance of control, and a relatively harmless expression of opposition. But the ubiquity of discussion in the DDR has, like the process of coordination in the Third Reich, a meaning that transcends the regime. It may be described as training in conflict, in an attitude that might bring to life social and political strife under more liberal conditions. It is striking to see how the other side of education for total dependence in the DDR is always the education for autonomy.

If it is true that conflict cannot be suppressed forever, the patterns and substitutes for its regulation in the DDR are also an index of the stability of the regime. The more successfully conflicts are absorbed and canalized, the more stable is the regime; the less this succeeds, the greater is the danger of its destruction by internal resistance and, ultimately, revolution. In this sense, the open border in Berlin was a stabilizing factor of the political rule of the Socialist Unity Party; and since its closure in 1961, it has had to be replaced systematically by inner reforms. There are many reasons, including the presence of patterns of conflict regulation, why the stability of the regime in the DDR must not be underestimated; but it follows from the very principle of suppressing opposition that this stability remains nevertheless precarious. We will return to this question when we come to examine whether the social changes of the DDR are of a lasting nature and where their political significance lies.

In terms of the four factors of our sociological theory of politics, the deepest visible changes of the DDR can unquestionably be observed in respect to the nature of the political class. Here postwar development in East Germany may be described as a systematic process of the formation of a leading stratum that is reliable in terms of the claim for disputed power. This has been at the same time a process of the emergence of a monopoly, the individual steps of which look like a textbook example of usurpation.

The very fact that the reconstruction of society in the East of Germany began in 1945 with the creation of a new political elite was a pointer to future developments. The substance of these developments might have seemed uncertain in the early stages, when the new political elite was still relatively heterogeneous; Communist, Social Democratic, and bourgeois parties existed side by side. But it was soon apparent that the radicals had merely overestimated the hour; heterogeneity was only a mistake on the part of the Soviet occupation power and the German Communists. For when it became evident that they would not succeed in copying the 1933 pattern of legal revolution, the planned revolution began. Its first steps consisted in the unification of the political class. After the enforced fusion of Communists and Social Democrats in 1946, the newly founded Socialist Unity Party turned to the suppression of the bourgeois parties. This process was supplemented by the creation of a number of satellite parties designed to mobilize hitherto undecided citizens. As a result, within less than five years a leadership group emerged whose inevitable internal diversity remained ineffectual in the face of the clear and undisputed claim of the Socialist Unity Party, and within it of the former Communists, for hegemony.

But unification of the political elite was merely the first step in a process that eventually brought about a new political class in the DDR. The second step was more difficult and more consequential; it led to the gradual fusion of elites from all sectors of society with the leadership of the party, or, where this did not succeed, to the subordination of all others to the party elite. Nationalization of the economy and its administration by state functionaries, politicization of the new army, reconstruction of the entire educational system, the legal system, the administration were some of the stages on this road. Only the church elites have managed to the present day to resist to some extent the monopolistic claims of the new political class. On the whole, the second step in creating a new elite succeeded in its authors' terms surprisingly quickly.

The result is a leading stratum whose properties and values today determine the picture of society in the DDR. In its social composition and orientation, the stratum has almost nothing in common with its historical predecessors or with the precarious political class of the Federal Republic. Almost without exception, it consists of new people. That most of them owe their elevated position to the regime they represent, adds to their political uniformity and holds them even to strictly unacceptable changes of ideological party lines.

Yet despite all communities of political orientation, and even of origin and schooling, no establishment of social form corresponds to the uniformity of political attitude. The DDR cannot afford an established elite any more than other totalitarian countries. As soon as concern about one's own position and the external and enforced, abstract cohesion of the elite is replaced by closer ties and communities, totalitarian rule loses its horror and is transformed into quasi-authoritarian patterns; as such it becomes milder, thus harder to defend and more threatened. Possibly there are such tendencies in the DDR; already, the "50 per cent clause" has been dropped in favor of children of the "intelligentsia," that is, the new state-supporting stratum; but even so the ability of members of the East German political class to rely on a lasting, indeed inheritable place at the top is still small.

Elites—or so German history would suggest—come and go. Especially if they are highly politicized and the position of their members depends on the survival of the regime, their own chance of survival in any kind of change is small. It is tempting to suggest, therefore, that the transformations at the top of East German society are but incidental and without lasting significance. While there are reasons for this suggestion, it is certainly not the whole truth. In the DDR as in every modern society, there are indispensable elites whose technical qualifications would guarantee them a place at the top under nearly all political conditions. Moreover, while the "reliable" core of the political class of the DDR would certainly be threatened by any change toward greater liberalism, it would be wrong to underestimate the lasting effect of its values: a mentality of upward mobility and achievement, confidence in the state, in plan and not market rationality, thus a modern illiberalism.

Under all conditions, the relation between elites and the ruling values of society is especially close. So far we have not spoken of the ideology of Marxism-Leninism and its variations. There was a reason for such abstinence. This ideology is much more interesting for the general staff of psychological warfare than it is for the sociologist. To be sure, the ideology has certain social consequences. It provides stereotypes by which people can, if not explain, then at least express unexplained processes in their own world as well as in that of others. Temporarily, the ideology may help to master internal contradictions as a consolation of philosophy in the face of a reality of suppression. It serves rival elite groups as a secret language of conflict. It creates a pseudoworld of problems that one can discuss forever without changing anything or threatening any real institution. However, this is also the reason why we shall continue to neglect the ideology of the DDR. Its relation to reality is indirect and faint, and where it acquires a real significance, it is as well to describe this without reference to the stereotypes of ideology.

One such significance may be found in the fact that there is an ideology at all that is supposed to be binding for all and in fact provides the central subject of discussion. The effect of this condition is considerable. Even political refugees from the DDR tend to sense a vacuum after a while where East German society had offered them a coherent ideology, at least as an object of criticism and hate. If one considers the often-asked question, "Does the West have an idea?" one is tempted to suspect that this vacuum is not only sensed by refugees from totalitarian countries, but that life in a society without a coherent and binding ideology, that is, life in a free society, makes any people feel uneasy under any circumstances. An ideology provides a stable point of orientation that allows the individual to regard himself as being in harmony or in disharmony with what is, and therefore saves him the strain of accepting the world as an open field into which he has placed his own designs.

Probably the substance of its ideology has its lasting significance for East German society too, if we free it of its stereotyped language. This would seem to be especially true of the principle of plan rationality, that is, a profound distrust of the strength of decentralized, autonomous agencies. Brecht was quite right in his description of the circle of plans; whoever begins to make them will tend to improve on a bad plan by a better one, but still a plan. Even marketlike mechanisms in the economy as they are gradually introduced through the back door seem to have little effect on the basic —and by no means merely official—attitude, which regards all tasks of social policy as tasks of substantive and detailed planning. This has many preconditions and consequences, among which the belief in the availability of certainty and the search for the expert planner are politically virulent. On this basis, a picture of order emerges, which involves denouncing all undirected structures as disorder. The validity of such values in the DDR helps to support the features of heteronomy and fear in the behavior of its people.

There is a third aspect of the changes of German values in the DDR that must not be overlooked in our context. This concerns the relation of private and public virtues. We have seen that withdrawal to one's private existence constitutes one form of resistance against the ruling regime. However, this withdrawal is seriously possible only for a few, and for all to a decreasing extent. Characteristically, a large part of the life of people in the DDR has to take place in public. To make sure of this, numerous patterns have been developed, among which, apart from permanent discussions, membership in organizations of many kinds is outstanding. It is difficult to speak of virtues in view of a public that is itself organized in a planlike manner and that serves to control the individual rather than to enable him to develop freely. But it is certain that there is little of the traditional German emphasis on private virtues left in the DDR, not only in the ruling values but also in the factual behavior of men. The institutional basis of this change leads us back to our first set of factors and to the process of co-ordination. It corresponds to the progress of public virtues or vices that the family has yielded much of its former significance to the educational institutions, and that people are pulled out of areas of private existence uncontrolled by the state as early and as thoroughly as possible.

The basic figure of change that characterizes the first two decades of East German society recurs in all four sets of factors. Its formulation provides a starting point for examining the questions of how stable these changes are and what prognosis they permit for the constitution of liberty in the DDR. Changes in the social context of political decision have far removed the German society of the DDR from its historical predecessors. Two types of layers of change may be distinguished in every field. On the one hand, the radical revolution of modernity has been completed. The structures that emerged have, in negative terms, drawn the final line under a process that led to the abolition of the social conditions of traditional authoritarianism, while in positive terms they have liberated all men equally from unwanted fetters of heritage and custom. The syndrome of equal opportunities, permanent discussion, privilege-free access to elite positions, and pronounced publicness of life is characteristic here.

On the other hand and simultaneously, however, all these changes concerning the form of social and political participation have been associated with a substance that subordinates them to the establishment of total power. Equality in the DDR is an equality of dependent comrades, not of adult citizens; discussion stops short of its liberal meaning, of decision; the privilege-free elite is a monopolistic political class; public values are dominated in substance by the claims of certainty and of the plan. It is easy to speak here of a perversion of modernity; in fact we are encountering merely one of two political consequences of the same process. Modern form with totalitarian substance—this is the principle of the changes in East German society.

Some may wonder whether we have not overestimated these changes here. It is popular to speak of the Soviet bayonets on which the survival of the DDR uncertainly rests; and many would like to believe that a change of political regime would make everything that has happened since 1945 disappear like a spook. However, this is a naïve and dangerous belief. What has happened in the DDR is more than the substitution of one leadership clique for another, which owes its position to the grace of alien powers. In fact, a society with its own peculiar structure has emerged. To be sure, the emergence of two Germanies after the war has taught us how quickly and deeply—and in what different directions—societies may change under the influence of external and internal forces. Thus it is quite possible, indeed probable, that East German society would undergo profound changes again if it were joined with the Federal Republic by free choice of the people, or merely developed a more liberal political system by itself. It is nevertheless possible to distinguish with some confidence sectors of society that are likely to be affected by such changes from others for which this is less true.

Examples provide a beginning. It is more likely that the leadership groups of the SED would disappear than that working-class children would lose their educational opportunities. It is more likely that a part, even a considerable part of nationalized industry would return to private hands than that social life in the country would once again assume its traditional closedness. It is more likely that people would abandon their confidence in great plans than that they would give up the chance of discussion.

Such statements might be extrapolated to a principle, which might look like this: Changes in the German society of the DDR are the more lasting and stable the more they involve the social form of modernity; they are the weaker and more threatened the more they concern the totalitarian substance.

Historical experiences as well as general considerations may be adduced in support of this thesis. Everywhere the revolution of modernity has produced its counterrevolution. Occasionally this counterrevolution has indeed taken societies a few steps back. But the journey back to the ancien régime has never lasted very long. On the other hand, the basis of equal publicness has given rise to varied structures and values, and these constitute one of the central issues of controversy in the modern world. They provide the substance of the antagonism of parties and open up at least two significantly different directions of development, both of which have been chosen by German societies after the war. To this extent the apparent optimism of the thesis developed here for the DDR must not be misunderstood. The greater precariousness of the totalitarian substance of many structures and values in East German society holds analogously for the liberal substance of these structures in the West as well; in both cases, what we have called substance is the unsteady superstructure of modernity.

But are the changes implied here at all probable? There is, of course, a basic reservation for any sociological analysis, including that of the two Germanies. External political and military interventions may change the context of societies overnight. They would not invalidate the thesis developed here for the DDR; but whether these interventions will occur, cannot be derived from traditional sociological analysis. Barring the sociology of international relations, our question concerns the internal legitimacy and stability of the regime and its probable future development; and here there are certain cues of prediction. Political communities organized in a plan-rational manner are under all conditions more strongly exposed to crises of legitimacy than those organized in market-rational ways. Whoever claims certainty may err much more consequentially than he who relies on government by conflict all along; whoever suppresses conflict has to be prepared for surprises. With this general reservation, however, it would appear that today the regime of the DDR is quite legitimate in terms of the assent, or at least the absence of active dissent, on the part of its citizens. This is also meant to be a statement about the stability of the political regime and of the social conditions supported by it.

In the eastern part of Germany the revolution of modernity has been nearly completed. It demanded extremely harsh, unpopular, and in this sense dangerous measures on the part of the ruling groups. Since more recent international developments have tended to expand the range of possible decisions somewhat for the regime, there is reason to believe that in the foreseeable future—and in the erratic form characteristic of tendentially totalitarian constitutions—changes are imminent in the area we have described as the unsteady superstructure of modernity.

However, these changes are very imprecisely described by the notion of "liberalization." They may well increase the chances of movement and participation for people and in that sense give more liberty. But this liberty has little to do with liberalism. There is reason to believe that the rulers of the regime will, if only out of the vested interest of their own survival, continue to replace the plan rationality of their control by marketlike forms of organization and seek, in the same connection, new and more subtle forms of canalizing conflicts.

The People's Chamber may become more lively, the spectrum of opinions expressed in the press wider; there may be even more discussion in all places; the private sphere of life may be extended again and, not without a subtle relation to this, new types of privilege in respect to educational and other opportunities may emerge; possibly there is going to be a certain amount of tolerated antagonism in the economy; the partisan character of the cultural industry may be reduced. But however many measures of this kind one devises, they do not add up to the constitution of liberty. Modernity is too strongly joined with co-ordination, publicness with the plan, tolerated discussion with control, and the whole system of the alliance of modernity and totalitarianism with the position of ruling groups to make this prospect likely. Thus the German Democratic Republic adds another negative response to the other answers of history to the question of democracy in Germany.

27. THE TWO GERMANIES:
THE GERMAN FEDERAL REPUBLIC

If one compares Frankfurt and Leipzig, Düsseldorf and Karl-Marx-Stadt, even East and West Berlin today, one is unlikely to conclude that these cities are all situated in the same country. Even apart from the most external, if by no means insignificant features, such as posters and street names, the number and shininess of cars, the quality and cut of people's clothes, there are visible, audible, recognizable differences of social worlds. The observation casts doubt on many easily formulated political demands, and it makes the sociologist wonder how such differences could emerge in but twenty years, for they constitute two entirely different answers to the same set of questions left by National Socialist Germany to its fragments. In any case, West Germany had to, and did, respond in its own way to the challenges to which East Germany gave its both modern and totalitarian or, better perhaps, plan-rational response.

Differences began with the way in which the two parts of Germany reacted to the social revolution of National Socialism. While in the East this revolution was continued and, if anything, accelerated and radicalized, certain developments in West Germany might be described as counterrevolutionary in this respect. As a reaction to the National Socialist revolution, but probably also as part of the search for reliable fixed points of social structure, West German society has chosen, in quite a few areas, the return to premodern structures. The narrowness and integrity of family ties was promoted by the state, even anchored in constitutions in the form of the parental prerogative. The *Länder* re-emerged and were equipped with greater rights than they had in the past; indeed a strong emphasis on the regional ties of men including the social acceptability of dialects is noticeable in the Federal Republic. Church membership with all its social implications found the interested support of many public agencies, so that the general tendency toward secularization was countered by a German tendency toward denominalization, which despite its improbability gained a surprising amount of ground.

It is very much part of the style of West German society to sing the song of the closed and narrow world, that is, to praise tiny village schools for their educational value, the traditional Gymnasium for its privileged position, to perpetuate an anachronistic country life by antiquated school primers and many millions of taxpayers' money subsidizing a world of yesterday, to devalue the hesitant move toward public values in the behavior of men. These are tendencies that have earned West German society the charge of "restoration" by its critics. But does this charge really hit the social changes of West German society after the war and their political potential?

If we begin the account of these changes once again with civic equality, one may be tempted at first sight to answer this question in the affirmative. In the Federal Republic, the realization of the equal basic status of all men stands in sharp contrast to the DDR. While in the East the social conditions of the role are present, but its legal and political potential is minimal, the Federal Republic recognizes the legal status of the citizen in its full range, but many of the social preconditions of its effective realization are lacking. Here the role that may be described as the epitome of modernity is once again —as before in the Weimar Republic—declaration rather than reality. We need merely summarize our analyses in this study to document this assertion.

So far as the legal status of the citizen is concerned, its establishment is remarkably comprehensive. There is general, equal, free, and secret suffrage; there is equality before the law. In the Federal Republic, the horizon of expectations associated with the citizen role has gained greatly in breadth by the new institution of justifiable basic rights. Thus it is no longer pure declaration if the Basic Law stipulates that the dignity of man is inviolable or that everybody has the right of free development of his personality, or that the rights of men and women are equal. These nice phrases have acquired immediate reality by the fact that a Federal Constitutional Court guards their application by the income-tax collector and the policeman, in political discussion and on the market place, indeed in military barracks and in prisons. Formally speaking, the citizen has stepped, in the Federal Republic, into the place of the *Volksgenosse*.

But we have also seen that this formal development constitutes but one side of modernity. It remains mute if it is not supported by substantive social changes. Such social changes, however, proceed extremely slowly in the Federal Republic. There is no political party that has made modernity the key-note of its program, and none that consistently works for it without saying so. Government policies in the fields of sub-sidies and social services are designed less to lay an effective basis for citizenship rights than to bring about a welfare state in the traditional sense. They continue to result in prevent-ing people from a modern rationality of choice by securing them forever at the place they happen to be: the peasant as peasant in a more and more retrograde agriculture, the miner as such in a declining trade, the refugee as refugee, and the old age pensioner as such. This is not the way to pro-mote initiative, free activity, mobility in a world of achievable positions, but to retard all these.

Principles of social policy, however, merely reflect the power of surviving traditions of behavior, which prevent people from making their own decisions. There are still many women who see their primary obligations in the world of chil-dren, kitchen, and church; workers put up with the conditions of their existence "below"; Catholics accept the narrow clo-sure of their existence, which is often further restricted by social and regional ties. Time and again interviews bring out a complete lack of motive toward the new possibilities of life, such as upward mobility, geographic mobility, changes of political orientation or social membership. The absence of motivation is often coupled with a lack of information about the possibilities of participation and appears sanctified by traditions invoked without question, so that a syndrome of minority results.

It would nevertheless be misleading to push our analysis too far in this direction. Although, apart from one small reservation, what has been said so far is correct, it does not describe the whole truth of equality in the German society of the Federal Republic. The small reservation is important; it concerns the comparison with the Weimar Republic. Between the Federal Republic and the Weimar Republic lies the inex-tinguishable social revolution of National Socialism, which has transformed the very structures in which the effective equality of citizenship rights is anchored. The fact that cer-tain sectors were never reached by this revolution, and that traces of restoration are recognizable in others, does not alter our conclusion that authoritarianism of the traditional kind has become impossible in German society. Indeed, the remainders of traditional ties and accepted minority are but a thin cover over the growing reality of civic equality. Comparatively minor initiatives suffice to move peasants and miners, women and Catholics, to modern attitudes and modes of behavior, that is, to make realization credible and mobilization acceptable to them, to motivate them for upward mobility by education and produce a general readiness to take the matters of life into their own hands. The growing demand for higher education is an infallible index here.

Although, therefore, the picture of civic equality is by no means as unidimensional for West Germany as it is for East Germany—which is regarded by many with wholly unjustified satisfaction—the tendency toward development is equally clear. It means the slow completion of modernity. This is the background before which the most significant single event for West German social development has to be seen, the economic miracle. While the DDR is shaped in its social reality by the process of the planned formation of a uniform, monopolistic elite dominated by its more narrowly political elements, the explosive development of its economy is the dominant and determinant feature of the short history of the German Federal Republic.

Speaking of the "economic miracle" and of the "explosiveness" of development means calling to mind the quantitative extent of the growth of productivity and gross national product, export and private consumption since 1948. This extent is indeed without precedent in economic history; its consequences are recognizable everywhere and reach deeply into the structures of society and the motives of men. But more astonishing still is the quality of West German economic development. Production began, as we have seen, at a low point not far removed from the early stages of industrialization. With justifiable exaggeration one might say that Germany after the war was once again given the burden and the chance of the industrial revolution. While East German society conducted this second industrialization once again in highly illiberal ways and thus remained bathed in the light of the state, West German society after 1948 made up, so to speak, for the errors Imperial Germany had committed. The miracle of West German economic development after 1948 is the comparatively liberal forms that produced it. At its beginning there was the courageous and successful decision of the then Economic Director and later Minister of Economic

Affairs Ludwig Erhard, a decision that at the time was regarded as foolhardy if not unjustifiable by most.

Upon closer inspection, the thesis of the liberal character
of economic development in postwar Germany clearly requires many a reservation and correction (and this not merely
because its instigator has since given himself over increasingly to the illiberal stereotypes of German tradition). There
could not be, and there was not a state-free economic development in Germany in 1948. The area of government
intervention by direct measures of planning and indirect measures of fiscal policy remained as wide as that of state ownership. Once again large enterprises and their combination
played a considerable part. But the countertrends are nevertheless unmistakable. They range from a lively competition
in many branches of industry to anti-trust legislation and
farther to the privatization of public property; even the almost
neurotic aversion of German politicians to the word "planning" is part of this tendency.

Considering the German past, the development of West
Germany's economy certainly took place in surprisingly liberal forms, and the consequences of this new turn may be
traced in the structures of society. In the economic field,
liberalism means competition, and competition is a form of
conflict. The principle of market rationality is always uncomfortable, and it has, as we know, only a weak tradition in
Germany. This is why the surprising aspects of postwar development must be found in the progress of this principle and
not in the continued effectiveness of its many restrictions. At
least for a while, economic competition in many branches of
West German business has done its job to the advantage of
the consumer.

Recognizable traces of a new style of conflict have entered
into the traditional authoritarian system of industrial relations; the metal industry above all provides a number of examples for the rational regulation of industrial conflict.
Changes in a similar direction are recognizable in most
other institutions. Slowly, the importance of dialogue and
discussion is growing in the educational system. The institution of the "army commissioner," a kind of military ombudsman, and the principle of the "citizen in uniform" document
new departures in the field of military organization. Even
courts of law are beginning to undergo a certain process of
"democratization" in our terms; today, prosecution and de-

fense are generally placed on the same level. Admittedly, the course of political conflict provides but very limited evidence for these observations; the clearer the tendency is toward a two-party system, the milder have the conflicts between the parties become. Even so, parliamentary democracy in the Federal Republic comes very much closer to the idea of government by conflict than the Weimar Republic ever did.

However, by and large the social effects of the economic miracle were least pronounced in the field of conflict regulation. The consequences of the liberal dynamics of West German economic development are much more striking in respect to the composition of elites. To begin with, the economic elites themselves differ considerably in their composition from their historical predecessors. Apart from the leaders of political parties, West German business leaders are the only upwardly mobile group in the political class of the Federal Republic (cf. 231).

There are many new men in this group who have acquired office and fortune since the war. Furthermore—and since this is harder to measure it must remain an assertion here—the weight of business leaders among the elites has greatly increased. Perhaps it was not very surprising that the second German industrialization in the western part of the country took its course against the state; the state was really no longer in existence, or in any case too weak to direct this process. Much the same holds for the relative position of the leaders of the two sectors, state and economy. At a time at which political leaders were either missing or extraordinarily weak, the leaders of the second most important institutional sector of modern societies, the economy, nolens volens found themselves in a position of great strength.

On the whole, they have not abused this position to advance monopolistic claims for themselves; to the present day, the business elites of the Federal Republic belong to the cartel of anxiety. But they have shaped the features of all leadership groups to a considerable extent. Ministers have come from and returned to business; the same holds for higher civil servants, for judges and the military, and even for professors. More important still, the style of business leadership, and above all a preference for the market in the place of the plan, has penetrated many non-economic sectors including public administration (to the dismay of all those who take the traditions of Prussia as their standard).

The top of society is increasingly bathed in an economic light, and unpleasant as this fact may appear to the backward-looking moralist, it is clearly useful for establishing the constitution of liberty.

Valid values are ruling values, that is, values that the rulers support with the force of the sanctions at their disposal. From the top of society, values informed by the patterns of economic life have spread throughout the whole of German society. No change is more striking for the outside observer who has visited Germany at regular intervals than that in people's values. Discipline, orderliness, subservience, cleanliness, industriousness, precision, and all the other virtues ascribed by many to the Germans as an echo of past splendor have already given way to a much less rigid set of values, among which economic success, a high income, the holiday trip, and the new car play a much larger part than the virtues of the past. Younger people especially display little of the much-praised and much-scorned respect for authority, and less of the disciplined virtues that for their fathers were allegedly sacred. A world of highly individual values has emerged, which puts the experienced happiness of the individual in first place and increasingly lets the so-called whole slip from sight. Perhaps there are some who still sense a vacuum where in earlier times and in the other Germany people were and are spellbound by a unified ideology; but generally this vacuum is soon filled with the pleasures of enjoying life.

Older people like to scorn the values indicated here. They talk about the materialism of people, their political apathy, the lost sense of the fatherland and the virtues of the fathers. But it would seem that politically the changes and tendencies of West German society discussed so far constitute the credit side of its balance. People who have grown accustomed to seeking individual happiness are unlikely candidates for totalitarian organization. Economic elites of a market order are ill-suited to the monopoly of political leadership groups that characterizes modern totalitarianism. Generally speaking, the principle of the market has a habit-forming effect even in its discomforts and may therefore persuade even those trained in more rigid patterns.

While the social suprastructure of equality is made up, in the German Democratic Republic, of the substance of totalitarian organization, it includes in the German Federal

Republic many elements of potential resistance against totalitarian control. Not prosperity as such, but the type of individual participation in its advantages is a source of antitotalitarian strength, because it is categorically opposed to the notion of planning every step of life and regards "the whole" as a marketlike, unplanned co-ordination of individual wishes.

There is no need to state this purely in negative terms. At some points, the qualitative economic miracle has furnished West German society with structures that are capable of supporting the constitution of liberty. However, a conclusion of this kind can be made only with great caution. The chances of liberal democracy in a German society have never been as great as they are in the German Federal Republic.

But here too they are restricted in numerous ways by old and new developments. After the credit side, we have to consider the debit side of West Germany's political sociology. We have already seen that one major post on this side of the balance consists of the deficiencies of the social foundation of citizenship. But the other factors also suggest many a critical question. Such concerns are not exactly alleviated by the fact that in respect to all three factors the burden of an illiberal past is further increased by new, specifically modern tendencies of illiberalism.

The social structure of conflict describes this condition. In the institutions of society and in the heads of people the echo of the authoritarian aversion to social conflict may still be heard. In politics, there are many who desire a grand coalition to put an end to party strife. In the economy, not only trade unionists associate the co-determination laws with the hope of an ultimate abolition of all industrial conflicts. There still are many who regard the public prosecutor as the most objective authority in the world, and teachers and professors as shareholders of certainty. Even a mildly inclined army commissioner could not claim that the citizen in uniform has already become real in the Federal Forces. Discussion has not gained much in popularity; this is even less the case with disputes, to say nothing of strikes. The idea is still alive in many Germans at least as a hidden hope that it would be possible to find the one man or the few who know the right answer to all questions.

This echo is audible at a time at which it is becoming increasingly difficult to formulate the dominate issues of political and economic conflict. As long as the foundations of equal citizenship are in dispute, aversion to conflict merely testifies to the German ideology of *Gemeinschaft;* but even in the Federal Republic the day is probably not too far off when conflict will assume the form of a "democratic class struggle," that is, of clashes about particular issues and their possible solutions and not about ideologies. There is, of course, one lasting subject of conflict in the modern world, but it concerns the external relations of societies and not their internal structure: that is, the conflict between the liberal and the totalitarian suprastructure of the civic equality of modernity. But it becomes increasingly difficult to describe the substance of the liberal suprastructure itself in its substance. Once the revolution of modernity is complete, government by conflict is a task that can no longer satisfy the imprecise ones and those who are looking for great tasks. The experience of other free societies may be sensed in the Federal Republic too: the constitution of liberty, hardly fully awake, is endangered again by the threats of the modern world.

In respect to the formation of a liberal elite, the difficulties are no smaller. The description of the cartel of anxiety to which we have devoted a chapter of this study, was in the first place a description of the Federal Republic. Even so, it had two sides, one of which concerns the German past, and the other the present and future of all developed societies. The anxiety of those who miss a tone-setting elite and therefore close their ranks uncertainly in order to preserve at least the status quo, is a result of the German past.

Explicitly authoritarian claims by certain groups also remind us of this past. In the leadership groups of public administration, the judiciary, the military, and to some extent also the church, such claims are still alive; at times the cartel of anxiety can hold them down only with difficulty. But already the memories and survivals of an active authoritarianism of the past are supplemented by the force of a new, hitherto unknown threat to liberal democracy. We have described this as a passive authoritarianism, an authoritarianism against the will of its leaders. This is the democracy without liberty under the rule of a political class that is, because of lack of participation and the absence of stable structures of social and political interest, pushed unwillingly into a position of undisputed leadership. The boredom of politics, which does not by-pass the Federal Republic, is not merely ancient minority, but also modern apathy.

Nowhere does this awkward alliance of old and new illiberalism become as apparent as in the value attitudes of people. Despite the qualitative effects of the economic miracle it is impossible to conclude that the public virtues have progressed very far in Germany. To the present day, the schools impart an image of the human personality that is free of all admixtures of the technical, economic, and social present. To the present day, self-sufficiency of the individual is regarded as a goal worth striving for. In so far as there have been changes in the rank order of family and school at all, these have at best been factual and do not involve the accepted ideology. Apparent political participation is still high in Germany, but it has also remained a very deceptive index for the institutionalization of those values that are directed to the ways in which people get along with one another. Here the statistics of traffic accidents provide a better, if less pleasing index. The fact that love for heroic loneliness may be deadly has not discouraged many Germans from it.

But there is also a new kind of turn against public values, which is determined equally by modernity and prosperity. At many points of this study we have pointed out the ambiguity of modernity. Traditional authoritarian structures not only resist the constitution of liberty, but also modern totalitarianism. But if we consider those virtues—or vices—of the affluent society by which we have characterized the Federal Republic, they reveal a very similar ambiguity. The search for individual enjoyment and happiness is an element of resistance to totalitarian claims. But it is also a very private kind of valuation, which hardly contributes to making the social community a lively and interesting place. Possibly the spread of this new privacy is one of the reasons why even the old democracies seem to pass through a phase of crisis; in any case the new privacy of the affluent society in the Federal Republic falls on the fertile ground of the old privacy of the industrial feudal society.

This old privacy was authoritarian in its political effect, and this suggests a further suspicion. Time and again we have encountered the possibility that a new, indeed novel authoritarianism will restrict the chances of the constitution of liberty. Once again this authoritarianism is based on the undisputed predominance of some and the non-participation of many. But a strange turnabout has occurred in respect to both. If the authoritarianism of the past was a result of the deliberate exercise of authority and unwanted non-participation, it seems today that the non-participation is wanted and the authority unintended. It is an authoritarianism of passivity.

Even repeated analysis in terms of the four factors in which the constitution of liberty has its social basis, does not lead to any simple answer to the question of whether the Federal Republic is democratic in its society or not. If anything, the faultings of German society in the past have become more complicated. Old and new, yesterday and today, still confront each other suddenly at many points of social structure. Certain changes are evident. The old order, which was still largely intact in Imperial Germany, that is, the continued significance of ascribed social positions, has dissolved in the melting pot of the social revolution of National Socialism. Today, despite all appearances, it is only remainders of structural minority that bar the path to modernity for German society.

To be sure, some faults still do effectively prevent the forces of liberalism awakened by the character of Germany's economic development after 1948 from becoming fully effective. While these faultings gradually give way to less ambiguous structures, which in theory should support the constitution of liberty, new obstacles emerge that once again threaten liberal democracy. The very social development that is a condition of the possibility of democracy also endangers it. Is it conceivable that, between the two authoritarianisms of the Imperial past and the future of the affluent society, Germany will altogether miss the chance of liberalism?

This question implies an answer that is not yet justified by the course of our argument. Three questions have to be answered still before we can regard this study as concluded for the time being. The first is the question whose significance is not confined to East German society: How stable and reliable are the changes of West German society that we have depicted here? The second question will then lead us back to our implied conclusion: What can be said, therefore, about the future of liberty in the Federal Republic? There will be many who will rightly regard this question as too restricted, indeed as based on an ill-considered renunciation: How about the chances of German reunification in one single society of liberty?

So far as the stability of the changes goes, our answer cannot be very different from that we gave for the DDR: The road to modernity remains beyond dispute, but its special character is variable. However, this formula states less about the Federal Republic than it does about the DDR. If we assume that it is impossible for a modern society to return to a traditional-authoritarian system, the greatest potential threat to the structure of West German society must be found in a totalitarianism of the Communist or the fascist type. Which changes in the Federal Republic would offer the greatest, and which the least resistance to such an attack?

From this extreme point of view, the liberalism of the patterns of economic development probably stands on relatively weak feet. Even the dominance of economic elites, uncertain in any case, may quickly turn into a new dependence on political groups. In any case, German society has not yet accepted the reality of conflict and the necessity of its rational regulation. Many of the most striking changes in the structure of the economy and society in the Federal Republic are therefore most liable to be undone again. This would not hold to the same extent, however, for those changes that concern the dominant patterns of people's behavior. The new privacy, that is, the individual search for happiness by people freed of the fetters of tradition and thrown into the affluent society, creates habits that it is hard to imagine would give way to the first attack of new changes. In so far as these habits have consequences for the character of elites and, more, for the treatment of social conflict, we find new structures of considerable stability in these fields too. It should be difficult to press West German society into the corset of the total organization of the individual for the purposes of the state.

But this is not a very convincing prognosis for the constitution of liberty in this society yet. That the chance of this constitution is greater today than it was in the past is a statement one can offer only with a bitter smile in view of the historical answers to the German Question. In fact, our analysis in the central parts of this study and in this last summary suggests a rather reserved judgment. The often-mentioned modern authoritarianism, which we have tried to describe from various angles, seems more likely than the establishment of the constitution of liberty in one of its historical forms.

Persistent faultings and specifically modern tendencies combine to create a political system that is authoritarian in effect if not in intention. A cartel of anxiety rules despite itself; the great majority of people deliberately renounces participation in the political process. Nothing essentially new happens, and the administration of the old does not arouse the interest of those involved. Parliamentary institutions continue to exist without being filled with the life for which they were designed. In other respects, too, the ritual of democratic procedure is respected. But it has become a mere ritual, unsupported by either a social or a political reality. If one considers the fundamental historicity of all things social, and the fact that the administration of the same never means the same for very long, one might suspect that this modern authoritarianism cannot be stable as such either. It may well be bound to generate within itself resistances that will periodically threaten it. But whether such threats produce new political forms or merely variations on the old ones is as yet an open question.

This dim perspective cannot, however, be our last word on the constitution of liberty in Western Germany. This study was based on a concept of democracy that cannot simply be handed over to a bygone past; rather, it was supposed to be applicable here and now. It would be wrong not to mention at the end of our analysis how problematical this concept has become in many countries, and especially in the Federal Republic, in view of the developments of the affluent society.

Liberal democracy as an historical force presented itself to countries with a different social structure as the political constitution of a non-totalitarian road to modernity. Germany missed this chance; there were never more than fragments of such liberalism in her political system and her social structure. Then there is the notion of liberal democracy as it grows out of modernity itself. It is government by conflict in a society of adult people, which builds into its institutions, despite the perfection of modernity, the principle of conflict as a medium of political decision and keeps it alive in its people. Here one has to speak of a mere notion; a reality cannot yet be called as witness. But this does not tell against the notion. In any case, its realization requires the reality of the structural elements we have discussed in this study, so that the task that is involved in bringing about the constitution of liberty under conditions of modernity is recognizable.

Thus we are left with a last question. In the concluding chapters of this study we have spoken of the "two Germanies." Many will find this formulation objectionable; but the fact that the truth raises objections must not prevent us from stating it. To some extent the German Federal Republic and the German Democratic Republic differ merely in the rhythm of their social development, in its deliberateness and radicalness. This is especially true of the egalitarian infrastructure of modernity, that is, the special preconditions of the realized role of the citizen. In detail, these differences are very significant; but they weigh lightly in view of the contradictory substance with which the form of equality has been filled on the two sides of the barbed wire. Even if one deducts the ultimately irrelevant peel of ideology, modernity is directed to rigid plan rationality in all sectors of East German society.

Public values, the formation of the new elite, steered conflicts are all perverted structures of freedom, which may not hold out against the attack of internal changes for very long but nevertheless impress features on society that are not easily extinguished. In West German society by contrast public values are missing, as are a self-confident elite and a sense of conflict turned into an institution. The market-rational direction of civic equality has provided the basis for a new privacy of human values. In this respect the distance is great between the two societies that twenty years ago were one.

This has, first of all, certain consequences for the probability and the course of reunification. Whatever the political chances and probabilities may be, socially the two Germanies are moving increasingly far apart. Even a slight loosening of the system of suppression in the DDR would not lead its society much closer to that of the Federal Republic, so long as the principle of plan rationality is maintained with all its constitutional consequences. At best one might suspect that with growing prosperity the new privacy, and thus the passive authoritarianism, will make headway in the east of Germany as well. Of course, what has developed apart in twenty years could presumably grow together again in twenty years as well. But if one looks at the social changes in the postwar period and their tendencies in the two Germanies, no centripetal force is recognizable in them which might enforce reunification from inside, by internal social forces.

This is no argument for or against German reunification; although it is an indication that, even if the immediate political obstacles and those economic and social ones that are accessible to political decision are cleared away, a mountain of less easily manipulable difficulties, which consist of social forces, would remain. The pivot of our analysis here is the question of democracy in Germany. What new answer to this question would a reunified Germany give?

Here speculation has free play. It must be taken with all caution therefore if I derive from our analysis the conclusion that in a reunified Germany too, if she were free to decide on her constitution, the chances of democracy would be greater than in the German past. The basis of this hope is the completed revolution of modernity. To say that the chances of freedom would be greater than they are in the DDR today does not amount to very much. For the Federal Republic, on the other hand, even the much-cited reunification in peace and freedom would involve certain dangers. The clash of planned publicness and new privacy, a tradition of rigid elite organization and the cartel of anxiety, of conflicts without decision and decisions without conflict, may have many consequences that weigh the balance in one or the other direction of modernity. There is a risk here that one can run if one wants to, and if one has an approximate idea of its extent. So far as reunification is concerned, the risk means simply that for the friend of the constitution of liberty this would create more problems than it would solve—and that the satisfactory solution of the problems created by it would be probable to the extent to which its predictable elements are previously recognized, discussed, and mastered in the Federal Republic.

This ends the course of our argument. The German Question is—to return to our starting point—not a political question put to others, but a social question put to ourselves. It demands from us not national sentiments, but social activities. Among all the answers that German society in the last hundred years has given to this question, that of the German Federal Republic comes closest to a socially founded constitution of liberty. But not even this answer is very satisfactory. Above all it is not the last answer yet to the question of democracy in Germany. Internal developments in the two Germanies of the present, and even more the possibility of their being joined again into one state and one society, promise new answers. Thus the German Question remains posed.

BIBLIOGRAPHY

Bibliography

Since it would obviously be arrogant even to try to offer a complete catalogue of books about the German Question—this literature has by now become almost as hard to master as the German Question itself—I have confined myself to a list of the books cited or used. This list may render a technical and a substantive service: by its continuous numbering it makes the identification of sources in the text more economical; at the same time it permits the critical reader to examine the indubitably considerable biases and limitations of the basis of information for this study. There is but one request I have in connection with such an examination. It is easy to find hundreds, perhaps thousands, of titles I might have used to support certain theses, render them more precise, differentiate them. Not to have used them in no case implies a critical stance to the authors concerned; at the same time it cannot, for the critic, imply criticism of my theses. Serious biases are present only where I have overlooked literature that contradicts my theses. Proof of such deficiencies is indeed an objection to this study.

Technically, one or two remarks about the bibliography may be in order. In the interest of brevity I have listed merely the main title of many works. All books are quoted from the edition (and language) mentioned here; translations into English are without exception my own.* Again in the interest of brevity, collections are as a rule mentioned but once, so that many authors quoted do not appear by name in this bibliography, because their contributions have appeared in collections. Some titles marked as Typescr. are in the hands of the author.

1   T. W. Adorno, E. Frenkel-Brunswik, D. J. Levinson, R. N. Sanford. *The Authoritarian Personality*. New York, 1950.
2   T. W. Adorno. *Aspekte der Hegelschen Philosophie*. Berlin-Frankfurt, 1957.
3   ——. *Jargon der Eigentlichkeit. Zur deutschen Ideologie*. Frankfurt, 1964.
3a A. Albrecht. "Rechtsstaat," *Staatslexikon,* ed. by the Görres-Gesellschaft, 6th ed., Vol. 6. Freiburg, 1961.
4   C. Amery. *Die Kapitulation oder deutscher Katholizismus heute*. Hamburg, 1963.

* In the case of books also published in English, the English titles are given in brackets.

5   C. Amery. "Dolchstoss im Wahljahr?," *Der Spiegel,* Vol. 19, No. 13 (1965).

6   H. Arendt. *Elemente und Ursprünge totaler Herrschaft.* Frankfurt, 1955 [*Origins of Totalitarianism.* New York, 1958].

7   ———. *Eichmann in Jerusalem.* Munich, 1964 [*Eichmann in Jerusalem.* New York, 1965].

8   R. Aron. *L'Opium des intellectuels.* Paris, 1955 [*Opium of the Intellectuals.* New York, 1962].

9   ———. "La définition libérale de la liberté," *European Journal of Sociology,* Vol. II, No. 2 (1961) and Vol. V, No. 2 (1964).

10 ———. *Die industrielle Gesellschaft.* Frankfurt, 1964.

11 ———. "Max Weber und die Machtpolitik," *Max Weber und die Soziologie heute.* Verhandlungen des 15. deutschen Soziologentages; Tübingen, 1965.

12 Ärztliche Pressestelle für Baden-Württemberg. "Warum immer ins Krankenhaus?," *Schwäbisches Tagblatt* (April 24, 1964).

13 K. S. Bader. *Die deutschen Juristen.* Tübingen, 1947.

14 W. von Baeyer-Katte et al. *Autoritarismus und Nationalismus—ein deutsches Problem?* Frankfurt, 1963.

15 F. Baur. "Introduction," *Bibliography of German Law.* Karlsruhe, 1964.

16 K. Bednarik. *Der junge Arbeiter von heute—ein neuer Typ.* Stuttgart, 1953.

17 R. Bendix. *Work and Authority in Industry.* New York, 1956.

18 B. R. Berelson, P. F. Lazarsfeld, W. N. McPhee. *Voting. A Study of Opinion Formation in a Presidential Campaign.* 2nd ed., Chicago, 1955.

19 O. Bezold, ed. *Die deutschen Parteiprogramme.* Munich, 1965.

20 T. J. H. Bishop. "The Social Origin of Winchester Boys, 1850–1950." Ph.D. thesis; London, 1963 (Typescr.).

21 P. Bockelmann. *Einführung in das Recht.* Munich, 1963.

22 F. Boese. *Geschichte des Vereins für Sozialpolitik, 1872–1932.* Berlin, 1939.

23 K. M. Bolte. *Sozialer Aufstieg und Abstieg.* Stuttgart, 1959.

24 ———. "Typen sozialer Schichtung in der Bundesrepublik Deutschland," *Hamburger Jahrbuch für Wirtschafts- und Gesellschaftspolitik.* 8th year; Tübingen, 1963.

25 K. E. Born. *Staat und Sozialpolitik seit Bismarcks Sturz.* Wiesbaden, 1957.

26 W. Bosch. *Die Sozialstruktur in West- und Mitteldeutschland.* Bonn, 1958.

27 K. D. Bracher, ed. *Staat und Politik.* 2nd ed.; Frankfurt, 1964 (Fischer-Lexikon No. 2).

28 K. D. Bracher, W. Sauer, G. Schulz. *Die nationalsozialistische Machtergreifung.* Cologne-Opladen, 1960.

29 K. D. Bracher. *Die Auflösung der Weimarer Republik.* Villingen, 1960.

30 ———. "Die Technik der nationalsozialistischen Machtergreifung," *Der Weg in die Diktatur, 1918–1933.* Munich, 1962.

31 ———. *Deutschland zwischen Demokratie und Diktatur.* Bern, 1964.

32 ———. *Theodor Heuss.* Tübingen, 1965.

33 E. K. Bramsted. *Aristocracy and the Middle Classes in Germany.* 2nd ed.; Chicago-London, 1964.

34 W. Buchanan, H. Cantril. *How Nations See Each Other.* Urbana, 1953.

35 K. Buchheim. *Leidensgeschichte des zivilen Geistes—oder die Demokratie in Deutschland.* Munich, 1951.

36 R. Burger. *Liegt die höhere Schule richtig?* Freiburg, 1963.

37 E. M. Butler. *The Tyranny of Greece over Germany.* 2nd ed.; Boston, 1958.

38 E. Cassirer. *The Myth of the State.* Garden City, 1955.

39 D. Claessens. *Familie und Wertsystem.* Berlin, 1962.

40 J. B. Conant. "Zwei Denkweisen. Ein Beitrag zur deutsch-amerikanischen Verständigung," *Hamburger Universitätsreden 21.* Hamburg, 1957 [*Two Modes of Thought.* New York, 1964].

41 W. Conze. *Die Zeit Wilhelms II. und die Weimarer Republik. Deutsche Geschichte, 1890–1933.* Tübingen-Stuttgart, 1964.

42 G. A. Craig. *The Politics of the Prussian Army, 1640–1945.* Oxford, 1955.

43 R. Dahrendorf, H. J. Lang. "Die Geheimwaffe des Führers. Ursprung, Verbreitung und Verwendung der 'Protokolle der Weisen von Zion.'" Hamburg, 1951 (Typescr.).

44 R. Dahrendorf. *Gesellschaft und Freiheit.* Munich, 1961.

45 ———. "Ausbildung einer Elite. Die deutsche Oberschicht und die Juristischen Fakultäten," *Der Monat,* No. 166 (1962).

46 ———. "Eine neue deutsche Oberschicht?," *Die neue Gesellschaft* (1962/I).

47 ———. "Conflict and Liberty. Some Remarks on the Social Structure of German Politics," *British Journal of Sociology,* Vol. XIV, No. 3 (1963).

48 ———. "Ungewissheit, Wissenschaft und Demokratie," *Argumentationen,* ed. by H. Delius and G. Patzig. Göttingen, 1964.

49 ———. "Zur Soziologie der juristischen Berufe in Deutschland," *Anwaltsblatt,* No. 8–9 (1964).

50 ———. "Recent Changes in the Class Structure of European

Societies," *A New Europe?*, ed. by S. Graubard. New York, 1964.

51 R. Dahrendorf. *Das Mitbestimmungsproblem in der deutschen Sozialforschung.* 2nd ed.; Munich, 1965.

52 ———. *Class and Class Conflict in Industrial Society.* 4th ed.; London, 1965.

53 ———. *Arbeiterkinder an deutschen Universitäten.* Tübingen, 1965.

54 *Das Grundgesetz der Bundesrepublik Deutschland.* Munich, 1961.

55 W. H. Dawson. *The Evolution of Modern Germany.* London-New York, 1908.

56 K. Demeter. *Das deutsche Offizierskorps in Gesellschaft und Staat, 1650–1945.* Frankfurt, 1962 [*The German Officer-corps: In Society and State.* New York, 1965].

57 K. W. Deutsch, L. J. Edinger. *Germany Rejoins the Powers.* Stanford, 1959.

58 Deutsches Institut für Bildung und Wissen. *Schule und pluralistische Gesellschaft.* Frankfurt, 1961.

59 J. Dewey. *Democracy and Education.* New York, 1961.

60 W. Dilthey. *Einleitung in die Geisteswissenschaften,* Gesammelte Schriften, Vol. 1; Stuttgart-Göttingen, 1959.

61 E. Durkheim. *L'Allemagne au-dessus de tout; La mentalité allemande et la guerre.* Paris, 1915.

62 L. J. Edinger. "Post-totalitarian Leadership: Elites in the German Federal Republic," *The American Political Science Review,* Vol. LIV, No. 1 (1960).

63 H. Eich. *Die unheimlichen Deutschen.* Düsseldorf-Wien, 1963 [*The Unloved Germans.* New York, 1965].

64 Fr. Engels. "Die Lage der arbeitenden Klasse in England," *Marx-Engels-Werke,* Vol. 1; Berlin, 1961.

65 E. H. Erikson. *Kindheit und Gesellschaft.* Stuttgart, 1961.

66 K. Erlinghagen. *Katholisches Bildungsdefizit in Deutschland.* Freiburg-Basel-Vienna, 1965.

67 Th. Eschenburg. *Herrschaft der Verbände?* Stuttgart, 1956.

68 ———. *Staat und Gesellschaft in Deutschland.* Stuttgart, 1960.

69 ———. *Die improvisierte Demokratie.* Munich, 1963.

70 E. Faul, ed. *Wahlen und Wähler in Westdeutschland.* Villingen, 1960.

71 Fr. Fischer. *Griff nach der Weltmacht.* Düsseldorf, 1961.

72 E. Fraenkel. *Zur Soziologie der Klassenjustiz.* Berlin, 1927.

73 ———. *Deutschland und die westliche Demokratien,* Stuttgart, 1964.

74 M. Friedman. *Essays in Positive Economics.* Chicago, 1953.

75 C. J. Friedrich. *Demokratie als Herrschafts- und Lebensform.* Heidelberg, 1959.

76 E. Fromm. *The Fear of Freedom.* 2nd ed.; London, 1960.

77 Fr. Fürstenberg. "Der Betriebsrat—Strukturanalyse einer Grenzinstitution," *Kölner Zeitschrift für Soziologie und Sozialpsychologie,* Vol. 10 (1958).

78 O. H. von der Gablentz. *Der Kampf um die rechte Ordnung.* Cologne-Opladen, 1964.

79 Th. Geiger. *Die soziale Schichtung des deutschen Volkes.* Stuttgart, 1932.

80 ———. *Die Klassengesellschaft im Schmelztiegel.* Cologne-Opladen, 1949.

81 ———. *Die Stellung der Intelligenz in der Gesellschaft.* Stuttgart, 1949.

82 H. Gerstein. *Studierende Mädchen.* Munich, 1965.

83 E. Goffman. *The Presentation of Self in Everyday Life.* New York, 1959.

84 ———. *Asylums.* Garden City, 1961.

85 H. E. Göppinger. "Strafe und Verbrechen," *Attempto.* Nachrichten für die Freunde der Universität Tübingen, No. 15 (1965).

86 J. Habermas, L. von Friedeburg, Chr. Oehler, Fr. Weltz. *Student und Politik.* Neuwied, 1961.

87 J. Habermas. *Strukturwandel der Öffentlichkeit.* Neuwied, 1962.

88 A. Hamilton, J. Madison, J. Jay. *The Federalist.* Cleveland-New York, 1961.

89 W. Hartenstein, K. Liepelt. "Party Members and Party Voters in Western Germany," *Acta Sociologica,* Vol. 6, Fasc. 1–2.

90 H. Hartmann. "Der zahlenmässige Beitrag der deutschen Hochschulen zur Gruppe der industriellen Führungskräfte," *Zeitschrift für die gesamte Staatswissenschaft,* Vol. 112, No. 1 (1956).

91 ———. *Unternehmer-Ausbildung.* Munich, 1958.

92 ———. *Authority and Organization in German Management.* Princeton, 1959.

93 U. von Hassell. *Vom anderen Deutschland. Tagebücher 1938–44.* 2nd ed.; Zürich-Freiburg, 1948.

94 F. A. Hayek. *The Constitution of Liberty.* London, 1960.

95 G. W. F. Hegel. *Grundlinien der Philosophie des Rechts.* (Hegels Sämtliche Werke, Vol. XII); Hamburg, 1955 [*The Philosophy of Right.* New York, 1942].

96 W. Hellpach. *Der deutsche Charakter.* Bonn, 1954.

97 J. Hitpass. *Einstellungen der Industriearbeiterschaft zu höherer Bildung.* Ratingen, 1965.

98 R. Hofstadter. *Anti-Intellectualism in American Life.* New York, 1963.

99 P. R. Hofstätter. "Die amerikanische und die deutsche Einsamkeit," *Verhandlungen des 13. deutschen Soziologentages.* Cologne-Opladen, 1957.

100   P. R. Hofstätter. *Gruppendynamik*. Hamburg, 1957.

101   ———. *Einführung in die Sozialpsychologie*. Stuttgart, 1959.

102   M. Horkheimer, ed. *Studien über Autorität und Familie.* Paris, 1936.

103   W. von Humboldt. *Schriften,* selected by W. Flemmer; Munich, 1964.

104   Institut für Demoskopie. *Jahrbuch 1958–1964*. Allensbach, 1965.

105   M. Janowitz. "Soziale Schichtung und Mobilität in Westdeutschland," *Kölner Zeitschrift für Soziologie und Sozialpsychologie,* Vol. 10 (1958).

106   C. Jantke. *Der vierte Stand.* Freiburg, 1955.

107   U. Jenny. "The Lonesomeness-Einsamkeit Conundrum." Tübingen, 1965 (Typescr.).

108   ———. "Öffentliche Tugenden als Erziehungsideal; Einige Materialien aus den Vereinigten Staaten." Tübingen, 1965 (Typescr.).

109   I. Kant. "Idee zu einer allgemeinen Geschichte in weltbürgerlicher Absicht," *Ausgewählte kleine Schriften.* Hamburg, 1965.

110   G. Kath. *Das soziale Bild der Studentenschaft.* Bonn, 1964.

111   E. Katz, P. Lazarsfeld. *Personal Influence.* Glencoe, 1955.

112   H. and W. Kaupen. "Der Einfluss gesellschaftlicher Wertvorstellungen auf die Struktur der deutschen Studentenschaft," *Kölner Zeitschrift für Soziologie und Sozialpsychologie,* Vol. 16, No. 1 (1964).

113   H. Kluth, U. Lohmar, R. Tartler. *Arbeiterjugend—gestern und heute.* Hamburg, 1955.

114   M. Knight. *The German Executive, 1890–1933.* Stanford, 1955.

115   J. H. Knoll. *Führungsauslese in Liberalismus und Demokratie.* Stuttgart, 1957.

116   J. Kob. *Erziehung in Elternhaus und Schule.* Stuttgart, 1963.

117   H. Kohn. *Wege und Irrwege. Vom Geist des deutschen Bürgertums.* Düsseldorf, 1962 [*The Mind of Germany*. New York, 1965].

118   H. Krausnick. "Stationen der Gleichschaltung," *Der Weg in die Diktatur, 1918–1933*. Munich, 1962 [*The Path to Dictatorship, 1918–1933*. Garden City, 1966].

119   L. Krieger. *The German Idea of Freedom.* Boston, 1957.

120   Chr. Graf von Krockow. *Die Entscheidung* (Göttinger Abhandlungen zur Soziologie, No. 3). Stuttgart, 1958.

121   J. P. Kruijt. "Sociologische beschouwingen over zuilen en verzuiling," *Socialisme en Democratie,* Vol. 1.

122   Fr. K. Kübler. "Der deutsche Richter und das demokratische Gesetz," *Archiv für die civilistische Praxis,* Vol. 162, No. 1–2 (1963).

123 E. Kuby. "Rot . . . Stopp . . . Grün . . . Anfahren . . . Scharf Bremsen," *Der Spiegel*, Vol. 15, No. 19 (1965).

124 F. Lassalle. *Ausgewählte Texte*, ed. by Th. Ramm. Stuttgart, 1962.

125 H. Laski. *A Grammar of Politics*. 4th ed.; London, 1960.

126 H. Lasswell. "Psychology of Hitlerism," *The Political Quarterly*, No. 4 (1933).

127 E. Lemberg. *Nationalismus*. Hamburg, 1964.

128 R. W. Leonhardt. *X-mal Deutschland*. Munich, 1961.

129 D. Lerner. *The Nazi Elite*. Stanford, 1951.

130 G. Linz. *Literarische Prominenz in der Bundesrepublik*. Olten-Freiburg, 1965.

131 S. M. Lipset. *Political Man*. New York, 1960.

132 ———. *The First New Nation*. New York, 1963.

133 D. Lockwood. "Arbitration and Industrial Conflict," *British Journal of Sociology*, Vol. VI (1955).

134 R. H. Lowie. *Toward Understanding Germany*. Chicago, 1954.

135 P. C. Ludz, ed. *Studien und Materialien zur Soziologie der DDR*. Kölner Zeitschrift für Soziologie und Sozialpsychologie, Special Issue No. 8 (1964).

136 Ch. Lütkens. "Die Schule als Mittelklasseninstitution," *Soziologie der Schule*. Kölner Zeitschrift für Soziologie und Sozialpsychologie, Special Issue No. 4 (1959).

137 E. W. Graf Lynar. *Deutsche Kriegsziele, 1914–1918*. Frankfurt-Berlin, 1964.

138 G. Mann. *Deutsche Geschichte des Neunzehnten und Zwanzigsten Jahrhunderts*. Frankfurt, 1958.

139 Th. Mann. *Betrachtungen eines Unpolitischen*. Berlin, 1918.

140 ———. *Rede über Deutschland und die Deutschen*. Berlin, 1947.

141 K. Mannheim. *Ideologie und Utopie*. Frankfurt, 1952 [*Ideology and Utopia*. New York, 1955].

142 T. H. Marshall. *Citizenship and Social Class*. Cambridge, 1950.

143 K. Marx. "Der achtzehnte Brumaire des Louis Bonaparte," *Marx-Engels-Werke*, Vol. 8; Berlin, 1960.

144 ———. "Das Kapital," *Marx-Engels-Werke*, Vols. 23, 24, 25; Berlin, 1963/64.

145 P. W. Massing. *Vorgeschichte des politischen Antisemitismus* (Frankfurter Beiträge zur Soziologie, Vol. 8). Frankfurt, 1959 [*Rehearsal for Destruction: Political Anti-Semitism in Imperial Germany*. New York, 1949].

146 E. Matthias. "Der Untergang der alten Sozialdemokratie, 1933," *Vierteljahrshefte für Zeitgeschichte*, Vol. 4 (1956).

147 ———. *Sozialdemokratie und Nation*. Stuttgart, 1952.

148 J. P. Mayer. *Max Weber and German Politics*. 2nd ed.; London, 1956.

149 W. H. McPherson. "Betrachtungen zur deutschen Arbeitsverfassung," *Wege zum sozialen Frieden,* ed. by H. D. Ortlieb and H. Schelsky. Stuttgart-Düsseldorf, 1954.

150 Fr. Meinecke. *Die deutsche Katastrophe.* Wiesbaden, 1955 [*The German Catastrophe.* Boston, 1963].

151 J. S. Mill. *On Liberty.* 11th ed.; London, 1960.

152 C. W. Mills. *Die amerikanische Elite.* Hamburg, 1962 [*Power Elite.* New York, 1956].

153 W. J. Mommsen. *Max Weber und die deutsche Politik.* Tübingen, 1959.

154 H. Moore, G. Kleining. "Das Bild der sozialen Wirklichkeit," *Kölner Zeitschrift für Soziologie und Sozialpsychologie,* Vol. XI, No. 3 (1959).

155 ——. "Das soziale Selbstbild der Gesellschaftsschichten in Deutschland," *Kölner Zeitschrift für Soziologie und Sozialpsychologie,* Vol. XII, No. 1 (1960).

156 H. J. Morgenthau, ed. *Germany and the Future of Europe.* Chicago, 1951.

157 R. Morsey. *Das Ende der Parteien, 1933.* Düsseldorf, 1960.

158 H. Mottek. *Studien zur Geschichte der industriellen Revolution in Deutschland.* Berlin, 1960.

159 H. Mursch. "Die Verkehrsunfälle in Deutschland," *Frankfurter Allgemeine Zeitung* (April 29, 1964).

160 O. Neuloh. *Die deutsche Betriebsverfassung und ihre Sozialformen bis zur Mitbestimmung.* Tübingen, 1956.

161 ——. *Der neue Betriebsstil.* Tübingen, 1960.

162 F. Neumann. *Behemoth—The Structure and Practice of National Socialism, 1933–1944.* New York, 1944.

163 ——. *The Democratic and the Authoritarian State.* Glencoe, 1957.

164 H. Neumeister. "Kinder in Deutschland," *Frankfurter Allgemeine Zeitung* (March 31, 1965).

165 E. Nolte. *Der Faschismus in seiner Epoche.* Munich, 1963 [*Three Faces of Fascism: Action Française, Italian Fascism, National Socialism.* New York, 1966].

166 T. Parsons. "Democracy and Social Structure in Pre-Nazi Germany," *Essays in Sociological Theory.* Glencoe, 1954.

167 R. Pechel. *Deutschenspiegel.* Berlin, 1946.

168 H. Peisert. "Regionalanalyse als Methode der Bildungsforschung," *Studien und Berichte aus dem Soziologischen Seminar der Universität Tübingen* (Report 5). Tübingen, 1965.

169 ——. "Studien zur Sozialstruktur der Bildungschancen in Deutschland." "Habilitation" thesis; Tübingen, 1965 (Typescr.).

170 Th. Pirker, S. Braun, B. Lutz, F. Hamelrath. *Arbeiter, Management, Mitbestimmung.* Stuttgart, 1955.
171 Th. Pirker. *Die SPD nach Hitler.* Munich, 1965.
172 H. Plessner. *Die verspätete Nation.* Stuttgart, 1959.
173 Fr. Pollock, *Gruppenexperiment, Ein Studienbericht.* Frankfurt, 1955.
174 Sir K. R. Popper. *The Open Society and Its Enemies.* London, 1949.
175 ———. *The Logic of Scientific Discovery.* New York, 1959.
176 ———. "On the Sources of Knowledge and of Ignorance," *Proceedings of the British Academy,* Vol. 46. London, 1960.
177 H. Popitz, H. P. Bahrdt, E. A. Jüres, H. Kesting. *Das Gesellschaftsbild des Arbeiters.* Tübingen, 1961.
178 Harry Pross. *Die Zerstörung der deutschen Politik.* Frankfurt, 1959.
179 Helge Pross. *Manager und Aktionäre in Deutschland.* Frankfurt, 1965.
180 E. Reigrotzki. *Soziale Verflechtungen in der Bundesrepublik.* Tübingen, 1956.
181 K. Renner. *Wandlungen der modernen Gesellschaft.* Vienna, 1953.
182 D. Riesman, N. Glazer, R. Denney. *Die einsame Masse.* Hamburg, 1958 [*The Lonely Crowd.* New Haven, 1950].
183 G. Ritter. *Das deutsche Problem.* Munich, 1962 [*The German Problem: Basic Questions of German Political Life, Past and Present.* Columbus, Ohio, 1965].
184 S. Rokkan. *Approaches to the Study of Political Participation.* Bergen, 1962.
185 W. Röpke. *Die deutsche Frage.* Erlenbach, 1945.
186 G. Roth. *The Social Democrats in Imperial Germany.* Englewood Cliffs, 1963.
187 H. Rothfels. *Die deutsche Opposition gegen Hitler.* Frankfurt-Hamburg, 1957 [*German Opposition to Hitler.* Chicago, 1962].
188 ———. *Bismarck und der Staat.* Stuttgart, 1958.
189 D. Rüschemeyer. "Rekrutierung, Ausbildung und Berufsstruktur," *Soziale Schichtung und soziale Mobilität.* Kölner Zeitschrift für Soziologie und Sozialpsychologie, Special Issue No. 5 (1961).
190 B. Russell. *Power. A New Social Analysis.* 7th ed.; London, 1957.
191 A. Sampson. *Anatomy of Britain.* London, 1962.
192 H. Schelsky. *Ortsbestimmung der deutschen Soziologie.* Düsseldorf-Cologne, 1959.
193 ———. *Einsamkeit und Freiheit.* Hamburg, 1963.
194 ———. *Auf der Suche nach Wirklichkeit.* Cologne-Düsseldorf, 1965.

195 E. K. Scheuch. "Sozialprestige und soziale Schichtung," *Soziale Schichtung und soziale Mobilität*. Kölner Zeitschrift für Soziologie und Sozialpsychologie, Special Issue No. 5 (1961).

196 A. O. Schorb, ed. *Für und wider den Rahmenplan*. Stuttgart, 1960.

197 J. A. Schumpeter. *Kapitalismus, Sozialismus und Demokratie*. Bern, 1946 [*Capitalism, Socialism and Democracy*. New York, 1950].

198 ———. *Aufsätze zur Soziologie*. Tübingen, 1953.

199 P. Sethe. *Deutsche Geschichte im letzten Jahrhundert*. Frankfurt, 1963.

200 W. Sombart. *Die deutsche Volkswirtschaft im 19. Jahrhundert und im Anfang des 20. Jahrhunderts*. Stuttgart, 1954.

201 U. Sonnenmann. *Das Land der unbegrenzten Zumutbarkeiten*. Hamburg-Reinbek, 1963.

202 H. Speier, W. P. Davison, eds. *West German Leadership and Foreign Policy*. Evanston, 1957.

203 J.-E. Spenlé. *Der deutsche Geist von Luther bis Nietzsche*. Meisenheim, 1949.

204 *Der Spiegel*. "Untersuchungshaft in Deutschland," Vol. 12, No. 18 (1964).

205 I. Staff, ed. *Justiz im dritten Reich*. Frankfurt, 1964.

206 Fr. Stampfer. *Die vierzehn Jahre der ersten deutschen Republik*. Hamburg, 1953.

207 Statistisches Amt, Kaiserliches. *Statistisches Jahrbuch für das Deutsche Reich, 1912*. Berlin, 1912.

208 Statistisches Bundesamt. *Statistisches Jahrbuch für die Bundesrepublik, 1963*. Stuttgart, 1964.

209 F. Stern. "The Political Consequences of the Unpolitical German," in: *History*, 3 (1960).

210 ———. *Kulturpessimismus als politische Gefahr*. Stuttgart, 1963 [*The Politics of Cultural Despair: A Study in the Rise of the Germanic Ideology*. Berkeley, 1961; Garden City, 1965].

211 ———. "War der Kriegsausbruch nur ein Betriebsunfall?," *Der Spiegel*, Vol. 18, No. 43 (1964).

212 G. Stolper, K. Häuser, K. Borchardt. *Deutsche Wirtschaft seit 1870*. Tübingen, 1964.

213 J. L. Talmon. *The Origins of Totalitarian Democracy*. London, 1955.

214 A. J. P. Taylor. *The Course of German History*. 2nd ed.; London, 1945.

215 H. Thierfelder. "Zur Soziologie der juristischen Berufe in Deutschland. Eine Erwiderung," *Deutsche Richterzeitung*, Vol. 43, No. 2 (1965).

216 A. de Tocqueville. *Democracy in America*. New York, 1956.

217 F. Tönnies. *Gemeinschaft und Gesellschaft.* Leipzig, 1887 [*Community and Society.* East Lansing, Michigan, 1957].

218 W. Tormin. *Zwischen Rätediktatur und sozialer Demokratie.* Düsseldorf, 1954.

219 H. von Treitschke. *Politik.* 4th ed.; Leipzig, 1918 [*Politics.* New York, 1963].

220 T. Veblen. *Imperial Germany and the Industrial Revolution.* New York, 1954.

221 E. Vermeil. *L'Allemagne contemporaine.* Paris, 1953.

222 R. Wassermann. "Unsere konservativen Richter," *Die Zeit* (March 13, 1964).

223 J. W. N. Watkins. "Epistemology and Politics," *Meetings of the Aristotelian Society* (December 9, 1957).

224 M. Weber. *Gesammelte Aufsätze zur Wissenschaftslehre.* Tübingen, 1951.

225 ———. *Gesammelte politische Schriften.* 2nd ed.; Tübingen, 1958.

226 W. E. Weyrauch. *The Personality of Lawyers.* New Haven-London, 1964.

227 E. Wiehn. "Vorzeitiger Schulabgang." Abgänge aus Untertertia u. Untersekunda von Oberschulen in Baden-Württemberg. Tübingen, 1965 (Typescr.).

228 Wirtschaftswissenschaftliches Institut der Gewerkschaften. *Wirtschafts- und sozialstatistisches Handbuch,* ed. by B. Gleitze. Cologne, 1960.

229 K. A. Wittfogel. *Oriental Despotism.* New Haven, 1957.

230 W. Woytinsky. *Die Welt in Zahlen.* Berlin, 1925.

231 W. Zapf, ed. *Beiträge zur Analyse der deutschen Oberschicht.* 2nd ed.; Munich, 1965.

232 W. Zapf. *Wandlungen der deutschen Elite, 1919–1961.* Munich, 1965.

Index